Contents

Abbreviations

BLS	Bureau of Labor Statistics, U.S. Department of Labor
CBO	Characteristics of Business Owners
CBP	County Business Patterns
CPS	Current Population Survey
D&B	Dun and Bradstreet Corporation
DMI	Dun's Market Identifier
EIN	Employer Identification Number
ES	Enterprise Statistics
ETA	Employment and Training Administration, U.S. Department of Labor
FICA	Federal Insurance Contributions Act
FUTA	Federal Unemployment Tax Act
IRS	Internal Revenue Service, U.S. Treasury Department
MSA	Metropolitan Statistical Area
NSSBF	National Survey of Small Business Finances
R&D	research and development
SBA	U.S. Small Business Administration
SBDB	Small Business Data Base
SIC	Standard Industrial Classification system
SIPP	Survey of Income and Program Participation
SMOBE	Survey of Minority-Owned Business Enterprises
UI	unemployment insurance
WOB	Survey of Women-Owned Business

1 Overview

Small firms are increasingly recognized as key job creators and inno-
vators in the economy. Not only did small firms generate virtually
all of the net new jobs between 1988 and 1990 in the United States,
but they helped mitigate the effects of the recent recession by con-
tinuing to create jobs. Small firms are expected to contribute about
70 percent of the new jobs in the nation's fastest growing industries
between 1990 and 2005, and about 66 percent of the 23.3 million
jobs projected to be created between 1990 and 2005.[1]

In general, the fastest growing industries are expected to include
health and business services, as well as industries related to the en-
vironment and care of disabled persons.

Despite small business' recognized importance in the economy,
the federal government has no single, current source of data by firm
size. One function of this handbook, therefore, is to pull together
the variety of data sources in order to present as complete and current a picture as possible. While firm size data are published every
five years by the Census Bureau, this information must be supple-
mented by other surveys for policy analysis purposes, and to obtain
more current estimates of the size of the small business population,
and changes in it.

Four kinds of data are presented here: (1) federal data published
on a regular basis, (2) federal data that are normally unpublished
but made available under contract to the Small Business Administration, (3) derived data not normally available for small firms but
adapted using a definition of small-business-dominated sectors, and
(4) special surveys in applied research areas conducted by the SBA.

---

1 In particular, growth is expected to be most robust in the following small-business-dominated sectors: residential care (4.5 percent annual growth), computer
and data processing services (4.4 percent), and health services (4.0 percent).
These projections are based upon Max L. Carey and James C. Franklin, "Industry
Output and Job Growth Continues Slow Into the Next Century" *Monthly Labor Re-
view* (November 1991), 45–63.

**How the
Handbook
Is Organized**

Business data sources available in the United States cover many types and sizes of businesses, in various locations, with various characteristics. Presented in sequence in this handbook are data covering: (1) all firms, (2) full-time firms with employees, (3) full-time self-employed persons, (4) firms by geographic location, and (5) current indicators of small business performance, such as incorporations, bankruptcies, and income.

Displayed first in this handbook are data available for all firms (Chapter 1). Much of the information available from the Internal Revenue Service (IRS) is of this type because no distinction can be made between taxpaying firms with and without employees, nor is there in the IRS data a distinction between full-time and part-time operations. Nevertheless, IRS data represent the most comprehensive estimates of the more than 20 million firms that comprise the entire small business population.[2]

Chapters 3 through 9 display data for a smaller subset of about six million firms that have employees and operate full time. Most business data sources in the United States cover this group of nonfarm businesses with employees. These data are available by firm employment and sales size from the Small Business Data Base for 1976 to 1990 (SBDB),[3] from Enterprise Statistics (ES) for 1977 to 1987, and from the unemployment insurance (UI) data of the U.S. Department of Labor's Employment and Training Administration for 1980 forward. Detailed financial information by firm size is provided (Chapter 9), and information on employee benefits by firm size (Chapters 7 and 8).

Chapters 2 through 6 contain information for firms that operate full-time and have employees, but for which limited firm size detail is available. Included in this category are data from the 1982 and 1987 Censuses of Women-Owned and Minority-Owned Business Enterprises, as well as data from the Census Bureau's Characteristics

---

2   Over 99 percent of business tax returns filed represent small businesses. Of the total, about 70 percent are sole proprietorships, 22 percent corporations, and 8 percent partnerships. Taken together, small business tax returns cover everything from 500-employee manufacturing operations to the income of persons operating part-time businesses.

3   The current data from the Small Business Data Base (SBDB) will be the final installment from the SBDB. The Dun and Bradstreet-based data base is being replaced with new longitudinal, dynamic data files developed from confidential microdata collected by the Census Bureau. The first of these files, which will measure business births and deaths, is expected to be produced during fiscal year 1994 and completed during fiscal year 1993. The files will cover the periods 1989 to1991 and 1991 to 1993.

of Business Owners data bases. In most instances, fewer than 10 percent of the firms in these categories have employees, a fact which limits the tabulations that can be displayed by firm size or geographic area.

Also included in these chapters are data from the Federal Reserve Board covering firms that operate full-time but do not have employees (Chapter 9). Other data, such as that taken from the SBA's December 1990 report, *A Status Report to Congress: Statistical Information on Women in Business*,[4] cover full-time businesses of the self-employed. In many instances, data on minority-owned and women-owned firms are also shown for all small firms with limited size detail.

Data on businesses operated by full-time self-employed persons are scarce. Except for tax data, almost all information on these businesses comes from samples, generally from Census surveys such as the Current Population Survey (CPS) and the Survey of Income and Program Participation (SIPP). Chapter 7 and Chapter 8 present data from previous CPS surveys on this full-time, self-employed business subset, as well as research results from recent contracts performed for the SBA.

Chapter 10 of the *Handbook* displays tables for selected current indicators of small business performance. These include business failures and business formation. In addition, historical data is shown where available, particularly that from the Employment and Training Administration (ETA). The ETA data are available quarterly by state and show firm openings and terminations, as well as "successor" firms which have been acquired or divested.

Chapter 11 presents miscellaneous data on such topics as research and development, intellectual property, and federal procurement from small businesses.

Definitions and Units of Measurement

The task of measuring the small business community, small firm employment and productivity, and the effects of various policies on small businesses is complicated by the variety of available data sources and the differences in the units they measure. Certain key definitions and measurement constraints need to be understood before conclusions are drawn based on available small business data.

First, a distinction must be made between "enterprises" and "es-

4   U.S. Small Business Administration, Office of Advocacy, *A Status Report to Congress: Statistical Information on Women in Business* (Washington, D.C.: U.S. Small Business Administration, 1990).

tablishments." An establishment is an individual business location; an enterprise or "firm" includes all establishments under the same ownership or control. Because the identity and size of a business are tied to its ownership, it is often important for small business policy analysis purposes that data be available by enterprise—rather than establishment—size.

Most federal data are available only for establishments, but data from the Census Bureau's Enterprise Statistics, from the Federal Procurement Data Center, and from the SBA's Small Business Data Base are available by enterprise size. Most of the survey-based research sponsored by the Office of Advocacy since 1978 has also been conducted by size of enterprise.[5] Both the Census Bureau and the Bureau of Labor Statistics have efforts underway to design sampling frames that will measure current economic changes on a firm or enterprise size basis.

Two additional units of business measurement are "reporting units" and "taxpaying units." Reporting units are firms that provide employment information to the U.S. Department of Labor's Employment and Training Administration and are permitted to combine data for all the establishments they own in a given county. These data are often available for entities containing more than a single establishment, but less than an enterprise; distributional information from reporting units must therefore be carefully qualified.[6] In addition, because data in the Unemployment Insurance system uses reporting units, new employer identification numbers (EINs)—used to identify new businesses— do not necessarily represent new small enterprises. Therefore, from this source, only approximate counts of new small business births and deaths are available by state.[7]

Data provided by the Internal Revenue Service are by "taxpaying unit," and may reflect an entire organization or part of a larger one. Because companies may file tax returns in the format that minimizes tax liability, returns may be filed by an entire enterprise (as for most single-unit small firms), or by a subsidiary or division of a larger organization. Fortunately, for policy analysts using these data, most small businesses are legally organized as proprietorships and partnerships, for which the distinctions between enterprises

---

5   See Executive Office of the President, *The State of Small Business: A Report of the President* (Washington, D.C.: U.S. Government Printing Office, 1992), 95–140.

6   Although the units reported on are not precisely defined, the data are valuable because of the trends they indicate.

7   More precise information about this data source is found in Chapter 3.

and establishments are less important.[8]

It is also important to understand the kinds of economic measures that are usually associated with a particular unit of analysis. For example, employment data are available for establishments, enterprises, and reporting units, but sales and other financial data are available only for enterprises (or for particular taxpaying units if different from the entire business enterprise). Data on some characteristics, such as benefits to employees, may also be available for subsidiaries within a company, if they operate as separate divisions. In this handbook, much of the nonfinancial data are presented for establishments by enterprise size, while financial data are on an enterprise basis unless otherwise specified.[9]

The data in this volume are arrayed either by employment size, asset size, or sales size of the firm. In most cases, it is better to measure firm size changes in terms of employment rather than in sales or assets, which must be adjusted for inflation. However, most financial data are arrayed by the asset or sales size of the firm and must be adjusted for inflation when comparisons are made between time periods.[10]

The distinction between dynamic and static measurements is also critical. Except for data from the Small Business Data Base, virtually all of the statistics reviewed in this publication are static; that is, they are "snapshots" of a variable taken at various points in time. A dynamic measure such as the SBDB, by contrast, can record the gross flows that contribute to the final, static snapshot.

For example, employment change can be derived as either the difference between the number of people at work at two points in time or as the result of two larger flows—jobs created minus jobs lost. The static shot shows a gain of just 2.7 million jobs between 1988

---

8 Because some small firms own subsidiaries, however, there is still some ambiguity as to which parts of the firms are observable in the taxpaying units.

9 In 1989, the Census Bureau undertook a survey which provided a better understanding of the kinds of economic and financial information that are available from different levels of business organizations, and how they vary by firm size. For further details, see U.S. Department of Commerce, Bureau of the Census, *1989 Recordkeeping Practices Survey* (Washington, D.C.: U.S. Government Printing Office, 1990).

10 Until recently, very little data were available on small firm finances. However, a detailed study conducted jointly by the Federal Reserve Board and the U.S. Small Business Administration, the 1989 National Survey of Small Firm Finances, has filled in some gaps in the knowledge of how entrepreneurs start and expand small firms. Summaries of these data are displayed in Chapter 9, along with other aggregate financial data applicable to the small business sector.

and 1990, but according to gross flow data, this was the result of 23.2 million jobs created through firm startups and expansions minus 20.5 million jobs lost through firm deaths and contractions. Comparative static data would indicate that small firms created relatively few jobs, but the underlying flows behind the comparative static measurements are much larger. On a national basis, it has been shown that to create one net new job, about four jobs must be created to more than replace three jobs that will be lost.[11] This is not unexpected in a growing, entrepreneurial climate.

In sum, dynamic gross flow data provide much more information about the health of the underlying economy, and can give policymakers a more complete picture of how small firms function to create jobs. Such data would be preferable if available, but most available federal data on small firms are based on comparative statics.

Measuring the Business Population from IRS Data

The broadest picture of the small business population is provided in comprehensive data from the Internal Revenue Service. In 1991, the most recent year for which IRS data are available, approximately 20.5 million business tax returns were filed (Table 1.1). Just under one-third of the business population are firms with employees that operate full time, most of which are small. Just over 40 percent of the business population are self-employed individuals who earn their living from full-time business pursuits, but choose to work for themselves. The remaining quarter of the business population consists of individuals who operate a business part-time. These may be consultants, sales representatives, or persons with full-time wage and salary jobs who have some part-time interest in a side business.[12] The relative size of this last group tends to be very sensitive to changes in the business cycle, rising during recessions and falling during recoveries.

Most data, especially financial and procurement data, are available only for the 5.7 million full-time firms with employees that represent about 28 percent of the business population. Coverage of Census surveys varies and some surveys, such as the Characteristics

---

11 See Bruce A. Kirchhoff and Bruce D. Phillips, "Employment Growth in the Decade of the Entrepreneur," unpublished paper presented at the Babson College–University of Pittsburgh Entrepreneurship Research Conference, Pittsburgh, Pennsylvania, April 17–19, 1991.

12 For a discussion of self-employment, see Executive Office of the President, *The State of Small Business: A Report of the President* (Washington, D.C.: U.S. Government Printing Office, 1986), 105–149.

of Business Owners, also include firms without employees that generally operate full-time. Chapter 2 displays the industrial distribution of full-time firms with employees, and the distribution of the full-time self-employed is discussed in Chapter 7. The distribution of the part-time self-employed is available only from historical, unpublished Current Population Survey Census tabulations.[13]

Legal Form of Organization

Of the 20.5 million nonfarm tax returns filed in 1991, 14.3 million (69.9 percent) were sole proprietorships, 4.5 million (21.9 percent) were corporations, and the remaining 1.7 million (8.2 percent) were organized as partnerships. By most definitions, virtually all proprietorships and partnerships are small businesses, while more than 95 percent of corporations with less than $25 million in sales or assets are small firms.

Determining the precise relationship between the three types of firms listed in Table 1.1 and their legal form of organization is problematic. Precise counts of firms by legal form of organization, cross-classified by employment size, are not readily available from tax data.[14] In addition, because sales is the only variable common to all three kinds of tax returns, sales per employee is the only financial variable that can be estimated for all three; data on assets per employee are available only for partnership and corporate returns.[15]

Trends in Tax Returns Filed

Some 13.6 million nonfarm business tax returns were filed in 1981 and 20.5 million returns were filed in 1991, for a compound annual increase of 4.2 percent during the decade (Table 1.2). By legal form of organization, the similar annual increases for proprietorship, partnership, and corporate returns were 4.4, 1.4, and 4.8 percent respectively. Clearly the corporate form of business ownership rose fastest during the 1980s, led by small subchapter S corporations. Women-owned proprietorships also increased rapidly, at about twice the rate of men-owned firms (see Chapter 5).[16]

13 See Chapter 8 for a discussion of the limited information available on this data set.

14 Exceptions are the 1979 and 1982 IRS Match File tabulations, which classified firms by legal form and employment size. However, similar files have not been developed since 1987 when the project on the 1982 files was completed. Further information about this file is found in U.S. Small Business Administration, Office of Advocacy, *Handbook of Small Business Data,* 1988 ed. (Washington, D.C.: U.S. Government Printing Office, 1988), 275–282.

15 Ratios of assets per employee and receipts per employee from the IRS Match Files are shown in *Handbook of Small Business Data,* 1988 ed., tables 7.2 and 7.3.

16 From 1979 to 1989, the latest year for which such data are available, women-

IRS data are used for various policy analysis purposes. Samples of unidentified tax returns are used to analyze the impact of changes in tax regulations. For example, during the debate on tax reform during the mid-1980s, a model was designed that made use of tax data to test the effects on small firms of various proposed changes in tax regulations. In addition, the IRS has used confidential tax files to study the growth characteristics of firms that received SBA guaranteed loans under the agency's major financing program, comparing these firms with similar firms that did not receive such loans.[17]

Limitations of IRS Data

Confidentiality restrictions prohibit the release of any tax data below the national level, or for detailed industrial subsets. By law, it must not be possible to identify any individual taxpayer from IRS data. Despite this limitation, the Statistics of Income Division of the Internal Revenue Service has done much to help provide a more complete picture of the aggregate small business universe. It is expected that future interagency agreements between the IRS and the SBA will make available more detailed information about the 14 million firms that do not have employees.[18]

Summary

The world of small business data is diverse, and a myriad of data sources each contribute to our understanding of different parts of the small business sector. While the most comprehensive data is available for firms with employees, alternative data sets must be consulted for information about nonemployer firms. These varied data sources are summarized in Table 1.3. While it is not possible to bring together in one place everything that is known about such a di-

---

owned nonfarm sole proprietorships rose at an annual rate of 12.6 percent, compared with 5.5 percent for male-owned nonfarm sole proprietorships. The population of jointly owned sole proprietorships—businesses generally owned by husbands and wives or two related individuals—also increased by 9.4 percent annually during this period. However, the number of jointly owned sole proprietorships—about 489,000 in 1989—constitutes less than 3 percent of the business population.

17 See U.S. Department of the Treasury, Internal Revenue Service, *Small Business Administration: 7(a) Loan Guaranty Study* (Washington, D.C.: U.S. Department of the Treasury, Internal Revenue Service, 1989). See also Price-Waterhouse, *Evaluation of the Small Business Administration's 7(a) Guaranteed Business Loan Program: Final Report* (Washington, D.C.: Price-Waterhouse, March 1992).

18 Other samples, such as the Current Population Survey of the Bureau of the Census and other longitudinal data sets have been used for extensive studies of the self-employed.

verse business universe, an examination of the many data sources in Table 1.3 indicates that the following chapters attempt to summarize much of the data that is publicly available about the small firm sector.

Chapter 1 Tables

Table 1.1 Distribution of Business Tax Returns, 1991

Type	Number	Percent
Full-time Businesses with Employees	5.7 million	27.8
Full-time Self-Employed Workers without Employees	8.9 million	43.4
Part-time Self-Employed Workers without Employees	5.9 million	28.8
Total	**20.5 million**	**100.0**

Source: Adapted from the U.S. Department of the Treasury, Internal Revenue Service, *Statistics of Income Bulletin* (Fall 1992).

Table 1.2 Nonfarm Business Tax Returns, 1981-1991 (Thousands)

Year	Corporations (Forms 1120 and 1120S)	Partnerships (Form 1065)	Proprietorships (Schedule C)	Total
1991[P]	4,488	1,681	14,326	20,495
1990	4,439	1,759	14,241	20,439
1989	4,197	1,780	13,529	19,506
1988	4,027	1,826	13,126	18,979
1987	3,829	1,824	12,633	18,286
1986	3,577	1,807	12,115	17,499
1985	3,437	1,755	11,767	16,959
1984	3,167	1,676	11,327	16,170
1983	3,078	1,613	10,507	15,198
1982	2,913	1,553	9,877	14,343
1981	2,813	1,458	9,345	13,616

P = Projected
Source: U.S. Department of the Treasury, Internal Revenue Service, *Statistics of Income Bulletin* (Spring 1991), table 19.

Table 1.3 Sources of Small Business Data Covered in the 1994 Handbook of Small Business Data

Source\Description	Availability	Latest
I. Published Federal Summary Data		
Enterprise Statistics (Number of firms, employment, payroll, sales)-(Census)	Every 5 years	1987
Women-Owned Businesses (Census) employment, payroll, sales[1]	Every 5 years	1987
Minority-Owned Businesses (Census) employment, payroll, sales[2]	Every 5 years	1987
Tax-Returns (Proprietors, Partnerships, Corporations-IRS)	Annual	1989
II. Unpublished Federal Summary Data		
Unemployment Insurance Data (Number of legal entities, births, deaths, successor firms)	Quarterly	4th quarter 1991
Small Business Data Base-(SBA) (Number of firms, establishments, employment, sales)	Biennial	1990
Federal Procurement Data Center-(DOD) (Federal contract actions >25K)	Annual	1990

[1]Available by state.

[2]Available by state.

Table 1.3 Sources of Small Business Data Covered in the 1994 Handbook of Small Business Data--Continued

Source\Description	Availability	Latest
Change in the Small Business Population (Number of firms, establishments, payroll, births, deaths-Census)[3]	Annual	1988-1990
Self-Employment-(Census) (Number of Self-employed individuals)[4]	Annual	1991
Sole Proprietorships Businesses By Gender (Number, receipts, by industry-IRS)	Annual	1989
Source Book for Corporations (Income Statement and Balance sheet items by asset class-IRS)	Annual	1989

III. Derived Data on Small Firms (Unpublished)

Small-business-dominated employment (Small Business Data Base, Bureau of Labor Statistics)	Quarterly	4th quarter 1991
Small business income Wage and Salary, proprietorship income, (Bureau of Economic Analysis)[5]	Quarterly	4th quarter 1991
Self-employment (Numbers, income, Bureau of Census, Current Population Survey)	Annual	1991

---

[3]Under contract to the U.S. Small Business Administration.

[4]Available by state.

[5]Available by state.

Table 1.3 Sources of Small Business Data Covered in the 1994 Handbook of Small Business Data--Continued

Source\Description	Availability	Latest
Business Failures (Number, liabilities-Dun and Bradstreet)	Monthly	1991
New Business Incorporations (Number-Dun and Bradstreet)[6]	Monthly	1991
Receipts in Small Business Dominated Service Sectors (Dollar volume, number of firms-Census)	Annual	1990

IV. Data Derived From SBA Survey Research

Federal Reserve Survey of Small Firm Finances* (Balance sheet information, sources of capital for 4,000 firms)	Once	1989
Health Benefits Data (Coverage by firm size)	Approximately every 3 years	1987
Pension Benefits Data (Provision by firm size)	Approximately every 3 years	1989
Characteristics of Business Owners (Sources of financing by business type-Census*)	Every 5 years	1987 (in progress)
Day-Care Provision by Firm Size	Once	1990

---

[6]Available by state.

*Cosponsorship with the U.S. Small Business Administration.

2 U.S. Data by Size of Firm

Introduction

The majority of national-level data by size of firm comes from three sources: *Enterprise Statistics*, which is published every five years by the Census Bureau of the U.S. Department of Commerce; for data to 1990, the U.S. Small Business Administration's Small Business Data Base (SBDB), which used data from Dun and Bradstreet's Dun's Market Identifier (DMI) file; and, starting with 1988 data, a replacement data set for the SBDB, using data from the Census Bureau.

Another major source of data is the Department of Commerce's *County Business Patterns*. However, these data are by size of establishment, not by size of firm. It is sometimes used for comparison purposes with the data by size of firm.

This chapter will present data from each of these sources. Because the data are from different sources, they are not strictly comparable. For the most part, however, the aggregate numbers are fairly close in magnitude for each of the sources. The SBDB is the source for tables on dynamic changes in the U.S. business population. New data from the Census Bureau are used to present tables on static representations of the U.S. business population. *Enterprise Statistics* tables are used for comparison with the other two data bases.

Small Business Data Base

The SBDB uses data edited from the DMI file of Dun and Bradstreet. The DMI file is edited and linked so that the SBDB can be used as a static as well as a dynamic data base. The SBDB covers almost 93 percent of all businesses with employees in the United States. Aggregate data on the number of firms by size of firms, the number of establishments, the industries in which firms are located (down to the four-digit SIC code level), as well as the location of firms (down to the MSA level) is available in the SBDB. In addition, the SBDB covers the corporate structure of firms. Therefore, data on headquarters as well as subsidiaries and branches is readily available.

Because the SBDB is a micro-level data base, dynamic data are available. The dynamic aspect of the SBDB makes it unique in the world of federal business statistics. It can be used to analyze dynamic shifts in the industrial composition of the U.S. economy. Jobs gained and lost could be analyzed on a state-by-state basis. Shifts of firms into and out of industries as well as regions could also be examined.

The SBDB was phased out in 1992 and replaced by data from the Census Bureau (see discussion below). Therefore, no data beyond 1990 will be available for analysis. The dynamic data base links data from 1976–1986, 1984–1988, and 1988–1990.

Census Bureau Data

For the future, the Census Bureau data created for the U.S. Small Business Administration will contain dynamic as well as static data, but for now the data are static or cross-sectional. The Census Bureau data are compiled from the Standard Statistical Establishment List data as well as the Master Establishment List. The data contain the number of firms, the number of employees, and the annual payroll of firms by size of firm. The data are also reported by major industrial sectors by state.

For state data, the number of firms within a state affiliated with a company are counted. (In other words, all the GM subsidiaries in one state are counted as one firm.) Only data from 1988–1990 are available now, but in the future data for two-year periods will be available.

Some state-by-industry detail is not available due to disclosure rules. If a company can be readily identified because of the small number of companies in an area, then the federal government cannot legally disclose this information. This may cause some problems when the data are examined at the state level, but at the national level there are fewer missing values to be estimated by the user.

Enterprise Statistics

Data from the Commerce Department's *Enterprise Statistics* are also static. The data are published every five years with a three- to four-year lag before publication. (For instance, immediately before the compilation of this publication began in 1992, *Enterprise Statistics* for 1987 was published.)

Enterprise Statistics provides the most comprehensive data available by size of firm published by the federal government. It contains data on the number of firms, the number of employees, the number of establishments, and the sales of firms by industry (at an expanded two-digit SIC code level).

County Business Patterns

The U.S. Department of Commerce publishes *County Business Patterns* (CBP) annually. A separate volume is devoted to counting the number of business establishments in every county in each state, the District of Columbia, and Puerto Rico. CBP publishes data on the number of establishments, the number of employees in mid-March, the annual payroll, and first quarter payroll. These data are by industry down to the three-digit, and often four-digit, SIC code level and by size of establishment.

In addition, a U.S. summary volume is published that details the number of business establishments by state and industry, the number of employees in mid-March, the annual payroll, and the first quarter payroll.

Highlights

- There were 4.9 million firms with employees in the United States in 1988. About 3.0 million firms had fewer than five employees. Only 12,824 firms had more than 500 employees.
- Small firms employed 47.9 million workers, while the approximately 13,000 large firms employed 40.0 million workers.
- The majority of nonfarm private sector U.S. workers were employed by firms in the service industry (29.1 percent), followed by manufacturing (21.9 percent) and retail trade (21.6 percent).
- Between 1982 and 1987, nonfarm private sector employment in U.S. industries grew by 11.5 million workers.
- Between 1982 and 1987, employment in small firms grew by 10.2 million workers.
- Between 1986 and 1988, small businesses created 44.9 percent of all jobs created.
- Between 1984 and 1988, 72 percent of all jobs created were due to births of new firms.

Chapter 2 Tables

Table 2.1 Nonfarm Private Firms, Employment, and Annual Payroll by Industrial Sector and Firm Size for the United States, 1988

Industry		Total	Employment Size of Firm							
			1-4	5-9	10-19	<20	20-99	100-499	<500	500+
Total	Number of Firms	4,954,645	2,979,905	923,580	540,988	4,444,473	430,640	66,708	4,941,821	12,824
	Employment	87,844,303	5,006,203	6,060,724	7,252,715	18,319,642	16,833,702	12,761,379	47,914,723	39,929,580
	Annual Payroll	$1,858,652,147	$108,800,891	$103,041,106	$130,326,463	$342,168,460	$315,751,201	$244,647,178	$902,566,839	$956,085,308
Ag Services	Number of Firms	78,324	53,786	14,047	6,940	74,773	3,078	353	78,204	120
	Employment	471,827	78,459	91,909	90,829	261,197	104,458	44,850	410,505	61,322
	Annual Payroll	$7,500,456	$1,399,691	$1,260,600	$1,377,522	$4,037,813	$1,526,414	$654,531	$6,218,758	$1,281,698
Mining	Number of Firms	25,035	13,545	4,100	3,174	20,819	3,156	628	24,603	432
	Employment	736,777	22,346	27,119	42,936	92,401	116,465	81,449	290,315	446,462
	Annual Payroll	$24,871,993	$680,373	$577,967	$977,766	$2,236,106	$2,881,147	$2,419,151	$7,536,404	$17,335,589
Construction	Number of Firms	572,317	355,556	106,921	61,577	524,054	42,822	4,661	571,537	780
	Employment	4,995,795	574,245	701,077	822,177	2,097,499	1,584,458	737,179	4,419,136	576,659
	Annual Payroll	$123,164,980	$13,198,064	$13,293,244	$17,795,533	$44,286,841	$40,108,035	$20,839,641	$105,234,517	$17,930,463
Manufacturing	Number of Firms	320,408	119,421	59,060	52,871	231,352	67,425	16,969	315,746	4,662
	Employment	19,234,894	209,521	396,378	720,707	1,326,606	2,780,917	3,091,008	7,198,531	12,036,363
	Annual Payroll	$513,349,110	$5,583,120	$7,203,974	$14,404,836	$27,191,930	$59,879,716	$67,878,074	$154,949,720	$358,399,390
TCPU	Number of Firms	173,108	97,992	30,644	20,779	149,415	18,790	3,364	171,569	1,539
	Employment	5,293,212	162,627	201,629	279,908	644,164	708,714	519,268	1,872,146	3,421,066
	Annual Payroll	$148,071,069	$3,321,363	$3,361,846	$4,993,892	$11,677,101	$14,302,570	$11,766,875	$37,746,546	$110,324,523
Wholesale	Number of Firms	368,169	181,502	76,046	54,098	311,646	45,556	7,809	365,011	3,158
	Employment	5,994,021	330,479	503,638	719,886	1,554,003	1,630,692	917,170	4,101,865	1,892,156
	Annual Payroll	$160,666,783	$8,971,303	$11,254,865	$16,827,445	$37,053,613	$39,632,125	$23,166,821	$99,852,559	$60,814,224
Retail	Number of Firms	1,094,188	600,339	227,277	140,412	968,028	110,832	12,591	1,091,451	2,737
	Employment	18,867,211	1,057,592	1,499,242	1,870,649	4,427,483	4,141,230	2,050,758	10,619,471	8,247,740
	Annual Payroll	$217,332,457	$13,574,986	$15,136,541	$19,454,550	$48,166,077	$50,076,684	$25,117,410	$123,360,171	$93,972,286
FIRE	Number of Firms	402,849	285,673	55,081	28,734	369,488	25,040	5,678	400,206	2,643
	Employment	6,662,355	460,691	355,692	381,002	1,197,385	953,639	828,560	2,979,584	3,682,771
	Annual Payroll	$176,104,171	$10,578,507	$7,466,807	$8,822,849	$26,868,163	$21,909,512	$19,882,167	$68,659,842	$107,444,329
Services	Number of Firms	1,834,660	1,163,501	344,196	172,228	1,679,925	123,465	24,828	1,828,218	6,442
	Employment	25,252,106	2,029,975	2,233,970	2,282,115	6,546,060	4,750,438	4,451,478	15,747,976	9,504,130
	Annual Payroll	$480,821,876	$49,046,657	$43,147,464	$45,376,089	$137,570,210	$84,943,346	$72,447,658	$294,961,214	$185,860,662
Unclassified	Number of Firms	122,416	109,371	7,732	3,256	120,359	1,799	192	122,350	66
	Employment	336,105	80,268	50,070	42,506	172,844	62,691	39,659	275,194	60,911
	Annual Payroll	$6,769,252	$2,446,827	$337,798	$295,981	$3,080,606	$491,652	$474,850	$4,047,108	$2,722,144

Note: Annual payroll in thousands of dollars.

Source: Adapted by the U.S. Small Business Administration, Office of Advocacy from unpublished data prepared under contract. The data was produced by merging the Company Organization Survey and the Standard Statistical Establishment List.

Table 2.2 Nonfarm Private Firms, Employment, and Annual Payroll by SBA Region and State, 1988

Region/State		Total	Employment Size of Firm 1-4	5-9	10-19	<20	20-99	100-499	<500	500+
United States	Number of Firms	4,954,645	2,979,905	923,580	540,988	4,444,473	430,640	66,708	4,941,821	12,824
	Employment	87,844,303	5,006,203	6,060,724	7,252,715	18,319,642	16,833,702	12,761,379	47,914,723	39,929,580
	Annual Payroll	$1,858,652,147	$108,800,891	$103,041,106	$130,326,463	$342,168,460	$315,751,201	$244,647,178	$902,566,839	$956,085,308
Region I	Number of Firms	327,294	187,772	60,354	35,585	283,711	30,340	6,991	321,042	6,252
	Employment	5,791,079	313,725	395,423	472,888	1,182,036	1,146,792	907,121	3,235,949	2,555,130
	Annual Payroll	$130,400,620	$7,686,003	$7,474,407	$9,477,715	$24,638,125	$23,498,766	$18,622,059	$66,758,950	$63,641,670
Connecticut	Number of Firms	82,378	47,399	15,144	8,992	71,535	7,490	1,709	80,734	1,644
	Employment	1,494,543	79,809	99,182	119,331	298,322	282,922	215,152	796,396	698,147
	Annual Payroll	$37,352,697	$2,246,898	$2,100,345	$2,722,071	$7,069,314	$6,419,376	$4,730,376	$18,219,066	$19,133,631
Maine	Number of Firms	31,107	19,088	5,516	3,003	27,607	2,353	547	30,507	600
	Employment	414,671	29,701	36,102	39,908	105,711	87,219	72,689	265,619	149,052
	Annual Payroll	$7,501,291	$552,688	$521,083	$647,904	$1,721,675	$1,431,798	$1,186,125	$4,339,598	$3,161,693
Massachusetts	Number of Firms	139,561	77,637	26,501	15,889	120,027	14,023	3,266	137,316	2,245
	Employment	2,810,546	132,531	173,928	211,645	518,104	538,832	444,164	1,501,100	1,309,446
	Annual Payroll	$64,713,142	$3,413,781	$3,436,814	$4,312,972	$11,163,567	$11,334,856	$9,482,353	$31,980,776	$32,732,366
New Hampshire	Number of Firms	30,993	17,968	5,595	3,305	26,868	2,752	634	30,254	739
	Employment	455,641	29,066	36,556	43,402	109,024	100,207	71,261	280,492	175,149
	Annual Payroll	$9,240,180	$640,070	$630,766	$796,766	$2,067,707	$1,904,143	$1,343,566	$5,315,416	$3,924,764
Rhode Island	Number of Firms	25,340	14,682	4,417	2,637	21,736	2,400	550	24,686	654
	Employment	406,149	24,837	28,887	35,360	89,084	90,805	68,829	248,718	157,431
	Annual Payroll	$7,788,396	$529,186	$496,443	$637,820	$1,663,449	$1,615,735	$1,273,979	$4,553,163	$3,235,233
Vermont	Number of Firms	17,915	10,998	3,181	1,759	15,938	1,322	285	17,545	370
	Employment	209,529	17,781	20,768	23,242	61,791	46,807	35,026	143,624	65,905
	Annual Payroll	$3,804,914	$303,380	$288,851	$360,182	$952,413	$792,858	$605,660	$2,350,931	$1,453,983
Region II	Number of Firms	598,793	370,358	102,856	59,176	532,390	49,832	10,498	592,720	6,073
	Employment	10,037,420	612,010	671,316	789,686	2,073,012	1,886,758	1,514,063	5,473,833	4,563,587
	Annual Payroll	$251,767,542	$15,777,436	$13,716,033	$17,154,103	$46,647,572	$42,292,335	$34,001,618	$122,941,525	$128,826,017
New Jersey	Number of Firms	187,451	113,021	32,776	19,125	164,922	16,310	3,644	184,876	2,575
	Employment	3,154,690	186,737	213,935	254,323	654,995	617,786	463,535	1,736,316	1,418,374
	Annual Payroll	$77,328,295	$4,883,567	$4,465,495	$5,586,089	$14,935,151	$14,147,474	$10,492,792	$39,575,417	$37,752,878
New York	Number of Firms	411,342	257,337	70,080	40,051	367,468	33,522	6,854	407,844	3,498
	Employment	6,882,730	425,273	457,381	535,363	1,418,017	1,268,972	1,050,528	3,737,517	3,145,213
	Annual Payroll	$174,439,247	$10,893,869	$9,250,538	$11,568,014	$31,712,421	$28,144,861	$23,508,826	$83,366,108	$91,073,139
Region III	Number of Firms	500,003	282,906	92,276	56,192	431,374	47,791	11,226	490,391	9,612
	Employment	9,409,816	480,119	604,741	747,422	1,832,282	1,780,372	1,445,294	5,057,948	4,351,868
	Annual Payroll	$194,919,804	$9,600,883	$10,053,425	$13,362,444	$33,016,752	$33,511,888	$27,608,356	$94,136,996	$100,782,808
Delaware	Number of Firms	15,214	8,275	2,737	1,673	12,685	1,466	383	14,534	680
	Employment	288,018	12,801	18,013	22,129	52,943	52,700	35,086	140,729	147,289
	Annual Payroll	$6,385,704	$274,260	$295,972	$387,883	$958,115	$945,554	$614,762	$2,518,431	$3,867,273

Table 2.2 Nonfarm Private Firms, Employment, and Annual Payroll by SBA Region and State, 1988--Continued

Region/State		Total	Employment Size of Firm 1-4	5-9	10-19	<20	20-99	100-499	<500	500+
District of Columbia	Number of Firms	17,071	8,402	2,876	1,985	13,263	2,109	824	16,196	875
	Employment	409,315	14,241	18,673	25,504	58,418	75,468	75,407	207,293	202,022
	Annual Payroll	$10,571,412	$528,461	$468,112	$630,200	$1,626,773	$1,823,259	$1,949,652	$5,399,684	$5,171,728
Maryland	Number of Firms	91,739	49,708	17,048	11,264	78,020	9,522	2,224	89,766	1,973
	Employment	1,718,051	82,305	112,239	150,110	344,654	355,380	272,086	970,120	747,931
	Annual Payroll	$36,269,898	$2,011,255	$1,995,240	$2,733,197	$6,739,692	$6,933,030	$5,397,950	$19,070,672	$17,199,226
Pennsylvania	Number of Firms	227,820	131,762	42,025	24,944	198,731	21,348	4,700	224,779	3,041
	Employment	4,373,383	226,679	275,401	332,909	834,989	816,974	691,026	2,342,989	2,030,394
	Annual Payroll	$89,897,402	$4,161,997	$4,475,966	$5,958,788	$14,596,751	$15,077,483	$12,759,076	$42,433,310	$47,464,092
Virginia	Number of Firms	116,652	66,113	21,868	13,166	101,147	10,785	2,527	114,459	2,193
	Employment	2,165,194	112,006	143,353	174,968	430,327	392,845	313,212	1,136,384	1,028,810
	Annual Payroll	$43,146,787	$2,168,400	$2,308,169	$3,032,297	$7,508,866	$7,195,172	$5,948,547	$20,652,585	$22,494,202
West Virginia	Number of Firms	31,507	18,646	5,722	3,160	27,528	2,561	568	30,657	850
	Employment	455,855	32,087	37,062	41,802	110,951	91,005	58,477	260,433	195,422
	Annual Payroll	$8,648,601	$456,510	$509,966	$620,079	$1,586,555	$1,537,390	$938,369	$4,062,314	$4,586,287
Region IV	Number of Firms	878,245	519,194	161,340	91,126	771,660	73,354	16,872	861,886	16,359
	Employment	15,042,886	878,104	1,054,415	1,208,070	3,140,589	2,723,160	2,066,773	7,930,522	7,112,364
	Annual Payroll	$274,806,197	$16,259,263	$16,300,686	$19,753,323	$52,313,272	$45,151,352	$34,105,520	$131,570,144	$143,236,053
Alabama	Number of Firms	70,245	40,551	13,023	7,408	60,982	6,219	1,378	68,579	1,666
	Employment	1,220,918	70,017	85,350	98,337	253,704	230,688	168,011	652,403	568,515
	Annual Payroll	$21,997,889	$1,090,600	$1,209,773	$1,535,232	$3,835,605	$3,692,831	$2,756,604	$10,285,040	$11,712,849
Florida	Number of Firms	289,277	176,854	52,926	29,235	259,015	22,683	4,501	286,199	3,078
	Employment	4,271,270	292,823	345,398	387,796	1,026,017	851,421	577,066	2,454,504	1,816,766
	Annual Payroll	$77,974,503	$6,284,688	$5,832,009	$6,663,338	$18,780,035	$14,422,435	$9,723,168	$42,925,638	$35,048,865
Georgia	Number of Firms	124,800	71,203	23,329	13,412	107,944	10,952	3,012	121,908	2,892
	Employment	2,356,650	119,420	152,885	177,716	450,021	401,553	319,549	1,171,123	1,185,527
	Annual Payroll	$46,502,384	$2,645,039	$2,521,666	$3,147,057	$8,313,762	$7,082,587	$5,636,102	$21,032,451	$25,469,933
Kentucky	Number of Firms	64,973	37,226	12,007	7,020	56,253	5,844	1,324	63,421	1,552
	Employment	1,092,902	64,737	78,453	92,982	236,172	215,325	151,524	603,021	489,881
	Annual Payroll	$19,852,273	$976,976	$1,088,112	$1,376,263	$3,441,351	$3,304,823	$2,403,941	$9,150,115	$10,702,158
Mississippi	Number of Firms	43,709	26,393	7,837	4,289	38,519	3,234	811	42,564	1,145
	Employment	674,890	45,595	51,194	56,639	153,428	116,710	98,867	369,005	305,885
	Annual Payroll	$10,720,832	$598,494	$668,298	$790,118	$2,056,910	$1,712,060	$1,405,584	$5,174,554	$5,546,278
North Carolina	Number of Firms	130,604	77,028	23,956	13,624	114,608	11,093	2,558	128,259	2,345
	Employment	2,507,479	131,116	156,499	180,709	468,324	414,912	352,107	1,235,343	1,272,136
	Annual Payroll	$45,234,202	$2,123,708	$2,299,199	$2,879,321	$7,302,228	$6,830,696	$5,666,501	$19,799,425	$25,434,777
South Carolina	Number of Firms	63,616	37,356	11,651	6,637	55,644	5,202	1,264	62,110	1,506
	Employment	1,157,629	64,300	75,945	87,801	228,046	187,739	153,708	569,493	588,136
	Annual Payroll	$19,972,583	$1,010,888	$1,062,472	$1,307,482	$3,380,842	$2,860,895	$2,432,997	$8,674,734	$11,297,849

Table 2.2 Nonfarm Private Firms, Employment, and Annual Payroll by SBA Region and State, 1988--Continued

Region/State		Total	1-4	5-9	10-19	<20	20-99	100-499	<500	500+
					Employment Size of Firm					
Tennessee	Number of Firms	91,021	52,583	16,611	9,501	78,695	8,127	2,024	88,846	2,175
	Employment	1,761,148	90,096	108,691	126,090	324,877	304,812	245,941	875,630	885,518
	Annual Payroll	$32,551,531	$1,528,870	$1,619,157	$2,054,512	$5,202,539	$5,245,025	$4,080,623	$14,528,187	$18,023,344
Region V	Number of Firms	885,757	496,925	167,009	103,017	766,951	86,199	18,681	871,831	13,926
	Employment	17,097,227	847,925	1,097,019	1,376,484	3,321,428	3,262,613	2,548,837	9,132,878	7,964,349
	Annual Payroll	$373,191,631	$17,929,624	$18,489,832	$24,704,613	$61,124,069	$61,932,368	$49,017,586	$172,074,023	$201,117,608
Illinois	Number of Firms	223,758	127,006	40,648	25,665	193,319	22,031	5,078	220,428	3,330
	Employment	4,375,941	213,589	267,274	342,143	823,006	829,514	657,320	2,309,840	2,066,101
	Annual Payroll	$101,287,191	$5,340,946	$5,035,698	$6,719,420	$17,096,064	$17,160,893	$13,918,643	$48,175,600	$53,111,591
Indiana	Number of Firms	102,527	56,879	19,576	11,787	88,242	9,922	2,313	100,477	2,050
	Employment	1,998,903	99,743	128,196	157,065	385,004	371,733	301,223	1,057,960	940,943
	Annual Payroll	$40,067,460	$1,774,180	$1,871,673	$2,490,005	$6,135,858	$6,460,331	$5,195,715	$17,791,904	$22,275,556
Michigan	Number of Firms	169,196	94,533	32,963	20,074	147,570	16,225	3,130	166,925	2,271
	Employment	3,207,562	160,281	216,918	268,941	646,140	618,817	440,603	1,705,560	1,502,002
	Annual Payroll	$75,678,529	$3,588,081	$3,815,262	$5,145,929	$12,549,272	$12,468,098	$8,815,875	$33,833,245	$41,845,284
Minnesota	Number of Firms	91,873	51,031	17,263	11,009	79,303	8,940	1,953	90,196	1,677
	Employment	1,700,092	85,441	113,760	147,223	346,424	337,429	271,506	955,359	744,733
	Annual Payroll	$35,783,844	$1,630,581	$1,872,276	$2,482,562	$5,985,419	$6,097,904	$5,131,944	$17,215,267	$18,568,577
Ohio	Number of Firms	196,942	110,437	37,434	22,702	170,573	19,274	4,193	194,040	2,902
	Employment	4,018,273	191,748	245,319	303,208	740,275	734,421	581,313	2,056,009	1,962,264
	Annual Payroll	$85,541,337	$3,919,030	$4,050,632	$5,351,166	$13,320,828	$13,494,603	$10,566,620	$37,382,051	$48,159,286
Wisconsin	Number of Firms	101,461	57,039	19,125	11,780	87,944	9,807	2,014	99,765	1,696
	Employment	1,796,456	97,123	125,552	157,904	380,579	370,699	296,872	1,048,150	748,306
	Annual Payroll	$34,833,270	$1,676,806	$1,844,291	$2,515,531	$6,036,628	$6,250,539	$5,388,789	$17,675,956	$17,157,314
Region VI	Number of Firms	567,975	340,733	102,405	57,912	501,050	46,965	10,176	558,191	9,784
	Employment	9,275,858	585,408	669,374	768,948	2,023,730	1,735,672	1,260,918	5,020,320	4,255,538
	Annual Payroll	$180,774,853	$11,280,686	$10,464,790	$12,595,567	$34,341,043	$28,831,141	$22,090,803	$85,262,987	$95,511,866
Arkansas	Number of Firms	44,958	27,126	8,026	4,464	39,616	3,422	811	43,849	1,109
	Employment	690,803	46,654	52,535	58,826	158,015	124,511	100,376	382,902	307,901
	Annual Payroll	$11,280,180	$699,360	$696,688	$865,826	$2,261,874	$1,809,606	$1,478,649	$5,550,129	$5,730,051
Louisiana	Number of Firms	73,661	42,608	13,682	7,769	64,059	6,559	1,438	72,056	1,605
	Employment	1,181,028	74,920	89,571	103,329	267,820	246,709	167,022	681,551	499,477
	Annual Payroll	$22,327,702	$1,420,188	$1,333,021	$1,641,869	$4,395,258	$3,937,534	$2,797,232	$11,130,024	$11,197,678
New Mexico	Number of Firms	30,061	17,534	5,379	3,235	26,148	2,436	557	29,141	920
	Employment	386,816	29,411	35,078	42,880	107,369	87,027	52,645	247,041	139,775
	Annual Payroll	$6,648,594	$451,099	$472,492	$599,705	$1,523,296	$1,266,165	$846,689	$3,636,150	$3,012,444
Oklahoma	Number of Firms	62,468	38,283	10,979	5,975	55,237	4,766	1,033	61,036	1,432
	Employment	875,890	66,109	71,441	79,070	216,620	173,634	117,084	507,338	368,552
	Annual Payroll	$16,423,170	$1,124,542	$1,084,347	$1,232,764	$3,441,653	$2,766,066	$2,025,098	$8,232,817	$8,190,353
Texas	Number of Firms	311,869	188,056	56,313	32,005	276,374	26,360	5,526	308,260	3,609
	Employment	5,450,518	321,660	368,214	426,017	1,115,891	979,280	723,415	2,818,586	2,631,932
	Annual Payroll	$112,815,027	$6,886,137	$6,181,374	$7,389,577	$20,457,088	$17,242,164	$13,464,486	$51,163,738	$61,651,289

Table 2.2 Nonfarm Private Firms, Employment, and Annual Payroll by SBA Region and State, 1988--Continued

Region/State		Total	1-4	5-9	10-19	<20	20-99	100-499	<500	500+
Region VII	Number of Firms	259,892	152,000	47,338	27,713	227,051	22,486	4,806	254,343	5,549
	Employment	4,190,537	262,012	309,966	367,015	938,993	821,257	568,918	2,329,168	1,861,369
	Annual Payroll	$78,519,683	$4,132,289	$4,471,172	$5,793,154	$14,396,615	$13,551,401	$9,639,548	$37,587,564	$40,932,119
Iowa	Number of Firms	60,325	35,346	11,300	6,426	53,072	5,044	1,039	59,155	1,170
	Employment	919,455	62,023	74,096	84,990	221,109	185,481	123,799	530,389	389,066
	Annual Payroll	$16,096,284	$893,559	$985,216	$1,261,884	$3,140,659	$2,852,623	$2,002,213	$7,995,495	$8,100,789
Kansas	Number of Firms	55,911	32,823	10,028	5,904	48,755	4,771	1,036	54,562	1,349
	Employment	834,337	57,228	65,587	78,149	200,964	172,784	112,264	486,012	348,325
	Annual Payroll	$15,724,502	$880,715	$953,966	$1,210,716	$3,025,397	$2,854,897	$1,923,548	$7,803,842	$7,920,660
Missouri	Number of Firms	106,519	62,092	19,054	11,462	92,608	9,703	2,085	104,396	2,123
	Employment	1,898,070	105,021	124,783	152,260	382,064	355,218	260,662	997,944	900,126
	Annual Payroll	$37,703,489	$1,828,732	$1,927,046	$2,541,988	$6,297,766	$6,214,936	$4,599,412	$17,112,114	$20,591,375
Nebraska	Number of Firms	37,137	21,739	6,956	3,921	32,616	2,968	646	36,230	907
	Employment	538,675	37,740	45,500	51,616	134,856	107,774	72,193	314,823	223,852
	Annual Payroll	$8,995,408	$529,283	$624,944	$778,566	$1,932,793	$1,628,945	$1,114,375	$4,676,113	$4,319,295
Region VIII	Number of Firms	180,122	108,887	31,946	17,681	158,514	13,659	3,228	175,401	4,721
	Employment	2,377,387	179,344	208,192	233,315	620,851	485,402	312,325	1,418,578	958,809
	Annual Payroll	$44,676,113	$3,164,412	$3,052,713	$3,590,876	$9,808,001	$7,873,225	$5,272,840	$22,954,066	$21,724,047
Colorado	Number of Firms	80,618	49,014	14,101	7,750	70,865	6,284	1,530	78,679	1,939
	Employment	1,167,137	81,061	91,983	102,365	275,409	225,178	151,321	651,908	515,229
	Annual Payroll	$24,036,151	$1,622,588	$1,516,785	$1,751,657	$4,891,030	$3,988,464	$2,670,096	$11,549,590	$12,486,561
Montana	Number of Firms	22,045	13,982	3,850	2,104	19,936	1,388	277	21,601	444
	Employment	203,707	22,827	24,947	27,775	75,549	47,798	25,061	148,408	55,299
	Annual Payroll	$3,221,787	$331,791	$305,293	$366,107	$1,003,191	$678,882	$398,945	$2,081,018	$1,140,769
North Dakota	Number of Firms	16,784	10,183	3,023	1,635	14,841	1,202	316	16,359	425
	Employment	184,166	16,869	19,585	21,616	58,070	42,926	29,368	130,364	53,802
	Annual Payroll	$2,913,690	$227,936	$253,117	$319,300	$800,353	$625,790	$431,456	$1,857,599	$1,056,091
South Dakota	Number of Firms	17,607	10,883	3,008	1,733	15,624	1,264	301	17,189	418
	Employment	193,790	17,646	19,599	22,854	60,099	44,847	29,169	134,115	59,675
	Annual Payroll	$2,889,369	$233,988	$248,194	$311,057	$793,239	$638,633	$453,381	$1,885,253	$1,004,116
Utah	Number of Firms	30,232	16,914	5,715	3,311	25,940	2,643	612	29,195	1,037
	Employment	507,189	27,831	37,511	43,683	109,025	96,119	66,102	271,246	235,943
	Annual Payroll	$9,358,721	$549,814	$530,487	$624,820	$1,705,121	$1,513,935	$1,110,096	$4,329,152	$5,029,569
Wyoming	Number of Firms	12,836	7,911	2,249	1,148	11,308	878	192	12,378	458
	Employment	121,398	13,110	14,567	15,022	42,699	28,534	11,304	82,537	38,861
	Annual Payroll	$2,258,395	$198,295	$198,837	$217,935	$615,067	$427,521	$208,866	$1,251,454	$1,006,941
Region IX	Number of Firms	722,603	426,951	129,987	79,150	636,088	66,149	12,834	715,071	7,532
	Employment	12,448,995	693,296	853,879	1,057,343	2,604,518	2,517,995	1,825,357	6,947,870	5,501,125
	Annual Payroll	$282,458,531	$19,811,212	$15,799,085	$19,938,505	$55,548,802	$50,178,801	$37,879,053	$143,606,656	$138,851,875
Arizona	Number of Firms	70,887	41,152	12,618	7,708	61,478	6,246	1,460	69,184	1,703
	Employment	1,174,785	67,150	82,752	102,237	252,139	231,354	157,582	641,075	533,710
	Annual Payroll	$22,332,829	$1,543,805	$1,307,256	$1,614,091	$4,465,152	$3,724,277	$2,684,535	$10,873,964	$11,458,865

Table 2.2 Nonfarm Private Firms, Employment, and Annual Payroll by SBA Region and State, 1988--Continued

Region/State		Total	1-4	5-9	Employment Size of Firm 10-19	<20	20-99	100-499	<500	500+
California	Number of Firms	604,939	359,911	108,621	66,195	534,727	55,566	10,309	600,602	4,337
	Employment	10,430,384	583,679	713,559	885,384	2,182,622	2,129,116	1,541,734	5,853,472	4,576,912
	Annual Payroll	$244,136,403	$17,176,643	$13,480,951	$17,140,088	$47,797,682	$43,641,442	$32,936,649	$124,375,773	$119,760,630
Hawaii	Number of Firms	23,068	12,707	4,449	2,707	19,863	2,157	469	22,489	579
	Employment	381,511	21,746	29,247	36,216	87,209	79,451	63,393	230,053	151,458
	Annual Payroll	$7,231,935	$527,028	$493,826	$595,691	$1,616,545	$1,359,558	$1,145,974	$4,122,077	$3,109,858
Nevada	Number of Firms	23,709	13,181	4,299	2,540	20,020	2,180	596	22,796	913
	Employment	462,315	20,721	28,321	33,506	82,548	78,074	62,648	223,270	239,045
	Annual Payroll	$8,757,364	$563,736	$517,052	$588,635	$1,669,423	$1,453,524	$1,111,895	$4,234,842	$4,522,522
Region X	Number of Firms	206,565	122,491	38,011	22,005	182,507	16,592	3,510	202,609	3,956
	Employment	2,863,901	200,914	248,934	290,370	740,218	598,192	412,149	1,750,559	1,113,342
	Annual Payroll	$58,415,353	$3,858,443	$3,915,651	$4,821,989	$12,596,083	$10,739,530	$7,888,444	$31,224,057	$27,191,296
Alaska	Number of Firms	12,229	7,491	2,195	1,177	10,863	782	226	11,871	358
	Employment	134,276	11,639	14,503	15,457	41,599	26,589	24,978	93,166	41,110
	Annual Payroll	$3,649,506	$342,737	$326,571	$355,120	$1,024,428	$661,088	$583,037	$2,268,553	$1,380,953
Idaho	Number of Firms	21,604	12,847	4,007	2,245	19,099	1,629	335	21,063	541
	Employment	265,444	21,402	26,145	29,365	76,912	57,262	30,407	164,581	100,863
	Annual Payroll	$4,673,727	$347,560	$350,943	$408,390	$1,106,893	$831,349	$458,040	$2,396,282	$2,277,445
Oregon	Number of Firms	67,316	39,644	12,452	7,224	59,320	5,486	1,167	65,973	1,343
	Employment	929,206	65,811	81,354	95,630	242,795	196,220	142,429	581,444	347,762
	Annual Payroll	$17,595,372	$1,195,006	$1,193,886	$1,485,696	$3,874,588	$3,387,721	$2,645,239	$9,907,548	$7,687,824
Washington	Number of Firms	105,416	62,509	19,357	11,359	93,225	8,695	1,782	103,702	1,714
	Employment	1,534,975	102,062	126,932	149,918	378,912	318,121	214,335	911,368	623,607
	Annual Payroll	$32,496,748	$1,973,140	$2,044,251	$2,572,783	$6,590,174	$5,859,372	$4,202,128	$16,651,674	$15,845,074

Note: The state and regional total do not sum to the U.S. total because firms are defined within states not across states. Therefore, it is likely that firms are counted more than once if they have operations in more than one state. Annual payroll in thousands of dollars.

Source: Adapted by the U.S. Small Business Administration, Office of Advocacy from unpublished data prepared under contract. The data was produced by merging the Company Organization Survey and the Standard Statistical Establishment List.

Table 2.3 Nonfarm Private Firms, Employment, and Annual Payroll by Industrial Sector and Firm Size, for the United States, 1989

Industry	Total	Employment Size of Firm							
		1-4	5-9	10-19	<20	20-99	100-499	<500	500+
All Industries									
Number of Firms	5,021,315	605,002	937,202	553,449	4,493,875	443,959	69,608	5,007,442	13,873
Employment	91,626,094	5,054,429	6,152,151	7,420,196	18,626,776	17,353,444	13,373,640	49,353,860	42,272,234
Annual Payroll	$1,989,941,554	$112,462,139	$108,002,714	$136,794,734	$357,259,587	$332,733,188	$264,144,335	$954,137,110	$1,035,804,444
Agriculture Service, Forestry, Fishing									
Number of Firms	83,431	57,011	15,019	7,473	79,503	3,449	357	83,309	122
Employment	498,774	81,589	98,364	97,999	277,952	117,346	46,761	442,059	56,715
Annual Payroll	$7,956,128	$1,542,798	$1,406,782	$1,491,561	$4,441,141	$1,753,092	$705,790	$6,900,023	$1,056,105
Mining									
Number of Firms	24,365	13,308	3,994	3,005	20,307	3,013	613	23,933	432
Employment	713,360	21,712	26,286	40,439	88,437	110,659	81,870	280,966	432,394
Annual Payroll	$25,005,283	$651,824	$588,421	$944,022	$2,184,267	$2,903,030	$2,549,010	$7,636,307	$17,368,976
Construction									
Number of Firms	589,025	367,479	108,634	63,166	539,279	44,246	4,704	588,229	796
Employment	5,135,544	589,987	711,928	842,031	2,143,946	1,638,001	761,389	4,543,336	592,208
Annual Payroll	$129,338,075	$13,808,634	$13,727,482	$18,500,632	$46,036,748	$42,161,458	$22,004,827	$110,203,033	$19,135,042
Manufacturing									
Number of Firms	324,139	121,318	59,761	53,121	234,200	67,910	17,251	319,361	4,778
Employment	19,534,078	213,262	401,622	726,743	1,341,627	2,821,448	3,161,091	7,324,166	12,209,912
Annual Payroll	$533,982,185	$5,777,952	$7,471,807	$14,819,975	$28,069,734	$61,747,150	$70,945,640	$160,762,524	$373,219,661
Transportation, Communications, Public Utilities									
Number of Firms	178,280	101,404	31,197	21,248	153,849	19,439	3,426	176,714	1,566
Employment	5,438,191	165,836	205,376	286,189	657,401	738,779	537,992	1,934,172	3,504,019
Annual Payroll	$154,037,389	$3,570,291	$3,563,083	$5,169,752	$12,303,126	$15,199,227	$12,398,283	$39,900,636	$114,136,753
Wholesale Trade									
Number of Firms	370,674	182,377	76,210	54,350	312,937	46,491	8,041	367,469	3,205
Employment	6,192,885	330,216	504,692	724,426	1,559,334	1,674,164	967,253	4,200,751	1,992,134
Annual Payroll	$171,384,401	$9,449,415	$11,645,424	$17,432,646	$38,527,485	$41,518,971	$25,066,273	$105,112,729	$66,271,672

Table 2.3 Nonfarm Private Firms, Employment, and Annual Payroll by Industrial Sector and Firm Size, for the United States, 1989--Continued

Industry	Total	Employment Size of Firm							
		1-4	5-9	10-19	<20	20-99	100-499	<500	500+
Finance, Insurance, Real Estate									
Number of Firms	409,605	290,422	56,719	29,043	375,644	25,513	5,695	406,852	2,753
Employment	6,819,379	466,787	362,930	385,812	1,215,529	966,970	841,770	3,024,269	3,795,110
Annual Payroll	185,205,243	10,781,241	7,979,176	9,160,519	27,920,936	22,906,444	20,655,088	71,482,468	113,722,775
Services									
Number of Firms	1,872,348	1,175,756	353,313	179,813	1,708,882	129,805	26,499	1,865,186	7,162
Employment	27,535,086	2,056,627	2,296,386	2,382,613	6,735,626	4,996,207	4,808,970	16,540,803	10,994,283
Annual Payroll	548,118,560	50,797,695	45,779,962	48,833,395	145,411,052	92,683,177	82,820,413	320,914,642	227,203,918
Unclassified									
Number of Firms	100,436	89,969	6,183	2,611	98,763	1,448	171	100,382	54
Employment	279,940	67,811	39,984	34,017	141,812	49,844	37,534	229,190	50,750
Annual Payroll	4,428,161	2,033,687	323,609	268,589	2,625,885	434,446	502,213	3,562,544	856,617

Note: Annual payroll in thousands of dollars.

Source: U.S. Small Business Administration, Office of Advocacy, based upon data prepared for the Small Business Administration, under contract by the U.S. Department of Commerce, Bureau of the Census, unpublished data. The data was produced by merging the Company Organization Survey and the Standard Statistical Establishment List.

Table 2.4 Nonfarm Private Firms, Employment and Annual Payroll by SBA Region and State, 1989

		Total	1-4	5-9	10-19	<20	20-99	100-499	<500	500+
United States	Firms	5,021,315	3,003,224	937,202	553,449	4,493,875	443,959	69,608	5,007,442	13,873
	Employment	91,626,094	5,054,429	6,152,151	7,420,196	18,626,776	17,353,444	13,373,640	49,353,860	42,272,234
	Annual Payroll	$1,989,941,554	$112,462,139	$108,002,714	$136,794,734	$357,259,587	$332,733,188	$264,144,335	$954,137,110	$1,035,804,444
Region I	Firms	328,801	187,616	60,881	35,911	284,408	30,689	7,125	322,222	6,579
	Employment	5,927,510	318,477	399,241	478,172	1,195,890	1,161,866	927,806	3,285,562	2,641,948
	Annual Payroll	$137,559,976	$7,625,246	$7,732,061	$9,731,929	$25,089,236	$24,126,497	$19,839,004	$69,054,737	$68,505,239
Connecticut	Firms	82,718	47,447	15,311	8,937	71,695	7,541	1,790	81,026	1,692
	Employment	1,498,730	81,040	100,469	118,746	300,255	283,184	221,856	805,295	693,435
	Annual Payroll	$39,366,303	$2,166,512	$2,239,841	$2,785,844	$7,192,197	$6,655,967	$5,228,645	$19,076,809	$20,289,494
Maine	Firms	31,603	19,154	5,605	3,185	27,944	2,492	538	30,974	629
	Employment	439,298	30,294	36,779	42,403	109,476	94,524	71,034	275,034	164,264
	Annual Payroll	$8,187,271	$570,836	$532,949	$683,017	$1,786,802	$1,535,593	$1,193,652	$4,516,047	$3,671,224
Massachusetts	Firms	139,998	77,790	26,440	15,942	120,172	14,182	3,276	137,630	2,368
	Employment	2,896,284	134,780	173,329	212,481	520,590	546,252	453,682	1,520,524	1,375,760
	Annual Payroll	$68,256,635	$3,403,632	$3,486,256	$4,389,959	$11,279,847	$11,626,128	$9,882,483	$32,788,458	$35,468,177
New Hampshire	Firms	30,722	17,569	5,695	3,351	26,615	2,669	651	29,935	787
	Employment	464,124	28,972	37,271	44,477	110,720	97,596	74,283	282,599	181,525
	Annual Payroll	$9,532,316	$613,601	$641,758	$818,859	$2,074,218	$1,811,378	$1,487,745	$5,373,341	$4,158,975
Rhode Island	Firms	25,594	14,616	4,574	2,688	21,878	2,442	571	24,891	703
	Employment	409,900	24,965	30,022	36,161	91,148	91,244	71,286	253,678	156,222
	Annual Payroll	$8,180,760	$558,262	$526,610	$675,718	$1,760,590	$1,661,764	$1,382,871	$4,805,225	$3,375,535
Vermont	Firms	18,166	11,040	3,256	1,808	16,104	1,363	299	17,766	400
	Employment	219,174	18,426	21,371	23,904	63,701	49,066	35,665	148,432	70,742
	Annual Payroll	$4,036,691	$312,403	$304,647	$378,532	$995,582	$835,667	$663,608	$2,494,857	$1,541,834
Region II	Firms	602,799	372,470	103,355	59,495	535,320	50,343	10,795	596,458	6,341
	Employment	7,094,547	429,429	460,396	539,532	1,429,357	1,295,828	1,086,678	3,811,863	3,282,684
	Annual Payroll	$265,172,783	$16,234,823	$14,336,456	$17,806,736	$48,378,015	$43,871,787	$36,555,035	$128,802,837	$136,369,946
New Jersey	Firms	188,785	114,130	32,850	19,067	166,047	16,261	3,812	186,120	2,665
	Employment	3,248,306	190,171	214,444	254,247	658,862	618,178	486,450	1,763,490	1,484,816
	Annual Payroll	$82,074,278	$5,112,500	$4,653,261	$5,784,698	$15,550,459	$14,448,247	$11,311,691	$41,310,397	$40,763,881
New York	Firms	414,014	258,340	70,505	40,428	369,273	34,082	6,983	410,338	3,676
	Employment	7,094,547	429,429	460,396	539,532	1,429,357	1,295,828	1,086,678	3,811,863	3,282,684
	Annual Payroll	$183,098,505	$11,122,323	$9,683,195	$12,022,038	$32,827,556	$29,423,540	$25,241,344	$87,492,440	$95,606,065
Region III	Firms	509,070	286,772	94,023	57,858	438,653	48,697	11,613	498,963	10,107
	Employment	9,773,192	489,630	616,335	770,760	1,876,725	1,813,517	1,503,716	5,193,958	4,579,234
	Annual Payroll	$209,144,481	$10,183,664	$10,592,545	$14,244,003	$35,020,212	$35,114,346	$29,620,980	$81,755,538	$109,388,943
Delaware	Firms	15,709	8,558	2,802	1,722	13,082	1,500	397	14,979	730
	Employment	301,748	13,463	18,379	22,654	54,496	53,524	35,315	143,335	158,413
	Annual Payroll	$7,088,656	$271,251	$314,823	$418,609	$1,004,683	$1,018,100	$661,788	$2,684,571	$4,404,085

Table 2.4 Nonfarm Private Firms, Employment and Annual Payroll by SBA Region and State, 1989--Continued

				Employment Size of Firm					
	Total	1-4	5-9	10-19	<20	20-99	100-499	<500	500+
District of Columbia Firms	16,866	8,253	2,828	1,996	13,077	2,061	812	15,950	916
Employment	426,982	14,181	18,529	25,776	58,486	72,461	76,692	207,639	219,343
Annual Payroll	$11,498,117	$562,304	$483,198	$673,007	$1,718,509	$1,904,957	$2,141,788	$5,765,254	$5,732,863
Maryland Firms	93,718	50,627	17,649	11,542	79,818	9,604	2,248	91,670	2,048
Employment	1,770,837	84,546	116,441	153,519	354,506	355,697	277,053	987,256	783,581
Annual Payroll	$38,705,421	$2,095,848	$2,131,542	$2,897,810	$7,125,200	$7,130,932	$5,636,350	$19,892,482	$18,812,939
Pennsylvania Firms	231,560	133,068	42,687	25,726	201,481	21,949	4,943	228,373	3,187
Employment	4,539,138	231,128	279,475	344,769	855,372	838,944	728,913	2,423,229	2,115,909
Annual Payroll	$96,172,025	$4,487,008	$4,700,700	$6,385,000	$15,572,708	$15,893,281	$13,905,637	$45,371,626	$50,800,399
Virginia Firms	119,513	67,616	22,305	13,682	103,603	10,948	2,621	117,172	2,341
Employment	2,266,831	113,989	146,001	181,971	441,961	399,045	324,810	1,165,816	1,101,015
Annual Payroll	$46,613,747	$2,293,570	$2,443,990	$3,242,099	$7,979,659	$7,573,827	$6,300,530	$21,854,016	$24,759,731
West Virginia Firms	31,704	18,650	5,752	3,190	27,592	2,635	592	30,819	885
Employment	467,656	32,323	37,510	42,071	111,904	93,846	60,933	266,683	200,973
Annual Payroll	$9,066,515	$473,683	$518,292	$627,478	$1,619,453	$1,593,249	$974,887	$4,187,589	$4,878,926
Region IV Firms	895,764	526,947	165,091	93,707	785,745	75,457	17,373	878,575	17,189
Employment	15,776,968	892,041	1,080,515	1,242,885	3,215,441	2,811,510	2,155,986	8,182,937	7,594,031
Annual Payroll	$296,217,277	$16,905,863	$17,141,866	$20,750,902	$54,798,631	$47,519,064	$36,230,009	$138,547,704	$157,669,573
Alabama Firms	71,101	40,534	13,328	7,662	61,524	6,408	1,427	69,359	1,742
Employment	1,303,358	70,012	87,300	101,297	258,609	238,927	179,991	677,527	625,831
Annual Payroll	$23,880,373	$1,104,831	$1,253,918	$1,593,293	$3,952,042	$3,901,209	$2,995,629	$10,848,880	$13,031,493
Florida Firms	297,488	181,693	54,319	30,263	266,275	23,310	4,640	294,225	3,263
Employment	4,499,478	298,358	355,008	401,061	1,054,427	881,763	610,329	2,546,519	1,952,959
Annual Payroll	$84,479,831	$6,632,357	$6,206,478	$7,064,418	$19,903,253	$15,214,014	$10,356,137	$45,473,404	$39,006,427
Georgia Firms	126,834	71,962	23,747	13,731	109,440	11,259	3,067	123,766	3,068
Employment	2,469,183	121,688	155,742	181,787	459,217	411,859	330,321	1,201,397	1,267,786
Annual Payroll	$49,908,709	$2,614,781	$2,625,644	$3,248,021	$8,488,446	$7,313,970	$5,929,195	$21,731,611	$28,177,098
Kentucky Firms	65,889	37,414	12,268	7,134	56,816	6,050	1,393	64,259	1,630
Employment	1,154,089	65,889	80,540	94,660	240,301	224,716	162,415	627,432	526,657
Annual Payroll	$21,333,175	$1,037,486	$1,149,769	$1,407,389	$3,594,644	$3,552,500	$2,622,723	$9,769,867	$11,563,308
Mississippi Firms	43,983	26,373	7,909	4,340	38,622	3,342	845	42,809	1,174
Employment	705,700	45,757	51,704	57,254	154,715	121,007	102,566	378,288	327,412
Annual Payroll	$11,505,577	$615,591	$675,049	$815,833	$2,106,473	$1,803,616	$1,502,311	$5,412,400	$6,093,177
North Carolina Firms	133,473	78,205	24,787	14,040	117,032	11,301	2,650	130,983	2,490
Employment	2,596,741	134,236	161,938	186,836	483,010	424,026	363,965	1,271,001	1,325,740
Annual Payroll	$48,473,932	$2,231,859	$2,431,639	$3,081,593	$7,745,091	$7,138,226	$6,037,320	$20,920,637	$27,553,295
South Carolina Firms	64,685	37,718	11,910	6,749	56,377	5,425	1,298	63,100	1,585
Employment	1,219,341	65,216	77,932	89,616	232,764	195,129	155,557	583,450	635,891
Annual Payroll	$21,849,854	$1,078,271	$1,115,411	$1,377,659	$3,571,341	$3,057,620	$2,515,406	$9,144,367	$12,705,487
Tennessee Firms	92,311	53,048	16,823	9,788	79,659	8,362	2,053	90,074	2,237
Employment	1,829,078	91,673	110,351	130,374	332,398	314,083	250,842	897,323	931,755
Annual Payroll	$34,785,826	$1,590,687	$1,683,958	$2,162,696	$5,437,341	$5,537,909	$4,271,288	$15,246,538	$19,539,288

Table 2.4 Nonfarm Private Firms, Employment and Annual Payroll by SBA Region and State, 1989--Continued

		Total	1-4	Employment Size of Firm 5-9	10-19	<20	20-99	100-499	<500	500+
Region V	Firms	899,307	500,381	169,979	105,302	775,662	89,541	19,460	884,663	14,644
	Employment	17,861,083	855,405	1,116,445	1,407,428	3,379,278	3,398,939	2,696,190	9,474,407	8,386,676
	Annual Payroll	$358,448,877	$93,154,907	$93,694,820	$98,239,453	$124,380,566	$125,903,481	$118,061,553	$207,636,986	$231,166,198
Illinois	Firms	226,916	128,112	41,209	26,097	195,418	22,726	5,266	223,410	3,506
	Employment	4,535,606	215,673	271,054	347,969	834,696	855,228	690,504	2,380,428	2,155,178
	Annual Payroll	$107,725,867	$5,512,614	$5,333,721	$7,045,056	$17,891,391	$17,954,762	$15,075,449	$50,921,602	$56,804,265
Indiana	Firms	104,156	57,078	19,936	12,251	89,265	10,294	2,410	101,969	2,187
	Employment	2,108,403	100,139	130,763	163,109	394,011	387,983	320,613	1,102,607	1,005,796
	Annual Payroll	$42,804,390	$1,741,467	$1,947,536	$2,603,570	$6,292,573	$6,802,500	$5,611,964	$18,707,037	$24,097,353
Michigan	Firms	173,169	96,144	33,804	20,466	150,414	17,081	3,289	170,784	2,385
	Employment	3,363,048	163,265	222,257	273,834	659,356	652,661	475,602	1,787,619	1,575,429
	Annual Payroll	$80,354,194	$80,354,194	$80,354,194	$80,354,194	$80,354,194	$80,354,194	$80,354,194	$80,354,194	$80,354,194
Minnesota	Firms	93,363	51,728	17,484	11,129	80,341	9,239	2,021	91,601	1,762
	Employment	1,785,979	86,368	114,823	148,503	349,694	350,619	285,671	985,984	799,995
	Annual Payroll	$38,133,765	$1,706,103	$1,843,187	$2,595,773	$6,145,063	$6,460,108	$5,590,995	$18,196,166	$19,937,599
Ohio	Firms	199,151	110,214	38,224	23,324	171,762	19,990	4,374	196,126	3,025
	Employment	4,179,287	192,525	250,653	312,527	755,705	766,264	613,377	2,135,346	2,043,941
	Annual Payroll	$89,430,548	$3,840,416	$4,216,069	$5,640,747	$13,697,232	$14,331,804	$11,428,838	$39,457,874	$49,972,674
Wisconsin	Firms	102,552	57,105	19,322	12,035	88,462	10,211	2,100	100,773	1,779
	Employment	1,888,760	97,435	126,895	161,486	385,816	386,184	310,423	1,082,423	806,337
	Annual Payroll	$37,552,056	$1,717,805	$1,953,116	$2,643,630	$6,314,551	$6,683,689	$5,723,434	$18,721,674	$18,830,382
Region VI	Firms	522,646	311,030	94,715	54,393	460,138	43,939	9,564	513,641	9,005
	Employment	8,916,648	533,395	618,857	723,649	1,875,901	1,633,912	1,200,169	4,709,982	4,206,666
	Annual Payroll	$179,844,781	$10,829,297	$10,077,828	$12,225,562	$33,132,687	$27,984,471	$21,824,811	$82,941,969	$96,902,812
Arkansas	Firms	45,481	27,263	8,126	4,611	40,000	3,501	826	44,327	1,154
	Employment	726,353	46,890	53,179	61,054	161,123	126,798	101,941	389,862	336,491
	Annual Payroll	$12,076,616	$724,916	$732,805	$915,917	$2,373,638	$1,871,283	$1,516,046	$5,760,967	$6,315,649
Louisiana	Firms	72,944	41,749	13,600	7,795	63,144	6,686	1,455	71,285	1,659
	Employment	1,223,313	73,114	88,779	103,564	265,457	252,867	171,408	689,732	533,581
	Annual Payroll	$23,391,074	$1,390,273	$1,349,622	$1,657,976	$4,397,871	$4,159,307	$2,921,757	$11,478,935	$11,912,139
New Mexico	Firms	30,364	17,817	5,325	3,156	26,298	2,520	584	29,402	962
	Employment	401,516	29,954	34,797	41,613	106,364	89,598	56,557	252,519	148,997
	Annual Payroll	$7,104,810	$482,365	$483,179	$612,959	$1,578,503	$1,328,143	$961,784	$3,868,430	$3,236,380
Oklahoma	Firms	62,258	37,571	11,094	6,201	54,866	4,854	1,072	60,792	1,466
	Employment	912,219	64,970	71,903	82,232	219,105	179,356	124,912	523,373	388,846
	Annual Payroll	$17,420,784	$1,117,348	$1,112,788	$1,303,882	$3,534,018	$2,918,694	$2,154,474	$8,607,186	$8,813,598
Texas	Firms	311,599	186,630	56,570	32,630	275,830	26,378	5,627	307,835	3,764
	Employment	5,653,247	318,467	370,199	435,186	1,123,852	985,293	745,351	2,854,496	2,798,751
	Annual Payroll	$119,851,497	$7,114,395	$6,399,434	$7,734,828	$21,248,657	$17,707,044	$14,270,750	$53,226,451	$66,625,046

Table 2.4 Nonfarm Private Firms, Employment and Annual Payroll by SBA Region and State, 1989--Continued

	Total	1-4	Employment Size of Firm 5-9	10-19	<20	20-99	100-499	<500	500+
Region VII									
Firms	261,463	151,994	47,696	28,005	227,695	22,988	4,989	255,672	5,791
Employment	4,390,725	262,755	312,547	371,666	946,968	844,017	597,981	2,388,966	2,000,762
Annual Payroll	$83,947,044	$4,272,169	$4,592,080	$6,051,274	$14,915,523	$14,241,015	$10,306,401	$39,462,937	$44,484,089
Iowa									
Firms	60,703	35,307	11,243	6,529	53,079	5,302	1,100	59,481	1,222
Employment	978,448	61,992	73,674	86,778	222,444	194,938	137,736	555,118	422,333
Annual Payroll	$17,445,042	$911,962	$995,416	$1,333,018	$3,240,396	$3,106,199	$2,216,341	$8,562,934	$8,882,090
Kansas									
Firms	55,751	32,335	10,224	5,932	48,491	4,773	1,098	54,362	1,389
Employment	866,597	56,477	66,878	78,617	201,972	173,801	122,442	498,215	368,182
Annual Payroll	$16,559,332	$895,133	$979,066	$1,262,452	$3,136,651	$2,898,284	$2,130,490	$8,165,425	$8,393,907
Missouri									
Firms	107,789	62,678	19,270	11,589	93,537	9,874	2,148	105,559	2,230
Employment	1,981,932	106,355	126,299	153,991	386,645	364,862	263,473	1,014,980	966,952
Annual Payroll	$40,278,605	$1,903,413	$1,975,396	$2,640,467	$6,519,276	$6,490,133	$4,748,424	$17,757,833	$22,520,772
Nebraska									
Firms	37,220	21,674	6,959	3,955	32,588	3,039	643	36,270	950.00
Employment	563,948	37,931	45,696	52,280	135,907	110,416	74,330	320,653	243295.00
Annual Payroll	$9,664,065	$561,661	$642,202	$815,337	$2,019,200	$1,746,399	$1,211,146	$4,976,745	$4,687,320
Region VIII									
Firms	180,423	108,193	31,913	18,042	158,148	14,194	3,261	175,603	4,820
Employment	2,488,799	178,679	208,266	238,312	625,257	509,251	326,180	1,460,688	1,028,111
Annual Payroll	$48,005,081	$3,260,233	$3,177,942	$3,751,254	$10,189,429	$8,429,757	$5,658,198	$24,277,384	$23,727,697
Colorado									
Firms	80,949	48,952	14,095	7,858	70,905	6,516	1,527	78,948	2,001
Employment	1,213,854	80,774	91,900	103,931	276,605	236,093	151,506	664,204	549,650
Annual Payroll	$25,746,080	$1,667,626	$1,582,084	$1,838,037	$5,087,747	$4,238,252	$2,780,277	$12,106,276	$13,639,804
Montana									
Firms	21,922	13,763	3,861	2,100	19,724	1,470	273	21,467	455
Employment	212,323	22,575	25,066	27,785	75,426	51,662	27,205	154,293	58,030
Annual Payroll	$3,448,849	$344,915	$319,256	$379,059	$1,043,230	$744,097	$455,627	$2,242,954	$1,205,895
North Dakota									
Firms	16,640	10,132	2,881	1,640	14,653	1,251	305	16,209	431
Employment	190,571	17,201	18,766	21,483	57,450	44,988	31,569	134,007	56,564
Annual Payroll	$3,101,553	$232,188	$252,365	$312,206	$796,759	$678,966	$471,604	$1,947,329	$1,154,224
South Dakota									
Firms	17,845	10,963	3,046	1,766	15,775	1,319	311	17,405	440.00
Employment	204,403	17,747	20,013	23,349	61,109	46,429	32,592	140,130	64273.00
Annual Payroll	$3,115,413	$240,789	$257,216	$325,768	$823,773	$672,189	$512,787	$2,008,749	$1,106,664
Utah									
Firms	30,232	16,527	5,771	3,498	25,796	2,748	639	29,183	1,049
Employment	541,593	27,421	37,800	46,373	111,594	101,015	69,538	282,147	259,446
Annual Payroll	$10,239,830	$571,257	$558,656	$678,065	$1,807,978	$1,646,022	$1,185,064	$4,639,064	$5,600,766
Wyoming									
Firms	12,835	7,856	2,259	1,180	11,295	890	206	12,391	444
Employment	126,055	12,961	14,721	15,391	43,073	29,064	13,770	85,907	40,148
Annual Payroll	$2,353,356	$203,458	$208,365	$218,119	$629,942	$450,231	$252,839	$1,333,012	$1,020,344

Table 2.4 Nonfarm Private Firms, Employment and Annual Payroll by SBA Region and State, 1989--Continued

			Employment Size of Firm						
	Total	1-4	5-9	10-19	<20	20-99	100-499	<500	500+
Region IX									
Firms	738,275	433,963	132,313	81,721	647,997	68,894	13,447	730,338	7,937
Employment	13,088,742	701,651	869,272	1,092,599	2,663,522	2,630,744	1,937,894	7,232,160	5,856,582
Annual Payroll	$308,562,575	$20,839,679	$16,838,702	$21,250,687	$58,929,068	$54,048,933	$41,948,533	$154,926,534	$153,636,041
Arizona									
Firms	71,084	41,037	12,792	7,555	61,384	6,382	1,525	69,291	1,793
Employment	1,220,236	67,088	83,775	99,868	250,731	236,240	166,134	653,105	567,131
Annual Payroll	$23,863,625	$1,575,284	$1,360,322	$1,627,286	$4,562,892	$3,833,978	$2,891,911	$11,288,781	$12,574,844
California									
Firms	618,577	366,166	110,525	68,575	545,266	57,938	10,778	613,982	4,595
Employment	10,957,357	591,052	726,393	918,089	2,235,534	2,225,413	1,634,902	6,095,849	4,861,508
Annual Payroll	$266,469,995	$18,088,169	$14,403,142	$18,236,874	$50,728,185	$47,084,464	$36,402,679	$134,215,328	$132,254,667
Hawaii									
Firms	23,573	12,937	4,492	2,809	20,238	2,258	481	22,977	596
Employment	410,568	21,984	29,506	37,851	89,341	84,586	69,029	242,956	167,612
Annual Payroll	$8,251,529	$538,589	$535,385	$682,014	$1,755,988	$1,547,911	$1,348,348	$4,652,247	$3,599,282
Nevada									
Firms	25,041	13,823	4,504	2,782	21,109	2,316	663	24,088	953
Employment	500,581	21,527	29,598	36,791	87,916	84,505	67,829	240,250	260,331
Annual Payroll	$9,977,426	$637,637	$539,853	$704,513	$1,882,003	$1,582,580	$1,305,595	$4,770,178	$5,207,248
Region X									
Firms	212,252	125,047	39,029	22,732	186,808	17,522	3,808	208,138	4,114
Employment	1,408,142	202,796	255,833	300,946	759,575	635,682	454,590	1,849,847	1,209,727
Annual Payroll	$65,486,754	$4,121,404	$4,221,483	$5,149,552	$13,492,439	$11,863,539	$9,044,194	$32,013,172	$31,086,582
Alaska									
Firms	12,957	8,033	2,227	1,249	11,509	840	235	12,584	373
Employment	145,300	11,703	14,518	16,438	42,659	29,425	25,709	97,793	47,507
Annual Payroll	$4,369,240	$381,695	$329,034	$377,721	$1,088,450	$737,427	$698,549	$2,524,426	$1,844,814
Idaho									
Firms	22,028	12,913	4,090	2,366	19,369	1,716	392	21,477	551
Employment	285,919	21,131	26,733	30,997	78,861	59,485	38,089	176,435	109,484
Annual Payroll	$5,228,736	$358,261	$371,439	$433,747	$1,163,447	$896,411	$592,244	$265,102	$2,576,634
Oregon									
Firms	68,703	40,027	12,822	7,432	60,281	5,798	1,233	67,312	1,391
Employment	976,923	66,709	83,881	98,724	249,314	209,698	154,742	613,754	363,169
Annual Payroll	$19,244,361	$1,238,526	$1,288,376	$1,571,358	$4,098,260	$3,733,268	$2,941,488	$10,773,016	$8,471,345
Washington									
Firms	108,564	64,074	19,890	11,685	95,649	9,168	1,948	106,765	1,799
Employment	1,651,432	103,253	130,701	154,787	388,741	337,074	236,050	961,865	689,567
Annual Payroll	$36,644,417	$2,142,922	$2,232,634	$2,766,726	$7,142,282	$6,496,433	$4,811,913	$18,450,628	$18,193,789

Note: The state and regional total do not sum to the U.S. total because firms are defined within states not across states. Therefore, it is likely that firms are counted more than once if they have operations in more than one state. Annual payroll in thousands of dollars.

Source: U.S. Small Business Administration, Office of Advocacy, based upon data prepared for the Small Business Administration, under contract by the U.S. Department of Commerce, Bureau of the Census, unpublished data. The data was produced by merging the Company Organization Survey and the Standard Statistical Establishment List.

Table 2.5 Nonfarm Private Firms, Employment, and Annual Payroll by Industrial Sector, and Firm Size, for the United States, 1990

Industry	Total	Employment Size of Firm							
		1-4	5-9	10-19	<20	20-99	100-499	<500	500+
All Industries									
Number of Firms	5,073,795	3,020,935	952,030	562,610	4,535,575	453,732	70,465	5,059,772	14,023
Employment	93,469,275	5,116,914	6,251,632	7,543,360	18,911,906	17,710,042	13,544,849	50,166,797	43,302,478
Annual Payroll	2,103,971,179	116,856,518	114,450,673	144,450,673	375,313,660	352,390,861	279,451,864	1,007,156,385	1,096,814,794
Agriculture, Service, Forestry, Fishing									
Number of Firms	87,939	59,421	16,173	8,098	83,692	3,745	372	87,809	130
Employment	534,125	86,338	105,997	106,592	298,927	127,895	50,545	477,367	56,758
Annual Payroll	8,724,020	1,623,390	1,518,039	1,654,922	4,796,351	1,997,351	811,286	7,604,988	1,119,032
Mining									
Number of Firms	24,309	13,250	3,925	3,058	20,233	3,015	629	23,877	432
Employment	723,420	21,593	25,820	41,225	88,638	111,605	87,423	287,666	435,754
Annual Payroll	26,671,410	714,999	615,773	1,026,685	2,357,457	3,072,475	2,868,747	8,298,679	18,372,731
Construction									
Number of Firms	597,272	372,677	110,619	63,297	546,593	45,030	4,885	596,508	764
Employment	5,258,524	603,801	724,903	844,033	2,172,737	1,663,237	791,975	4,627,949	630,575
Annual Payroll	132,972,138	13,652,646	14,074,052	18,684,004	46,410,702	42,908,394	23,212,001	112,531,097	20,441,041
Manufacturing									
Number of Firms	327,036	124,543	60,470	53,158	238,171	67,301	16,870	322,342	4,694
Employment	19,167,922	220,326	406,418	726,867	1,355,611	2,785,692	3,078,746	7,218,049	11,949,873
Annual Payroll	543,898,226	5,946,451	7,856,582	15,420,205	29,223,238	63,652,275	73,081,434	165,956,947	377,941,279
Transportation, Communications, Public Utilities									
Number of Firms	180,900	102,820	31,795	21,257	155,872	19,943	3,465	179,280	1,620
Employment	5,594,752	169,014	209,478	286,172	664,664	762,043	553,068	1,979,775	3,614,977
Annual Payroll	165,930,849	3,753,427	3,704,771	5,321,895	12,780,093	16,124,647	13,157,314	42,062,054	123,868,795
Wholesale Trade									
Number of Firms	374,283	186,019	75,610	54,588	316,217	46,849	8,007	371,073	3,210
Employment	6,332,437	333,939	499,958	728,860	1,562,757	1,693,941	977,453	4,234,151	2,098,286
Annual Payroll	181,249,158	9,758,638	12,018,618	18,170,863	39,948,119	43,541,669	26,398,140	109,887,928	71,361,230

Table 2.5 Nonfarm Private Firms, Employment, and Annual Payroll by Industrial Sector, and Firm Size, for the United States, 1990--Continued

Industry	Total	Employment Size of Firm							
		1-4	5-9	10-19	<20	20-99	100-499	<500	500+
Retail Trade									
Number of Firms	1,109,703	605,787	229,751	144,174	979,712	114,275	12,855	1,106,842	2,861
Employment	19,861,604	1,061,152	1,515,594	1,923,026	4,499,772	4,273,110	2,134,371	10,907,253	8,954,351
Annual Payroll	242,369,258	14,446,638	16,164,655	21,058,903	51,670,196	53,201,028	27,284,284	132,155,508	110,213,750
Finance, Insurance, Real Estate									
Number of Firms	419,963	298,358	57,674	29,544	385,576	25,866	5,760	417,202	2,761
Employment	6,983,931	476,299	373,535	393,382	1,243,216	984,655	864,224	3,092,095	3,891,836
Annual Payroll	198,342,124	11,472,515	8,371,080	9,617,129	29,460,724	23,967,871	22,487,793	57,916,388	122,425,736
Services									
Number of Firms	1,921,767	1,200,505	363,345	186,433	1,750,283	136,760	27,386	1,914,429	7,338
Employment	28,880,444	2,098,685	2,364,281	2,472,307	6,935,273	5,283,645	5,003,879	17,222,797	11,657,647
Annual Payroll	601,553,639	54,417,414	49,459,256	53,307,079	157,183,749	103,701,939	90,119,588	351,005,276	250,548,363
Unclassified									
Number of Firms	64,767	58,305	3,975	1,594	63,874	783	64	64,721	46
Employment	132,116	45,767	25,648	20,896	92,311	24,219	3,165	119,695	12,421
Annual Payroll	2,260,357	1,070,400	223,643	188,988	1,483,031	223,212	31,277	1,737,520	522,837

Note: Annual payroll in thousands of dollars.

Source: U.S. Small Business Administration, Office of Advocacy, based upon data prepared for the Small Business Administration, under contract by the U.S. Department of Commerce Bureau of the Census, unpublished data. The data was produced by merging the Company Organization Survey and the Standard Statistical Establishment List.

Table 2.6 Nonfarm Private Firms, Employment and Annual Payroll by Firm Size, SBA Region and State, 1990

				Employment Size of Firm					
		Total	1-4	5-9	10-19	< 20	20-99	100-499	< 500	500+
United States	Number of Firms	5,073,795	3,020,935	952,030	562,610	4,535,575	453,732	70,465	5,059,772	14,023
	Employment	93,469,275	5,116,914	6,251,632	7,543,360	18,911,906	17,710,042	13,544,849	50,166,797	43,302,478
	Annual Payroll	$2,103,971,179	5,116,856,518	$114,006,469	$144,450,673	$375,313,660	$352,390,861	$279,451,864	$1,007,156,385	$1,096,814,794
Region I	Number of Firms	319,933	183,997	58,628	34,850	277,475	28,928	6,865	313,268	6,665
	Employment	5,728,555	315,370	383,307	464,625	1,163,302	1,084,525	883,391	3,131,218	2,597,337
	Annual Payroll	$139,300,693	$7,561,459	$7,675,354	$9,832,321	$25,069,134	$23,503,384	$19,816,215	$68,388,733	$70,911,960
Connecticut	Number of Firms	81,129	46,567	14,889	8,954	70,410	7,256	1,745	79,411	1,718
	Employment	1,481,786	80,402	97,370	119,264	297,036	270,112	213,263	780,411	701,375
	Annual Payroll	$40,507,189	$2,165,963	$2,212,606	$2,902,116	$7,280,685	$6,611,658	$5,175,206	$19,067,549	$21,439,640
Maine	Number of Firms	30,747	18,728	5,421	3,056	27,205	2,389	514	30,108	639
	Employment	424,027	30,267	35,428	40,702	106,397	86,772	70,458	263,627	160,400
	Annual Payroll	$8,222,663	$552,012	$547,786	$683,353	$1,783,151	$1,478,752	$1,233,677	$4,495,580	$3,727,083
Massachusetts	Number of Firms	135,585	76,269	25,241	15,306	116,816	13,220	3,171	133,207	2,378
	Employment	2,772,586	133,215	164,936	204,052	502,203	506,119	433,084	1,441,406	1,331,180
	Annual Payroll	$68,739,961	$3,376,067	$3,432,682	$4,408,665	$11,217,414	$11,251,190	$10,029,858	$32,498,462	$36,241,499
New Hampshire	Number of Firms	29,392	17,054	5,391	3,072	25,517	2,469	600	28,586	806
	Employment	441,480	28,354	35,332	40,733	104,419	89,737	66,556	260,712	180,768
	Annual Payroll	$9,559,059	$610,654	$632,790	$770,316	$2,013,760	$1,733,174	$1,370,879	$5,117,813	$4,441,246
Rhode Island	Number of Firms	25,110	14,465	4,442	2,664	21,571	2,277	543	24,391	719
	Employment	393,456	24,800	29,163	35,949	89,912	84,106	65,608	239,626	153,830
	Annual Payroll	$8,151,778	$544,707	$536,671	$686,260	$1,767,638	$1,595,067	$1,339,943	$4,702,648	$3,449,130
Vermont	Number of Firms	17,970	10,914	3,244	1,798	15,956	1,317	292	17,565	405
	Employment	215,220	18,332	21,078	23,925	63,335	47,679	34,422	145,436	69,784
	Annual Payroll	$4,120,043	$312,056	$312,819	$381,611	$1,006,486	$833,543	$666,652	$2,506,681	$1,613,362
Region II	Number of Firms	600,456	371,321	103,177	59,113	533,611	49,815	10,639	594,065	6,391
	Employment	10,293,275	618,201	673,583	789,525	2,081,309	1,891,918	1,551,484	5,524,711	4,768,564
	Annual Payroll	$277,139,945	$16,635,878	$14,888,517	$18,493,879	$50,018,274	$45,558,150	$37,783,453	$133,359,877	$143,780,068
New Jersey	Number of Firms	187,958	113,797	32,847	18,885	165,529	16,061	3,648	185,238	2,720
	Employment	3,219,629	189,856	214,542	251,952	656,350	609,516	468,408	1,734,274	1,485,355
	Annual Payroll	$85,408,883	$5,164,152	$4,845,894	$5,996,851	$16,006,897	$14,942,583	$11,265,384	$42,214,864	$43,194,019
New York	Number of Firms	412,498	257,524	70,330	40,228	368,082	33,754	6,991	408,827	3,671
	Employment	7,073,646	428,345	459,041	537,573	1,424,959	1,282,402	1,083,076	3,790,437	3,283,209
	Annual Payroll	$191,731,062	$11,471,726	$10,042,623	$12,497,028	$34,011,377	$30,615,567	$26,518,069	$91,145,013	$100,586,049
Region III	Number of Firms	515,441	289,022	96,194	58,428	443,644	49,703	11,713	505,060	10,381
	Employment	9,951,208	498,963	631,640	778,537	1,909,140	1,850,804	1,505,201	5,265,145	4,686,063
	Annual Payroll	$221,357,526	$10,479,903	$11,271,138	$14,919,771	$36,670,812	$37,110,379	$31,056,939	$104,818,130	$116,539,396
Delaware	Number of Firms	16,323	8,873	2,925	1,823	13,621	1,535	405	15,561	762
	Employment	311,016	13,961	19,398	23,858	57,217	54,918	36,091	148,226	162,790
	Annual Payroll	$7,545,568	$314,442	$331,797	$458,906	$1,105,145	$1,071,012	$728,650	$2,904,807	$4,640,761

Table 2.6 Nonfarm Private Firms, Employment and Annual Payroll by Firm Size, SBA Region and State, 1990--Continued

		Total	1-4	5-9	10-19	Employment Size of Firm < 20	20-99	100-499	< 500	500+
District of Columbia	Number of Firms	16,474	7,972	2,711	1,944	12,627	2,079	823	15,529	945
	Employment	426,734	13,573	17,739	25,109	56,421	72,598	78,408	207,427	219,307
	Annual Payroll	$12,393,438	$544,484	$484,231	$697,571	$1,726,286	$1,971,586	$2,297,270	$5,995,142	$6,398,296
Maryland	Number of Firms	95,935	51,959	18,188	11,635	81,782	9,781	2,286	93,849	2,086
	Employment	1,810,872	87,312	119,967	155,028	362,307	362,237	277,566	1,002,110	808,762
	Annual Payroll	$41,101,164	$2,193,793	$2,291,679	$3,040,561	$7,526,033	$7,514,698	$5,825,124	$20,865,855	$20,235,309
Pennsylvania	Number of Firms	233,521	133,321	43,476	26,028	202,825	22,505	4,931	230,261	3,260
	Employment	4,598,597	234,500	285,205	348,483	868,188	857,909	717,894	2,443,991	2,154,606
	Annual Payroll	$101,449,327	$4,593,450	$4,993,889	$6,674,115	$16,261,454	$16,914,358	$14,476,574	$47,652,386	$53,796,941
Virginia	Number of Firms	121,339	68,364	23,038	13,754	105,156	11,151	2,626	118,933	2,406
	Employment	2,321,472	117,227	151,241	183,061	451,529	408,734	327,774	1,188,037	1,133,435
	Annual Payroll	$49,191,018	$2,356,207	$2,619,072	$3,363,415	$8,338,694	$8,031,549	$6,538,110	$22,908,353	$26,282,665
West Virginia	Number of Firms	31,849	18,533	5,856	3,244	27,633	2,652	642	30,927	922
	Employment	482,517	32,390	38,090	42,998	113,478	94,408	67,468	275,354	207,163
	Annual Payroll	$9,677,011	$477,527	$550,470	$685,203	$1,713,200	$1,607,176	$1,171,211	$4,491,587	$5,185,424
Region IV	Number of Firms	908,274	531,844	168,178	95,977	795,999	77,081	17,643	890,723	17,551
	Employment	16,168,273	907,602	1,100,873	1,273,248	3,281,723	2,873,259	2,181,834	8,336,816	7,831,457
	Annual Payroll	$314,194,727	$17,795,627	$18,132,566	$22,066,489	$57,994,682	$50,319,943	$38,240,103	$146,554,728	$167,639,999
Alabama	Number of Firms	71,450	40,065	13,673	7,915	61,653	6,532	1,474	69,659	1,791
	Employment	1,340,644	70,487	89,687	104,621	264,795	243,160	185,352	693,307	647,337
	Annual Payroll	$25,620,230	$1,136,430	$1,350,062	$1,710,059	$4,196,551	$4,184,757	$3,098,577	$11,479,885	$14,140,345
Florida	Number of Firms	302,847	185,212	55,593	30,515	271,320	23,521	4,694	299,535	3,312
	Employment	4,607,903	306,376	363,494	405,006	1,074,876	888,348	613,789	2,577,013	2,030,890
	Annual Payroll	$89,566,848	$6,986,194	$6,586,373	$7,441,654	$21,014,221	$15,803,534	$10,996,151	$47,813,906	$41,752,942
Georgia	Number of Firms	128,054	72,742	23,795	13,948	110,485	11,407	3,073	124,965	3,089
	Employment	2,498,736	124,246	155,943	184,201	464,390	415,431	325,652	1,205,473	1,293,263
	Annual Payroll	$52,463,307	$2,758,366	$2,735,451	$3,431,484	$8,925,301	$7,740,151	$6,254,011	$22,919,463	$29,543,844
Kentucky	Number of Firms	66,604	37,138	12,591	7,470	57,199	6,284	1,424	64,907	1,697
	Employment	1,185,978	64,861	82,614	99,346	246,821	233,010	166,494	646,325	539,653
	Annual Payroll	$22,553,766	$1,039,995	$1,207,375	$1,527,011	$3,774,381	$3,833,406	$2,744,912	$10,352,699	$12,201,067
Mississippi	Number of Firms	44,484	26,583	7,917	4,517	39,017	3,419	841	43,277	1,207
	Employment	724,749	45,921	51,944	59,782	157,647	125,816	103,308	386,771	337,978
	Annual Payroll	$12,335,906	$664,542	$688,848	$870,892	$2,224,282	$1,965,146	$1,563,464	$5,752,892	$6,583,014
North Carolina	Number of Firms	135,925	79,099	25,398	14,459	118,956	11,707	2,725	133,388	2,537
	Employment	2,675,033	137,302	165,994	192,700	495,996	437,788	367,676	1,301,460	1,373,573
	Annual Payroll	$51,322,095	$2,404,756	$2,590,955	$3,240,362	$8,236,073	$7,619,718	$6,367,380	$22,223,171	$29,098,924
South Carolina	Number of Firms	66,074	38,016	12,360	7,046	57,422	5,703	1,340	64,465	1,609
	Employment	1,266,293	65,994	81,070	93,158	240,222	206,685	164,587	611,494	654,799
	Annual Payroll	$23,563,523	$1,123,712	$1,221,511	$1,514,236	$3,859,459	$3,334,117	$2,748,237	$9,941,813	$13,621,710
Tennessee	Number of Firms	92,836	52,989	16,851	10,107	79,947	8,508	2,072	90,527	2,309
	Employment	1,868,937	92,415	110,127	134,434	336,976	323,021	254,976	914,973	953,964
	Annual Payroll	$36,769,052	$1,681,632	$1,751,991	$2,330,791	$5,764,414	$5,839,114	$4,467,371	$16,070,899	$20,698,153

Table 2.6 Nonfarm Private Firms, Employment and Annual Payroll by Firm Size, SBA Region and State, 1990--Continued

		Total	1-4	5-9	10-19	< 20	20-99	100-499	< 500	500+
Region V	Number of Firms	913,093	506,288	173,695	107,028	787,011	91,420	19,652	898,083	15,010
	Employment	18,236,286	868,401	1,141,536	1,432,102	3,442,039	3,476,248	2,724,802	9,643,089	8,593,197
	Annual Payroll	$417,179,398	$18,783,969	$20,445,898	$27,167,433	$66,397,300	$69,540,520	$56,229,070	$192,166,890	$225,012,508
Illinois	Number of Firms	230,830	130,121	42,166	26,537	198,824	23,073	5,322	227,219	3,611
	Employment	4,647,135	219,916	277,659	354,571	852,146	868,836	701,340	2,422,322	2,224,813
	Annual Payroll	$114,487,799	$5,718,436	$5,611,232	$7,451,593	$18,781,261	$19,026,942	$16,023,957	$53,832,160	$60,655,639
Indiana	Number of Firms	105,883	57,579	20,681	12,394	90,654	10,500	2,468	103,622	2,261
	Employment	2,150,168	101,409	135,624	165,529	402,562	396,649	324,390	1,123,601	1,026,567
	Annual Payroll	$45,057,638	$1,806,145	$2,094,833	$2,712,274	$6,613,252	$7,273,027	$5,977,545	$19,863,824	$25,193,814
Michigan	Number of Firms	175,884	97,409	34,653	20,891	152,953	17,236	3,257	173,446	2,438
	Employment	3,411,489	166,402	227,515	279,771	673,688	659,676	470,584	1,803,948	1,607,541
	Annual Payroll	$83,175,942	$3,712,416	$4,243,082	$5,566,480	$13,521,978	$13,852,916	$9,985,002	$37,359,896	$45,816,046
Minnesota	Number of Firms	95,520	52,869	17,882	11,359	82,110	9,577	2,036	93,723	1,797
	Employment	1,832,236	87,985	117,591	152,284	357,860	364,495	292,846	1,015,201	817,035
	Annual Payroll	$40,272,064	$1,855,815	$1,968,609	$2,727,462	$6,549,886	$6,915,569	$5,959,279	$19,424,734	$20,847,330
Ohio	Number of Firms	200,705	110,531	38,658	23,543	172,732	20,471	4,419	197,622	3,083
	Employment	4,246,402	193,602	253,679	314,933	762,214	786,013	613,020	2,161,247	2,085,155
	Annual Payroll	$93,908,597	$3,855,925	$4,461,241	$5,873,357	$14,190,523	$15,261,518	$12,048,714	$41,500,755	$52,407,842
Wisconsin	Number of Firms	104,271	57,779	19,655	12,304	89,738	10,563	2,150	102,451	1,820
	Employment	1,948,856	99,087	129,468	165,014	393,569	400,579	322,622	1,116,770	832,086
	Annual Payroll	$40,277,358	$1,837,232	$2,066,901	$2,836,267	$6,740,400	$7,210,548	$6,234,573	$20,185,521	$20,091,837
Region VI	Number of Firms	529,934	313,029	96,452	55,942	465,423	45,423	9,914	520,760	9,174
	Employment	9,245,742	536,470	630,411	744,284	1,911,165	1,695,586	1,265,276	4,872,027	4,373,715
	Annual Payroll	$194,799,621	$11,541,521	$10,768,518	$13,116,789	$35,426,828	$30,228,097	$24,243,948	$89,898,873	$104,900,748
Arkansas	Number of Firms	45,984	27,118	8,411	4,711	40,240	3,743	812	44,795	1,189
	Employment	750,877	47,061	54,853	62,484	164,398	135,602	98,318	398,318	352,559
	Annual Payroll	$13,079,962	$776,877	$782,845	$960,904	$2,520,626	$2,097,869	$1,520,409	$6,138,904	$6,941,058
Louisiana	Number of Firms	73,204	41,608	13,493	8,007	63,108	6,897	1,502	71,507	1,697
	Employment	1,271,285	73,309	88,146	106,533	267,988	264,364	179,985	712,337	558,948
	Annual Payroll	$25,522,526	$1,462,900	$1,415,315	$1,799,816	$4,678,031	$4,541,876	$3,262,934	$12,482,841	$13,035,685
New Mexico	Number of Firms	30,730	17,861	5,499	3,246	26,606	2,556	587	29,749	981
	Employment	418,138	30,093	36,012	42,745	108,850	91,605	60,501	260,956	157,182
	Annual Payroll	$7,639,003	$495,502	$520,559	$646,261	$1,662,322	$1,422,361	$1,018,719	$4,103,402	$3,535,601
Oklahoma	Number of Firms	63,152	37,861	11,306	6,303	55,470	5,062	1,122	61,654	1,498
	Employment	940,800	65,379	73,880	83,771	223,030	186,068	130,773	539,871	400,929
	Annual Payroll	$18,719,222	$1,217,648	$1,189,634	$1,383,559	$3,790,841	$3,159,758	$2,371,317	$9,321,916	$9,397,306
Texas	Number of Firms	316,864	188,581	57,743	33,675	279,999	27,165	5,891	313,055	3,809
	Employment	5,864,642	320,628	377,520	448,751	1,146,899	1,017,947	795,699	2,960,545	2,904,097
	Annual Payroll	$129,838,908	$7,588,594	$6,860,165	$8,326,249	$22,775,008	$19,006,233	$16,070,569	$57,851,810	$71,987,098
Region VII	Number of Firms	264,308	152,621	48,107	28,698	229,426	23,804	5,117	258,347	5,961
	Employment	4,502,183	264,882	314,910	380,295	960,087	875,627	620,688	2,456,402	2,045,781
	Annual Payroll	$88,726,765	$4,383,795	$4,835,533	$6,347,635	$15,566,963	$15,223,991	$11,067,182	$41,858,136	$46,868,629

Employment Size of Firm

Table 2.6 Nonfarm Private Firms, Employment and Annual Payroll by Firm Size, SBA Region and State, 1990--Continued

		Total	1-4	5-9	10-19	< 20	20-99	100-499	< 500	500+
						Employment Size of Firm				
Iowa	Number of Firms	61,404	35,315	11,415	6,786	53,516	5,501	1,131	60,148	1,256
	Employment	1,007,900	62,045	74,471	89,896	226,412	201,572	143,074	571,058	436,842
	Annual Payroll	$18,631,850	$943,398	$1,067,916	$1,419,331	$3,430,645	$3,339,661	$2,415,958	$9,186,264	$9,445,586
Kansas	Number of Firms	55,893	32,277	10,102	5,964	48,343	4,978	1,128	54,449	1,444
	Employment	893,799	55,831	66,219	78,635	200,685	180,733	127,283	508,701	385,098
	Annual Payroll	$17,486,890	$907,486	$1,013,367	$1,303,499	$3,224,352	$3,144,622	$2,311,163	$8,680,137	$8,806,753
Missouri	Number of Firms	109,446	63,361	19,638	11,840	94,839	10,118	2,207	107,164	2,282
	Employment	2,013,440	108,761	128,580	157,678	395,019	375,401	272,899	1,043,319	970,121
	Annual Payroll	$42,132,115	$1,960,899	$2,079,530	$2,754,147	$6,794,576	$6,831,660	$5,033,128	$18,659,364	$23,472,751
Nebraska	Number of Firms	37,565	21,668	6,952	4,108	32,728	3,207	651	36,586	979
	Employment	587,044	38,245	45,640	54,086	137,971	117,921	77,432	333,324	253,720
	Annual Payroll	$10,475,910	$572,012	$674,720	$870,658	$2,117,390	$1,908,048	$1,306,933	$5,332,371	$5,143,539
Region VIII	Number of Firms	183,698	109,281	32,606	18,653	160,540	14,932	3,273	178,745	4,953
	Employment	2,584,184	180,711	213,069	247,757	641,537	539,857	338,730	1,520,124	1,064,060
	Annual Payroll	$51,446,407	$3,413,514	$3,373,390	$4,075,771	$10,862,675	$9,280,646	$6,130,173	$26,273,494	$25,172,913
Colorado	Number of Firms	82,749	49,912	14,478	8,032	72,422	6,749	1,533	80,704	2,045
	Employment	1,248,009	82,038	94,536	106,614	283,188	245,969	156,617	685,774	562,235
	Annual Payroll	$27,459,806	$1,767,406	$1,705,440	$1,985,843	$5,458,689	$4,620,759	$3,087,336	$13,166,784	$14,293,022
Montana	Number of Firms	22,223	13,856	3,863	2,190	19,909	1,569	274	21,752	471
	Employment	221,851	22,947	25,277	29,218	77,442	55,098	27,602	160,142	61,709
	Annual Payroll	$3,688,313	$355,434	$327,121	$410,030	$1,092,585	$820,881	$464,888	$2,378,354	$1,309,959
North Dakota	Number of Firms	16,615	9,918	2,984	1,695	14,597	1,282	298	16,177	438
	Employment	196,407	16,767	19,388	22,464	58,619	47,000	32,522	138,141	58,266
	Annual Payroll	$3,273,308	$232,462	$258,789	$333,432	$824,683	$734,690	$511,625	$2,070,998	$1,202,310
South Dakota	Number of Firms	18,258	10,988	3,179	1,864	16,031	1,449	316	17,796	462
	Employment	215,104	17,998	20,753	24,736	63,487	51,692	34,125	149,304	65,800
	Annual Payroll	$3,396,357	$254,940	$277,499	$345,491	$877,930	$772,167	$562,348	$2,212,445	$1,183,912
Utah	Number of Firms	30,891	16,757	5,796	3,638	26,191	2,963	644	29,798	1,093
	Employment	570,761	28,031	38,060	48,442	114,533	109,904	72,428	296,865	273,896
	Annual Payroll	$11,061,370	$599,827	$584,437	$754,784	$1,939,048	$1,835,872	$1,229,512	$5,004,432	$6,056,938
Wyoming	Number of Firms	12,962	7,850	2,306	1,234	11,390	920	208	12,518	444
	Employment	132,052	12,930	15,055	16,283	44,268	30,194	15,436	89,898	42,154
	Annual Payroll	$2,567,253	$203,445	$220,104	$246,191	$669,740	$496,277	$274,464	$1,440,481	$1,126,772
Region IX	Number of Firms	750,562	437,698	136,066	83,508	657,272	71,338	13,779	742,389	8,173
	Employment	13,522,843	717,926	895,488	1,115,821	2,729,235	2,733,341	1,990,179	7,452,755	6,070,088
	Annual Payroll	$328,664,188	$21,894,529	$18,022,629	$22,735,546	$62,652,704	$58,352,633	$44,828,652	$165,833,989	$162,830,199
Arizona	Number of Firms	71,586	41,255	12,861	7,703	61,819	6,336	1,567	69,722	1,864
	Employment	1,236,131	67,817	84,303	101,761	253,881	234,000	173,369	661,250	574,881
	Annual Payroll	$24,947,945	$1,634,381	$1,446,530	$1,751,416	$4,832,327	$3,962,914	$3,105,712	$11,900,953	$13,046,992

Table 2.6 Nonfarm Private Firms, Employment and Annual Payroll by Firm Size, SBA Region and State, 1990--Continued

						Employment Size of Firm				
		Total	1-4	5-9	10-19	< 20	20-99	100-499	< 500	500+
California	Number of Firms	628,547	368,886	113,875	70,001	552,762	60,097	11,014	623,873	4,674
	Employment	11,317,447	604,710	749,814	936,884	2,291,408	2,317,811	1,669,878	6,279,097	5,038,350
	Annual Payroll	$283,208,683	$18,980,042	$15,380,956	$19,446,765	$53,807,763	$50,761,562	$38,723,411	$143,292,736	$139,915,947
Hawaii	Number of Firms	24,386	13,430	4,601	2,855	20,886	2,355	523	23,764	622
	Employment	432,663	22,931	30,223	38,143	91,297	87,652	75,147	254,096	178,567
	Annual Payroll	$9,296,865	$637,465	$594,080	$755,416	$1,986,961	$1,752,733	$1,586,391	$5,326,085	$3,970,780
Nevada	Number of Firms	26,043	14,127	4,729	2,949	21,805	2,550	675	25,030	1,013
	Employment	536,602	22,468	31,148	39,033	92,649	93,878	71,785	258,312	278,290
	Annual Payroll	$11,210,695	$642,641	$601,063	$781,949	$2,025,653	$1,875,424	$1,413,138	$5,314,215	$5,896,480
Region X	Number of Firms	218,925	127,112	40,648	23,912	191,672	18,924	3,992	214,588	4,337
	Employment	3,236,726	208,388	266,815	317,166	792,369	688,877	483,264	1,964,510	1,272,216
	Annual Payroll	$71,161,909	$4,366,323	$4,592,926	$5,695,039	$14,654,288	$13,273,118	$10,076,129	$38,003,535	$33,158,374
Alaska	Number of Firms	12,843	7,659	2,304	1,358	11,321	874	238	12,433	410
	Employment	157,798	11,914	15,165	17,942	45,021	30,830	27,862	103,713	54,085
	Annual Payroll	$4,663,266	$384,249	$352,776	$421,117	$1,158,142	$777,276	$761,990	$2,697,408	$1,965,858
Idaho	Number of Firms	22,976	13,222	4,371	2,521	20,114	1,896	383	22,393	583
	Employment	300,163	22,088	28,598	33,274	83,960	66,760	38,334	189,054	111,109
	Annual Payroll	$5,607,460	$374,358	$403,603	$487,286	$1,265,247	$1,052,323	$623,855	$2,941,425	$2,666,035
Oregon	Number of Firms	69,860	40,252	13,061	7,650	60,963	6,162	1,294	68,419	1,441
	Employment	1,017,415	67,499	85,495	101,631	254,625	222,501	162,337	639,463	377,952
	Annual Payroll	$20,729,997	$1,327,393	$1,382,558	$1,706,340	$4,416,291	$4,068,066	$3,211,575	$11,695,932	$9,034,065
Washington	Number of Firms	113,246	65,979	20,912	12,383	99,274	9,992	2,077	111,343	1,903
	Employment	1,761,350	106,887	137,557	164,319	408,763	368,786	254,731	1,032,280	729,070
	Annual Payroll	$40,161,186	$2,280,323	$2,453,989	$3,080,296	$7,814,608	$7,375,453	$5,478,709	$20,668,770	$19,492,416

Note: The state and regional total do not sum to the U.S. total because firms are defined within states not across states. Therefore, it is likely that firms are counted more than once if they have operations in more than one state. Annual payroll in thousands of dollars.

Source: U.S. Small Business Administration, Office of Advocacy, based upon data prepared for the Small Business Administration, under contract by the U.S. Department of Commerce, Bureau of the Census, unpublished data. The data was produced by merging the Company Organization Survey and the Standard Statistical Establishment List.

Table 2.7 Nonfarm Private Establishments, Employment, and Annual Payroll by Firm Employment Size, 1990

Item	Total	1-4	5-9	10-19	<20	20-99	100-499	<500	500+
All Private Nonfarm Industries									
Establishments	6,175,559	3,032,253	970,580	599,529	4,602,362	590,496	254,747	5,447,605	727,954
Percent	100	49.1	15.7	9.7	74.5	9.6	4.1	88.2	11.8
Employment	93,469,275	5,116,914	6,251,632	7,543,360	18,911,906	17,710,042	13,544,849	50,166,797	43,302,478
Percent	100	5.5	6.7	8.1	20.2	18.9	14.5	53.7	46.3
Avg.Empl./Estab.	15.1	1.7	6.4	12.6	4.1	30.0	53.2	9.2	59.5
Annual Payroll ($Mill.)	2,103,971	116,857	114,006	144,451	375,314	352,391	279,452	1,007,156	1,096,815
Percent	100	5.6	5.4	6.9	17.8	16.7	13.3	47.9	52.1
Avg. Annual Wage	22,510	22,837	18,236	19,149	19,845	19,898	20,632	20,076	25,329
Agricultural Services, Forestry, and Fishing, SIC 07,08,09									
Establishments	89,206	59,424	16,183	8,134	83,741	3,895	548	88,184	1,022
Percent	100	66.6	18.1	9.1	93.9	4.4	0.6	98.9	1.1
Employment	534,125	86,338	105,997	106,592	298,927	127,895	50,545	477,367	56,758
Percent	100	16.2	19.8	20	56	23.9	9.5	89.4	10.6
Avg.Empl./Estab.	6.0	1.5	6.5	13.1	3.6	32.8	92.2	5.4	55.5
Annual Payroll ($Mill.)	8,724	1,623	1,518	1,655	4,796	1,997	811	7,605	1,119
Percent	100	18.6	17.4	19	55	22.9	9.3	87.2	12.8
Avg. Annual Wage	16,333	18,803	14,322	15,526	16,045	15,617	16,051	15,931	19,716
Mining (Includes Oil, Gas, Quarries, etc.), SIC 10,12,13,14									
Establishments	30,943	13,308	3,995	3,208	20,511	3,616	1,714	25,841	5,102
Percent	100.0	43.0	12.9	10.4	66.3	11.7	5.5	83.5	16.5
Employment	723,420	21,593	25,820	41,225	88,638	111,605	87,423	287,666	435,754
Percent	100.0	3.0	3.6	5.7	12.3	15.4	12.1	39.8	60.2
Avg.Empl./Estab.	23.4	1.6	6.5	12.9	4.3	30.9	51.0	11.1	85.4
Annual Payroll ($Mill.)	26,671	715	616	1,027	2,357	3,072	2,869	8,299	18,373
Percent	100.0	2.7	2.3	3.8	8.8	11.5	10.8	31.1	68.9
Avg. Annual Wage	36,868	33,113	23,849	24,904	26,596	27,530	32,815	28,848	42,163
Construction, SIC 15,16,17									
Establishments	603,534	372,732	110,684	63,459	546,875	45,837	6,350	599,062	4,472
Percent	100.0	61.8	18.3	10.5	90.6	7.6	1.1	99.3	0.7
Employment	5,258,524	603,801	724,903	844,033	2,172,737	1,663,237	791,975	4,627,949	630,575
Percent	100.0	11.5	13.8	16.1	41.3	31.6	15.1	88.0	12.0
Avg.Empl./Estab.	8.7	1.6	6.5	13.3	4.0	36.3	124.7	7.7	141.0
Annual Payroll ($Mill.)	132,972	13,653	14,074	18,684	46,411	42,908	23,212	112,531	20,441
Percent	100	10.3	10.6	14.1	34.9	32.3	17.5	84.6	15.4
Avg. Annual Wage	25,287	22,611	19,415	22,137	21,360	25,798	29,309	24,316	32,417

Table 2.7 Nonfarm Private Establishments, Employment, and Annual Payroll by Firm Employment Size, 1990--Continued

Item	Total	Employment Size of Firm							
		1-4	5-9	10-19	<20	20-99	100-499	<500	500+
Manufacturing, SIC 2,3									
Establishments	385,933	124,583	60,546	53,422	238,551	71,311	28,705	338,567	47,366
Percent	100.0	32.3	15.7	13.8	61.8	18.5	7.4	87.7	12.3
Employment	19,167,922	220,326	406,418	726,867	1,353,611	2,785,692	3,078,746	7,218,049	11,949,873
Percent	100.0	1.1	2.1	3.8	7.1	14.5	16.1	37.7	62.3
Avg.Empl./Estab.	49.7	1.8	6.7	13.6	5.7	39.1	107.3	21.3	252.3
Annual Payroll ($Mill.)	543,898	5,946	7,857	15,420	29,223	63,652	73,081	165,957	377,941
Percent	100.0	1.1	1.4	2.8	5.4	11.7	13.4	30.5	69.5
Avg. Annual Wage	28,375	26,989	19,331	21,215	21,589	22,850	23,737	22,992	31,627
Transportation, Communication, and Public Utilities, SIC 4									
Establishments	484,482	206,076	64,390	44,366	314,832	47,266	20,594	382,692	101,790
Percent	100.0	42.5	13.3	9.2	65.0	9.8	4.3	79.0	21.0
Employment	11,189,504	338,028	412,664	563,971	1,329,328	1,524,086	1,106,136	3,959,550	7,229,954
Percent	100.0	3.0	3.7	5.0	11.9	13.6	9.9	35.4	64.6
Avg.Empl./Estab.	23.1	1.6	6.4	12.7	4.2	32.2	53.7	10.3	71.0
Annual Payroll ($Mill.)	331,862	7,507	7,279	10,479	25,560	32,249	26,315	84,124	247,738
Percent	100.0	2.3	2.2	3.2	7.7	9.7	7.9	25.3	74.7
Avg. Annual Wage	29,658	22,208	17,640	18,581	19,228	21,160	23,790	21,246	34,265
Wholesale Trade - SIC 50, 51									
Establishments	484,619	187,069	77,740	59,655	324,464	67,691	28,337	420,492	64,127
Percent	100.0	38.6	16.0	12.3	67.0	14.0	5.8	86.8	13.2
Employment	6,332,437	333,939	499,958	728,860	1,562,757	1,693,941	977,453	4,234,151	2,098,286
Percent	100.0	5.3	7.9	11.5	24.7	26.8	15.4	66.9	33.1
Avg.Empl./Estab.	13.1	1.8	6.4	12.2	4.8	25.0	34.5	10.1	32.7
Annual Payroll ($Mill.)	181,249	9,759	12,019	18,171	39,948	43,542	26,398	109,888	71,361
Percent	100.0	5.4	6.6	10.0	22.0	24.0	14.6	60.6	39.4
Avg. Annual Wage	28,622	29,223	24,039	24,931	25,563	25,704	27,007	25,953	34,009
Retail Trade - SIC 52-59									
Establishments	1,574,905	611,053	237,727	159,980	1,008,760	165,286	81,048	1,255,094	319,811
Percent	100.0	38.8	15.1	10.2	64.1	10.5	5.1	79.7	20.3
Employment	19,861,604	1,061,152	1,515,594	1,923,026	4,499,772	4,273,110	2,134,371	10,907,253	8,954,351
Percent	100.0	5.3	7.6	9.7	22.7	21.5	10.7	54.9	45.1
Avg.Empl./Estab.	12.6	1.7	6.4	12.0	4.5	25.9	26.3	8.7	28.0
Annual Payroll ($Mill.)	242,369	14,447	16,165	21,059	51,670	53,201	27,284	132,156	110,214
Percent	100.0	6.0	6.7	8.7	21.3	22.0	11.3	54.5	45.5
Avg. Annual Wage	12,203	13,614	10,666	10,951	11,483	12,450	12,783	12,116	12,308

Table 2.7 Nonfarm Private Establishments, Employment, and Annual Payroll by Firm Employment Size, 1990--Continued

Item	Total	EMPLOYMENT SIZE OF FIRM							
		1-4	5-9	10-19	<20	20-99	100-499	<500	500+

Finance, Insurance, and Real Estate, SIC 60-69

Item	Total	1-4	5-9	10-19	<20	20-99	100-499	<500	500+
Establishments	563,761	298,602	57,964	30,067	386,633	31,296	22,209	440,138	123,623
Percent	100.0	53.0	10.3	5.3	68.6	5.6	3.9	78.1	21.9
Employment	6,983,931	476,299	373,535	393,382	1,243,216	984,655	864,224	3,092,095	3,891,836
Percent	100.0	6.8	5.3	5.6	17.8	14.1	12.4	44.3	55.7
Avg.Empl./Estab.	12.4	1.6	6.4	13.1	3.2	31.5	38.9	7.0	31.5
Annual Payroll ($Mill.)	198,342	11,473	8,371	9,617	29,461	23,968	22,488	75,916	122,426
Percent	100.0	5.8	4.2	4.8	14.9	12.1	11.3	38.3	61.7
Avg. Annual Wage	28,400	24,087	22,410	24,447	23,697	24,341	26,021	24,552	31,457

Services, SIC 70-89

Item	Total	1-4	5-9	10-19	<20	20-99	100-499	<500	500+
Establishments	2,135,627	1,204,139	369,571	197,827	1,771,537	177,148	75,475	2,024,160	111,467
Percent	100.0	56.4	17.3	9.3	83.0	8.3	3.5	94.8	5.2
Employment	28,880,444	2,098,685	2,364,281	2,472,307	6,935,273	5,283,645	5,003,879	17,222,797	11,657,647
Percent	100.0	7.3	8.2	8.6	24.0	18.3	17.3	59.6	40.4
Avg.Empl./Estab.	13.5	1.7	6.4	12.5	3.9	29.8	66.3	8.5	104.6
Annual Payroll ($Mill.)	601,554	54,417	49,459	53,307	157,184	103,702	90,120	351,005	250,548
Percent	100.0	9.0	8.2	8.9	26.1	17.2	15.0	58.3	41.7
Avg. Annual Wage	20,829	25,929	20,919	21,562	22,664	19,627	18,010	20,380	21,492

Source: U. S. Department of Commerce, Bureau of the Census, special tabulations for the Office of Advocacy, Small Business Administration, March 1993. Table prepared in June 1993.

Table 2.8 Total and Small Business Employment, 1982 and 1987

SIC	Industry	Total Employment		Employment in Small Firms (<500)		Employment in Small Firms (Percent)		Change in Employment (Percent)	
		1982	1987	1982	1987	1982	1987	Total	Small Business
	Total, All Covered Industries	53,053,089	68,140,605	28,461,873	38,631,208	53.6	56.7	28.4	35.7
2	Mining	815,667	473,296	455,243	284,606	55.8	60.1	-42.0	-37.5
3	Construction	4,321,677	5,116,642	3,517,906	4,517,344	81.4	88.3	18.4	28.4
4	Manufacturing	22,007,978	21,447,990	6,654,698	7,073,709	30.2	33.0	-2.5	6.3
5	Selected Transportation	N.A.	1,891,611		1,162,233		61.4		
6	Wholesale Trade	4,120,876	4,756,294	3,609,199	4,016,989	87.6	84.5	15.4	11.3
7	Retail Trade	14,845,081	18,622,014	9,154,072	10,529,386	61.7	56.5	25.4	15.0
9	Services	6,941,810	15,832,758	5,070,755	11,046,941	73.0	69.8	128.1	117.9
10	Metal Mining	39,671	39,036	10,001	9,155	25.2	23.5	-1.6	-8.5
13	Oil and Gas Extraction	493,518	213,141	314,981	161,948	63.8	76.0	-56.8	-48.6
14	Nonmetal Minerals, Except Fuels	76,277	70,258	50,310	56,140	66.0	79.9	-7.9	11.6
15	General Building Contractors	1,058,128	1,322,819	905,266	1,162,027	85.6	87.8	25.0	28.4
16	Heavy Construction Contractors	932,680	895,424	472,672	607,067	50.7	67.8	-4.0	28.4
17	Special Trade Contractors	2,330,869	2,906,399	2,139,968	2,748,250	91.8	94.6	24.7	28.4
20	Food and Kindred Products	2,305,029	1,790,057	547,949	493,723	23.8	27.6	-22.3	-9.9
21	Tobacco Manufactures	167,388	203,387	3,916	2,812	2.3	1.4	21.5	-28.2
22	Textile Mill Products	787,808	780,356	222,432	218,814	28.2	28.0	-0.9	-1.6
23	Apparel and Other Textile Products	1,146,691	1,077,775	702,140	635,612	61.2	59.0	-6.0	-9.5
24	Lumber and Wood Products	491,415	639,640	380,949	479,318	77.5	74.9	30.2	25.8
25	Furniture and Fixtures	444,625	572,995	236,880	270,502	53.3	47.2	28.9	14.2
26	Paper and Allied Products	712,726	878,382	159,380	202,029	22.4	23.0	23.2	26.8
27	Printing and Publishing	1,492,575	1,742,353	712,584	820,872	47.7	47.1	16.7	15.2
28	Chemicals and Allied Products	1,265,014	1,155,773	178,633	194,411	14.1	16.8	-8.6	8.8
29	Petroleum and Coal Products	800,036	452,770	35,393	22,612	4.4	5.0	-43.4	-36.1
30	Rubber and Misc. Plastic Products	673,436	796,289	314,190	391,649	46.6	49.2	18.2	24.7
31	Leather and Leather Products	206,436	98,825	73,402	46,385	35.6	46.9	-52.1	-36.8
32	Stone, Clay, and Glass Products	678,191	618,609	238,871	256,366	35.2	41.4	-8.8	7.3
33	Primary Metal Industries	1,074,848	812,529	192,039	203,930	17.9	25.1	-24.4	6.2
34	Fabricated Metal Products	1,369,774	1,363,681	760,784	806,948	55.5	59.2	-0.4	6.1
35	Machinery, Except Electric	2,595,516	2,101,652	865,427	869,932	33.3	41.4	-19.0	0.5
36	Electric and Electronic Equipment	2,490,275	2,362,462	408,707	617,634	16.4	26.1	-5.1	51.1

Table 2.8 Total and Small Business Employment, 1982 and 1987--Continued

SIC	Industry	Total Employment		Employment in Small Firms (<500)		Employment in Small Firms (Percent)		Change in Employment (Percent)	
		1982	1987	1982	1987	1982	1987	Total	Small Business
39	Miscellaneous Manufacturing Industries	385,397	365,438	243,005	265,408	63.1	72.6	-5.2	9.2
50	Wholesale Trade--Durable Goods	2,344,344	2,820,897	2,133,306	2,382,425	91.0	84.5	20.3	11.7
51	Wholesale Trade--Nondurable Goods	1,776,532	1,982,576	1,475,893	1,590,851	83.1	80.2	11.6	7.8
52	Building Material and Garden Supplies	498,162	654,783	410,434	495,458	82.4	75.7	31.4	20.7
53	General Merchandise Stores	2,253,136	2,588,938	150,726	120,465	6.7	4.7	14.9	-20.1
54	Food Stores	2,641,818	3,065,304	1,189,564	1,296,084	45.0	42.3	16.0	9.0
55	Auto Dealers and Service Stations	1,556,812	1,975,053	1,479,372	1,828,275	95.0	92.6	26.9	23.6
56	Apparel and Accessory Stores	863,915	1,089,597	585,685	553,618	67.8	50.8	26.1	-5.5
57	Furniture and Home Furnishing Stores	551,821	713,726	482,099	572,696	87.4	80.2	29.3	18.8
58	Eating and Drinking Places	4,656,811	6,374,480	3,428,166	4,116,768	73.6	64.6	36.9	20.1
59	Miscellaneous Retail	1,822,606	2,203,842	1,428,026	1,586,300	78.4	72.0	20.9	11.1
70	Hotels and Other Lodging Places	1,091,806	1,335,710	641,483	726,719	58.8	54.4	22.3	13.3
72	Personal Services	971,286	1,216,970	817,636	905,503	84.2	74.4	25.3	10.7
73	Business Services	2,956,507	5,249,508	2,010,131	2,946,698	68.0	56.1	77.6	46.6
75	Auto Repair, Services and Garages	542,028	1,009,167	484,806	851,068	89.4	84.3	86.2	75.5
78	Motion Pictures	232,157	295,287	114,837	154,098	49.5	52.2	27.2	34.2
79	Amusement and Recreation Services	578,469	666,725	450,757	515,884	77.9	77.4	15.3	14.4
80	Health Services	2,408,387	3,472,717	2,096,802	2,552,269	87.1	73.5	44.2	21.7
81	Legal Services	569,557	808,865	551,105	618,124	96.8	76.4	42.0	12.2
82	Selected Educational Services	65,640	107,958	58,198	90,891	88.7	84.2	64.5	56.2
89	Miscellaneous Services	1,122,708	1,605,107	831,965	1,520,921	74.1	94.8	43.0	82.8

N.A. = Not applicable. 1987 Enterprise Statistics data were calculated using 1987 SIC codes; 1982 Enterprise Statistics data were calculated using 1977 SIC codes. Because of SIC code migration between the two time periods much historical data are not strictly comparable.

Source: U.S. Department of Commerce, Bureau of the Census, *1987 Enterprise Statistics*, vol. 3, *Company Summary*, ES87-3 (Washington, D.C.: U.S. Government Printing Office, 1991), Table 3 and Table 12.

Table 2.9 Enterprises by Enterprise Size and Industry, 1987

SIC Code	Industry	Total				Employment Size of Firm								
			0	1-4	5-9	10-19	20-49	50-99	< 100	100-499	<500	500-999	1,000-9,999	10,000+
	Total, All Industries	3,878,866	330,815	1,900,185	783,793	452,986	269,305	81,914	3,818,998	51,076	3,870,074	4,590	3,718	484
10	Metal Mining	598	103	240	98	56	51	15	563	22	585	6	7	0
12	Coal Mining	2,850	158	731	502	650	546	138	2,725	88	2,813	14	21	2
13	Oil and Gas Extraction	18,179	1,896	9,617	2,930	1,905	1,224	375	17,947	194	18,141	21	17	0
14	Nonmetallic Minerals, Except Fuels	3,518	215	1,201	797	678	420	104	3,415	94	3,509	7	2	0
15	General Building Contractors	156,005	3,134	94,369	31,765	15,626	8,036	2,001	154,931	956	155,887	72	45	1
16	Heavy Construction, General Contractors	35,369	595	14,115	7,271	5,898	4,754	1,582	34,215	1,026	35,241	71	53	4
17	Special Trade Contractors	337,820	6,343	188,477	74,924	40,009	20,842	4,906	335,501	2,175	337,676	105	39	0
20	Food and Kindred Products	15,150	982	3,755	2,459	2,496	2,524	1,227	13,443	1,295	14,738	205	180	27
21	Tobacco Products	92	4	30	9	10	8	7	68	12	80	3	6	3
22	Textile Mill Products	4,764	162	990	605	760	942	512	3,971	601	4,572	89	92	11
23	Apparel and Other Textile Products	20,982	978	5,775	3,216	3,393	3,975	1,865	19,202	1,519	20,721	164	92	5
24	Lumber and Wood Products	31,494	2,262	12,128	6,504	5,021	3,525	1,145	30,585	814	31,399	54	38	3
25	Furniture and Fixtures	10,525	537	3,239	1,889	1,716	1,645	750	9,776	622	10,398	65	57	5
26	Paper and Allied Products	3,975	110	576	475	728	1,001	483	3,373	473	3,846	46	65	18
27	Publishing and Printing	56,840	3,894	22,512	12,468	8,483	5,879	1,970	55,206	1,339	56,545	118	101	20
28	Chemicals and Allied Products	7,682	347	2,146	1,469	1,350	1,209	491	7,012	474	7,486	67	22	28
29	Petroleum and Coal Products	1,057	42	282	203	163	179	70	939	73	1,012	12		11
30	Rubber and Miscellaneous Plastics Products	11,316	459	2,382	1,754	2,039	2,388	1,164	10,186	934	11,120	114	76	6
31	Leather and Leather Products	1,879	88	561	292	289	293	158	1,681	167	1,848	22	9	0
32	Stone, Clay, and Glass Products	12,124	677	3,552	2,338	2,310	1,938	692	11,507	497	12,004	54	60	6
33	Primary Metal Industries	4,897	159	909	723	872	1,019	477	4,159	561	4,720	83	80	14
34	Fabricated Metal Products	31,181	1,175	7,441	5,977	6,245	6,083	2,379	29,300	1,616	30,916	143	111	11
35	Machinery, Except Electrical	47,465	2,419	15,358	10,181	8,858	6,570	2,194	45,580	1,525	47,105	186	156	18
36	Electrical and Other Electronic Equipment	12,818	629	3,252	2,030	2,024	2,279	1,167	11,381	1,123	12,504	131	159	24
37	Transportation Equipment	8,727	590	2,425	1,460	1,459	1,373	636	7,943	584	8,527	86	82	32
38	Instruments and Related Products	8,407	469	2,388	1,569	1,340	1,322	579	7,667	558	8,225	74	83	25
39	Miscellaneous Manufacturing Industries	15,745	1,256	5,986	2,977	2,402	1,882	695	15,198	460	15,658	56	31	0
42	Trucking and Warehousing	87,929	10,812	42,605	14,407	10,177	6,739	1,948	86,688	1,080	87,768	86	65	10
44	Water Transportation	5,844	796	2,430	1,095	692	477	166	5,656	142	5,798	25	20	1
47	Transportation Services	31,582	2,832	16,069	7,623	3,073	1,346	370	31,313	240	31,553	16	13	0
50	Wholesale Trade-Durable Goods	224,515	14,532	95,658	51,049	34,794	20,319	5,356	221,708	2,563	224,271	145	96	3
51	Wholesale Trade-Nondurable Goods	130,161	9,354	56,193	26,907	18,834	12,848	3,774	127,910	2,042	129,952	123	79	7
52	Building Materials and Garden Supplies	58,239	4,318	25,818	14,561	8,563	3,773	781	57,814	364	58,178	27	31	3

Table 2.9 Enterprises by Enterprise Size and Industry, 1987--Continued

SIC Code	Industry	Total	0	1-4	5-9	10-19	20-49	50-99	<100	100-499	<500	500-999	1,000-9,999	10,000+
53	General Merchandise Stores	12,609	1,184	6,696	2,376	1,192	600	203	12,251	202	12,453	42	86	28
54	Food Stores	130,615	14,410	57,179	27,043	17,597	9,975	2,580	128,784	1,482	130,266	149	171	29
55	Automotive Dealers and Service Stations	159,566	11,563	70,090	35,083	21,211	14,003	5,371	157,321	2,140	159,461	65	40	0
56	Apparel and Accessory Stores	72,846	7,154	37,538	15,991	7,281	3,302	845	72,111	585	72,696	65	74	11
57	Furniture and Home Furnishing Stores	81,063	7,160	41,234	18,578	9,242	3,655	684	80,553	436	80,989	43	30	1
58	Eating and Drinking Places	302,813	40,930	99,996	58,468	47,776	38,694	11,300	297,164	5,010	302,174	397	211	31
59	Miscellaneous Retail	251,962	25,324	133,988	55,340	25,216	9,041	1,825	250,734	1,030	251,764	91	93	14
70	Hotels, Camps, and Other Lodging Places	40,528	6,586	14,947	5,920	5,059	4,065	1,961	38,538	1,717	40,255	157	108	8
72	Personal Services	160,035	15,541	93,140	31,020	13,443	5,110	1,141	159,395	559	159,954	42	36	3
73	Business Services	216,143	27,259	104,364	36,998	22,819	14,268	5,051	210,759	4,468	215,227	509	380	27
75	Automotive Repair, Services, and Garages	131,032	13,637	75,256	26,589	10,959	3,681	593	130,715	274	130,989	20	20	3
76	Miscellaneous Repair Services	60,504	6,340	36,719	10,617	4,664	1,724	323	60,387	106	60,493	9	2	0
78	Motion Pictures	28,130	3,829	14,615	5,363	2,630	1,179	270	27,886	203	28,089	18	19	4
79	Amusement and Recreation Services	57,780	11,402	23,021	9,407	7,020	4,851	1,264	56,965	716	57,681	62	34	3
80	Health Services	381,768	22,688	218,519	90,910	31,066	10,948	4,075	378,206	3,197	381,403	213	138	14
81	Legal Services	134,677	9,864	90,815	18,848	8,909	4,405	1,042	133,883	713	134,596	66	15	0
82	Selected Educational Services	8,929	1,199	4,380	1,422	971	593	221	8,786	129	8,915	8	6	0
83	Social Services	37,479	4,381	16,560	7,973	5,322	2,569	469	37,274	185	37,459	11	8	1
87	Engineering and Management Services	189,006	22,167	104,909	31,650	16,983	8,942	2,449	187,100	1,667	188,767	128	102	9
89	Services n.e.c.	21,652	5,870	13,009	1,670	713	291	70	21,623	24	21,647	5	0	0

n.e.c.= Not elsewhere classified

Note: Data exclude government employment. This table excludes agriculture and finance.

Source: Adapted from the U.S. Department of Commerce, Bureau of the Census, *1987 Enterprise Statistics*, Vol. 3, *Company Summary*, ES87-3 (Washington, D.C.: U.S. Government Printing Office, 1991), Table 3.

Table 2.10 Nonfarm Establishment Employment by Industrial Sector and Firm Size, 1990 (Thousands)

	Total	1-4	5-9	10-19	20-49	50-99	<100	100-499	<500	500-999	1,000-4,999	5,000-9,999	10,000+	500+
Total, All Industries														
Employment	94,881.00	9,585.87	7,330.02	6,892.60	10,176.46	7,680.63	41,665.58	12,706.74	54,372.32	3,874.81	9,455.77	4,230.93	22,947.19	40,508.70
Percent	100.00	10.10	7.73	7.26	10.73	8.10	43.91	13.39	57.31	4.08	9.97	4.46	24.19	42.69
Agriculture, Forestry, Fishing														
Employment	1,271.00	407.90	213.30	138.40	146.40	79.90	985.90	109.60	1,095.50	32.20	61.30	15.70	66.00	175.20
Percent	100.00	32.09	16.78	10.89	11.52	6.29	77.57	8.62	86.19	2.53	4.82	1.24	5.19	13.78
Mining														
Employment	752.00	45.80	44.00	46.20	60.70	40.60	237.30	76.20	313.50	29.40	104.60	45.60	259.00	438.60
Percent	100.00	6.09	5.85	6.14	8.07	5.40	31.56	10.13	41.69	3.91	13.91	6.06	34.44	58.32
Construction														
Employment	5,238.00	1,184.30	777.30	736.20	892.80	508.00	4,098.60	617.60	4,716.20	112.50	155.30	51.30	202.80	521.90
Percent	100.00	22.61	14.84	14.05	17.04	9.70	78.25	11.79	90.04	2.15	2.96	0.98	3.87	9.96
Manufacturing														
Employment	21,306.00	423.60	574.20	801.80	1,501.80	1,350.70	4,652.10	3,014.10	7,666.20	1,148.40	2,764.20	1,488.50	8,238.40	13,639.50
Percent	100.00	1.99	2.70	3.76	7.05	6.34	21.83	14.15	35.98	5.39	12.97	6.99	38.67	64.02
Transportation, Communications, Public Utilities														
Employment	5,478.00	267.60	268.50	303.70	452.30	328.80	1,620.90	585.90	2,206.80	212.30	610.70	271.40	2,176.90	3,271.30
Percent	100.00	4.88	4.90	5.54	8.26	6.00	29.59	10.70	40.28	3.88	11.15	4.95	39.74	59.72
Wholesale Trade														
Employment	6,214.00	661.80	699.30	706.10	860.30	525.30	3,452.80	788.60	4,241.40	216.10	509.70	196.20	1,050.50	1,972.50
Percent	100.00	10.65	11.25	11.36	13.84	8.45	55.56	12.69	68.26	3.48	8.20	3.16	16.91	31.74
Retail Trade														
Employment	16,942.00	2,434.10	1,948.90	1,659.80	2,258.70	1,405.50	9,707.00	1,355.30	11,062.30	347.20	847.20	480.40	4,205.30	5,880.10
Percent	100.00	14.37	11.50	9.80	13.33	8.30	57.30	8.00	65.30	2.05	5.00	2.84	24.82	34.71
Finance, Insurance, Real Estate														
Employment	7,667.00	752.10	493.90	454.90	630.10	417.00	2,748.00	808.10	3,556.10	324.10	885.10	598.10	2,303.80	4,111.10
Percent	100.00	9.81	6.44	5.93	8.22	5.44	35.84	10.54	46.38	4.23	11.54	7.80	30.05	53.62
Services														
Employment	30,012.00	3,408.70	2,310.50	2,045.50	3,373.30	3,024.80	14,162.80	5,351.30	19,514.10	1,452.60	3,517.60	1,083.60	4,444.40	10,498.20
Percent	100.00	11.36	7.70	6.82	11.24	10.08	47.19	17.83	65.02	4.84	11.72	3.61	14.81	34.98

Employment Size of Firm

Note: Establishment employment is assigned to industry divisions according to the SIC code of the establishment, and to the employment size class of the enterprise that owns the establishment. Excludes farm and government. Files have been re-benchmarked and are therefore not necessarily comparable with historical data.

Source: U.S. Small Business Administration, Office of Advocacy, Small Business Data Base, USEEM file, version 8, 1991.

Table 2.11 Job Creation by Selected Firm Size, SBA Region, and State, 1988-1990

	Small Firms (<500 Employees)		Large Firms (500+ Employees)	
	Net New Jobs	Percent of Total	Net New Jobs	Percent of Total
U.S. Total	3,165,694	100.0	-408,336	0.0
Region I	153,033	100.0	-100,958	0.0
Connecticut	78,925	100.0	-10,154	0.0
Maine	23,655	85.2	4,118	14.8
Massachusetts	16,333	100.0	-70,374	0.0
New Hampshire	9,445	100.0	-10,488	0.0
Rhode Island	8,063	100.0	-6,669	0.0
Vermont	16,612	100.0	-7,391	0.0
Region II	82,370	100.0	-131,611	0.0
New York	116,825	100.0	-83,089	0.0
New Jersey	-34,455	0.0	-48,522	0.0
Region III	189,521	74.0	66,627	26.0
Delaware	12,636	30.4	28,939	69.6
District of Columbia	8,469	100.0	-10,815	0.0
Maryland	7,511	13.5	48,136	86.5
Pennsylvania	50,006	100.0	-20,067	0.0
Virginia	96,156	100.0	23	0.0
West Virginia	14,743	41.9	20,411	58.1
Region IV	200,647	100.0	-74,367	0.0
Alabama	18,942	97.0	583	3.0
Florida	-1,210	0.0	-21,661	0.0
Georgia	-19,298	0.0	-14,553	0.0
Kentucky	11,617	52.5	10,530	47.5
Mississippi	16,779	57.4	12,465	42.6
North Carolina	87,951	100.0	-20,086	0.0
South Carolina	37,539	100.0	-26,037	0.0
Tennessee	48,327	100.0	-15,628	0.0
Region V	622,110	100.0	-224,109	0.0
Illinois	189,160	100.0	-34,911	0.0
Indiana	85,750	100.0	-33,504	0.0
Michigan	88,966	100.0	-17,625	0.0
Minnesota	59,346	100.0	-17,428	0.0
Ohio	114,130	100.0	-116,819	0.0
Wisconsin	84,758	100.0	-3,822	0.0
Region VI	537,999	100.0	-40,592	0.0
Arkansas	6,572	58.5	4,664	41.5
Louisiana	15,752	100.0	-20,432	0.0
New Mexico	26,820	100.0	-10,113	0.0
Oklahoma	9,141	100.0	-1,451	0.0
Texas	479,714	100.0	-13,260	0.0
Region VII	242,713	100.0	-34,423	0.0
Iowa	130,742	96.3	5,079	3.7
Kansas	43,991	63.5	25,245	36.5
Missouri	33,816	100.0	-65,648	0.0
Nebraska	34,164	100.0	-99	0.0
Region VIII	195,455	100.0	-19,996	0.0
Colorado	79,173	100.0	-128	0.0
Montana	17,630	100.0	-1,405	0.0
North Dakota	23,040	100.0	-931	0.0
South Dakota	27,800	100.0	-1,911	0.0
Utah	35,776	73.8	12,702	26.2
Wyoming	12,036	100.0	-2,919	0.0
Region IX	675,375	100.0	-1,888	0.0
Arizona	78,423	72.5	29,775	27.5
California	558,059	100.0	-72,331	0.0
Hawaii	16,811	66.3	8,547	33.7
Nevada	22,082	40.7	32,121	59.3

Table 2.11   Job Creation by Selected Firm Size, SBA Region, and State, 1988-1990--Continued

	Small Firms (<500 Employees)		Large Firms (500+ Employees)	
	Net New Jobs	Percent of Total	Net New Jobs	Percent of Total
Region X	266,471	88.2	35,531	11.8
Alaska	9,941	95.9	421	4.1
Idaho	31,033	99.0	299	1.0
Oregon	82,308	90.1	9,070	9.9
Washington	143,189	84.8	25,741	15.2

Source: U.S. Small Business Administration, Office of Advocacy, Small Business Data Base, 1988-1990 USELM file, version 7, 1991.

Table 2.12 Job Creation by Industrial Sector and Firm Size, 1986-1988 (Data in 000)

| Firm Size | Total, All Sizes | Employment Size of Firm | | | | |
		<20	20-99	100-499	<500	500+
Total All Industries	6,169	1,488	573	707	2,768	3,402
Agriculture Forestry, Fishing	39	47	7	0	54	-15
Mining	-152	-9	-23	-19	-52	-100
Construction	195	290	-4	-39	246	-51
Manufacturing	858	214	81	72	367	491
Transportation, Comm., Utilities	245	76	24	12	112	133
Wholesale Trade	285	126	5	19	150	136
Retail Trade	1,483	116	107	162	385	1,099
Finance, Insurance, and Real Estate	579	135	54	50	240	339
Services	2,636	495	322	450	1,267	1,369

Share of Jobs Created

| Firm Size | Total, All Sizes | Employment Size of Firm | | | | |
		<20	20-99	100-499	<500	500+
Total All Industries	100.0	24.1	9.3	11.5	44.9	55.1
Agriculture Forestry, Fishing	100.0	120.5	17.9	0.01	38.4	-38.4
Mining N/A						
Construction	100.0	148.7	-2.1	-20.0	26.6	-26.6
Manufacturing	100.0	24.9	9.4	8.4	42.8	57.2
Transportation, Comm., Utilities	100.0	31.0	9.8	4.9	45.7	54.3
Wholesale Trade	100.0	44.2	1.8	6.7	52.6	47.4
Retail Trade	100.0	7.8	7.2	10.9	26.0	74.0
Finance, Insurance Real Estate	100.0	23.3	9.3	8.6	41.5	58.5
Services	100.0	15.8	12.2	17.1	48.1	51.9

Note: Detail my not add to totals due to rounding.

Source: U.S. Small Business Administration, Office of Advocacy, Small Business Data Base, USEEM file, v.8, unpublished data.

Table 2.13 Job Creation by Major Industry and Firm Size, 1984-1988 (Data in 000)

| | Total All Sizes | Employment Size of Firm | | | | |
		1-19	20-99	100-499	<500	500+
Industry						
Total All Industries	11,143	3,124	1,297	987	5,408	5,735
Agriculture, Forestry, Fishing	107	94	11	0	104	3
Mining	-288	-13	-52	-50	-115	-172
Construction	442	574	60	-63	572	-129
Manufacturing	829	427	182	-28	580	248
Transportation, Communications, and Public Utilities	829	160	68	50	278	550
Wholesale Trade	662	298	38	40	377	285
Retail Trade	2,716	282	216	302	800	1,915
Finance, Insurance, and Real Estate	xx,50	283	131	134	548	702
Services	4,597	1,019	644	602	2,264	2,333

Share of Jobs Created

| | Total All Sizes | Employment Size of Firm | | | | |
		1-19	20-99	100-499	<500	500+
Total All Industries	100.0	28.0	11.6	8.9	48.5	51.5
Agriculture, Forestry, Fishing	100.0	87.9	10.3	-0.0	97.2	2.8
Mining	N\A					
Construction	100.0	129.9	13.6	14.3	129.4	-29.4
Manufacturing	100.0	51.5	22.0	-3.4	70.0	30.0
Transportation Comm., Utilities	100.0	19.3	8.2	6.0	33.5	66.5
Wholesale Trade	100.0	45.0	5.7	6.0	56.9	43.1
Retail Trade	100.0	10.4	8.0	11.1	29.5	70.5
Finance, Insurance, and Real Estate	100.0	22.6	10.5	10.7	43.8	56.2
Services	100.0	22.2	14.0	13.1	49.2	51.8

Note: Detail may not add to totals due to rounding.

Source: U.S. Small Business Administration, Office of Advocacy, Small Business Data Base, USEEM FILE, v.8, unpublished data.

Table 2.14 Source of New Jobs By Time Period, Type, and Major Industry: 1984-1988

		Total All Causes	Jobs Due to Births	Jobs Due to Expansions
Total, All Industries				
	1984-1988	100.0	71.5	29.5
	1984-1986	100.0	63.4	36.6
	1986-1988	100.0	71.0	29.0
Agriculture Forestry, and Fishing				
	1984-1988	100.0	68.1	31.9
	1984-1986	100.0	61.7	38.3
	1986-1988	100.0	66.1	33.9
Mining				
	1984-1986	100.0	75.9	24.1
	1984-1986	100.0	67.0	23.0
	1986-1988	100.0	73.3	26.7
Construction				
	1984-1988	100.0	61.3	38.7
	1984-1986	100.0	52.1	47.9
	1986-1988	100.0	58.4	41.6
Manufacturing				
	1984-1988	100.0	70.6	39.4
	1984-1986	100.0	61.6	38.4
	1986-1988	100.0	71.3	28.7
Transportation, Communications, Utilities				
	1984-1988	100.0	72.2	27.8
	1984-1986	100.0	68.5	36.5
	1986-1988	100.0	69.6	30.4
Wholesale Trade				
	1984-1988	100.0	65.8	34.2
	1984-1986	100.0	60.0	40.0
	1986-1988	100.0	64.0	36.0
Retail Trade				
	1984-1988	100.0	78.4	21.6
	1984-1986	100.0	71.0	29.0
	1986-1988	100.0	79.4	30.6
Finance, Insurance, and Real Estate				
	1984-1988	100.0	66.5	33.5
	1984-1986	100.0	59.2	41.8
	1986-1988	100.0	62.9	37.1
Services				
	1984-1988	100.0	72.2	27.8
	1984-1988	100.0	62.8	37.2
	1986-1988	100.0	71.8	28.2

Source: U.S. Small Business Administration, Office of Advocacy, Small Business Data Base USELM file, v.8, unpublished data.

Table 2.15 Components of Employment Growth (Thousands), 1984-1988

	Total, All Sizes	Employment Size of Firm				
		<20	20-99	100-499	<500	500+
Employment Base Year (1984)	85,824	16,368	14,760	12,812	43,940	41,885
+ Births	28,659	5,827	3,822	3,709	13,358	15,302
+ Expansions	11,407	3,336	2,348	1,638	7,323	4,084
- Deaths	-22,048	-5,004	-3,604	-3,262	-11,870	-10,177
- Contractions	-6,875	-1,035	-1,268	-1,099	-3,402	-3,473
Net Employment Change	11,143	3,124	1,297	987	5,408	5,735
Employment Term. Year (1988)	96,967	19,492	16,057	13,799	49,348	47,620

Note: Detail may not add to totals due to rounding.

Source: U.S. Small Business Administration, Office of Advocacy, Small Business Data Base, USELM file, v.8, unpublished data.

Table 2.16 Net Change in the Number of Establishments by Firm Size, 1986-1988 (Percent)

	Total	1-19	20-99	100-499	<500	500+
			Employment Size of Firm			
Total, All Industries	<u>4.32</u>	<u>2.15</u>	<u>2.01</u>	<u>7.77</u>	<u>2.49</u>	<u>20.40</u>
Agriculture, Forestry, and Fishing	5.20	5.26	4.92	5.32	5.23	3.69
Mining	-8.68	-8.38	-10.20	-11.32	-8.95	-7.09
Construction	3.05	3.55	-1.22	0.20	3.03	3.91
Manufacturing	1.74	2.65	-2.57	1.02	1.25	4.60
Transportation, Communications Utilities	3.61	2.90	-0.25	1.04	2.09	8.93
Wholesale Trade	0.76	-0.42	-2.05	1.35	0.08	7.71
Retail Trade	4.19	-1.57	2.47	14.06	-0.21	42.40
Finance, Insurance Real Estate	5.79	5.25	5.19	5.40	5.25	8.05
Services	8.09	5.47	7.86	14.66	6.43	27.36

Source: U.S. Small Business Administration Office of Advocacy, Small Business Data Base, USEEM file, v.8, unpublished data.

Table 2.17 Enterprises by Enterprise Size and Detailed Industry, 1988

Industry	Total	1-4	5-9	10-19	20-49	50-99	<100	100-499	<500	500<1K	1K<5K	5K<10K	10K+	500+
Total	4,003,980	2,050,947	933,595	500,145	319,311	106,418	3,910,416	77,528	3,987,944	7,804	6,503	859	870	16,036
01 Agriculture Product-Crops	41,570	26,311	9,217	3,250	1,879	514	41,171	348	41,519	30	19	1	1	51
02 Agriculture Product-Livestock	19,938	12,402	4,998	1,493	735	181	19,809	99	19,908	21	7	2	0	30
07 Agricultural Services	51,145	30,971	11,690	5,369	2,296	499	50,825	292	51,117	18	9	0	1	28
08 Forestry	1,254	736	267	133	82	20	1,238	11	1,249	2	3	0	5	
09 Fishing, Hunting, Trapping	1,276	758	275	120	85	27	1,265	10	1,275	0	1	0	0	1
10 Metal Mining	969	435	213	122	86	35	891	47	938	13	14	1	3	31
11 Anthracite Mining	164	50	45	37	24	4	160	3	163	1	0	0	0	1
12 Bitum Coal and Lignite Mining	2,889	661	532	837	567	148	2,745	114	2,859	13	13	2	2	30
13 Oil and Gas Extraction	25,769	14,316	5,763	3,036	1,725	523	25,363	315	25,678	38	33	6	14	91
14 Nonmetal Minerals, Except Fuels	2,796	847	730	580	398	113	2,668	104	2,772	12	9	2	1	24
15 General Building Contractor	201,239	132,993	36,823	18,108	9,414	2,455	199,793	1,288	201,081	95	56	5	2	158
16 Heavy Construction Contract	32,397	12,959	7,764	5,192	3,981	1,370	31,266	1,003	32,269	74	44	8	2	128
17 Special Trade Contractors	325,981	190,890	69,103	37,340	20,873	5,245	323,451	2,371	325,822	107	47	2	3	159
20 Food and Kindred Products	17,841	4,461	4,026	3,313	2,927	1,361	16,088	1,358	17,446	193	152	22	28	395
21 Tobacco Manufacturers	79	22	12	9	10	7	60	9	69	2	5	0	3	10
22 Textile Mill Products	8,258	2,323	1,417	1,307	1,474	733	7,254	779	8,033	110	93	11	11	225
23 Apparel and Other	22,378	6,813	3,953	3,516	3,845	2,027	20,154	1,878	22,032	186	139	13	8	346
24 Lumber and Wood Products	27,078	9,438	6,537	5,095	3,691	1,343	26,104	861	26,965	67	40	2	4	113
25 Furniture and Fixtures	13,114	4,153	3,027	2,348	1,929	819	12,276	686	12,962	77	58	15	2	152
26 Paper and Allied Products	5,040	777	780	931	1,206	642	4,336	553	4,889	61	61	10	19	151
27 Printing and Publishing	63,776	25,363	18,319	9,877	6,331	2,131	62,021	1,445	63,466	140	124	28	18	310
28 Chemicals and Allied Products	12,159	3,277	2,953	2,259	1,946	794	11,229	662	11,891	91	115	19	43	268
29 Petroleum and Coal Products	1,529	383	394	260	250	102	1,389	90	1,479	14	21	8	7	50
30 Rubber and Miscellaneous Plastic Products	12,108	2,713	2,248	2,172	2,467	1,194	10,794	1,102	11,896	118	72	12	10	212
31 Leather and Leather Products	2,807	1,042	487	395	391	213	2,528	229	2,757	20	27	3	0	50
32 Stone, Clay, and Glass Products	14,136	4,328	3,482	2,667	2,138	796	13,411	590	14,001	62	53	10	10	135
33 Primary Metal Industries	6,848	1,314	1,302	1,296	1,428	629	5,969	673	6,642	76	96	19	15	206
34 Fabricated Metal Products	34,500	8,395	7,470	7,089	6,687	2,690	32,331	1,839	34,170	187	123	8	12	330
35 Machinery, Except Electrical	60,053	20,024	15,260	11,266	8,272	2,761	57,583	1,962	59,545	223	201	36	48	508
36 Electric and Electronic Equipment	19,469	4,953	3,964	3,442	3,537	1,527	17,423	1,590	19,013	201	197	18	40	456

Table 2.17 Enterprises by Enterprise Size and Detailed Industry, 1988--Continued

Industry	Total	1-4	5-9	10-19	20-49	50-99	<100	100-499	<500	500<1K	1K<5K	5K<10K	10K+	500+
37 Transportation Equipment	10,783	3,280	2,356	1,821	1,657	705	9,819	708	10,527	104	90	19	43	256
38 Instruments and Related Products	12,259	3,724	2,812	2,263	1,885	740	11,424	658	12,082	72	78	17	10	177
39 Miscellaneous Manufacturing Industries	25,853	11,134	6,184	3,971	2,749	986	25,024	707	25,731	63	51	3	5	122
40 Railroad Transportation	310	44	83	61	41	27	256	26	282	10	8	2	8	28
41 Local and Interurban Passenger Transportation	10,744	3,166	2,172	1,956	2,084	761	10,139	525	10,664	41	32	4	3	80
42 Trucking and Warehousing	70,938	34,644	15,216	10,221	7,061	2,209	69,351	1,403	70,754	98	71	8	8	184
44 Water Transportation	6,646	3,241	1,510	864	607	206	6,428	168	6,596	23	25	2	0	50
45 Transportation by Air	5,946	2,726	1,534	794	525	156	5,735	143	5,878	21	30	6	11	68
46 Pipe Lines, Except Natural	97	29	20	8	22	8	87	7	94	3	0	0	0	3
47 Transportation Services	27,314	10,854	9,663	4,089	1,801	498	26,905	336	27,241	35	36	0	2	73
48 Communication	11,574	2,500	2,766	3,127	2,019	572	10,984	466	11,450	54	45	8	17	124
49 Electric, Gas, and Sanitation Services	10,776	3,530	2,599	1,755	1,531	649	10,064	458	10,522	66	126	28	34	254
50 Wholesale Trade-Durable Goods	270,834	126,296	75,822	39,019	20,944	5,420	267,501	2,979	270,480	201	137	10	6	354
51 Wholesale Trade-Nondurable Goods	156,576	76,196	39,674	21,162	12,971	3,906	153,909	2,356	156,265	164	120	13	14	311
52 Building Materials and Garden Supplies	70,318	37,900	19,786	8,140	3,366	710	69,902	359	70,261	26	22	6	3	57
53 General Merchandise Stores	19,105	10,965	4,263	1,775	923	400	18,326	577	18,903	71	83	19	29	202
54 Food Stores	110,942	53,453	29,778	13,838	9,076	2,736	108,881	1,701	110,582	161	139	30	30	360
55 Auto Dealers and Service Stations	136,065	61,014	36,038	17,510	13,878	5,523	133,963	2,002	135,965	59	36	4	1	100
56 Apparel and Accessory Stores	108,061	72,272	24,361	7,022	2,938	716	107,309	601	107,910	55	78	4	14	151
57 Furniture and Home Furnishing Stores	119,349	74,610	28,974	10,511	3,921	786	118,802	464	119,266	44	30	5	4	83
58 Eating and Drinking Places	194,284	49,708	53,900	41,025	33,658	10,338	188,629	4,961	193,590	408	236	26	24	694
59 Miscellaneous Retail	307,492	195,759	73,130	25,795	9,419	2,012	306,115	1,148	307,263	108	99	10	12	229
60 Banking	14,682	1,287	2,646	3,739	4,074	1,575	13,321	1,022	14,343	117	150	36	36	339
61 Credit Agencies Other than Banks	20,933	7,666	5,196	3,142	2,530	1,111	19,645	1,032	20,677	133	106	12	5	256
62 Security, Commodity Brokers and Services	14,112	6,994	3,496	1,679	1,040	403	13,612	368	13,980	71	41	11	9	132
63 Insurance Carriers	6,687	1,900	1,579	1,117	844	407	5,847	483	6,330	110	165	37	45	357
64 Insurance Agents, Brokers and Services	37,293	17,392	10,834	5,282	2,718	685	36,911	332	37,243	22	18	7	3	50
65 Real Estate	188,280	121,869	33,829	16,900	10,135	2,973	185,706	2,289	187,995	181	93	8	3	285
66 Combined Real Estate, Insurance	3,872	2,226	873	421	224	72	3,816	41	3,857	7	7	1	0	15
67 Holdings and Other Investment Offices	16,817	10,685	2,754	1,364	907	429	16,139	505	16,644	75	79	15	4	173
70 Hotels and Other Lodging Places	39,013	18,681	7,296	4,883	4,066	1,942	36,868	1,864	38,732	162	96	11	12	281

Table 2.17 Enterprises by Enterprise Size and Detailed Industry, 1988--Continued

Industry	Total	1-4	5-9	10-19	20-49	50-99	<100	100-499	<500	500<1K	1K<5K	5K<10K	10K+	500+
72 Personal Services	106,277	64,758	24,463	10,479	4,660	1,146	105,506	682	106,188	47	31	7	4	89
73 Business Services	293,646	166,048	62,059	32,736	19,508	6,412	286,763	5,754	292,517	624	427	45	33	1,129
75 Auto Repair, Services, and Garages	110,036	67,674	28,152	9,867	3,401	572	109,666	316	109,982	27	21	3	3	54
76 Miscellaneous Repair Services	83,324	62,479	13,650	4,788	1,857	396	83,170	141	83,311	10	3	0	0	13
78 Motion Pictures	12,897	6,840	3,038	1,796	762	230	12,666	187	12,853	18	17	5	4	44
79 Amusement and Recreation Services	44,441	20,416	9,551	6,696	5,087	1,639	43,389	932	44,321	68	40	6	6	120
80 Health Services	93,546	35,935	21,012	12,589	8,998	5,973	84,507	6,738	91,245	990	1,188	83	40	2,301
81 Legal Services	29,961	11,482	7,542	5,180	3,678	1,120	29,002	840	29,842	88	31	0	0	119
82 Educational Services	21,683	4,651	2,950	3,061	3,737	2,319	16,718	4,071	20,789	456	332	54	52	894
83 Social Services	27,834	6,216	6,150	5,702	5,065	2,333	25,466	2,151	27,617	145	63	6	3	217
84 Museums, Botanical, Zoological Garden	1,416	486	332	230	216	79	1,343	69	1,412	3	0	1	0	4
86 Membership Organizations	56,812	24,427	14,047	8,517	5,986	1,933	54,910	1,546	56,456	208	122	14	12	356
88 Private Households	236	169	48	9	6	3	235	1	236	0	0	0	0	0
89 Miscellaneous Service	65,356	29,513	16,406	10,382	6,062	1,699	64,062	1,100	65,162	103	69	11	11	194

Source: U.S. Small Business Administration, Office of Advocacy, Small Business Data Base, 1988 USELM file, unpublished data.

Table 2.18 Nonfarm Establishments by Firm Size and Industry Division, 1987

Industry	Total	1-4	5-9	10-19	20-49	50-99	<100	100-499	500-999	1,000-4,999	5,000-9,999	10,000+	500+
Total, United States													
Establishments	5,339,947	2,538,096	926,370	608,221	400,340	157,709	4,631,096	204,923	62,168	132,826	60,462	251,466	506,932
Percent	100.0	48.95	17.35	11.73	7.72	3.04	89.32	3.89	1.20	2.56	1.17	4.85	9.78
Agricultural Services, Forestry, and Fishing													
Establishments	126,982	77,927	27,649	11,159	7,603	1,756	126,094	819	58	11	0	0	69
Percent	100.0	61.37	21.77	8.79	5.99	1.38	99.30	0.64	0.05	0.01	0.00	0.00	0.05
Mining													
Establishments	32,074	14,216	4,418	3,530	2,845	1,138	26,147	1,866	651	1,775	1,252	383	4,061
Percent	100.0	44.32	13.77	11.01	8.87	3.55	81.52	5.82	2.03	5.53	3.90	1.19	12.66
Construction													
Establishments	539,171	307,088	114,066	61,840	34,669	9,600	527,263	7,168	1,555	1,958	647	580	4,740
Percent	100.0	56.96	21.16	11.47	6.43	1.78	97.79	1.33	0.29	0.36	0.12	0.11	0.88
Manufacturing													
Establishments	473,353	113,012	58,799	52,600	49,111	23,595	297,117	36,278	12,451	32,070	17,975	77,462	6,457
Percent	100.0	23.87	12.42	11.11	10.38	4.98	62.77	7.66	2.63	6.78	3.80	16.36	29.57
Selected Transportation													
Establishments	147,611	75,757	23,596	15,071	10,622	4,305	129,351	5,889	1,965	4,525	1,283	4,598	12,371
Percent	100.0	51.3	15.99	10.21	7.20	2.92	87.63	3.99	1.33	3.07	0.87	3.11	8.38
Wholesale Trade													
Establishments	431,869	176,220	80,590	61,152	48,896	21,733	389,501	24,331	5,901	8,523	1,135	2,478	18,037
Percent	100.0	40.93	18.24	14.16	11.32	5.03	90.19	5.63	1.37	1.97	0.26	0.57	4.18
Retail Trade													
Establishments	1,489,922	588,384	232,080	158,082	116,548	51,346	1,151,440	75,291	27,196	58,439	28,031	143,896	257,561
Percent	100.0	39.62	15.97	10.65	7.85	3.46	77.54	5.11	1.83	3.94	1.85	9.69	17.35
Finance, Insurance, and Real Estate													
Establishments	481,271	220,737	94,216	100,411	47,079	10,656	473,099	6,885	724	532	28	7	1,291
Percent	100.0	45.87	19.58	20.86	9.78	2.21	98.30	1.43	0.15	0.11	0.01	0.00	0.27
Services													
Establishments	1,622,694	964,205	285,956	144,316	82,967	33,580	1,511,089	42,766	11,667	24,994	10,111	22,072	68,844
Percent	100.0	59.42	17.62	8.90	5.11	2.07	93.12	2.64	0.72	1.54	0.62	1.36	4.24

Note: Data exclude government employment.

Source: U.S. Department of Commerce, Bureau of the Census, 1987 Enterprise Statistics, vol. 3, Company Summary, E.S.87-3. (Washington, D.C.: U.S. Government Printing Office, 1991). For Agricultural Services and Finance, the U.S. Small Business Administration, Office of Advocacy, Small Business Data Base, USEEM file, version 7, 1990.

Table 2.19 Small Firm Share of Employment and Sales by Major Industry, 1977-1987

	Employment Share	Sales Share*
Total, All Industries		
1977	52.5	51.8
1982	55.8	51.6
1987	56.7	53.5
Agriculture, Forestry, Fishing		
1984	80.4	86.9
1986	79.2	85.3
1988	81.4	85.8
Mining		
1977	44.3	36.9
1982	55.8	48.9
1987	60.1	52.3
Construction		
1977	82.1	81.6
1982	81.4	76.6
1987	88.3	85.3
Manufacturing		
1977	29.0	22.5
1982	30.3	21.6
1987	33.0	24.3
Transportation Communication		
1984	34.4	22.1
1986	33.1	24.7
1988	33.5	24.1
Wholesale Trade		
1977	88.8	85.0
1982	87.6	84.5
1987	84.5	79.7
Retail Trade		
1977	62.3	63.4
1982	61.7	61.1
1987	56.5	57.6
Finance, Insurance, Real Estate**		
1984	47.7	32.7
1986	45.5	28.0
1988	45.1	18.2
Services		
1977	75.7	75.1
1982	77.2	75.5
1987	69.8	71.7

Source: U.S. Department of Commerce, Bureau of the Census, Enterprise Statistics 1977,82,87, Table 3,(Washington, D.C.: U.S. Government Printing Office 1981,1986,1991). Data for Transportation and Finance are unavailable for all three time periods. Services is limited to industries covered in all three volumes.

Table 2.20 Age of Business by Type in the Small Business Data Base: 1988

Age in Years	All Firms	Percent	Women-Owned Firms	Percent	Export Firms	Percent
All Firms	4,672,981	100.0	203,118	100.0	43,412	100.0
<2	180,679	3.9	10,663	5.2	1,617	3.7
2<4	402,587	8.6	24,329	12.0	3,965	9.1
4<6	492,771	10.5	28,139	13.9	4,919	11.3
6<8	476,535	10.2	26,073	12.8	4,358	10.0
8<10	399,500	8.5	21,026	10.4	3,822	8.8
10<16	1,068,618	22.9	47,669	23.5	9,165	21.1
16<20	576,522	12.3	19,346	9.5	4,900	11.3
>20	1,075,869	23.1	25,873	12.7	10,666	24.7
< 10		41.7		54.3		42.9
> 10		58.3		46.7		57.1

Note: Age of firm is only reported for enterprises.

Source: U.S. Small Business Administration, Office of Advocacy, Small Business Data Base, USEEM file, v.8, unpublished data.

Table 2.21 Small Business Birth, Death, and Net Growth Rates: 1980-1988

[Represents any concern which is independently owned and operated and has fewer than 500 employees. Minus sign (-) indicates decrease.]

Item	Birth Rate[1]	Death Rate[2]	Net Growth[3]
All Industries			
1980-1982	9.5	9.1	0.4
1982-1984	10.2	8.9	1.3
1984-1986	10.6	9.6	1.0
1986-1988	11.0	9.8	1.2
Construction			
1980-1982	8.9	9.6	-0.7
1982-1984	10.8	10.5	0.3
1984-1986	10.9	10.0	0.9
1986-1988	11.4	9.8	1.5
Manufacturing			
1980-1982	8.1	7.3	0.8
1982-1984	8.8	7.1	1.7
1984-1986	8.7	8.2	0.5
1986-1988	9.3	8.7	0.6
Wholesale trade			
1980-1982	9.1	7.5	1.6
1982-1984	9.9	7.5	2.4
1984-1986	9.8	8.8	1.0
1986-1988	9.4	9.3	0.0
Retail trade			
1980-1982	8.5	9.6	-1.1
1982-1984	8.9	9.5	-0.6
1984-1986	9.8	10.3	-0.6
1986-1988	10.4	10.5	-0.1
Services			
1980-1982	11.4	9.3	2.1
1982-1984	11.8	8.7	3.1
1984-1986	11.7	9.4	2.4
1986-1988	13.0	9.8	3.2

*All rates are annualized.

[1]Business birth rate represents the number of establishments formed during the specified period relative to the number of establishments in the initial year.

[2]Business death rate represents the number of number of establishments that disappear (close) during the specified period relative to the number of establishments in the initial year.

[3]Net growth rate is the birth rate less the death rate.

Source: U.S. Small Business Administration, Office of Advocacy, Small Business Data Base (SBDB), U.S. Establishment Longitudinal Microdata (USELM) file. (The USELM file is a longitudinal, stratified and weighted sample of the SBDB's cross-sectional universe file, the U.S. Establishment and Enterprise Microdata (USEEM) file.

3 Employment and Size of Reporting Unit Data from the Employment and Training Administration

A new source of data has been developed by the Small Business Administration's Office of Advocacy using information from the unemployment insurance (UI) offices in each state. These statistics are collected in the states and transmitted to the Employment and Training Administration of the U.S. Department of Labor; the data are used for the quarterly report on employment and wages.

The reporting system relies on compliance by employers in reporting new hires and terminations of employment, so that unemployment insurance (FUTA) payments can be assessed accurately. In addition to monitoring employee changes, the state UI offices track firms that go into and out of business—that is, new firms that open UI accounts, and firms that terminate or cease paying UI taxes. Firms that change owners, known as "successor" firms, are also tracked.

UI data cover civilian nonagricultural firms with employees that are subject to the FUTA laws. Data are collected by size of reporting unit. A reporting unit can include more than one establishment if located in the same county and industry.[1]

The SBA's Office of Advocacy has assembled a longitudinal file of UI summary data by employment and size of reporting unit.

---

1 In recent years, the Bureau of Labor Statistics has undertaken a massive program to break out individual establishments from reporting units. This program is virtually complete in most states, and data is now being reported by establishment. Historically, however, the data is by size of reporting unit. Reporting units and establishments are very close in definition for firms with less than 10 employees, but are less representative as size of reporting unit increases. (For example, in 1987 reporting units with under 10 employees contributed 14.3 percent of total employment, while firms with less than 10 employees contributed 15.7 percent of total employment. However, when size is increased to 100 employees or less, reporting units contributed 51.2 percent of total employment, while firms with less than 100 employees provided 42.4 percent of total employment. Therefore data on reporting units only substitutes for small firm data for firms with under approximately 50 employees.)

These data are also available by major federal region so that the components of growth over time can be disaggregated by region.

In discussion, the term "firm/reporting unit" should be used. This is because UI data for very small firm sizes legitimately refer to small enterprises, but once units are larger than 50 employees, establishments owned by larger enterprises tend to be included in the reports. Therefore, the larger the reporting unit, the less likely it is to represent an independent small business.

Two types of tabular data are shown in this chapter: employment data and data on the number of firms/reporting units by employment size class, shown by fiscal and/or calendar year. The first five tables portray the components of firm change—new, successor, and terminated firms—for the 1981–1991 period, with particular emphasis on 1990–1991 changes.[2] Tables 3.6 through 3.9 express the annual change data as regional firm birth and death rates, while tables 3.10 through 3.12 present similar data for employment changes.

Summary

A new data series, developed from unemployment insurance data from the Employment and Training Administration, shows that about 30 percent of businesses either start or stop in the United States each year. Most of the new firm growth that occurred during 1990–1991 did so in the western regions of the country, in which net business formation exceeded 3 percent annually.

Over the longer term, 1978–1988 period, employment grew fastest in firms/reporting units of 50 to 99 employees, perhaps indicative of the need for increased scale economies in service-producing sectors to reach efficiency. In general, the growth of small firms/reporting units have increased in the downsizing manufacturing sector, and large firms have grown in service producing sectors, such as retail trade.

By region, net business formation turned from highly positive to highly negative after 1988 in New England and in the northeastern states, while no observable cycles in business formation were observed in Regions V, VII, and X. In the Midwest (SBA Region V), net business formation remained much below the national average during the 1980s, while in the western and southwestern states comprising SBA Regions VII and X it generally remained above the national average.

2   As explained in the previous footnote, the words "firm change" really refer to changes in the number of reporting units. Changes in reporting units are useful proxies for firm changes only for reporting units of less than 50 employees.

Now that new summary time-series employment data have also recently become available from the UI system, it will be important to compare both employment growth and net business formation over time. How do the two vary, and what do they reveal about small business patterns of regional growth?

Chapter 3 Tables

Table 3.1 Number of Firms and Components of Firm Change: SBA Region I, 1982-1992

Successor Firms

	1982	1983	1984	1985	1986	1987	1988	1989	1990	1991	1992	Percent Change 1982-1992
Region I, Total	7,665	8,843	8,361	8,784	10,257	11,453	10,973	10,729	8,534	8,008	7,647	-0.2
Connecticut	2,593	2,515	2,550	2,646	3,060	3,229	3,391	3,203	2,729	2,505	2,241	-13.6
Maine	973	854	1,024	795	1,161	1,225	1,246	1,196	763	902	876	-10.0
Massachusetts	2,649	3,684	2,943	3,111	3,495	3,560	3,601	3,557	2,766	2,440	2,237	-15.6
New Hampshire	609	1,006	971	1,088	1,170	1,274	1,162	1,096	933	816	794	30.4
Rhode Island	184	156	166	175	595	759	695	805	657	752	850	362.0
Vermont	657	628	707	969	776	1,406	878	872	686	593	649	-1.2

New Firms

	1982	1983	1984	1985	1986	1987	1988	1989	1990	1991	1992	Percent Change 1982-1992
Region I, Total	28,887	36,101	37,364	37,808	42,600	45,175	46,752	42,692	37,435	37,534	35,669	23.5
Connecticut	7,186	8,345	8,762	8,863	9,887	10,650	11,320	10,653	9,399	8,470	8,358	16.3
Maine	2,488	2,819	3,453	2,522	4,451	4,571	4,702	4,475	3,978	3,533	3,832	54.0
Massachusetts	11,950	17,092	16,348	15,595	17,154	18,506	19,010	17,101	14,697	12,953	13,675	14.4
New Hampshire	2,898	3,356	4,029	4,580	5,423	5,594	4,986	4,528	4,278	3,922	3,962	36.7
Rhode Island	2,838	2,916	3,258	3,628	3,222	3,679	4,101	3,520	2,900	6,458	3,772	32.9
Vermont	1,527	1,573	1,514	2,620	2,463	2,175	2,633	2,415	2,183	2,198	2,070	35.6

Terminations

	1982	1983	1984	1985	1986	1987	1988	1989	1990	1991	1992	Percent Change 1982-1992
Region I, Total	34,922	42,258	37,200	35,124	41,312	42,037	45,158	47,238	46,838	48,274	44,509	27.5
Connecticut	13,868	9,263	10,078	9,073	9,496	10,481	11,931	11,741	11,994	12,242	12,017	-13.3
Maine	689	7,899	4,078	4,064	4,081	4,392	4,366	4,683	4,737	4,593	3,876	462.6
Massachusetts	12,231	17,069	13,815	12,601	18,200	16,063	17,385	18,415	17,539	18,914	17,263	41.1
New Hampshire	3,122	3,418	3,576	3,741	3,925	4,666	5,262	5,491	6,018	5,599	5,317	70.3
Rhode Island	3,108	2,840	3,859	3,040	3,120	3,671	3,511	3,993	3,863	3,963	3,858	24.1
Vermont	1,904	1,769	1,794	2,605	2,490	2,764	2,703	2,915	2,687	2,963	2,178	14.4

Firms at End of Year

	1982	1983	1984	1985	1986	1987	1988	1989	1990	1991	1992	Percent Change 1982-1992
Region I, Total	293,580	296,266	304,791	316,259	327,804	342,395	354,962	361,145	360,276	357,544	356,351	21.4
Connecticut	77,987	79,584	80,818	83,254	86,705	90,103	92,883	94,998	95,132	93,865	92,447	18.5
Maine	32,501	28,275	28,674	27,927	29,458	30,862	32,444	33,432	33,436	33,278	34,110	5.0
Massachusetts	120,862	124,569	130,045	136,150	138,599	144,602	149,828	152,071	151,995	148,474	147,123	21.7
New Hampshire	23,544	24,488	25,912	27,839	30,507	32,709	33,595	33,728	32,921	32,060	31,499	33.8
Rhode Island	24,471	24,703	24,268	25,031	25,728	26,495	27,780	28,112	27,806	31,053	31,817	30.0
Vermont	14,215	14,647	15,074	16,058	16,807	17,624	18,432	18,804	18,986	18,814	19,355	36.2

Source: State Employment Security Agency quarterly reports to the U.S. Department of Labor, Employment and Training Administration edited by the Small Business Administration, Office of Advocacy.

Table 3.2 Number of Firms and Components of Firm Change: SBA Region II, 1982-1992

	1982	1983	1984	1985	1986	1987	1988	1989	1990	1991	1992	Percent Change 1982-1992
Successor Firms												
Region II, Total	14,337	12,455	13,244	11,841	15,025	14,750	13,928	13,410	11,756	10,424	10,489	-26.8
New Jersey	4,871	4,177	4,181	3,750	4,909	4,826	4,294	3,877	3,393	3,287	3,476	-28.6
New York	9,466	8,278	9,063	8,091	10,116	9,924	9,634	9,533	8,363	7,137	7,013	-25.9
New Firms												
Region II, Total	66,925	70,603	76,950	79,788	87,343	89,803	87,943	82,349	79,391	70,845	72,037	7.6
New Jersey	19,926	20,554	21,579	24,511	28,544	29,215	27,988	25,603	24,610	21,273	21,560	8.2
New York	46,999	50,049	55,371	55,277	58,799	60,588	59,955	56,746	54,781	49,572	50,477	7.4
Terminations												
Region II, Total	77,154	74,521	71,731	78,915	90,948	87,707	88,155	90,875	89,165	89,487	90,961	17.9
New Jersey	22,203	22,087	21,085	22,814	26,504	26,981	25,432	26,645	25,538	27,472	28,961	30.4
New York	54,951	52,434	50,646	56,101	64,444	60,726	62,723	64,230	63,627	62,015	62,000	12.8
Firms at End of Year												
Region II, Total	558,333	566,870	585,333	598,047	609,467	626,313	640,029	644,913	646,895	638,677	629,512	12.7
New Jersey	166,573	169,217	173,892	179,339	186,288	193,348	200,198	203,033	205,498	202,586	198,661	19.3
New York	391,760	397,653	411,441	418,708	423,179	432,965	439,831	441,880	441,397	436,091	430,851	10.0

Source: State Employment Security Agency quarterly reports to the U.S. Department of Labor, Employment and Training Administration edited by the Small Business Administration, Office of Advocacy.

Table 3.3 Number of Firms and Components of Firm Change: SBA Region III, 1982-1992

Successor Firms

	1982	1983	1984	1985	1986	1987	1988	1989	1990	1991	1992	Percent Change 1982-1992
Region III, Total	10,612	8,739	8,238	9,311	9,626	10,621	9,716	11,317	10,340	10,467	9,807	-7.6
Delaware	305	333	266	232	290	383	341	365	281	294	302	-1.0
District of Columbia	177	0	0	30	123	132	132	152	156	186	61	-65.5
Maryland	1,743	1,128	1,220	1,167	1,298	1,274	1,238	1,111	1,044	966	890	-48.9
Pennsylvania	3,879	3,269	2,942	3,491	3,583	4,058	3,468	5,264	4,536	4,748	4,510	16.3
Virginia	3,566	3,149	2,933	3,409	3,461	3,843	3,559	3,552	3,558	3,493	3,294	-7.6
West Virginia	942	860	877	982	871	931	978	873	765	780	750	-20.4

New Firms

	1982	1983	1984	1985	1986	1987	1988	1989	1990	1991	1992	Percent Change 1982-1992
Region III, Total	55,820	60,898	67,620	66,881	70,014	78,541	76,531	80,901	74,444	71,926	73,092	30.9
Delaware	1,595	1,966	1,996	1,882	2,133	2,742	2,587	2,484	2,083	2,731	2,617	64.1
District of Columbia	2,381	3,209	3,232	3,215	3,161	3,380	3,388	3,862	3,226	3,202	4,627	94.3
Maryland	12,321	14,684	16,353	16,488	17,116	19,934	19,392	19,177	18,923	17,987	17,995	46.1
Pennsylvania	22,752	23,274	25,793	26,247	26,936	25,809	27,214	30,857	26,125	25,562	25,255	11.0
Virginia	13,419	14,068	16,076	14,821	16,853	22,316	19,898	20,462	19,856	18,354	18,425	37.3
West Virginia	3,352	3,697	4,170	4,228	3,815	4,360	4,052	4,059	4,231	4,090	4,173	24.5

Terminations

	1982	1983	1984	1985	1986	1987	1988	1989	1990	1991	1992	Percent Change 1982-1992
Region III, Total	62,725	59,733	60,704	62,479	66,014	72,379	76,395	73,637	76,857	79,463	77,204	23.1
Delaware	1,643	2,112	1,702	1,912	1,914	2,159	2,206	1,793	1,422	2,490	1,749	6.5
District of Columbia	2,658	1,892	3,193	3,320	3,304	3,647	3,620	4,340	3,715	3,998	3,125	17.6
Maryland	12,331	11,860	12,955	13,977	14,071	15,539	16,201	16,198	17,945	18,842	18,426	49.4
Pennsylvania	27,595	22,791	25,939	24,667	24,978	27,760	29,100	28,019	27,929	29,668	29,731	7.7
Virginia	13,515	16,577	12,655	13,261	17,157	18,715	20,527	18,333	21,438	19,820	19,809	46.6
West Virginia	4,983	4,501	4,260	5,342	4,590	4,559	4,741	4,954	4,408	4,645	4,364	-12.4

Firms at End of Year

	1982	1983	1984	1985	1986	1987	1988	1989	1990	1991	1992	Percent Change 1982-1992
Region III, Total	444,624	454,528	469,682	483,395	497,021	513,804	523,656	542,237	550,164	553,094	558,789	25.7
Delaware	13,630	13,817	14,377	14,579	15,088	16,054	16,776	17,832	18,774	19,309	20,479	50.2
District of Columbia	20,498	21,815	21,854	21,779	21,759	21,624	21,524	21,198	20,865	20,255	21,818	6.4
Maryland	80,022	83,974	88,592	92,270	96,613	102,282	106,711	110,801	112,823	112,934	113,393	41.7
Pennsylvania	201,996	205,748	208,544	213,615	219,156	221,263	222,845	230,947	233,679	234,321	234,355	16.0
Virginia	95,744	96,384	102,738	107,707	110,864	118,308	121,238	126,919	128,895	130,922	132,832	38.7
West Virginia	32,734	32,790	33,577	33,445	33,541	34,273	34,562	34,540	35,128	35,353	35,912	9.7

Source: State Employment Security Agency quarterly reports to the U.S. Department of Labor, Employment and Training Administration edited by the Small Business Administration, Office of Advocacy.

Table 3.4 Number of Firms and Components of Firm Change: SBA Region IV, 1982-1992

Successor Firms

	1982	1983	1984	1985	1986	1987	1988	1989	1990	1991	1992	Percent Change 1982-1992
Region IV, Total	31,870	30,046	30,401	31,874	36,601	36,192	34,640	35,597	34,332	31,391	32,617	2.3
Alabama	3,039	2,682	2,494	2,800	3,559	3,220	3,058	3,062	2,773	2,965	2,879	-5.3
Florida	11,015	9,850	9,946	10,249	11,235	11,289	10,973	11,004	10,274	9,247	8,442	-23.4
Georgia	4,200	3,932	3,938	4,438	4,456	4,862	4,831	4,859	4,730	4,314	4,380	4.3
Kentucky	3,316	3,652	3,854	3,702	4,034	3,956	3,860	3,814	4,129	3,397	3,549	7.0
Mississippi	1,776	1,802	1,828	1,951	1,979	1,955	1,785	1,916	1,737	1,577	1,639	-7.7
North Carolina	4,695	4,776	4,674	4,900	6,375	5,360	5,252	5,770	5,205	4,826	6,613	40.9
South Carolina	2,330	2,259	2,480	2,367	2,549	3,048	2,736	2,741	2,698	2,745	2,625	12.7
Tennessee	1,499	1,093	1,187	1,467	2,414	2,502	2,145	2,431	2,786	2,320	2,490	66.1

New Firms

	1982	1983	1984	1985	1986	1987	1988	1989	1990	1991	1992	Percent Change 1982-1992
Region IV, Total	101,432	111,072	120,412	132,510	133,842	137,936	136,484	137,709	140,172	133,857	140,623	38.6
Alabama	7,119	7,224	7,571	8,729	10,684	9,555	9,512	9,236	9,260	8,737	9,122	28.1
Florida	36,284	38,599	43,503	46,921	47,056	48,802	48,092	51,117	48,391	50,357	51,522	42.0
Georgia	14,723	16,904	18,630	19,604	19,731	21,975	21,326	20,661	22,309	20,738	22,532	53.0
Kentucky	6,560	7,769	7,243	7,406	8,463	8,371	8,480	8,208	7,730	7,550	8,111	23.6
Mississippi	4,892	5,388	5,609	5,795	5,542	5,732	5,554	5,712	5,620	5,191	5,654	15.6
North Carolina	11,973	14,088	14,871	17,438	18,902	17,728	19,654	19,279	19,652	19,152	21,277	77.7
South Carolina	6,929	7,303	8,505	8,929	8,870	10,267	9,655	9,136	9,913	8,706	8,585	23.9
Tennessee	12,952	13,797	14,480	17,688	14,594	15,506	14,211	14,360	17,297	13,426	13,820	6.7

Terminations

	1982	1983	1984	1985	1986	1987	1988	1989	1990	1991	1992	Percent Change 1982-1992
Region IV, Total	124,425	118,176	115,406	125,793	140,242	145,143	145,917	153,502	159,141	160,386	161,762	30.0
Alabama	10,203	9,737	8,368	8,334	10,191	10,877	11,174	11,404	10,927	14,478	11,710	14.8
Florida	41,138	37,597	39,043	41,292	49,038	49,044	49,452	51,683	54,009	55,539	55,317	34.5
Georgia	17,468	16,502	16,030	17,247	18,630	19,717	21,268	24,136	24,448	24,527	25,481	45.9
Kentucky	10,117	9,961	9,598	10,385	11,031	11,368	10,686	11,079	11,276	10,356	10,691	5.7
Mississippi	6,482	7,176	6,146	6,761	6,870	7,925	7,131	7,334	7,200	6,768	6,997	7.9
North Carolina	15,872	15,424	14,405	16,578	20,323	20,166	21,748	22,153	21,643	22,882	26,103	64.5
South Carolina	8,748	8,268	8,496	8,524	9,636	10,750	10,406	10,280	10,736	10,785	10,605	21.2
Tennessee	14,397	13,511	13,320	16,672	14,523	15,296	14,052	15,433	18,902	15,051	14,858	3.2

Table 3.4 Number of Firms and Components of Firm Change: SBA Region IV, 1982-1992--Continued

	Firms at End of Year											Percent Change 1982-1992
Region IV, Total	734,761	757,703	793,110	831,701	861,902	890,887	916,094	935,898	951,261	956,123	967,601	31.7
Alabama	65,882	66,051	67,748	70,943	74,995	76,893	78,289	79,183	80,289	77,513	77,804	18.1
Florida	225,234	236,086	250,492	266,370	275,623	286,670	296,283	306,721	311,377	315,442	320,089	42.1
Georgia	103,614	107,948	114,486	121,281	126,838	133,958	138,847	140,231	142,822	143,347	144,778	39.7
Kentucky	62,095	63,555	65,054	65,777	67,243	68,202	69,856	70,799	71,382	71,973	72,942	17.5
Mississippi	42,749	42,763	44,054	45,039	45,690	45,452	45,660	45,954	46,111	46,111	46,407	8.6
North Carolina	103,506	106,946	112,086	117,846	122,800	125,722	128,880	131,776	134,990	136,086	137,873	33.2
South Carolina	54,264	55,558	58,047	60,819	62,602	65,167	67,152	68,749	70,624	71,290	71,895	32.5
Tennessee	77,417	78,796	81,143	83,626	86,111	88,823	91,127	92,485	93,666	94,361	95,813	23.8

Source: State Employment Security Agency quarterly reports to the U.S. Department of Labor, Employment and Training Administration edited by the Small Business Administration, Office of Advocacy.

Table 3.5 Number of Firms and Components of Firm Change: SBA Region V, 1982-1992

Successor Firms

	1982	1983	1984	1985	1986	1987	1988	1989	1990	1991	1992	Percent Change 1982-1992
Region V, Total	36,009	31,819	26,259	26,190	30,223	25,971	24,724	25,085	24,343	20,585	19,897	-44.7
Illinois	14,928	9,789	5,725	5,308	9,269	6,690	5,354	5,217	4,568	4,086	3,894	-73.9
Indiana	3,880	3,715	3,660	3,755	3,471	2,757	4,019	3,791	3,652	2,015	2,598	-33.0
Michigan	5,198	5,060	4,693	4,660	4,896	4,896	4,859	5,082	4,674	3,802	3,950	-24.0
Minnesota	3,713	3,604	3,969	3,704	3,585	3,557	3,188	3,122	3,423	3,387	2,984	-19.6
Ohio	5,036	6,411	5,850	6,138	6,297	5,557	4,729	5,004	5,314	4,707	3,641	-27.7
Wisconsin	3,254	3,240	2,362	2,625	2,705	2,514	2,575	2,869	2,712	2,588	2,830	-13.0

New Firms

	1982	1983	1984	1985	1986	1987	1988	1989	1990	1991	1992	Percent Change 1982-1992
Region V, Total	83,033	82,624	93,260	89,904	99,624	98,415	94,894	100,752	97,867	96,541	98,078	18.1
Illinois	28,296	25,355	28,771	25,459	37,051	31,669	28,689	29,992	27,952	25,267	26,995	-4.6
Indiana	7,983	8,250	8,186	9,753	9,419	12,133	10,242	11,755	10,993	13,351	13,239	65.8
Michigan	15,068	14,564	18,213	16,429	13,452	13,452	16,395	18,167	16,804	16,730	16,836	11.7
Minnesota	8,019	8,309	10,680	10,220	10,590	10,545	10,232	10,257	11,525	10,730	10,828	35.0
Ohio	15,778	16,173	17,484	17,969	18,586	20,306	18,582	20,211	20,286	19,737	19,218	21.8
Wisconsin	7,889	9,973	9,926	10,074	10,526	10,310	10,754	10,370	10,307	10,726	10,962	39.0

Terminations

	1982	1983	1984	1985	1986	1987	1988	1989	1990	1991	1992	Percent Change 1982-1992
Region V, Total	105,468	104,893	100,526	117,144	111,822	103,517	100,669	116,674	117,549	104,090	105,759	0.3
Illinois	25,380	30,110	28,979	44,824	37,159	32,423	28,553	34,661	29,173	26,771	31,250	23.1
Indiana	11,758	12,049	10,687	11,817	10,896	8,638	12,636	16,338	10,632	15,919	13,462	14.5
Michigan	20,798	18,132	11,170	14,837	16,596	16,596	16,372	21,645	28,676	15,055	18,010	-13.4
Minnesota	11,279	11,046	11,660	12,177	13,092	13,038	11,829	11,097	13,614	12,500	11,014	-2.3
Ohio	20,906	22,437	29,461	23,588	21,841	21,617	19,520	20,897	23,863	22,490	20,287	-3.0
Wisconsin	15,347	11,119	8,569	9,901	12,238	11,205	11,759	12,036	11,591	11,355	11,736	-23.5

Firms at End of Year

	1982	1983	1984	1985	1986	1987	1988	1989	1990	1991	1992	Percent Change 1982-1992
Region V, Total	845,903	855,453	874,446	873,416	891,441	912,310	931,259	940,422	945,083	958,119	970,295	14.7
Illinois	225,513	230,547	236,064	222,027	231,188	237,124	242,614	243,162	246,509	249,091	248,690	10.3
Indiana	93,219	93,135	94,294	95,985	97,979	104,231	105,856	105,064	109,077	108,524	110,899	19.0
Michigan	156,454	157,946	169,682	175,934	177,686	179,438	184,320	185,924	178,726	184,203	186,979	19.5
Minnesota	87,104	87,971	90,960	92,707	93,790	94,854	96,445	98,727	100,061	101,678	104,476	19.9
Ohio	196,028	196,175	190,048	190,567	193,609	197,855	201,646	205,964	207,701	209,655	212,227	8.3
Wisconsin	87,585	89,679	93,398	96,196	97,189	98,808	100,378	101,581	103,009	104,968	107,024	22.2

Source: State Employment Security Agency quarterly reports to the U.S. Department of Labor, Employment and Training Administration edited by the Small Business Administration, Office of Advocacy.

Table 3.6 Number of Firms and Components of Firm Change: SBA Region VI, 1982-1992

Successor Firms

	1982	1983	1984	1985	1986	1987	1988	1989	1990	1991	1992	Percent Change 1982-1992
Region VI, Total	22,195	20,569	19,969	20,459	16,925	18,433	15,643	16,286	16,544	17,297	17,249	-22.3
Arkansas	2,567	2,011	1,643	969	1,032	1,254	1,031	1,367	1,372	1,658	1,690	-34.2
Louisiana	3,651	3,423	3,066	2,687	2,275	2,197	2,209	2,611	2,414	2,520	3,216	-11.9
New Mexico	1,535	1,361	1,203	1,495	1,372	1,218	1,197	1,275	1,066	1,080	972	-36.7
Oklahoma	2,587	2,719	2,431	1,970	1,829	1,869	1,604	1,799	1,524	1,496	1,642	-36.5
Texas	11,855	11,055	11,626	13,338	10,417	11,895	9,602	9,234	10,168	10,543	9,729	-17.9

New Firms

	1982	1983	1984	1985	1986	1987	1988	1989	1990	1991	1992	Percent Change 1982-1992
Region VI, Total	76,005	77,079	80,349	92,850	78,673	83,825	75,407	74,236	77,014	77,569	77,221	1.6
Arkansas	5,046	5,917	6,985	7,715	7,372	7,230	6,694	6,692	6,484	6,270	7,201	42.7
Louisiana	12,715	10,553	11,434	11,780	10,496	9,201	8,814	9,054	8,321	8,484	9,104	-28.4
New Mexico	4,073	4,514	4,620	4,747	4,543	4,074	4,681	4,565	4,721	4,326	4,562	12.0
Oklahoma	9,519	10,617	10,064	10,168	9,562	8,071	8,037	7,806	8,069	8,038	8,070	-15.2
Texas	44,652	45,478	47,246	58,440	46,700	55,249	47,181	46,119	49,419	50,451	48,284	8.1

Terminations

	1982	1983	1984	1985	1986	1987	1988	1989	1990	1991	1992	Percent Change 1982-1992
Region VI, Total	76,161	88,091	90,163	97,451	98,380	106,767	95,708	89,776	86,306	85,214	81,466	7.0
Arkansas	7,281	7,645	7,348	7,429	8,179	7,936	8,211	8,771	7,252	7,348	6,982	-4.1
Louisiana	13,392	13,280	12,252	14,504	13,153	13,975	12,596	12,178	10,883	10,536	10,719	-20.0
New Mexico	4,909	4,721	4,464	5,515	5,830	5,563	5,459	5,598	4,943	5,242	4,876	-0.7
Oklahoma	9,405	13,573	12,754	11,273	12,968	12,130	11,321	8,919	9,397	8,856	8,640	-8.1
Texas	41,174	48,872	53,345	58,730	58,250	67,163	58,121	54,310	53,831	53,232	50,249	22.0

Firms at End of Year

	1982	1983	1984	1985	1986	1987	1988	1989	1990	1991	1992	Percent Change 1982-1992
Region VI, Total	512,582	522,139	532,294	548,152	545,370	540,861	536,203	536,949	544,201	553,853	566,767	10.6
Arkansas	45,982	46,265	47,545	48,800	49,025	49,573	49,087	48,375	48,979	49,559	51,468	11.9
Louisiana	82,735	83,431	85,679	85,642	85,260	82,683	81,110	80,597	80,449	80,917	82,428	-0.4
New Mexico	29,208	30,362	31,721	32,448	32,553	32,262	32,681	32,923	33,767	33,931	34,589	18.4
Oklahoma	66,850	66,613	66,354	67,219	65,642	63,452	61,772	62,458	62,654	63,332	64,404	-3.7
Texas	287,807	295,468	300,995	314,043	312,910	312,891	311,553	312,596	318,352	326,114	333,878	16.0

Source: State Employment Security Agency quarterly reports to the U.S. Department of Labor, Employment and Training Administration edited by the Small Business Administration, Office of Advocacy.

Table 3.7 Number of Firms and Components of Firm Change: SBA Region VII, 1982-1992

Successor Firms

	1982	1983	1984	1985	1986	1987	1988	1989	1990	1991	1992	Percent Change 1982-1992
Region VII, Total	11,401	11,004	11,414	11,003	10,983	11,263	10,944	11,194	9,934	10,035	10,268	-9.9
Missouri	5,077	4,974	5,363	5,190	5,445	5,589	5,486	5,424	4,809	4,784	4,833	-4.8
Iowa	2,630	2,604	2,640	2,448	2,234	2,390	2,176	2,377	1,976	2,297	2,614	-0.6
Kansas	2,205	2,001	1,933	2,033	2,095	1,987	1,984	2,090	1,929	1,837	1,682	-23.7
Nebraska	1,489	1,425	1,478	1,332	1,209	1,297	1,298	1,303	1,220	1,117	1,139	-23.5

New Firms

	1982	1983	1984	1985	1986	1987	1988	1989	1990	1991	1992	Percent Change 1982-1992
Region VII, Total	26,058	26,885	29,723	30,205	30,398	30,240	30,399	30,532	29,721	29,252	29,501	13.2
Missouri	10,032	10,914	12,607	13,352	14,106	13,789	14,065	13,976	13,336	12,822	13,240	32.0
Iowa	4,656	5,160	5,401	5,260	4,890	5,644	5,479	5,664	5,526	6,041	5,617	20.6
Kansas	6,425	6,668	7,170	7,323	7,271	6,801	6,976	6,779	6,716	6,381	6,348	-1.2
Nebraska	4,945	4,143	4,545	4,270	4,131	4,006	3,879	4,113	4,143	4,008	4,296	-13.1

Terminations

	1982	1983	1984	1985	1986	1987	1988	1989	1990	1991	1992	Percent Change 1982-1992
Region VII, Total	35,449	36,330	39,566	38,917	40,423	40,836	38,592	38,769	38,577	37,772	37,498	5.8
Missouri	14,230	16,295	18,314	15,717	16,888	17,796	17,294	16,870	16,674	16,764	17,022	19.6
Iowa	8,284	7,828	8,395	8,608	8,525	8,503	7,484	7,686	6,971	7,410	7,542	-9.0
Kansas	7,984	7,730	7,724	8,671	9,054	8,926	8,601	8,958	8,788	8,303	7,364	-7.8
Nebraska	4,951	4,477	5,133	5,921	5,956	5,611	5,213	5,255	6,144	5,295	5,570	12.5

Firms at End of Year

	1982	1983	1984	1985	1986	1987	1988	1989	1990	1991	1992	Percent Change 1982-1992
Region VII, Total	270,161	271,720	273,291	275,582	276,540	277,207	279,958	282,915	283,993	285,508	287,779	6.5
Missouri	112342	111,935	111,591	114,416	117,079	118,661	120,918	123,448	124,919	125,761	126,812	12.9
Iowa	64,087	64,023	63,669	62,769	61,368	60,899	61,070	61,425	61,956	62,884	63,573	-0.8
Kansas	55,269	56,208	57,587	58,272	58,584	58,446	58,805	58,716	58,573	58,488	59,154	7.0
Nebraska	38,463	39,554	40,444	40,125	39,509	39,201	39,165	39,326	38,545	38,375	38,240	-0.6

Source: State Employment Security Agency quarterly reports to the U.S. Department of Labor, Employment and Training Administration edited by the Small Business Administration, Office of Advocacy.

Table 3.8 Number of Firms and Components of Firm Change: SBA Region VIII, 1982-1992

Successor Firms

	1982	1983	1984	1985	1986	1987	1988	1989	1990	1991	1992	Percent Change 1982-1992
Region VIII, Total	7,115	7,509	7,299	7,456	8,083	6,682	6,493	7,250	6,673	6,600	7,056	-0.8
Colorado	2,112	2,219	1,824	2,094	2,458	1,330	1,218	1,725	1,492	1,486	1,252	-40.7
Montana	1,373	1,627	1,615	1,727	1,867	1,432	1,303	1,247	1,327	1,380	1,497	9.0
North Dakota	622	641	756	702	732	794	763	715	685	619	686	10.3
South Dakota	550	616	606	606	650	659	598	678	606	597	669	21.6
Utah	1,473	1,559	1,685	1,593	1,748	2,220	1,947	2,017	1,968	1,883	2,106	43.0
Wyoming	985	847	813	734	628	247	664	868	595	635	846	-14.1

New Firms

	1982	1983	1984	1985	1986	1987	1988	1989	1990	1991	1992	Percent Change 1982-1992
Region VIII, Total	29,202	28,566	28,890	26,892	27,034	27,148	23,118	25,290	24,216	23,983	29,000	-0.7
Colorado	15,730	14,104	13,952	13,096	14,381	14,293	10,871	12,819	11,962	11,732	14,808	-5.9
Montana	2,746	3,147	3,009	2,525	2,515	2,482	2,495	2,419	2,295	2,299	2,653	-3.4
North Dakota	1,890	2,090	1,777	1,552	1,527	1,623	1,587	1,490	1,392	1,335	1,395	-26.2
South Dakota	1,610	1,744	1,911	1,894	1,890	1,924	1,803	1,967	2,026	1,790	2,069	28.5
Utah	4,975	5,241	6,120	5,869	4,812	5,051	4,580	4,457	4,662	5,071	5,962	19.8
Wyoming	2,251	2,240	2,121	1,956	1,909	1,775	1,782	2,138	1,879	1,756	2,113	-6.1

Terminations

	1982	1983	1984	1985	1986	1987	1988	1989	1990	1991	1992	Percent Change 1982-1992
Region VIII, Total	31,233	32,176	30,699	34,320	33,369	27,729	30,001	33,299	29,626	27,209	29,241	-6.4
Colorado	13,933	14,112	11,427	15,224	14,092	8,736	12,625	15,722	12,864	11,236	13,011	-6.6
Montana	3,665	3,955	4,142	4,415	4,642	4,556	3,813	3,613	3,453	3,345	3,536	-3.5
North Dakota	2,426	2,552	2,652	2,317	2,607	2,561	2,108	2,297	2,265	1,944	2,010	-17.1
South Dakota	2,174	2,330	2,337	2,308	2,549	2,368	2,280	2,162	2,370	2,194	2,375	9.2
Utah	6,312	6,281	7,025	7,018	6,494	7,171	6,781	6,271	5,774	5,754	6,112	-3.2
Wyoming	2,723	2,946	3,116	3,038	2,985	2,337	2,394	3,234	2,900	2,736	2,197	-19.3

Firms at End of Year

	1982	1983	1984	1985	1986	1987	1988	1989	1990	1991	1992	Percent Change 1982-1992
Region VIII, Total	180,162	184,061	189,551	189,579	191,327	197,428	197,038	196,279	197,542	200,916	207,721	15.3
Colorado	74,383	76,594	80,943	80,909	83,656	90,543	90,007	88,829	89,419	91,401	94,450	27.0
Montana	23,498	24,317	24,799	24,636	24,376	23,734	23,719	23,772	23,941	24,275	24,889	5.9
North Dakota	18,299	18,478	18,359	18,296	17,948	17,804	18,046	17,954	17,766	17,776	17,847	-2.5
South Dakota	17,414	17,444	17,624	17,816	17,807	18,022	18,143	18,626	18,888	19,081	19,444	11.7
Utah	29,973	30,492	31,272	31,716	31,782	31,882	31,628	31,831	32,687	33,887	35,833	19.6
Wyoming	16,595	16,736	16,554	16,206	15,758	15,443	15,495	15,267	14,841	14,496	15,258	-8.1

Source: State Employment Security Agency quarterly reports to the U.S. Department of Labor, Employment and Training Administration edited by the Small Business Administration, Office of Advocacy.

Table 3.9 Number of Firms and Components of Firm Change: SBA Region IX, 1982-1992

Successor Firms

	1982	1983	1984	1985	1986	1987	1988	1989	1990	1991	1992	Percent Change 1982-1992
Region IX, Total	33,862	30,306	29,464	29,986	27,874	18,233	15,441	14,349	15,507	13,305	12,108	-64.2
Arizona	4,698	5,118	4,845	4,553	5,429	5,635	5,077	4,756	5,393	4,722	4,941	5.2
California	27,213	23,332	22,717	23,505	20,531	10,749	8,603	7,715	8,279	6,586	5,141	-81.1
Hawaii	711	645	639	570	506	574	553	551	630	561	549	-22.8
Nevada	1,240	1,211	1,263	1,358	1,408	1,275	1,208	1,327	1,205	1,436	1,477	19.1

New Firms

	1982	1983	1984	1985	1986	1987	1988	1989	1990	1991	1992	Percent Change 1982-1992
Region IX, Total	104,286	109,140	122,824	123,017	121,202	121,332	123,627	129,753	157,497	147,726	137,745	32.1
Arizona	8,036	8,956	10,152	10,176	11,550	11,423	10,279	9,545	9,832	9,070	9,847	22.5
California	89,881	93,463	105,605	105,499	102,327	102,137	104,998	111,674	139,146	130,531	119,734	33.2
Hawaii	2,946	3,009	3,206	3,272	3,239	3,453	3,527	3,514	3,585	3,214	3,238	9.9
Nevada	3,423	3,712	3,861	4,070	4,086	4,319	4,823	5,020	4,934	4,911	4,926	43.9

Terminations

	1982	1983	1984	1985	1986	1987	1988	1989	1990	1991	1992	Percent Change 1982-1992
Region IX, Total	123,189	125,029	104,608	121,319	150,634	65,246	109,033	153,940	158,275	146,170	146,207	18.7
Arizona	11,307	10,325	10,707	10,455	14,132	13,528	13,250	13,392	14,235	13,011	12,531	10.8
California	104,005	106,268	86,215	102,880	128,356	43,894	87,586	132,141	135,767	124,345	124,137	19.4
Hawaii	3,295	3,572	3,438	3,478	3,200	3,230	3,633	3,390	3,385	3,486	3,612	9.6
Nevada	4,582	4,864	4,248	4,506	4,946	4,594	4,564	5,017	4,888	5,328	5,927	29.4

Firms at End of Year

	1982	1983	1984	1985	1986	1987	1988	1989	1990	1991	1992	Percent Change 1982-1992
Region IX, Total	700,341	714,758	762,438	794,122	792,564	866,883	896,918	887,080	901,817	916,678	920,324	31.4
Arizona	56,414	60,163	64,453	68,727	71,574	75,104	77,210	78,119	79,109	79,890	82,147	45.6
California	600,524	611,051	653,158	679,282	673,784	742,776	768,791	756,039	767,697	780,469	781,207	30.1
Hawaii	22,441	22,523	22,930	23,294	23,839	24,636	25,083	25,758	26,588	26,877	27,052	20.5
Nevada	20,962	21,021	21,897	22,819	23,367	24,367	25,834	27,164	28,423	29,442	29,918	42.7

Source: State Employment Security Agency quarterly reports to the U.S. Department of Labor, Employment and Training Administration edited by the Small Business Administration, Office of Advocacy.

Table 3.10 Number of Firms and Components of Firm Change: SBA Region X, 1982-1992

Successor Firms

	1982	1983	1984	1985	1986	1987	1988	1989	1990	1991	1992	Percent Change 1982-1992
Region X, Total	10,133	9,917	9,426	9,433	9,645	9,584	10,564	7,810	8,058	9,671	10,625	4.9
Alaska	172	362	390	356	379	342	281	268	327	303	236	37.2
Idaho	803	790	909	930	876	816	793	734	742	749	1,085	35.1
Oregon	2,987	2,674	2,662	2,787	2,682	2,805	3,889	1,451	1,475	3,745	4,256	42.5
Washington	6,171	6,091	5,465	5,360	5,708	5,621	5,601	5,357	5,514	4,874	5,048	-18.2

New Firms

	1982	1983	1984	1985	1986	1987	1988	1989	1990	1991	1992	Percent Change 1982-1992
Region X, Total	24,162	29,954	33,420	34,647	33,790	35,859	37,866	40,440	51,367	37,204	43,218	78.9
Alaska	1,301	3,562	4,107	3,754	3,917	4,544	4,970	3,137	2,688	2,356	2,472	90.0
Idaho	2,758	3,259	3,650	3,253	3,072	3,108	3,338	3,414	3,853	3,655	4,130	49.7
Oregon	8,334	9,316	10,217	12,116	10,850	10,742	9,870	13,255	15,504	10,521	10,299	23.6
Washington	11,769	13,817	15,446	15,524	15,951	17,465	19,688	20,634	29,322	20,672	26,317	123.6

Terminations

	1982	1983	1984	1985	1986	1987	1988	1989	1990	1991	1992	Percent Change 1982-1992
Region X, Total	35,868	35,718	34,982	42,621	41,017	39,484	39,885	39,676	41,727	42,380	43,265	20.6
Alaska	947	3,283	3,200	3,712	5,278	5,733	5,781	3,552	3,382	2,581	2,110	122.8
Idaho	3,840	3,648	3,778	3,862	4,090	3,710	3,269	3,835	3,337	3,500	4,028	4.9
Oregon	12,635	12,451	11,567	13,650	12,792	12,410	11,390	11,792	11,921	13,347	11,799	-6.6
Washington	18,446	16,336	16,437	21,397	18,857	17,631	19,445	20,497	23,087	22,952	25,328	37.3

Firms at End of Year

	1982	1983	1984	1985	1986	1987	1988	1989	1990	1991	1992	Percent Change 1982-1992
Region X, Total	197,750	201,873	209,737	211,196	213,614	219,573	228,118	236,892	254,590	259,085	269,663	36.4
Alaska	13,552	14,163	15,460	15,858	14,876	14,029	13,499	13,552	13,185	13,263	13,861	2.3
Idaho	22,201	22,602	23,383	23,704	23,562	23,776	24,638	24,951	26,209	27,113	28,300	27.5
Oregon	65,885	65,424	66,736	67,989	68,729	69,866	72,235	75,149	80,207	81,126	83,882	27.3
Washington	96,112	99,684	104,158	103,645	106,447	111,902	117,746	123,240	134,989	137,583	143,620	49.4

Source: State Employment Security Agency quarterly reports to the U.S. Department of Labor, Employment and Training Administration edited by the Small Business Administration, Office of Advocacy.

4 Changing Characteristics of Workers in Small and Large Firms

Introduction

Independent small businesses employ about half of the nation's private sector labor force. Small businesses have made substantial contributions to job retention and generation during both economic downturns and expansions. An understanding of the extent of this contribution can be gained by examining changes in the work force by size of business between 1979 and 1983—a period of two recessions—and between 1983 and 1988, the period of the longest peacetime expansion in U.S. history.

Data Sources

Data from the Current Population Survey (CPS), conducted by the Bureau of the Census, provide an opportunity to analyze changes in the characteristics of the work force and size of business over the 10-year period between 1979 and 1988. The CPS household survey is conducted on a monthly basis; the May surveys for the three years 1979, 1983, and 1988 permit an analysis of demographic characteristics over the business cycle. This means that change can be analyzed over two different segments: 1979 to 1983, a period which began with an economic expansion and ended with a severe recession; and 1983 to 1988, a period of extended economic growth. These data provide demographic and employment information about workers by size of firm and provide data that can be used to examine the dynamics of change in employee characteristics by firm size or by industry.

Highlights

- Economic conditions between 1979 and 1988 affected the hiring and retention of workers in small and large firms.
- Small firms were more likely than large firms to hire the unemployed.
- Although the proportion of younger workers declined in firms of all sizes, net job losses for younger workers were lower in small firms than in large firms.

- Women were equally likely to be employed in small firms as in large firms during the decade of the 1980s. However, the female proportion of the work force increased more rapidly in large firms.

- The proportion of Vietnam veterans in the small business work force rose between 1979 and 1983, especially in the smallest firms, but fell between 1983 and 1988 as the more mature Vietnam veterans moved into larger firms.

- The proportion of workers that were married declined between 1979 and 1988 across all firm sizes—a reflection of changing values and economic conditions.

Chapter 4 Tables

Table 4.1 Change in Distribution of Wage-and-Salary Workers[1] by Firm Size, 1979, 1983 and 1988

	Total All Firms	Employment Size of Enterprise					
		1-9	10-24	1-24	25-99	100-499	500+
May 1979							
Number (Thousands)	54,551	NA	NA	16,224	8,093	6,771	23,463
Percent	100.0			29.8	14.8	12.4	43.0
May 1983							
Number (Thousands)	59,205	NA	NA	17,921	8,309	8,030	24,945
Percent	100.0			30.3	14.0	13.6	42.1
May 1988							
Number (Thousands)	74,523	12,493	7,629	20,122	10,732	9,933	33,736
Percent	100.0	16.8	10.2	27.0	14.4	13.3	45.3
Percent Change							
1979-1983	8.5	NA	NA	10.5	2.7	18.6	6.3
1983-1988	25.9	NA	NA	12.3	29.2	23.7	35.2
1979-1988	36.6	NA	NA	24.0	32.6	46.7	43.8

Data on the smallest firm sizes (1-9) and (10-24) are not available (NA) for 1979 and 1983.

Includes only employed private wage-and-salary workers, aged 16 years and older. Workers in the agricultural and private household sectors have been excluded, as have government workers and members of the Armed Forces. Further, the total does not include about 14 percent of private wage-and-salary workers in the CPS who did not know the answer to the CPS questions about firm size. The self-employed are no included here.

Source: U.S. Department of Commerce, Bureau of the Census, Current Population Survey, May 1979, May 1983 and May 1988, unpublished data.

Table 4.2   Composition of Employment by Age of Worker and Firm Size, 1979, 1983 and 1988
(Percent)

Age	All Firms	Employment Size of Enterprise						
		1-24	25-99	100-499	500+	Under 100	100 and Over	Under 500
16-24								
1979	25.1	29.7	25.8	24.4	21.8	28.4	22.4	27.6
1983	22.3	27.9	24.3	21.2	18.0	26.7	18.8	25.4
1988	19.2	22.8	21.0	17.0	17.0	22.2	17.0	20.9
25-44								
1979	46.9	42.8	44.3	48.7	50.0	43.4	49.7	44.5
1983	51.5	46.0	50.4	54.1	54.8	47.4	54.6	49.0
1988	55.5	50.4	54.8	58.1	58.1	51.9	58.1	53.4
45-64								
1979	25.9	23.3	27.0	25.0	27.7	24.5	27.1	24.6
1983	24.2	22.5	23.4	22.8	26.2	22.8	25.4	22.8
1988	23.2	22.9	21.8	23.0	23.9	22.5	23.7	22.6
65+								
1979	2.1	4.2	2.9	1.9	0.5	3.7	0.8	3.3
1983	2.0	3.6	1.9	1.9	1.0	3.1	1.2	2.8
1988	2.1	3.9	2.4	1.9	1.0	3.4	1.2	3.1
Total								
1979	100.0	100.0	100.0	100.0	100.0	100.0	100.0	100.0
1983	100.0	100.0	100.0	100.0	100.0	100.0	100.0	100.0
1988	100.0	100.0	100.0	100.0	100.0	100.0	100.0	100.0

Source: U.S. Department of Commerce, Bureau of the Census, <u>Current Population Survey</u>,
May 1979, May 1983, and May 1988, unpublished data.

Table 4.3   Percentage Distribution of Younger and Elderly Workers by Firm Size, 1979, 1983 and 1988

Age	Total All Firms	Employment Size of Enterprise						
		1-24	25-99	100-499	500+	Under 100	100 and Over	Under 500
Younger (16-24)								
1979	100.0	35.2	15.3	12.1	37.4	50.5	49.5	62.6
1983	100.0	37.8	15.3	12.9	34.0	53.1	46.9	66.0
1988	100.0	32.2	15.8	11.8	40.2	48.0	52.0	59.8
Elderly (65+)								
1979	100.0	58.2	19.9	11.3	10.6	78.1	21.9	89.4
1983	100.0	53.9	13.1	12.4	20.6	67.0	33.0	79.4
1988	100.0	50.1	16.4	11.9	21.6	66.5	33.5	78.4

Source: U.S. Department of Commerce, Bureau of the Census, Current Population Survey, May 1979, May 1983, and May 1988, unpublished data.

Table 4.4   Employment by Age of Worker and Firm Size 1979, 1983 and 1988 (Percent)

Age	All Firms	1-24	25-99	100-499	500+	Under 100	100 and Over	Under 500
16-19								
1979	8.5	11.9	10.3	6.7	6.1	11.4	6.2	10.4
1983	6.5	9.6	7.1	5.2	4.5	8.8	4.7	8.0
1988	6.4	8.1	5.7	4.7	6.1	7.3	5.7	6.6
20-24								
1979	16.6	17.8	15.5	17.7	15.8	17.0	16.2	17.2
1983	15.8	18.2	17.2	16.0	13.5	17.9	14.1	17.4
1988	12.8	14.7	15.3	12.3	11.0	14.9	11.3	14.3
25-34								
1979	27.7	24.4	26.8	30.1	29.7	25.2	29.8	26.3
1983	30.7	28.6	31.2	32.0	31.5	29.4	31.6	30.0
1988	32.1	29.8	32.8	34.7	32.4	30.8	33.0	31.8
35-44								
1979	19.1	18.4	17.5	18.6	20.3	18.1	19.9	18.2
1983	20.8	17.5	19.2	22.1	23.3	18.0	23.0	19.0
1988	23.4	20.6	22.0	23.5	25.6	21.1	25.1	21.7
45-54								
1979	15.4	13.2	16.0	14.6	17.0	14.1	16.5	14.2
1983	14.2	13.0	13.4	13.8	15.5	13.2	15.1	13.3
1988	14.8	13.8	13.3	15.1	15.7	13.6	15.6	14.0
55-64								
1979	10.6	10.1	11.0	10.4	10.6	10.5	10.6	10.4
1983	10.0	9.5	10.0	9.0	10.7	9.6	10.3	9.5
1988	8.4	9.1	8.5	7.8	8.2	8.9	8.1	8.6
65+								
1979	2.1	4.2	2.9	1.9	0.5	3.7	0.8	3.3
1983	2.0	3.6	1.9	1.9	1.0	3.1	1.2	2.8
1988	2.1	3.9	2.4	1.9	1.0	3.4	1.2	3.0
Total								
1979	100.0	100.0	100.0	100.0	100.0	100.0	100.0	100.0
1983	100.0	100.0	100.0	100.0	100.0	100.0	100.0	100.0
1988	100.0	100.0	100.0	100.0	100.0	100.0	100.0	100.0

Source: U.S. Department of Commerce, Bureau of the Census, <u>Current Population Survey</u>, May 1979, May 1983, and May 1988, unpublished data.

Table 4.5 Composition and Percentage Distribution of Employment by Gender of Worker and Firm Size 1979, 1983 and 1988 (Percent)

| Gender | All Firms | Employment Size of Enterprise | | | | | | |
		1-24	25-99	100-499	500+	Under 100	100 and Over	Under 500
1979								
Men	60.2	56.8	59.1	57.5	63.7	57.6	62.3	57.5
Women	39.8	43.2	40.9	42.5	36.3	42.4	37.7	42.5
Total	100.0	100.0	100.0	100.0	100.0	100.0	100.0	100.0
Men	100.0	28.1	14.6	11.8	45.5	42.7	57.3	54.5
Women	100.0	32.3	15.2	13.3	39.2	47.5	52.5	60.8
1983								
Men	56.6	55.7	56.2	54.5	58.1	55.9	57.2	55.6
Women	43.4	44.3	43.8	45.5	41.9	44.1	42.8	44.4
Total	100.0	100.0	100.0	100.0	100.0	100.0	100.0	100.0
Men	100.0	29.8	13.9	13.1	43.2	43.7	56.3	56.8
Women	100.0	30.9	14.2	14.2	40.7	45.1	54.9	59.3
1988								
Men	56.0	55.2	57.5	54.4	56.5	56.0	56.0	55.6
Women	44.0	44.8	42.5	45.6	43.5	44.0	44.0	44.4
Total	100.0	100.0	100.0	100.0	100.0	100.0	100.0	100.0
Men	100.0	26.6	14.8	12.9	45.7	41.4	58.6	54.3
Women	100.0	27.5	13.9	13.8	44.8	41.4	58.6	55.2

Source: U.S. Department of Commerce, Bureau of the Census, <u>Current Population Survey</u>, May 1979, May 1983, and May 1988, unpublished data.

Table 4.6   Composition of Employment by Marital Status of Workers and Firm Size, 1979, 1983 and 1988   (Percent)

Marital Status[1]	All Firms	Employment Size of Enterprise						
		1-24	25-99	100-499	500+	Under 100	100 and Over	Under 500
Married Persons as a Percent of Total Employees in Firms								
1979	63.1	59.5	62.2	63.0	65.9	60.4	62.2	61.0
1983	60.6	56.6	58.1	61.8	63.9	57.0	63.4	58.1
1988	58.9	57.0	56.6	60.0	60.5	56.9	60.4	57.6

[1]Married (Spouse Present) as compared with All Other.

Source: U.S. Department of Commerce, Bureau of the Census, <u>Current Population Survey</u>, May 1979, May 1983, and May 1988, unpublished data.

Table 4.7   Race and Percentage Distribution of Wage-and-Salary Workers by Firm Size, 1979, 1983 and 1988   (Percent)

Race	All Firms	Employment Size of Enterprise						
		1-24	25-99	100-499	500+	Under 100	100 and Over	Under 500
1979								
White	91.0	92.2	91.1	90.7	90.2	91.8	90.4	91.6
Black	7.2	6.3	6.9	7.5	7.9	6.5	7.8	6.7
Other	1.8	1.5	2.0	1.8	1.9	1.7	1.8	1.7
Total	100.0	100.0	100.0	100.0	100.0	100.0	100.0	100.0
White	100.0	30.1	14.9	12.4	42.6	45.0	55.0	57.4
Black	100.0	25.8	14.2	12.9	47.1	40.0	60.0	52.9
Other	100.0	25.9	16.6	12.5	45.0	42.5	57.5	54.9
1983								
White	90.0	91.3	90.8	90.2	88.8	91.1	89.1	90.9
Black	7.6	6.2	6.7	8.0	8.8	6.4	8.6	6.8
Other	2.4	2.5	2.5	1.8	2.4	2.5	2.3	2.3
Total	100.0	100.0	100.0	100.0	100.0	100.0	100.0	100.0
White	100.0	30.7	14.2	13.6	41.5	44.9	55.1	58.5
Black	100.0	24.7	12.5	14.3	48.5	37.2	62.8	51.5
Other	100.0	32.0	14.5	10.3	43.2	46.5	53.5	56.7
1988								
White	88.6	91.9	89.3	88.1	86.6	91.0	86.9	90.3
Black	8.5	5.5	6.7	9.4	10.6	5.9	10.4	6.8
Other	2.9	2.6	4.0	2.5	2.8	3.1	2.7	2.9
Total	100.0	100.0	100.0	100.0	100.0	100.0	100.0	100.0
White	100.0	28.0	14.5	13.3	44.2	42.5	57.5	55.8
Black	100.0	17.4	11.3	14.8	56.5	28.7	71.3	43.5
Other	100.0	24.2	20.1	11.4	44.3	44.3	55.7	55.8

Source: U.S. Department of Commerce, Bureau of the Census, <u>Current Population Survey</u>, May 1979, May 1983, and May 1988, unpublished data.

Table 4.8 Wage-and-Salary Workers of Hispanic Origin by Firm Size, 1979, 1983 and 1988
(Percent)

Origin[*]	All Firms	Employment Size of Enterprise						
		1-24	25-99	100-499	500+	Under 100	100 and Over	Under 500
1979								
Non-Hispanic	95.5	95.4	93.5	94.5	96.5	94.8	96.0	94.7
Hispanic	4.5	4.6	6.5	5.5	3.5	5.2	4.0	5.3
Total	100.0	100.0	100.0	100.0	100.0	100.0	100.0	100.0
1983								
Non-Hispanic	94.6	94.0	93.4	94.1	95.5	93.8	95.2	93.9
Hispanic	5.4	6.0	6.6	5.9	4.5	6.2	4.8	6.1
Total	100.0	100.0	100.0	100.0	100.0	100.0	100.0	100.0
1988								
Non-Hispanic	93.6	92.5	92.8	94.4	94.3	92.6	94.3	93.0
Hispanic	6.4	7.5	7.2	5.6	5.7	7.4	5.7	7.0
Total	100.0	100.0	100.0	100.0	100.0	100.0	100.0	100.0

[*]Persons of Hispanic origin may be any race.

Source: U.S. Department of Commerce, Bureau of the Census, <u>Current Population Survey</u>,
May 1979, May 1983, and May 1988, unpublished data.

Table 4.9   Wage-and-Salary Workers by Educational Attainment and Firm Size
1979, 1983 and 1988   (Percent)

| | All Firms | Employment Size of Enterprise | | | | | | |
		1-24	25-99	100-499	500+	Under 100	100 and Over	Under 500
Less than 4 Years of High School								
1979	22.0	26.4	26.1	22.0	17.6	26.3	18.6	25.3
1983	17.2	21.8	20.3	16.5	13.1	21.4	13.9	20.2
1988	16.1	18.6	18.7	15.7	13.9	18.6	14.3	17.9
4 Years of High School to 3 Years of College								
1979	62.0	60.1	59.5	61.0	64.5	59.9	63.7	60.2
1983	62.8	61.6	62.4	62.9	63.8	61.9	63.6	62.1
1988	63.0	63.8	61.4	62.3	63.3	63.0	63.0	62.8
4 Years or More of College								
1979	16.0	13.5	14.4	17.0	17.9	13.8	17.7	14.5
1983	20.0	16.6	17.3	20.6	23.1	16.7	22.5	17.7
1988	20.9	17.6	19.9	22.0	22.8	18.4	22.7	19.3
Total								
1979	100.0	100.0	100.0	100.0	100.0	100.0	100.0	100.0
1983	100.0	100.0	100.0	100.0	100.0	100.0	100.0	100.0
1988	100.0	100.0	100.0	100.0	100.0	100.0	100.0	100.0

Source: U.S. Department of Commerce, Bureau of the Census, Current Population Survey, May 1979, May 1983, and May 1988, unpublished data.

Table 4.10 Distribution of Vietnam Veteran[1] Employment by Firm Size 1979, 1983 and 1988
(Percent)

| | All Firms | Employment Size of Enterprise | | | | | | |
		1-24	25-99	100-499	500+	Under 100	100 and Over	Under 500
Vietnam Veterans as a Percent of Total Employees in Firms								
1979	7.8	5.9	7.1	7.9	9.2	6.3	8.9	6.7
1983	6.9	4.7	6.0	6.5	8.9	5.1	8.3	5.4
1988	5.8	3.9	4.8	5.4	7.3	4.2	6.9	4.5
Distribution of Vietnam Veterans by Firm Size								
1979	100.0	22.7	13.6	12.7	51.0	36.3	63.7	49.0
1983	100.0	20.5	12.3	12.8	54.4	32.8	67.2	45.6
1988	100.0	18.4	11.9	12.5	57.2	30.3	69.7	42.8

[1]Males only.

Source: U.S. Department of Commerce, Bureau of the Census, <u>Current Population Survey</u>, May 1979, May 1983, and May 1988, unpublished data.

Table 4.11   Distribution of Wage-and-Salary Workers by Firm Size and Region, 1979, 1983 and 1988 (Percent)

Region	Total All Firms	Employment Size of Enterprise						
		1-24	25-99	100-499	500+	Under 100	100 and Over	Under 500
Northeast								
1979	23.5	21.2	23.6	25.6	24.4	22.0	24.7	22.8
1983	22.6	20.0	20.7	25.4	24.3	20.2	24.6	21.4
1988	21.1	20.0	22.7	24.1	20.4	20.9	21.3	21.7
Midwest								
1979	28.3	26.5	27.0	27.7	30.1	26.7	29.6	26.9
1983	26.8	25.0	28.4	27.7	27.2	26.1	27.3	26.4
1988	25.5	23.1	24.7	26.1	27.0	23.7	26.8	24.2
South								
1979	29.4	31.8	29.6	28.4	28.1	31.1	28.1	30.5
1983	31.5	33.5	31.6	30.0	30.5	32.9	30.4	32.2
1988	33.6	35.3	30.9	31.8	33.9	33.8	33.4	33.3
West								
1979	18.8	20.5	19.8	18.3	17.4	20.2	17.6	19.8
1983	19.1	21.5	19.3	16.9	18.0	20.8	17.7	20.0
1988	19.8	21.6	21.7	18.0	18.7	21.6	18.5	20.8
Total								
1979	100.0	100.0	100.0	100.0	100.0	100.0	100.0	100.0
1983	100.0	100.0	100.0	100.0	100.0	100.0	100.0	100.0
1988	100.0	100.0	100.0	100.0	100.0	100.0	100.0	100.0

Source: U.S. Department of Commerce, Bureau of the Census, Current Population Survey, May 1979, May 1983, and May 1988, unpublished data.

Table 4.12   Distribution of Wage and Salary Workers by Firm Size and Region, 1988 (Percent)

Division	Total All Firms	Employment Size of Enterprise						
		1-24	25-99	100-499	500+	Under 100	100 and Over	Under 500
New England	5.9	6.0	6.0	6.0	5.7	6.0	5.8	6.0
Middle Atlantic	15.3	14.0	16.7	18.2	14.7	14.9	15.5	15.7
East North Central	17.7	15.3	17.0	18.8	18.9	15.9	18.9	16.6
West North Central	7.8	7.7	7.8	7.3	8.0	7.7	7.9	7.6
South Atlantic	17.7	18.3	15.7	16.6	18.4	17.4	17.9	17.2
East South Central	5.4	5.2	5.3	6.4	5.3	5.2	5.6	5.5
West South Central	10.4	11.9	9.8	8.8	10.3	11.1	9.9	10.6
Mountain	5.2	6.0	5.6	3.5	5.1	6.0	4.8	5.3
Pacific	14.6	15.6	16.1	14.4	13.6	15.8	13.7	15.5
Total	100.0	100.0	100.0	100.0	100.0	100.0	100.0	100.0

Source: U.S. Department of Commerce, Bureau of the Census, Current Population Survey, May 1988, unpublished data.

Table 4.13 Distribution of Wage and Salary Workers by Firm Size and Selected States, 1988 (Percent)

	Total All Firms	Employment Size of Enterprise						
		1-24	25-99	100-499	500+	Under 100	100 and Over	Under 500
California	100.0	28.7	16.3	13.2	41.8	45.0	55.0	58.2
New York	100.0	25.9	16.5	17.2	40.4	42.4	57.6	59.6
Texas	100.0	29.2	13.8	11.4	45.6	43.0	57.0	54.4
Florida	100.0	36.0	12.2	11.2	40.6	48.2	51.8	59.4
Massachusetts	100.0	29.3	15.3	13.3	42.1	44.6	55.4	57.8
Pennsylvania	100.0	22.1	17.3	16.7	43.9	39.4	60.6	56.1
Illinois	100.0	24.1	14.0	12.6	49.3	38.1	61.9	50.6
Ohio	100.0	19.6	14.0	14.0	52.4	33.6	66.4	47.6
Michigan	100.0	23.3	15.7	12.7	48.3	39.0	61.0	51.7
New Jersey	100.0	26.7	11.9	11.9	49.5	38.6	61.4	50.5
North Carolina	100.0	25.4	13.4	13.8	47.4	38.8	61.2	52.6
Indiana	100.0	23.3	10.6	19.2	46.9	33.9	66.1	53.1
All other States	100.0	27.5	14.0	12.7	45.8	41.5	58.5	54.2

Source: U.S. Department of Commerce, Bureau of the Census, Current Population Survey, May 1988, unpublished data.

Table 4.14 Composition of Employment by Firm Size and Selected States, 1988 (Percent)

| | Total All Firms | Employment Size of Enterprise | | | | | | |
		1-24	25-99	100-499	500+	Under 100	100 and Over	Under 500
California	10.9	11.6	12.3	10.8	10.1	11.8	10.2	11.6
New York	6.7	6.4	7.6	8.6	5.9	6.8	6.6	7.3
Texas	6.7	7.2	6.4	5.7	6.7	6.9	6.5	6.7
Florida	5.5	7.3	4.6	4.6	4.9	6.4	4.8	5.9
Massachusetts	2.5	2.8	2.7	2.5	2.4	2.7	2.4	2.7
Pennsylvania	5.1	4.2	6.2	6.4	5.0	4.9	5.3	5.2
Illinois	4.7	4.2	4.6	4.5	5.2	4.4	5.0	4.4
Ohio	4.3	3.1	4.2	4.5	5.0	3.5	4.9	3.8
Michigan	3.9	3.4	4.3	3.8	4.2	3.7	4.1	3.7
New Jersey	3.5	3.4	2.9	3.1	3.8	3.2	3.7	3.2
North Carolina	3.1	2.9	2.9	3.2	3.2	2.9	3.2	2.9
Indiana	2.4	2.1	1.8	3.5	2.5	2.0	2.7	2.3
All other States	40.7	41.4	39.5	38.8	41.1	40.8	40.6	40.3
Total	100.0	100.0	100.0	100.0	100.0	100.0	100.0	100.0

Source: U.S. Department of Commerce, Bureau of the Census, <u>Current Population Survey</u>, May 1988, unpublished data.

Table 4.15   Distribution of Wage and Salary Workers by Firm Size and Metropolitan Area and Central City, 1979, 1983 and 1988 (Percent)

| | Total All Firms | Employment Size of Enterprise | | | | | | |
		1-24	25-99	100-499	500+	Under 100	100 and Over	Under 500
Metropolitan Area								
1979	75.0	68.7	77.7	77.6	77.6	71.7	77.6	73.0
1983	74.6	69.7	73.0	75.6	78.2	70.7	77.6	71.9
1988	81.4	77.5	81.1	80.5	84.0	78.8	83.2	79.2
Non-Metropolitan Area								
1979	25.0	31.3	22.3	22.4	22.4	28.3	22.4	27.0
1983	25.4	30.3	27.0	24.4	21.8	29.3	22.4	28.1
1988	18.6	22.5	18.9	19.5	16.0	21.2	16.8	20.8
Total								
1979	100.0	100.0	100.0	100.0	100.0	100.0	100.0	100.0
1983	100.0	100.0	100.0	100.0	100.0	100.0	100.0	100.0
1988	100.0	100.0	100.0	100.0	100.0	100.0	100.0	100.0
Central City								
1979	37.3	38.0	40.6	40.7	34.7	38.9	36.1	39.3
1983	37.1	37.3	38.9	38.1	36.0	37.8	36.5	37.9
1988	35.9	36.5	37.9	36.3	34.9	37.0	35.2	36.8
Remainder of Metropolitan Area								
1979	62.7	62.0	59.4	59.3	65.3	61.1	63.9	60.7
1983	62.9	62.7	61.1	61.9	64.0	62.2	63.5	62.1
1988	64.1	63.5	62.1	63.7	65.1	63.0	64.8	63.2
Total								
1979	100.0	100.0	100.0	100.0	100.0	100.0	100.0	100.0
1983	100.0	100.0	100.0	100.0	100.0	100.0	100.0	100.0
1988	100.0	100.0	100.0	100.0	100.0	100.0	100.0	100.0

Source: U.S. Department of Commerce, Bureau of the Census, Current Population Survey, May 1979, May 1983, and May 1988, unpublished data.

Table 4.16 Demographic Characteristics of Wage and Salary Workers in Very Small Firms by Employment Size of Firm, 1988 (Percent)

	Total All Firms	Employment Size of Enterprise					
		1-9	10-24	25-49	50-99	Under 100	100 and Over
Age							
16-19	6.4	8.3	7.9	5.8	5.5	7.3	5.7
20-24	12.8	14.2	15.4	15.4	15.3	14.9	11.3
25-34	32.1	28.3	32.4	33.0	32.4	30.8	33.0
35-44	23.4	20.4	20.8	23.0	20.7	21.1	25.1
45-54	14.8	13.9	13.7	12.1	14.8	13.6	15.6
55-64	8.4	10.4	6.8	8.5	8.6	8.9	8.1
65+	2.1	4.5	3.0	2.2	2.7	3.4	1.2
Total	100.0	100.0	100.0	100.0	100.0	100.0	100.0
Age Distribution							
Younger (16-24)	100.0	19.7	12.5	9.0	6.8	48.0	52.0
Elderly (65+)	100.0	35.5	14.6	8.5	7.9	66.5	33.5
Gender							
Men	56.0	54.7	56.1	58.2	56.6	56.0	56.0
Women	44.0	45.3	43.9	41.8	43.4	44.0	44.0
Total	100.0	100.0	100.0	100.0	100.0	100.0	100.0
Gender Distribution							
Men	100.0	16.4	10.2	8.5	6.3	41.4	58.6
Women	100.0	17.3	10.2	7.7	6.2	41.4	58.6
Marital Status							
Married, Spouse Present	58.9	57.5	56.3	56.6	56.5	56.9	60.4
Other	41.1	42.5	43.7	43.4	43.5	43.1	39.6
Total	100.0	100.0	100.0	100.0	100.0	100.0	100.0
Race							
White	88.6	92.3	91.4	88.8	90.0	91.0	86.9
Black	8.5	5.2	5.9	6.2	7.4	5.9	10.4
Other	2.9	2.5	2.7	5.0	2.6	3.1	2.7
Total	100.0	100.0	100.0	100.0	100.0	100.0	100.0
Origin*							
Hispanic	6.4	6.6	9.0	8.2	5.9	7.4	5.7
Non-Hispanic	93.6	93.4	91.0	91.8	94.1	92.6	94.3
Total	100.0	100.0	100.0	100.0	100.0	100.0	100.0
Years of Education							
< 12	16.1	18.9	18.1	19.4	17.7	18.6	14.3
12-15	63.0	64.2	63.2	60.2	62.9	63.0	63.0
≥ 16	20.9	16.9	18.7	20.4	19.4	18.4	22.7
Total	100.0	100.0	100.0	100.0	100.0	100.0	100.0
Vietnam Veterans							
Vietnam Veterans	5.8	3.6	4.4	5.3	4.1	4.2	6.9
All Others	94.2	96.4	95.6	94.7	95.9	95.8	93.1
Total	100.0	100.0	100.0	100.0	100.0	100.0	100.0
Veteran Distribution							
Vietnam Veterans	100.0	10.5	7.9	7.4	4.5	30.3	69.7
All Others	100.0	17.2	10.4	8.2	6.3	42.1	57.9

Source: U.S. Department of Commerce, Bureau of the Census, <u>Current Population Survey</u>, May 1988, unpublished data.

Table 4.17 Location Characteristics of Wage-and-Salary Workers in Very Small Firms by Employment Size of Firm, 1988 (Percent)

	Total All Firms	Employment Size of Enterprise					
		1-9	10-24	25-49	50-99	Under 100	100 and Over
Region							
Northeast	21.1	20.5	19.3	23.5	21.7	20.9	21.3
Midwest	25.5	22.2	24.4	24.0	25.7	23.7	26.8
South	33.6	36.9	32.8	30.5	31.3	33.8	33.4
West	19.8	20.4	23.5	22.0	21.3	21.6	18.5
Total	100.0	100.0	100.0	100.0	100.0	100.0	100.0
Sub-Regional Divisions							
New England	5.9	6.1	5.9	5.8	6.4	6.0	5.8
Mid Atlantic	15.3	14.4	13.4	17.7	15.3	14.9	15.5
East North Central	17.7	14.9	16.1	16.5	17.6	15.9	18.9
West North Central	7.8	7.4	8.3	7.5	8.1	7.7	7.9
South Atlantic	17.7	18.3	18.4	15.2	16.4	17.4	17.9
East South Central	5.4	5.5	4.6	4.6	6.3	5.2	5.6
West South Central	10.4	13.1	9.8	10.7	8.6	11.1	9.9
Mountain	5.2	6.0	6.0	5.0	6.4	6.0	4.8
Pacific	14.6	14.4	17.5	17.0	14.9	15.8	13.7
Total	100.0	100.0	100.0	100.0	100.0	100.0	100.0
Selected States							
California	10.9	10.8	12.9	13.5	10.8	11.8	10.2
New York	6.7	6.3	6.5	8.1	7.0	6.8	6.6
Texas	6.7	7.9	6.1	7.2	5.4	6.9	6.5
Pennsylvania	5.1	4.6	3.5	6.3	6.0	4.9	5.3
Illinois	4.7	3.8	5.0	4.9	4.2	4.4	5.0
Ohio	4.3	3.5	2.5	3.8	4.7	3.5	4.9
Florida	5.5	7.2	7.4	4.5	4.9	6.4	4.8
Michigan	3.9	3.3	3.5	3.4	5.4	3.7	4.1
New Jersey	3.5	3.5	3.3	3.3	2.3	3.2	3.7
North Carolina	3.1	2.7	3.2	2.7	3.1	2.9	3.2
Massachusetts	2.6	2.9	2.6	2.7	2.7	2.7	2.4
Indiana	2.4	2.2	1.9	2.0	1.5	2.0	2.7
All Other	40.7	41.3	41.6	37.6	42.0	40.8	40.6
Total	100.0	100.0	100.0	100.0	100.0	100.0	100.0
Area							
Metropolitan	81.4	76.0	80.0	82.7	78.9	78.8	83.2
Non-Metropolitan	18.6	24.0	20.0	17.3	21.1	21.2	16.8
Total	100.0	100.0	100.0	100.0	100.0	100.0	100.0
Central City	29.2	27.8	29.1	32.7	28.1	29.1	29.3
Non-Central City	70.8	72.2	70.9	67.3	71.9	70.9	70.7
Total	100.0	100.0	100.0	100.0	100.0	100.0	100.0
Central City	35.9	36.6	36.3	39.6	35.6	37.0	35.2
Remainder MSA	64.1	63.4	63.7	60.4	64.4	63.0	64.8
Total	100.0	100.0	100.0	100.0	100.0	100.0	100.0

*   Persons of Hispanic origin may be any race.
** Full-time (FT) workers are those who worked a regular schedule of more than 35 hours per week; part-time (PT) workers are those who worked less than 35 hours per week; Full-year (FY) workers are those who worked 50 to 52 weeks per year; part-year workers are those who worked less than 50 weeks per year.

Regions and Sub-regional Divisions as defined by the U.S. Bureau of the Census.

MSA denotes Metropolitan Statistical Areas.

Source: U.S. Department of Commerce, Bureau of the Census, Current Population Survey, May 1988, unpublished data.

Table 4.18 Occupational Distribution of Wage-and-Salary Workers by Firm Size, 1983 and 1988 (Percent)

Major Occupation*	All Firms	Employment Size of Enterprise						
		1-24	25-99	100-499	500+	Under 100	100 and Over	Under 500
Managerial and Professional								
1983	21.1	17.5	20.4	24.4	22.8	18.4	23.2	19.8
1988	23.9	22.2	24.8	25.7	24.0	23.1	24.4	23.7
Technical, Sales, and Administrative Support, including Clerical								
1983	34.7	34.1	31.5	32.9	36.6	33.3	35.7	33.3
1988	32.9	33.3	30.3	30.6	34.1	32.3	33.3	31.9
Service								
1983	11.8	15.7	14.0	11.7	8.4	15.1	9.2	14.3
1988	11.0	14.0	12.6	10.0	9.0	13.5	9.2	12.6
Precision Production, Craft, and Repair								
1983	13.1	14.9	13.1	10.9	12.6	14.4	12.2	13.5
1988	13.7	16.3	13.6	11.6	12.9	15.4	12.6	14.5
Operators, Fabricators, and Laborers								
1983	18.5	15.7	20.4	20.0	19.5	17.2	19.6	17.8
1988	17.9	13.1	17.7	21.3	19.8	14.7	20.2	16.3
Farming, Forestry, and Fishing								
1983	0.8	2.1	0.6	0.1	0.1	1.6	0.1	1.3
1988	0.6	1.1	1.0	0.8	0.2	1.0	0.3	1.0
Total								
1983	100.0	100.0	100.0	100.0	100.0	100.0	100.0	100.0
1988	100.0	100.0	100.0	100.0	100.0	100.0	100.0	100.0

*Occupation categories for 1979 are different.

Source: U.S. Department of Commerce, Bureau of the Census, <u>Current Population Survey</u>, May 1983 and May 1988, unpublished data.

Table 4.19 Employment by Industry and Firm Size, 1979, 1983 and 1988 (Percent)

Industry Division	All Firms	Employment Size of Enterprise						
		1-24	25-99	100-499	500+	Under 100	100 and Over	Under 500
Mining								
1979	1.2	0.3	0.7	1.1	2.0	0.3	1.8	0.6
1983	1.2	0.4	0.6	1.1	1.9	0.5	1.7	0.6
1988	0.9	0.5	0.7	1.1	1.1	0.5	1.1	0.7
Construction								
1979	6.7	12.6	9.0	6.8	1.8	11.4	2.9	10.4
1983	6.0	11.5	8.5	4.3	1.7	10.6	2.3	9.1
1988	6.4	13.4	8.9	6.3	1.5	11.8	2.6	10.4
Manufacturing, Durable								
1979	18.8	5.2	13.9	18.6	30.0	8.1	27.4	10.4
1983	15.7	6.3	13.2	15.4	23.6	8.4	21.6	10.1
1988	15.0	5.8	13.2	15.9	20.8	8.4	19.7	10.2
Manufacturing, Non-Durable								
1979	10.9	3.7	11.2	14.6	14.7	6.2	14.7	8.0
1983	10.5	4.5	9.3	13.2	14.4	6.0	14.1	7.7
1988	10.5	4.5	8.4	13.4	13.9	5.9	13.8	7.7
Transportation, Communications and Public Utilities								
1979	7.4	3.9	5.2	4.7	11.4	4.4	9.9	4.4
1983	6.9	3.0	5.3	6.3	10.5	3.7	9.5	4.3
1988	7.3	3.9	5.7	5.2	10.6	4.5	9.3	4.7
Wholesale Trade								
1979	5.5	6.1	7.9	7.9	3.5	6.7	4.5	6.9
1983	5.8	6.9	9.0	6.7	3.6	7.6	4.4	7.4
1988	4.9	5.5	8.2	5.7	3.2	6.4	3.8	6.3
Retail Trade								
1979	19.9	28.3	22.4	13.9	15.1	26.4	14.8	23.6
1983	20.4	26.4	20.9	15.1	17.6	24.6	17.0	22.4
1988	20.1	25.8	19.1	12.1	19.2	23.5	17.6	20.7
Finance, Insurance & Real Estate								
1979	7.4	6.5	7.4	7.8	7.8	6.8	7.8	7.1
1983	7.8	5.2	7.6	8.7	9.5	6.0	9.3	6.6
1988	8.9	6.9	7.4	8.8	10.6	7.1	10.2	7.5
Miscellaneous Services								
1979	22.2	33.4	22.3	24.6	13.7	29.7	16.2	28.6
1983	25.7	35.8	25.6	29.2	17.2	32.6	20.1	31.8
1988	26.0	33.7	28.4	31.5	19.1	31.9	21.9	31.8
Total								
1979	100.0	100.0	100.0	100.0	100.0	100.0	100.0	100.0
1983	100.0	100.0	100.0	100.0	100.0	100.0	100.0	100.0
1988	100.0	100.0	100.0	100.0	100.0	100.0	100.0	100.0

Data exclude agriculture.

Source: U.S. Department of Commerce, Bureau of the Census, <u>Current Population Survey</u>, May 1979, May 1983, and May 1988, unpublished data.

Table 4.20 Wage-and-Salary Workers by Industry and Firm Size, 1979, 1983 and 1988 (Thousands)

	Total All Firms	Employment Size of Enterprise					
		1-9	10-24	1-24	25-99	100-499	500+
All Industries							
1979	54,551	NA	NA	16,224	8,093	6,771	23,463
1983	59,209	NA	NA	17,922	8,310	8,031	24,946
1988	74,523	12,493	7,629	20,122	10,732	9,933	33,736
Mining							
1979	643	NA	NA	42	57	74	470
1983	684	NA	NA	76	53	90	465
1988	635	63	29	91	73	104	367
Construction							
1979	3,658	NA	NA	2,048	729	459	422
1983	3,542	NA	NA	2,063	704	346	429
1988	4,783	1,744	952	2,696	956	622	509
Manufacturing, Durable							
1979	10,269	NA	NA	841	1,122	1,261	7,045
1983	9,324	NA	NA	1,120	1,095	1,234	5,875
1988	11,192	473	698	1,171	1,420	1,583	7,018
Manufacturing, Non-Durable							
1979	5,940	NA	NA	596	905	991	3,448
1983	6,236	NA	NA	805	776	1,062	3,593
1988	7,828	453	461	914	903	1,326	4,685
Transportation, Communications and Public Utilities							
1979	4,050	NA	NA	641	421	317	2,671
1983	4,100	NA	NA	537	441	503	2,619
1988	5,478	441	346	787	609	519	3,563
Wholesale Trade							
1979	2,988	NA	NA	983	640	533	832
1983	3,423	NA	NA	1,242	745	541	895
1988	3,635	610	493	1,103	880	570	1,082
Retail Trade							
1979	10,878	NA	NA	4,599	1,810	939	3,530
1983	12,070	NA	NA	4,724	1,739	1,211	4,396
1988	14,945	3,243	1,948	5,191	2,055	1,202	6,497
Finance, Insurance & Real Estate							
1979	4,017	NA	NA	1,059	604	531	1,823
1983	4,640	NA	NA	935	626	697	2,382
1988	6,620	858	526	1,384	790	878	3,568
Miscellaneous Services							
1979	12,110	NA	NA	5,416	1,805	1,666	3,223
1983	15,191	NA	NA	6,420	2,130	2,348	4,293
1988	19,406	4,609	2,176	6,785	3,045	3,129	6,447

Data are not available (NA) for the very smallest firms in 1979 and 1983.

Data exclude agriculture.

Source: U.S. Department of Commerce, Bureau of the Census, Current Population Survey, May 1979, May 1983, and May 1988, unpublished data.

Table 4.21 Employment in Goods- or Services-Producing Firms by Firm Size, 1979, 1983 and 1988 (Percent)

	All Firms	Employment Size of Enterprise						
		1-24	25-99	100-499	500+	Under 100	100 and Over	Under 500
Employed in Goods-Producing Firms								
1979	37.6	21.7	34.8	41.1	48.5	26.1	46.9	29.4
1983	33.4	22.7	31.6	34.0	41.5	25.5	39.7	27.5
1988	32.8	24.2	31.2	36.6	37.3	26.7	37.1	29.1
Employed in Services-Producing Firms								
1979	62.4	78.3	65.2	58.9	51.5	73.9	53.1	70.6
1983	66.6	77.3	68.4	66.0	58.5	74.5	60.3	72.5
1988	67.2	75.8	68.8	63.4	62.7	73.3	62.9	70.9
Total								
1979	100.0	100.0	100.0	100.0	100.0	100.0	100.0	100.0
1983	100.0	100.0	100.0	100.0	100.0	100.0	100.0	100.0
1988	100.0	100.0	100.0	100.0	100.0	100.0	100.0	100.0

Source: U.S. Department of Commerce, Bureau of the Census, Current Population Survey, May 1979, May 1983, and May 1988, unpublished data.

Table 4.22 Labor Force Participation of Wage-and-Salary Workers by Firm Size, 1979, 1983 and 1988 (Percent)

	All Firms	Employment Size of Enterprise						
		1-24	25-99	100-499	500+	Under 100	100 and Over	Under 500
Labor Force Status 1978, 1982, 1987								
In Labor Force								
1978*	74.2	65.1	70.5	75.9	81.2	66.9	80.0	68.9
1982*	78.4	71.2	77.2	79.4	83.6	73.1	82.6	74.6
1987*	79.1	71.7	76.9	81.7	83.3	73.5	83.0	75.5
Out of Labor Force								
1978*	25.8	34.9	29.5	24.1	18.8	33.1	20.0	31.1
1982*	21.6	28.8	22.8	20.6	16.4	26.9	17.4	25.4
1987*	20.9	28.3	23.1	18.3	16.7	26.5	17.0	24.5
Total								
1978*	100.0	100.0	100.0	100.0	100.0	100.0	100.0	100.0
1982*	100.0	100.0	100.0	100.0	100.0	100.0	100.0	100.0
1987*	100.0	100.0	100.0	100.0	100.0	100.0	100.0	100.0
Weeks Worked in 1978, 1982, 1987								
1-26 Weeks								
1978*	10.3	14.8	11.9	8.9	7.2	13.8	7.6	12.7
1982*	9.9	14.9	10.3	8.7	6.7	13.4	7.2	12.3
1987*	8.6	12.7	9.0	7.8	6.5	11.4	6.8	10.5
27-47 Weeks								
1978*	16.4	21.4	18.6	16.6	12.3	20.5	13.3	19.6
1982*	16.0	20.6	19.4	14.1	12.4	20.2	12.8	18.8
1987*	13.6	16.3	16.6	14.4	10.9	16.4	11.7	15.9
50-52[1] Weeks								
1978*	73.3	63.8	69.5	74.5	80.5	65.7	79.1	67.7
1982*	74.1	64.5	70.3	77.2	80.9	66.4	80.0	68.9
1987*	77.8	71.0	74.4	77.8	82.6	72.2	81.5	73.6
Total								
1978*	100.0	100.0	100.0	100.0	100.0	100.0	100.0	100.0
1982*	100.0	100.0	100.0	100.0	100.0	100.0	100.0	100.0
1987*	100.0	100.0	100.0	100.0	100.0	100.0	100.0	100.0

[1]Full year workers.

*Questions asked in 1979, 1983, or 1988 but answers refer to previous year-- 1978, 1982, or 1987.

Source: U.S. Department of Commerce, Bureau of the Census, Current Population Survey, May 1979, May 1983, and May 1988, unpublished data.

Table 4.23 Employment Status of Wage-and-Salary Workers by Firm Size, 1979, 1983 and 1988 (Percent)

| | All Firms | Employment Size of Enterprise | | | | | | |
		1-24	25-99	100-499	500+	Under 100	100 and Over	Under 500
Wage-and-Salary								
1978*	96.0	89.2	96.9	98.5	99.6	91.8	99.3	93.3
1982*	96.7	91.8	97.2	98.3	99.4	93.5	99.1	94.7
1987*	95.2	85.7	96.2	98.8	99.2	89.3	99.1	91.7
Self-Employed (Incorporated)								
1978*	2.8	7.8	2.2	0.9	0.1	5.9	0.3	4.8
1982*	2.3	6.2	1.7	1.1	0.2	4.8	0.4	3.9
1987*	3.4	10.7	2.7	0.7	0.2	7.9	0.3	6.1
Self-Employed (Unincorporated, Farm and Other)								
1978*	1.2	3.0	0.9	0.6	0.3	2.3	0.4	1.9
1982*	1.0	2.0	1.1	0.6	0.4	1.7	0.5	1.4
1987*	1.4	3.6	1.1	0.5	0.6	2.8	0.6	2.2
Total								
1978*	100.0	100.0	100.0	100.0	100.0	100.0	100.0	100.0
1982*	100.0	100.0	100.0	100.0	100.0	100.0	100.0	100.0
1987*	100.0	100.0	100.0	100.0	100.0	100.0	100.0	100.0

Note: *Includes 1978 status for only those workers employed in 1979, 1982 status for only those workers employed in 1983, and 1987 status for only those workers employed in 1988.

Source: U.S. Department of Commerce, Bureau of the Census, Current Population Survey, May 1979, May 1983, and May 1988, unpublished data.

Table 4.24 Union Contract of Wage-and-Salary Workers by Firm Size, 1979, 1983 and 1988 (Percent)

	All Firms	Employment Size of Enterprise						
		1-24	25-99	100-499	500+	Under 100	100 and Over	Under 500
Covered by Union Contract								
1979	22.8	6.6	17.1	23.9	35.8	10.1	33.1	13.1
1983	18.8	4.7	14.7	19.4	30.1	7.9	27.5	10.6
1988	13.9	3.1	8.6	13.4	21.1	5.2	19.4	7.4

Source: U.S. Department of Commerce, Bureau of the Census, <u>Current Population Survey</u>, May 1979, May 1983, and May 1988, unpublished data.

Table 4.25   Full-Time[1] and Full-Year[2] Status of Wage-and-Salary Workers by Firm Size, 1979, 1983 and 1988   (Percent)

| Status | Total All Firms | Employment Size of Enterprise | | | | | | |
		1-24	25-99	100-499	500+	Under 100	100 and Over	Under 500
1978*								
FT,FY	66.5	53.6	62.6	69.1	75.7	56.6	74.2	59.4
PT,FY	6.8	10.3	6.8	5.4	4.8	9.1	4.9	8.3
FT,PY	17.1	20.0	20.2	18.6	13.6	20.1	14.8	19.7
PT,PY	9.6	16.1	10.4	6.9	5.9	14.2	6.1	12.6
All Workers	100.0	100.0	100.0	100.0	100.0	100.0	100.0	100.0
1982*								
FT,FY	64.4	50.4	61.4	67.9	73.8	54.0	72.4	57.3
PT,FY	9.7	14.1	8.9	9.3	7.1	12.4	7.6	11.7
FT,PY	16.6	21.0	19.5	15.8	12.9	20.5	13.6	19.4
PT,PY	9.3	14.5	10.2	7.0	6.2	13.1	6.4	11.6
All Workers	100.0	100.0	100.0	100.0	100.0	100.0	100.0	100.0
1987*								
FT,FY	69.6	58.4	67.1	71.2	76.2	61.4	75.1	63.9
PT,FY	8.2	12.6	7.2	6.6	6.4	10.7	6.5	9.7
FT,PY	13.9	16.8	17.4	15.2	10.9	17.0	11.8	16.5
PT,PY	8.3	12.2	8.3	7.0	6.5	10.9	6.6	9.9
All Workers	100.0	100.0	100.0	100.0	100.0	100.0	100.0	100.0

[1]Full-time (FT) workers are those who worked a regular schedule of more than 35 hours per week; part-time (PT) workers are those who worked less than 35 hours per week.

2Full-year (FY) workers are those who worked from 50 to 52 weeks per year; part-year workers are those who worked less than 50 weeks per year.

Note: *Includes 1978 status for only those workers employed in 1979, 1982 status for only those workers employed in 1983, and 1987 status for only those workers employed in 1988.

Source: U.S. Department of Commerce, Bureau of the Census, Current Population Survey, May 1979, May 1983, and May 1988, unpublished data.

Table 4.26 Distribution of Employment Tenure of Wage-and-Salary Workers by Firm Size, 1979, 1983 and 1988 (Percent)

			Employment Size of Enterprise					
	All Firms	1-24	25-99	100-499	500+	Under 100	100 and Over	Under 500
Number of Employers								
Per Employee 1978, 1982, 1987								
One Employer								
1978*	82.7	78.6	79.7	82.5	86.5	78.9	85.6	79.7
1982*	86.6	81.6	85.0	85.7	90.9	82.7	89.6	83.4
1987*	83.3	80.7	80.6	81.9	86.1	80.7	85.1	81.0
Two or More Employers								
1978*	17.3	21.4	20.3	17.5	13.5	21.1	14.4	20.3
1982*	13.4	18.4	15.0	14.3	9.1	17.3	10.4	16.6
1987*	16.7	19.3	19.4	18.1	13.9	19.3	14.9	19.0
Total								
1978*	100.0	100.0	100.0	100.0	100.0	100.0	100.0	100.0
1982*	100.0	100.0	100.0	100.0	100.0	100.0	100.0	100.0
1987*	100.0	100.0	100.0	100.0	100.0	100.0	100.0	100.0
Years Workers were with								
Current Employer 1979, 1983, 1988								
Less than one Year								
1979	24.4	33.1	28.8	22.5	17.5	31.7	18.6	29.7
1983	19.8	29.4	21.9	18.3	12.8	27.0	14.1	25.0
1988	19.9	25.9	22.2	17.8	16.3	24.6	16.6	22.9
One or More Years								
1979	75.6	66.9	71.2	77.5	82.5	68.3	81.4	70.3
1983	80.2	70.6	78.1	81.7	87.2	73.0	85.9	75.0
1988	80.1	74.1	77.8	82.2	83.7	75.4	83.4	77.1
Total								
1979	100.0	100.0	100.0	100.0	100.0	100.0	100.0	100.0
1983	100.0	100.0	100.0	100.0	100.0	100.0	100.0	100.0
1988	100.0	100.0	100.0	100.0	100.0	100.0	100.0	100.0

Note: *Includes 1978 status for only those workers employed in 1979, 1982 status for only those workers employed in 1983, and 1987 status for only those workers employed in 1988.

Source: U.S. Department of Commerce, Bureau of the Census, Current Population Survey, May 1979, May 1983, and May 1988, unpublished data.

Table 4.27 Employment Status of Wage-and-Salary Workers by Firm Size, 1979, 1983 and 1988 (Percent)

	All Firms	1-24	25-99	100-499	500+	Under 100	100 and Over	Under 500
				Employment Size of Enterprise				
Employment Status 1978, 1982, 1987								
Unemployed in Prior Year								
1978*	11.3	13.7	12.5	12.3	9.1	13.3	9.8	13.1
1982*	14.8	18.5	18.0	13.5	11.5	18.3	12.0	17.2
1987*	10.1	12.8	11.9	11.4	7.6	12.5	8.4	12.2
Not Unemployed in Prior Year								
1978*	88.7	86.3	87.5	87.7	90.9	86.7	90.2	86.9
1982*	85.2	81.5	82.0	86.5	88.5	81.7	88.0	82.8
1987*	89.9	87.2	88.1	88.6	92.4	87.5	91.6	87.8
Total								
1978*	100.0	100.0	100.0	100.0	100.0	100.0	100.0	100.0
1982*	100.0	100.0	100.0	100.0	100.0	100.0	100.0	100.0
1987*	100.0	100.0	100.0	100.0	100.0	100.0	100.0	100.0
Distribution of Unemployed Workers by Number of Weeks Unemployed in 1978, 1982, 1987**								
1-4 Weeks								
1978	29.3	27.0	26.2	31.9	32.1	26.7	32.1	27.8
1982	9.8	14.9	10.3	8.7	6.6	13.4	7.1	12.3
1987	22.9	21.9	23.1	19.3	25.5	22.3	23.6	21.6
5-14 Weeks								
1978	38.8	35.4	41.7	37.1	41.7	37.4	40.4	37.3
1982	6.4	8.7	8.2	5.6	4.4	8.5	4.7	7.8
1987	40.4	37.3	46.6	46.2	37.8	40.4	40.4	41.7
15+ Weeks								
1978	31.9	37.6	32.1	31.0	26.2	35.9	27.5	34.9
1982	83.8	76.4	81.5	85.7	89.0	78.1	88.1	79.9
1987	36.7	40.8	30.3	34.5	36.7	37.3	36.0	36.7
Total								
1978	100.0	100.0	100.0	100.0	100.0	100.0	100.0	100.0
1982	100.0	100.0	100.0	100.0	100.0	100.0	100.0	100.0
1987	100.0	100.0	100.0	100.0	100.0	100.0	100.0	100.0

**Unemployed or looking for work for one or more weeks in previous years.

Note: *Includes 1978 status for only those workers employed in 1979, 1982 status for only those workers employed in 1983, and 1987 status for only those workers employed in 1988.

Source: U.S. Department of Commerce, Bureau of the Census, Current Population Survey, May 1979, May 1983, and May 1988, unpublished data.

Table 4.28 Economic Characteristics of Wage and Salary Workers in Very Small Firms by Employment Size of Firm, 1988 (Percent)

	Total All Firms	Employment Size of Enterprise					
		1-9	10-24	25-49	50-99	Under 100	100 and Over
Major Occupation							
Managerial and Professional	23.9	21.3	23.8	25.1	24.3	23.1	24.4
Technical, Sales, and Administrative Support, Including Clerical	32.9	34.2	32.0	30.3	30.1	32.3	33.3
Service	11.0	13.4	14.7	12.5	12.8	13.5	9.2
Precision Production, Craft, and Repair	13.7	16.4	16.2	13.3	14.1	15.4	12.6
Operators, Fabricators, and Laborers	17.9	13.1	13.1	17.5	18.1	14.7	20.2
Farming, Forestry, and Fishing	0.6	1.6	0.2	1.3	0.6	1.0	0.3
Total	100.0	100.0	100.0	100.0	100.0	100.0	100.0
Major Industry							
Mining	0.9	0.5	0.4	0.9	0.4	0.5	1.1
Construction	6.4	14.0	12.5	9.5	8.2	11.8	2.6
Manufacturing, Durable	15.0	3.8	9.1	10.8	16.4	8.4	19.7
Manufacturing, Non-Durable	10.5	3.6	6.0	8.4	8.4	5.9	13.8
Transportation, Communications and Public Utilities	7.3	3.5	4.5	5.9	5.4	4.5	9.3
Wholesale Trade	4.9	4.9	6.5	8.5	7.8	6.4	3.8
Retail Trade	20.1	25.9	25.5	21.4	16.2	23.5	17.6
Finance, Insurance & Real Estate	8.9	6.9	7.0	6.5	8.5	7.1	10.2
Miscellaneous Services	26.0	36.9	28.5	28.1	28.7	31.9	21.9
Total	100.0	100.0	100.0	100.0	100.0	100.0	100.0
Employed in Goods-Producing Firms	32.8	21.9	28.0	29.6	33.4	26.7	37.1
Employed in Service-Producing Firms	67.2	78.1	72.0	70.4	66.6	73.3	62.9
Workers in Labor Force	79.1	70.2	74.2	76.0	78.0	73.5	83.0
Weeks Worked in 1987							
1-26 Weeks	8.6	13.5	11.3	10.3	7.3	11.4	6.8
27-47 Weeks	13.6	16.3	16.4	17.1	16.1	16.5	11.7
50-52[1] Weeks	77.8	70.1	72.4	72.6	76.6	72.2	81.6
Total	100.0	100.0	100.0	100.0	100.0	100.0	100.0
Employment Status							
Wage-and-Salary	95.2	82.7	90.2	95.5	97.0	89.3	99.1
Self-Employed (Incorporated)	3.4	13.2	6.8	3.0	2.3	7.9	0.3
Self-Employed (Unincorporated)	1.4	4.1	3.0	1.5	0.7	2.8	0.6
Total	100.0	100.0	100.0	100.0	100.0	100.0	100.0
Workers Covered by Union Contract	13.9	1.7	5.3	8.7	8.4	5.2	19.4
Full-Time[1] and Full-Year[2] Status, 1987							
Full-Time, Full Year	69.6	55.8	62.5	65.0	69.8	61.4	75.1
Part-Time, Full Year	8.2	14.3	9.9	7.6	6.8	10.7	6.5
Full-Time, Part Year	13.9	16.9	16.7	18.7	15.6	17.0	11.8
Part-Time, Part Year	8.3	13.0	10.9	8.7	7.8	10.9	6.6
Total	100.0	100.0	100.0	100.0	100.0	100.0	100.0

[1]Full-time (FT) workers are those who worked a regular schedule of more than 35 hours per week; part-time (PT) workers are those who worked less than 35 hours per week.

[2]Full-year (FY) workers are those who worked from 50 to 52 weeks per year; part-year workers are those who worked less than 50 weeks per year.

Table 4.28 Economic Characteristics of Wage and Salary Workers in Very Small Firms by Employment Size of Firm, 1988 (Percent)--Continued

		Employment Size of Enterprise					
	Total All Firms	1-9	10-24	25-49	50-99	Under 100	100 and Over
Two or More Employers in 1987	16.7	20.0	18.3	19.0	19.9	19.3	14.9
One or More Years with Current Employer	80.1	73.2	75.5	79.1	76.2	75.4	83.4
Unemployed in 1987	10.1	12.7	12.9	12.3	11.4	12.5	8.4
Distribution of Unemployed Workers by Number of Weeks Unemployed in 1987							
1-4 Weeks	22.9	19.6	25.6	24.0	21.9	22.3	23.6
5-14 Weeks	40.4	37.6	36.9	42.9	51.9	40.4	40.4
15+ Weeks	36.7	42.8	37.5	33.1	26.2	37.3	36.0
Total	100.0	100.0	100.0	100.0	100.0	100.0	100.0

Source: U.S. Department of Commerce, Bureau of the Census, Current Population Survey, May 1988, unpublished data.

Table 4.29 Earnings of Wage-and-Salary Workers by Employment Size of Firm, 1987 (Percent)

| Estimated Hourly Rates | All Firms | Employment Size of Firm | | | | | | |
		1-24	25-99	100-499	500+	Under 100	100+	Under 500
≤ $5.00/hr.	21.8	34.3	23.8	17.7	16.0	30.3	16.4	27.0
$5.01 to $10.00/hr.	41.1	45.5	45.0	46.9	36.0	45.3	38.5	45.8
≥ $10.01/hr.	37.1	20.2	31.2	35.4	48.0	24.4	45.1	27.2
Total	100.0	100.0	100.0	100.0	100.0	100.0	100.0	100.0

Source: U.S. Small Business Administration, Office of Advocacy. Tabulations by Sheldon Haber of unpublished data from the U.S. Department of Commerce, Bureau of the Census, <u>Current Population Survey</u>, May 1988.

Table 4.30 Earnings of Wage-and-Salary Workers by Employment Size of Firm, 1987 (Percent)

	All Firms	Employment Size of Firm					
		1-9	10-24	25-49	50-99	100-499	500+
≤ $5.00/hr.	21.8	37.8	28.9	25.4	21.7	17.7	16.0
$5.01 to $10.00/hr.	41.1	44.4	47.2	44.9	45.1	46.9	36.0
≥ $10.01/hr.	37.1	17.8	23.9	29.7	35.2	35.4	48.0
Total	100.0	100.0	100.0	100.0	100.0	100.0	100.0

Source: U.S. Small Business Administration, Office of Advocacy. Tabulations by Sheldon Haber of unpublished data from the U.S. Department of Commerce, Bureau of the Census, Current Population Survey, May 1988.

5 Women-Owned Businesses

Introduction

This section of the *Handbook* examines the size and growth of the women-owned business population using data from three sources: (1) the Survey of Women-Owned Business (WOB), produced by the Bureau of the Census; (2) the National Survey of Small Business Finances, a one-time survey conducted in 1987 by the Federal Reserve Board of Governors and the SBA; and (3) data on women-owned, men-owned, and jointly owned sole proprietorships compiled for the SBA by the Internal Revenue Service. While none of these data sources provide a complete picture of the women-owned business population, each provides insight on some important developments in the status of women-owned businesses.[1]

The 1982 and 1987 Surveys of Women-Owned Business

The Census Bureau's Survey of Women-Owned Business is the most comprehensive source of data on women-owned businesses collected on a regular basis. Every five years since 1972, the Census Bureau, as a special program of its economic censuses, releases basic statistics on women-owned businesses, as well as statistics on businesses owned by blacks and other minorities.[2] These statistics cover women-owned sole proprietorships, partnerships, and subchapter S corporations, but do not cover regular corporations, which are typically the largest businesses.[3] (Unless otherwise specified, the discussion presented in this chapter does not pertain to regular corporations owned by women.) Although the Census data coverage is

1 For a discussion of the various sources of data on women-owned businesses, see U.S. Small Business Administration, Office of Advocacy, *A Status Report to Congress: Statistical Information on Women in Business* (Washington, D.C.: U.S. Small Business Administration, 1990).

2 The Census Bureau classifies a business as woman-owned if 50 percent or more of the business' owners are women. By this classification scheme, jointly owned sole proprietorships are counted among women-owned businesses.

3 Beginning with 1987, the Census data also exclude businesses with less than $500 in annual receipts.

incomplete, it is the most comprehensive of its kind.

National Survey of Small Business Finances

The Federal Reserve Board of Governors, with SBA cooperation, conducted the National Survey of Small Business Finances (NSSBF) to collect information on the financial structure of small businesses. A byproduct of this survey was the only federally produced estimate of the number and receipts of regular (1120C) corporations owned by women. According to the NSSBF, there were 184,103 regular corporations owned by women in 1987, with total receipts of approximately $198.8 billion.

Combining the 1987 NSSBF figures on women-owned regular corporations with the 1987 Census data on women-owned sole proprietorships, partnerships, and subchapter S corporations creates crude but uniquely comprehensive estimates of the total number of women-owned businesses and their annual receipts. The combined Census and NSSBF data reveal that in 1987 there were approximately 4.3 million women-owned businesses, with total receipts of $476.9 billion. These estimates—contrasted with Census and IRS universe estimates of the 1987 U.S. business population—establish an approximate lower bound for women-owned business' share of businesses and business receipts: as of 1987, about 26.6 percent of U.S. businesses were women-owned, accounting for roughly 4.5 percent of total U.S. business receipts.[4]

Internal Revenue Service

The IRS assists the Small Business Administration to enable more timely tracking of women-owned businesses and to track these businesses over the interim years not covered by the Census Bureau's Survey of Women-Owned Business. Every year, under an interagency agreement with the IRS, the SBA's Office of Advocacy purchases customized tabulations based on a random sample of nonfarm sole proprietorship income tax returns.[5] At present, IRS/SBA

---

4 The Census Bureau reports that there were 13,695,480 sole proprietorships, partnerships, and subchapter S corporations (with receipts of $500 or more) in 1987, with combined 1987 receipts of $1.995 trillion. The Internal Revenue Service reports that there were 2,484,228 regular (1120C) corporations with total receipts of $8.61 trillion in 1987.

5 On the basis of the first names of sole proprietors appearing on Form 1040C income tax returns, the IRS classifies nonfarm sole proprietorships as women-owned, men-owned, or jointly owned. The IRS provides the SBA with tabulations of the number, annual receipts, and net income of sole proprietorships by gender of ownership, geographic location (SBA region), and industry group.

data on women-owned, men-owned, and jointly owned sole proprietorships are available for every year between 1977 and 1989, except 1978.

Chapter 5 Tables

Table 5.1 Number and Receipts of Women-Owned Businesses by Legal Form of Organization, 1987

Legal Form of Organization	Number of Businesses	Percent of Total	Total Receipts (Millions of Dollars)	Percent of Total
Total, All Forms	4,114,787	100.0	278,138	100.0
Sole Proprietorships	3,722,544	90.5	80,627	10.5
Partnerships	155,760	3.8	29,265	29.0
Subchapter S Corporations	236,483	5.8	168,246	60.5

Source: Adapted by the U.S. Small Business Administration, Office of Advocacy, from U.S. Department of Commerce, Bureau of the Census, <u>Women-Owned Businesses, 1987</u> (Washington, D.C.: U.S. Government Printing Office, 1990), Table 7.

Table 5.2 Number and Receipts of Women-Owned Businesses by Industry, 1982 and 1987

Industry	1982				1987			
	Number of Firms	Percent of Total	Receipts (Thousands of Dollars)	Percent of Total	Number of Firms	Percent of Total	Receipts (Thousands of Dollars)	Percent of Total
Total, All Industries	2,612,621	100.00	98,291,513	100.00	4,112,787	100.00	278,138,117	100.00
Agriculture, Forestry, Fishing	19,497	0.75	685,728	0.70	47,979	1.17	1,932,818	0.69
Mining	19,832	0.76	2,220,945	2.26	26,420	0.64	1,933,822	0.70
Construction	58,991	2.26	4,564,914	4.64	94,308	2.29	20,302,124	7.30
Manufacturing	44,909	1.72	5,302,877	5.40	93,960	2.28	30,914,089	11.11
Transportation, Communications, Public Utilities	38,944	1.49	3,228,923	3.29	79,768	1.94	10,936,278	3.93
Wholesale Trade	32,059	1.23	9,189,524	9.35	82,513	2.01	42,804,558	15.39
Retail Trade	631,309	24.16	35,861,430	36.48	796,692	19.37	85,417,525	30.71
Finance, Insurance, Real Estate	246,403	9.43	6,369,932	6.48	437,360	10.63	17,833,402	6.41
Services	1,284,837	49.18	26,277,751	26.73	2,269,028	55.17	61,123,430	21.98
Unclassified	235,840	9.03	4,589,489	4.67	184,759	4.49	4,940,071	1.78

Source: Adapted by the U.S. Small Business Administration, Office of Advocacy, from U.S. Department of Commerce, Bureau of the Census, Women-Owned Businesses, 1987 (Washington, D.C.: U.S. Government Printing Office, 1990), Table 1.

Table 5.3 Number and Receipts of Women-Owned Businesses, 1982
and 1987

	Number of Businesses		Percent Change, 1982-1987	Rank
	1982	1987		
Total, All Industries	2,612,621	4,112,787	57.42	
Agriculture	19,497	47,979	146.08	2
Mining	19,832	26,420	33.22	8
Construction	58,991	94,308	59.87	7
Manufacturing	44,909	93,960	109.22	3
Transportation, Communications, Public Utilities	8,944	79,768	104.83	4
Wholesale Trade	32,059	82,513	157.38	1
Retail Trade	631,309	796,692	26.20	9
Finance, Insurance, Real Estate	246,403	437,360	77.50	5
Services	1,284,837	2,269,028	76.60	6
Unclassified	235,840	184,759	-21.66	—

	Receipts (Thousands of Dollars)		Percent Change, 1982-1987	Rank
	1982	1987		
Total, All Industries	98,291,513	278,138,117	182.97	
Agriculture	685,728	1,932,818	181.86	5
Mining	2,220,945	1,933,822	-12.93	9
Construction	4,564,914	20,302,124	344.74	3
Manufacturing	5,302,877	30,914,089	482.97	1
Transportation, Communications, Public Utilities	3,228,923	10,936,278	238.70	4
Wholesale Trade	9,189,524	42,804,558	365.80	2
Retail Trade	35,861,430	85,417,525	138.19	7
Finance, Insurance, Real Estate	6,369,932	17,833,402	179.96	6
Services	26,277,751	61,123,430	132.61	8
Unclassified	4,589,489	4,940,071	7.64	—

Source: Department of Commerce, Bureau of the Census, Women-Owned
Businesses, 1987 (Washington, D.C.: U.S. Government Printing Office, 1987),
Table 1.

Table 5.4   Women-Owned Firms by SBA Region and State, 1982 and
1987

Region/State	1982	1987	Percent Change, 1982-1987	Rank
U.S. Total	2,612,621	4,114,787	57.5	
Region I	141,073	247,254	75.3	
Massachusetts	63,162	111,376	76.3	5
Rhode Island	8,032	14,517	80.7	3
New Hampshire	11,912	22,713	90.7	1
Maine	14,473	23,922	65.3	13
Connecticut	35,450	60,924	71.9	7
Vermont	8,044	13,802	71.6	8
Region II	239,728	402,285	67.8	
New Jersey	63,243	117,373	85.6	2
New York	176,485	284,912	61.4	16
Region III	241,737	386,932	60.1	
Delaware	5,702	9,727	70.6	9
Maryland	48,371	81,891	69.3	10
Virginia	56,882	94,416	66.0	11
Pennsylvania	106,159	167,362	57.7	20
District of Columbia	8,893	10,987	23.6	51
West Virginia	15,730	22,549	43.4	43
Region IV	395,543	643,443	62.7	
North Carolina	57,374	93,532	63.0	14
Florida	125,392	221,361	76.5	4
Georgia	53,254	88,050	65.3	12
South Carolina	27,055	42,604	57.5	21
Alabama	30,856	48,018	55.6	27
Tennessee	44,643	67,448	51.1	30
Mississippi	20,411	28,976	42.0	45
Kentucky	36,558	53,454	46.2	36
Region V	462,592	712,370	54.0	
Illinois	110,278	177,057	60.6	18
Wisconsin	44,413	69,185	55.8	26
Minnesota	56,234	88,137	56.7	22
Michigan	87,133	133,958	53.7	28
Indiana	62,015	89,949	45.0	40
Ohio	102,519	154,084	50.3	32
Region VI	328,016	478,546	45.9	
New Mexico	16,287	25,397	55.9	24
Arkansas	24,463	35,469	45.0	41
Texas	199,758	298,138	49.3	33
Oklahoma	49,193	63,690	29.5	49
Louisiana	38,315	55,852	45.8	37
Region VII	149,693	227,040	51.7	
Missouri	54,080	87,658	62.1	15
Iowa	36,097	53,592	48.5	34
Kansas	36,770	53,505	45.5	39
Nebraska	22,746	32,285	41.9	46

Table 5.4 Women-Owned Firms by SBA Region and State, 1982 and
1987--Continued

Region/State	1982	1987	Percent Change, 1982-1987	Rank
Region VIII	115,734	173,827	50.2	
Colorado	57,370	89,411	55.9	25
Utah	19,072	29,810	56.3	23
South Dakota	9,367	13,374	42.8	44
Montana	12,762	17,747	39.1	48
North Dakota	8,770	12,689	44.7	42
Wyoming	8,393	10,796	28.6	50
Region IX	415,838	660,915	58.9	
Nevada	11,676	18,831	61.3	17
Arizona	35,085	60,567	72.6	6
California	354,662	559,821	57.9	19
Hawaii	14,415	21,696	50.5	31
Region X	122,667	182,175	48.5	
Oregon	40,479	58,941	45.6	38
Washington	59,296	90,285	52.3	29
Alaska	9,489	13,976	47.3	35
Idaho	13,403	18,973	41.6	47

Source: Adapted by the U.S. Small Business Administration,
Office of Advocacy, from U.S. Department of Commerce, Bureau
of the Census, <u>Women-Owned Business, 1987</u> (Washington, D.C.:
U.S. Government Printing Office, 1990), Table 2.

Table 5.5 Receipts of Women-Owned Businesses by SBA Region
and State, 1982 and 1987

Region/State	1982	1987	Percent Change, 1982-1987	Rank
U.S. Total	98,291,513	278,138,117	183.0	
Region I	4,528,317	22,058,201	387.1	
Massachusetts	1,777,802	11,139,810	526.6	1
Rhode Island	270,337	1,340,182	395.7	2
New Hampshire	391,716	1,857,769	374.3	3
Maine	420,461	1,634,638	288.8	4
Connecticut	1,401,205	5,319,710	279.7	6
Vermont	266,796	766,092	187.2	21
Region II	11,925,504	43,523,437	265.0	
New Jersey	3,573,040	13,553,517	279.3	7
New York	8,352,464	29,969,920	258.8	10
Region III	8,614,942	27,440,819	218.5	
Delaware	195,636	753,238	285.0	5
Maryland	1,529,902	5,508,587	260.1	9
Virginia	1,753,387	5,951,516	239.4	12
Pennsylvania	4,186,425	13,339,231	218.6	13
District of Columbia	333,941	774,019	131.8	34
West Virginia	615,651	1,114,228	81.0	46
Region IV	14,992,022	45,642,288	204.4	
North Carolina	1,859,606	6,813,158	266.4	8
Florida	4,788,745	16,828,094	251.4	11
Georgia	1,847,866	5,873,682	217.9	14
South Carolina	983,220	2,949,555	200.0	18
Alabama	1,267,621	3,624,355	185.9	22
Tennessee	1,707,491	4,226,269	147.5	30
Mississippi	954,839	2,062,007	116.0	37
Kentucky	1,582,634	3,265,168	106.3	40
Region V	17,476,050	49,217,474	181.6	
Illinois	4,566,694	13,884,278	204.0	17
Wisconsin	1,562,095	4,667,000	198.8	19
Minnesota	1,750,867	4,991,493	185.1	23
Michigan	2,789,692	7,889,112	182.8	25
Indiana	3,191,676	8,913,422	179.3	26
Ohio	3,615,026	8,872,169	145.4	31
Region VI	14,043,650	22,468,498	60.0	
New Mexico	575,980	1,166,312	102.4	41
Arkansas	1,069,343	2,007,652	87.8	44
Texas	8,074,340	13,384,958	65.8	49
Oklahoma	2,123,012	2,947,868	38.9	50
Louisiana	2,200,975	2,961,708	34.6	51
Region VII	5,078,033	12,563,583	147.4	
Missouri	1,989,406	5,349,139	168.9	27
Iowa	1,136,994	2,904,611	155.5	29
Kansas	1,234,950	2,660,785	115.5	38
Nebraska	716,683	1,649,048	130.1	35

Table 5.5 Receipts of Women-Owned Businesses by SBA Region and State, 1982 and 1987--Continued

Region/State	1982	1987	Percent Change, 1982-1987	Rank
Region VIII	4,013,723	8,405,006	109.4	
Colorado	1,829,435	4,260,547	132.9	33
Utah	664,597	1,392,426	109.5	39
South Dakota	368,044	726,047	97.3	42
Montana	499,100	930,377	86.4	45
North Dakota	340,081	571,701	68.1	47
Wyoming	312,466	523,908	67.7	48
Region IX	13,856,877	36,208,229	161.3	
Nevada	450,174	1,413,558	214.0	16
Arizona	1,027,306	2,910,886	183.4	24
California	12,022,899	31,026,855	158.1	28
Hawaii	356,498	856,930	140.4	32
Region X	3,762,395	10,610,582	182.0	
Oregon	1,357,284	4,279,167	215.3	15
Washington	1,598,681	4,689,046	193.3	20
Alaska	378,943	829,326	118.9	36
Idaho	427,487	813,043	90.2	43

Source: Adapted by the U.S. Small Business Administration, Office of Advocacy, from U.S. Department of Commerce, Bureau of the Census, Women-Owned Businesses, 1987 (Washington, D.C.: U.S. Government Printing Office, 1990), Table 2.

Table 5.6 Number and Receipts of Women-Owned Businesses with Paid Employees by
Industry Division, 1982 and 1987[*]

Industry	1982				1987			
	Firms	Percent of Total	Receipts	Percent of Total	Firms	Percent of Total	Receipts	Percent of Total
Total	311,662	100.0	65,347,449	100.0	618,198	100.0	223,916,218	100.0
Agriculture, Forestry, Fishing	2,843	0.9	408,226	0.6	9,377	1.5	1,291,282	0.6
Mining	1,335	0.4	1,323,490	2.0	1,942	0.3	1,428,180	0.6
Construction	13,321	4.3	3,304,870	5.1	36,178	5.9	17,832,436	8.0
Manufacturing	10,239	3.3	4,759,355	7.3	26,989	4.4	29,933,879	13.4
Transportation, Communications, Public Utilities	8,431	2.7	2,500,610	3.8	19,083	3.1	9,488,317	4.2
Wholesale	8,704	2.8	8,241,442	12.6	22,691	3.7	40,324,930	18.0
Retail	119,453	38.3	26,769,866	41.0	199,302	32.2	74,424,387	33.2
Finance, Insurance, Real Estate	16,483	5.3	2,830,331	4.3	36,741	5.9	9,236,301	4.1
Services	122,002	39.1	14,149,174	21.7	253,276	41.0	38,670,269	17.3
unclassified	8,851	2.8	1,060,085	1.6	12,619	2.0	1,286,237	0.6

[*] Receipts are in thousands of dollars.

Source: Adapted by the U.S. Small Business Administration, Office of Advocacy, from U.S.
Department of Commerce, Bureau of the Census, Women-Owned Businesses, 1987 (Washington,
D.C.: U.S. Government Printing Office, 1990), Table 1.

Table 5.7 Percent Change in the Number and Receipts of Women-Owned Businesses with Paid Employees, by Industry Division, 1982-1987 (Receipts Are in Thousands of Dollars)*

	Firms			Receipts		
	1982	1987	Percent Change, 1982-1987	1982	1987	Percent Change, 1982-1987
Total	311,662	618,198	98.4	65,347,449	223,916,218	242.7
Agriculture, Forestry, Fishing	2,843	9,377	229.8	408,226	1,291,282	216.3
Mining	1,335	1,942	45.5	1,323,490	1,428,180	7.9
Construction	13,321	36,178	171.6	3,304,870	17,832,436	439.6
Manufacturing	10,239	26,989	163.6	4,759,355	29,933,879	528.9
Transportation, Communications, Public Utilities	8,431	19,083	126.3	2,500,610	9,488,317	279.4
Wholesale	8,704	22,691	160.7	8,241,442	40,324,930	389.3
Retail	119,453	199,302	66.8	26,769,866	74,424,387	178.0
Finance, Insurance, Real Estate	16,483	36,741	122.9	2,830,331	9,236,301	226.3
Services	122,002	253,276	107.6	14,149,174	38,670,269	173.3
Unclassified	8,851	12,619	42.6	1,060,085	1,286,237	21.3

* Receipts are in thousands of dollars.

Source: Adapted by the U.S. Small Business Administration, Office of Advocacy, from U.S. Department of Commerce, Bureau of the Census, Women-Owned Businesses, 1987 (Washington, D.C.: U.S. Government Printing Office, 1990), Table 1.

Table 5.8 Nonfarm Sole Proprietorships by Gender of Ownership and Industry Group, 1980 and 1989

Industry	1980			1989			Percent Change, 1980-1989	
	All Nonfarm Businesses	Women-Owned Businesses	Women's Share of Total	All Nonfarm Businesses	Women-Owned Businesses	Women's Share of Total	All Nonfarm Businesses	Women-Owned Businesses
Total, All Industries	9,730,019	2,535,240	26.1	15,920,964	4,977,142	31.3	63.6	96.3
Agriculture, Forestry, and Fishing	307,720	30,811	10.0	306,589	59,361	19.4	-0.4	92.7
Mining, Construction, and Manufacturing	1,409,280	84,221	6.0	2,500,203	243,113	9.7	77.4	188.7
Transportation, Communications, and Public Utilities	438,795	27,696	6.3	657,862	80,677	12.3	49.9	191.3
Wholesale and Retail Trade	2,527,084	824,771	32.6	2,822,327	1,014,619	35.9	11.7	23.0
Finance, Insurance, and Real Estate	1,048,966	354,801	33.8	1,376,034	482,304	35.1	31.2	35.9
Services	3,918,166	1,212,940	31.0	8,257,949	3,097,068	37.5	110.8	155.3

Note: Detail may not add to totals due to disclosure rules regarding the release of taxpayer information. Data for 1989 are preliminary.

Source: Special tabulations prepared by the U.S. Department of the Treasury, Internal Revenue Service, under contract to the U.S. Small Business Administration, Office of Advocacy, January 1992.

Table 5.9 Receipts of Nonfarm Sole Proprietorships by Gender of Ownership and Industry Group, 1980 and 1989 (Thousands of Dollars)

Industry	1980			1989			Percent Change, 1980-1989	
	All Nonfarm Businesses	Women-Owned Businesses	Women's Share of Total	All Nonfarm Businesses	Women-Owned Businesses	Women's Share of Total	All Nonfarm Businesses	Women-Owned Businesses
Total, All Industries	411,205,713	36,376,570	8.8	692,810,919	89,033,875	12.9	68.5	144.8
Agriculture, Forestry, and Fishing	6,433,612	234,280	3.6	13,245,250	1,333,621	10.1	105.9	469.2
Mining, Construction, and Manufacturing	71,248,141	1,977,303	2.8	126,286,063	4,909,646	3.9	77.2	148.3
Transportation, Communications, and Public Utilities	19,965,525	698,144	3.5	31,819,936	2,446,889	7.7	59.4	250.5
Wholesale and Retail Trade	202,283,802	18,937,581	9.4	228,263,146	27,040,123	11.8	12.8	42.8
Finance, Insurance, and Real Estate	21,530,768	3,640,416	16.9	49,465,189	9,872,990	20.0	129.7	171.2
Services	89,743,865	10,888,846	12.1	243,731,334	43,430,604	17.8	171.6	298.9

Note: Detail may not add to totals due to disclosure rules regarding the release of taxpayer information. Data for 1989 are preliminary.

Source: Special tabulations prepared by the U.S. Department of the Treasury, Internal Revenue Service, under contract to the U.S. Small Business Administration, Office of Advocacy, January 1992.

Table 5.10 Nonfarm Sole Proprietorships by Gender of Ownership and SBA Region, 1980 and 1989

Region	1980			1989			Percent Change, 1980-1989	
	All Nonfarm Businesses	Women-Owned Businesses	Women's Share of Total	All Nonfarm Businesses	Women-Owned Businesses	Women's Share of Total	All Nonfarm Businesses	Women-Owned Businesses
U.S. Total	9,730,019	2,535,240	26.1	15,920,961	4,977,144	31.3	63.6	96.3
Region I	512,401	120,273	23.5	856,493	252,773	29.5	67.2	110.2
Region II	807,319	195,756	24.2	1,336,596	420,737	31.5	65.6	114.9
Region III	866,848	231,216	26.7	1,475,750	518,538	35.1	70.2	124.3
Region IV	1,480,801	370,354	25.0	2,554,396	705,019	27.6	72.5	90.4
Region V	1,774,893	481,945	27.2	2,678,752	848,336	31.7	50.9	76.0
Region VI	1,237,802	277,022	22.4	1,968,820	562,344	28.6	59.1	103.0
Region VII	602,859	166,643	27.6	927,036	315,468	34.0	53.8	89.3
Region VIII	431,948	115,755	26.8	614,669	189,202	30.8	42.3	63.5
Region IX	1,513,668	446,169	29.5	2,778,511	922,365	33.2	83.6	106.7
Region X	484,626	123,924	25.6	729,938	242,362	33.2	50.6	95.6

Note: Detail may not add to totals due to disclosure rules regarding the release of information for specific taxpayers. SBA regions, which correspond to federal regions, are defined as follows: Region I: Connecticut, Maine, Massachusetts, New Hampshire, Rhode Island, Vermont; Region II: New Jersey, New York; Region III: Delaware, District of Columbia, Maryland, Pennsylvania, Virginia, West Virginia; Region IV: Alabama, Florida, Georgia, Kentucky, Mississippi, North Carolina, South Carolina, Tennessee; Region V: Illinois, Indiana, Michigan, Minnesota, Ohio, Wisconsin; Region VI: Arkansas, Louisiana, New Mexico, Oklahoma, Texas; Region VII: Iowa, Kansas, Missouri, Nebraska; Region VIII: Colorado, Montana, North Dakota, South Dakota, Utah, Wyoming; Region IX: Arizona, California, Hawaii, Nevada; and, Region X: Alaska, Idaho, Oregon, Washington. Data for 1989 are preliminary.

Source: Special tabulations prepared by the U.S. Department of the Treasury, Internal Revenue Service, under contract to the U.S. Small Business Administration, Office of Advocacy, January 1992.

Table 5.11 Receipts of Nonfarm Sole Proprietorships by Gender of Ownership and SBA Region, 1980 and 1989 (Thousands of Dollars)

Region	1980			1989			Percent Change, 1980-1989	
	All Nonfarm Businesses	Women-Owned Businesses	Women's Share of Total	All Nonfarm Businesses	Women-Owned Businesses	Women's Share of Total	All Nonfarm Businesses	Women-Owned Businesses
U.S. Total	411,205,713	36,376,570	8.8	692,810,919	89,033,875	12.9	68.5	144.8
Region I	19,394,807	1,521,698	7.8	36,155,955	4,102,842	11.3	86.4	169.6
Region II	30,900,154	3,065,589	9.9	57,075,404	8,010,727	14.0	84.7	161.3
Region III	37,319,189	3,408,915	9.1	63,566,451	9,726,697	15.3	70.3	185.3
Region IV	66,605,226	5,515,772	8.3	104,503,530	12,784,535	12.2	56.9	131.8
Region V	73,456,559	6,463,322	8.8	100,129,385	12,258,754	12.2	36.3	89.7
Region VI	57,683,340	4,538,872	7.9	79,605,357	8,305,868	10.4	38.0	83.0
Region VII	26,636,767	2,080,737	7.8	37,975,916	4,818,757	12.7	42.6	131.6
Region VIII	16,337,108	1,206,690	7.4	21,107,591	2,199,111	10.4	29.2	82.2
Region IX	64,684,469	6,989,048	10.8	156,463,848	23,012,106	14.7	141.9	229.3
Region X	17,823,850	1,528,716	8.6	36,227,481	3,814,479	10.5	103.3	149.5

Note: Detail may not add to totals due to disclosure rules regarding the release of information for specific taxpayers. SBA regions, which correspond to federal regions, are defined as follows: Region I: Connecticut, Maine, Massachusetts, New Hampshire, Rhode Island, Vermont; Region II: New Jersey, New York; Region III: Delaware, District of Columbia, Maryland, Pennsylvania, Virginia, West Virginia; Region IV: Alabama, Florida, Georgia, Kentucky, Mississippi, North Carolina, South Carolina, Tennessee; Region V: Illinois, Indiana, Michigan, Minnesota, Ohio, Wisconsin; Region VI: Arkansas, Louisiana, New Mexico, Oklahoma, Texas; Region VII: Iowa, Kansas, Missouri, Nebraska; Region VIII: Colorado, Montana, North Dakota, South Dakota, Utah, Wyoming; Region IX: Arizona, California, Hawaii, Nevada; and, Region X: Alaska, Idaho, Oregon, Washington. Data for 1989 are preliminary.

Source: Special tabulations prepared by the U.S. Department of the Treasury, Internal Revenue Service, under contract to the U.S. Small Business Administration, Office of Advocacy, January 1992.

6   Minority-Owned Businesses

Introduction

Newly available data from the Census Bureau's 1987 Survey of Minority-Owned Business Enterprises allow a detailed look at some of the changes that occurred among minority-owned businesses.[1]

Survey of Minority-Owned Business Enterprises

The Survey of Minority-Owned Business Enterprises (SMOBE) is a special program conducted every five years by the U.S. Bureau of the Census as part of its economic censuses. The SMOBE program covers businesses owned by individuals who are members of the following nonwhite ethnic and racial groups:

- American Indians and Alaska Natives, the latter group being further divided by the Census Bureau into Eskimos and Aleuts;
- Asian Americans and Pacific Islanders, which includes Asian Indians, Chinese, Filipinos, Hawaiians, Japanese, Koreans, Vietnamese, and other Asians and Pacific Islanders;
- Blacks; and
- Hispanics, which includes Cubans, European Spanish, Mexicans, Puerto Ricans, other Central or South Americans, and other Hispanics.

It is important to note that these minority groups are not mutually exclusive, since a person can be a member of more than one ethnic or racial group.

The coverage of the Census Bureau's SMOBE program is restricted to sole proprietorships, partnerships, and subchapter S corpora-

---

1   The analytical literature on minority entrepreneurship is vast. For a comprehensive look at minority entrepreneurship, see "Minority Business and Entrepreneurship" in U.S. Small Business Administration, Office of Advocacy, *Small Business in the American Economy* (Washington, D.C.: U.S. Government Printing Office, 1988), 165–191. The SBA has sponsored many studies on various aspects of minority entrepreneurship. Summaries of these studies can be found in U.S. Small Business Administration, Office of Advocacy, *Catalog of Completed Research Studies,* 1990 ed. (Washington, D.C.: U.S. Small Business Administration, 1990).

tions. The SMOBE data do not cover regular (1120C) corporations owned by minorities.[2] Unless otherwise specified, this chapter deals only with businesses that fall within this population.

The SMOBE yields cross-sectional data on the number, receipts, and employment of minority-owned businesses.[3] These data are published by legal form of organization, by industry (down to the two-digit SIC code level of detail), and by geographic location (down to county level of detail, for counties with sufficient numbers of minority-owned businesses).

In mid-1991, the Census Bureau completed publication of its SMOBE statistics for 1987.[4] This chapter highlights the changes in selected aspects of the minority-owned business population between 1982 and 1987 as revealed by the 1987 SMOBE data.

2   Regular corporations tend to be the largest businesses. The SMOBE also excluded businesses with 1987 receipts of less than $500.

3   The 1982 and 1987 Characteristics of Business Owners surveys, follow-on surveys to the SMOBE, contain a wealth of additional information of the characteristics of minority business owners and their businesses. See U.S. Department of Commerce, Bureau of the Census, *1982 Characteristics of Business Owners,* CBO82-1 (Washington, D.C.: U.S. Government Printing Office, 1987).

4   See U.S. Department of Commerce, Bureau of the Census, *1987 Survey of Minority-Owned Business Enterprises,* 4 vols. (Washington, D.C.: U.S. Government Printing Office, 1990–1991). The individual volumes are: *Black* (MB87-1); *Hispanic* (MB87-2); *Asian Americans, American Indians, and Other Minorities* (MB87-3); and *Summary* (MB87-4). Due to changes made in coverage of the SMOBE program, data reported from prior surveys are not comparable over time.

Chapter 6 Tables

Table 6.1   Number and Receipts of Minority-Owned Businesses, by Ethnic Category of Owner, 1987

	Number of Firms	Receipts (in Thousands)	Per Firm
All Businesses[1]	13,695,480	1,994,808,000	145,654
Men	9,850,693	1,716,669,883	174,269
Women	4,114,787	278,138,117	67,595
All Minority-Owned Businesses			
Total[2]	1,213,750	77,839,943	64,132
Men	825,441	59,846,993	72,503
Women	388,309	17,992,950	46,337
Black	424,165	19,762,876	46,592
Men	265,887	13,232,364	49,767
Women	158,278	6,530,512	41,260
Hispanic	422,373	24,731,600	58,554
Men	307,348	20,403,191	66,385
Women	115,025	4,328,409	37,630
American Indian and Alaska Native	21,380	911,279	42,623
Men	15,072	711,166	47,185
Women	6,308	200,113	31,724
Asian and Pacific Islander	355,331	33,124,326	93,221
Men	243,442	25,988,493	106,754
Women	111,889	7,135,833	63,776

[1]Includes all businesses--regardless of owners' race or ethnicity--that fall within the scope of the Census Bureau's sampling universe.

[2]These are the correct numbers for businesses and associated receipts aggregated across minority subgroups. That is, these totals do not contain any double-counting of Hispanic-owned businesses or receipts.

Note: Regular (1120C) corporations are not included in these figures.

Source: Adapted by the U.S. Small Business Administration, Office of Advocacy, from data published in U.S. Department of Commerce, Bureau of the Census, 1987 Survey of Minority-Owned Business Enterprises, vol. 4, Summary, MB87-4 (Washington, D.C.: U.S. Government Printing Office, 1991), Table B.

Table 6.2 Number and Receipts of Minority-Owned Businesses, by Legal Form of Organization, 1987

Legal Form	Businesses		Receipts	
	Number	Percent of Total	Amount (Thousands of Dollars)	Percent of Total
Total, All Forms	1,213,750	100.0	77,839,943	100.0
Sole Proprietorships	1,129,705	93.1	46,164,026	59.3
Partnerships	41,833	3.4	8,374,968	10.8
1120S Corporations	42,212	3.5	23,300,949	29.9

Source: Adapted by the U.S. Small Business Administration, Office of Advocacy, from data published in: U.S. Department of Commerce, Bureau of the Census, <u>1987 Survey of Minority-Owned Business Enterprises</u>, vol. 4, <u>Summary</u>, MB87-4 (Washington, D.C.: U.S. Government Printing Office, 1991), Table 7.

Table 6.3 Number of Businesses per 1,000 Persons, by Ethnic Group, 1987

Demographic Group	Number of Businesses	Number of Persons	Number of Businesses Per 1,000 Persons
American Indian and Alaska Native	21,380	1,959,234	10.9
Asian American and Pacific Islander	355,331	7,273,662	48.9
Black	424,165	29,986,060	14.2
Hispanic	422,373	22,354,059	18.9

Note: Data on number of Businesses are for 1987. Data on number of persons--which include persons of all ages--are for 1990.

Source: Adapted by the U.S. Small Business Administration, Office of Advocacy, from data published in: U.S. Department of Commerce, Bureau of the Census, 1987 Survey of Minority-Owned Business Enterprises, vol. 4, Summary, MB87-4 (Washington, D.C.: U.S. Government Printing Office, 1991), Table A.

Table 6.4 Number and Receipts of Businesses Owned by Asian Americans, American Indians, and Other Minorities, by Industry, 1982 and 1987

	Number of Firms		Percent Change,	Receipts (in Thousands)		Change,
	1982	1987	1982-1987	1982	1987	1982-1987
Total, All Industries	201,264	376,711	87.2	13,148,315	34,035,605	158.9
Agriculture, Forestry, Fishing	9,828	13,387	36.2	228,687	469,755	105.4
Mining	342	466	36.3	24,380	19,176	-21.3
Construction	7,592	16,223	113.7	416,546	1,379,974	231.3
Manufacturing	3,483	11,032	216.7	286,694	1,524,959	431.9
Transportation, Communications, Public Utilities	4,826	12,857	166.4	220,317	735,766	234.0
Wholesale Trade	3,458	11,014	218.5	808,055	4,224,910	422.8
Retail Trade	57,175	91,851	60.6	,168,511	13,583,839	120.2
Finance, Insurance, Real Estate	12,709	27,911	119.6	425,058	1,107,047	160.4
Services	85,191	172,946	103.0	3,905,566	10,059,033	157.6
Unclassified	16,658	19,024	14.2	664,499	931,146	40.1

Source: Adapted by the U.S. Small Business Administration, Office of Advocacy, from data published in: U.S. Department of Commerce, Bureau of the Census, *1987 Survey of Minority-Owned Business Enterprises*, vol. 3, *Asian Americans, American Indians, and Other Minorities*, MB87-3 (Washington, D.C.: U.S. Government Printing Office, 1991), Table 1.

Table 6.5   Industrial Distribution of Businesses Owned by American Indians and Alaska Natives, 1987

Ethnicity	Total, All Industries	Agriculture	Mining	Construction	Manufacturing	Transportation, Communications, Public Utilities	Wholesale Trade	Retail Trade	Finance, Insurance, Real Estate	Services	Unclassified
Aleut											
Number	1,143	671	0	40	8	48	10	91	29	210	36
Percent	100.00	58.71	0.00	3.50	0.70	4.20	0.87	7.96	2.54	18.37	3.15
Eskimo											
Number	2,353	1,613	6	43	28	50	10	157	23	262	161
Percent	100.00	68.55	0.25	1.83	1.19	2.12	0.42	6.67	0.98	11.13	6.84
American Indian											
Number	17,884	1,377	100	2,749	875	819	340	2,842	562	7,132	1,088
Percent	100.00	7.70	0.56	15.37	4.89	4.58	1.90	15.89	3.14	39.88	6.08
Total											
Number	21,380	3,661	106	2,832	911	917	360	3,090	614	7,604	1,285
Percent	100.00	17.12	0.50	13.25	4.26	4.29	1.68	14.45	2.87	35.57	6.01

Source: Adapted by the U.S. Small Business Administration, Office of Advocacy, from data published in: U.S. Department of Commerce, Bureau of the Census, 1987 Survey of Minority-Owned Business Enterprises, vol. 3, Asian Americans, American Indians, and Other Minorities, MB87-3 (Washington, D.C.: U.S. Government Printing Office, 1991), Table 2.

Table 6.6 Industrial Distribution of Receipts of Businesses Owned by American Indians and Alaska Natives, 1987

Ethnicity	Total, All Industries	Industry Division									
		Agriculture	Mining	Construction	Manufacturing	Transportation, Communications, Public Utilities	Wholesale Trade	Retail Trade	Finance, Insurance, Real Estate	Services	Unclassified
Aleut											
Receipts[1]	53,301	34,207	0	590	NA	1,680	NA	5,564	1,238	3,547	2,296
Percent	100.00	64.18	0.00	1.11	NA	3.15	NA	10.44	2.32	6.65	4.31
Eskimo											
Receipts[1]	54,554	23,274	59	7,182	NA	931	NA	12,282	955	5,834	3,401
Percent	100.00	42.66	0.11	13.16	NA	1.71	NA	22.51	1.75	10.69	6.23
American Indian											
Receipts[1]	803,424	46,965	4,003	148,012	60,221	41,675	34,585	250,240	17,999	168,784	30,940
Percent	100.00	5.85	0.50	18.42	7.50	5.19	4.30	31.15	2.24	21.01	3.85
Total											
Receipts[1]	911,279	104,446	4,062	155,784	60,221	44,286	34,585	268,086	20,192	178,165	36,637
Percent	100.00	11.46	0.45	17.10	6.61	4.86	3.80	29.42	2.22	19.55	4.02

NA = Data not available because of public disclosure restrictions.

[1]Figures for receipts represent thousands of dollars.

Source: Adapted by the U.S. Small Business Administration, Office of Advocacy, from data published in: U.S. Department of Commerce, Bureau of the Census, *1987 Survey of Minority-Owned Business Enterprises*, vol. 3, Asian Americans, American Indians, and Other Minorities, MB87-3 (Washington, D.C.: U.S. Government Printing Office, 1991), Table 2.

Table 6.7 Industrial Distribution of Businesses Owned by Asian Americans and Pacific Islanders, 1987

Ethnicity	Total, All Industries	Agriculture	Mining	Construction	Manufacturing	Transportation, Communications, Public Utilities	Wholesale Trade	Retail Trade	Finance, Insurance, Real Estate	Services	Unclassified
Asian Indian											
Number	52,266	358	112	1,199	878	2,812	1,634	9,314	3,537	29,787	2,635
Percent	100.00	0.68	0.21	2.29	1.68	5.38	3.13	17.82	6.77	56.99	5.04
Chinese											
Number	89,717	774	100	3,298	2,685	2,576	3,510	25,803	8,906	37,232	4,833
Percent	100.00	0.86	0.11	3.68	2.99	2.87	3.91	28.76	9.93	41.50	5.39
Japanese											
Number	53,372	4,407	69	2,128	1,383	1,352	1,826	9,051	4,227	26,291	2,638
Percent	100.00	8.26	0.13	3.99	2.59	2.53	3.42	16.96	7.92	49.26	4.94
Korean											
Number	69,304	557	16	3,249	1,905	1,582	1,908	26,161	2,736	28,604	2,586
Percent	100.00	0.80	0.02	4.69	2.75	2.28	2.75	37.75	3.95	41.27	3.73
Vietnamese											
Number	25,671	2,230	6	823	1,947	708	330	6,646	1,132	10,461	1,388
Percent	100.00	8.69	0.02	3.21	7.58	2.76	1.29	25.89	4.41	40.75	5.41
Filipino											
Number	40,412	739	24	1,448	643	1,432	793	6,099	5,145	21,846	2,243
Percent	100.00	1.83	0.06	3.58	1.59	3.54	1.96	15.09	12.73	54.06	5.55
Hawaiian											
Number	4,279	247	8	384	126	149	93	689	286	2,077	220
Percent	100.00	5.77	0.19	8.97	2.94	3.48	2.17	16.10	6.68	48.54	5.14
Other Asian and Pacific Islander											
Number	20,310	414	25	862	554	1,329	560	4,998	1,328	9,044	1,196
Percent	100.00	2.04	0.12	4.24	2.73	6.54	2.76	24.61	6.54	44.53	5.89
Total											
Number	355,331	9,726	360	13,391	10,121	11,940	10,654	88,761	27,297	165,342	17,739
Percent	100.00	2.74	0.10	3.77	2.85	3.36	3.00	24.98	7.68	46.53	4.99

Source: Adapted by the U.S. Small Business Administration, Office of Advocacy, from data published in: U.S. Department of Commerce, Bureau of the Census, 1987 Survey of Minority-Owned Business Enterprises, vol. 3, Asian Americans, American Indians, and Other Minorities, MB87-3 (Washington, D.C.: U.S. Government Printing Office, 1991), Table 2.

Table 6.8 Industrial Distribution of Receipts of Businesses Owned by Asian Americans and Pacific Islanders, 1987

Ethnicity	Total, All Industries	Agriculture	Mining	Construction	Manufacturing	Transportation, Communications, Public Utilities	Wholesale Trade	Retail Trade	Finance, Insurance, Real Estate	Services	Unclassified
Asian Indian											
Receipts[1]	6,714,684	19,278	2,071	177,070	241,067	158,605	879,785	1,935,454	182,676	2,917,588	201,090
Percent	100.00	0.29	0.03	2.64	3.59	2.36	13.10	28.82	2.72	43.45	2.99
Chinese											
Receipts[1]	9,609,592	37,495	2,809	333,144	494,044	175,923	1,429,316	4,268,139	429,065	2,186,744	252,913
Percent	100.00	0.39	0.03	3.47	5.14	1.83	14.87	44.42	4.46	22.76	2.63
Japanese											
Receipts[1]	3,837,255	145,348	2,550	216,294	165,002	104,773	511,116	1,289,714	163,531	1,138,326	100,501
Percent	100.00	3.79	0.07	5.64	4.30	2.73	13.32	33.61	4.26	29.67	2.62
Korean											
Receipts[1]	7,682,668	27,871	NA	218,721	334,092	87,446	876,122	4,064,114	116,020	1,773,886	NA
Percent	100.00	0.36	NA	2.85	4.35	1.14	11.40	52.90	1.51	23.09	NA
Vietnamese											
Receipts[1]	1,360,974	86,698	68	26,953	103,274	19,723	95,612	624,988	26,247	330,780	46,631
Percent	100.00	6.37	0.00	1.98	7.59	1.45	7.03	45.92	1.93	24.30	3.43
Filipino											
Receipts[1]	1,914,133	26,900	3,161	84,540	56,721	76,520	157,518	442,980	102,119	910,854	52,820
Percent	100.00	1.41	0.17	4.42	2.96	4.00	8.23	.14	5.34	47.59	2.76
Hawaiian											
Receipts[1]	221,176	8,841	NA	43,478	20,564	9,928	8,741	38,205	16,981	65,409	NA
Percent	100.00	4.00	NA	19.66	9.30	4.49	3.95	17.27	7.68	29.57	NA

Table 6.8 Industrial Distribution of Receipts of Businesses Owned by Asian Americans and Pacific Islanders, 1987--Continued

Ethnicity	Total, All Industries	Agriculture	Mining	Construction	Manufacturing	Industry Division Transportation, Communications, Public Utilities	Wholesale Trade	Retail Trade	Finance, Insurance, Real Estate	Services	Unclassified
Other Asian and Pacific Islander											
Receipts[1]	1,783,844	12,878	495	123,990	46,632	58,562	230,642	652,159	50,116	557,281	51,089
Percent	100.00	0.72	0.03	6.95	2.61	3.28	12.93	36.56	2.81	31.24	2.86
Total											
Receipts[1]	33,124,326	365,309	10,700	1,100,241	1,461,396	691,480	4,188,852	13,315,753	1,086,755	9,880,868	705,044
Percent	100.00	1.10	0.03	3.32	4.41	2.09	12.65	40.20	3.28	29.83	2.13

NA = Data not available because of public disclosure restrictions.

[1]Figures for receipts represent thousands of dollars.

Source: Adapted by the U.S. Small Business Administration, Office of Advocacy, from data published in: U.S. Department of Commerce, Bureau of the Census, 1987 Survey of Minority-Owned Business Enterprises, vol. 3, Asian Americans, American Indians, and Other Minorities, MB87-3 (Washington, D.C.: U.S. Government Printing Office, 1991), Table 2.

Table 6.9 Number and Receipts of Black-Owned Businesses by Industry, 1982 and 1987

	Number of Firms 1982	1987	Percent Change, 1982-1987	Receipts (Thousands of Dollars) 1982	1987	Change, 1982-1987
Total, All Industries	308,260	424,165	37.6	9,061,601	19,762,876	118.1
Agriculture, Forestry, Fishing	4,592	7,316	59.3	126,979	216,742	70.7
Mining	270	322	19.3	NA	54,071	NA
Construction	22,459	36,763	63.7	828,843	2,174,399	162.3
Manufacturing	3,707	8,004	115.9	344,719	1,023,104	196.8
Transportation, Communications, Public Utilities	23,907	36,958	54.6	733,232	1,573,342	114.6
Wholesale Trade	3,119	5,519	76.9	431,941	1,327,479	207.3
Retail Trade	70,811	66,229	-6.5	3,481,069	5,889,654	69.2
Finance, Insurance, Real Estate	12,957	26,989	108.3	280,305	804,252	186.9
Services	136,664	209,547	53.3	2,834,513	6,120,084	115.9
Unclassified	29,774	26,518	-10.9	NA	579,749	NA

NA = Data not available because of public disclosure restrictions.

Source: Adapted by the U.S. Small Business Administration, Office of Advocacy, from data published in: U.S. Department of Commerce, Bureau of the Census, <u>1987 Survey of Minority-Owned Business Enterprises</u>, vol. 1, <u>Black</u>, MB87-1 (Washington, D.C.: U.S. Government Printing Office, 1991), Table 1.

Table 6.10 Number and Receipts of Hispanic-Owned Businesses by Industry, 1982 and 1987

	Number of Firms		Percent Change,	Receipts (in Thousands)		Change,
	1982	1987	1982-1987	1982	1987	1982-1987
Total, All Industries	233,971	422,373	80.5	11,759,133	24,731,600	110.3
Agriculture, Forestry, Fishing	6,976	16,365	134.6	NA	694,937	NA
Mining	387	829	114.2	34,765	29,836	-14.2
Construction	26,298	55,516	111.1	,294,800	3,438,708	165.6
Manufacturing	3,938	11,090	181.6	480,333	1,449,913	201.9
Transportation, Communications, Public Utilities	12,957	26,955	108.0	566,877	1,380,981	143.6
Wholesale Trade	3,359	10,154	202.3	766,654	2,445,416	219.0
Retail Trade	53,334	69,911	31.1	4,408,413	7,643,850	73.4
Finance, Insurance, Real Estate	10,284	22,106	115.0	302,190	864,282	186.0
Services	92,759	184,372	98.8	2,983,923	6,031,406	102.1
Unclassified	23,679	25,075	5.9	NA	752,271	NA

NA = Data not available because of public disclosure restrictions.

Source: Adapted by the U.S. Small Business Administration, Office of Advocacy, from data published in: U.S. Department of Commerce, Bureau of the Census, 1987 Survey of Minority-Owned Business Enterprises, vol. 2, Hispanic, MB87-2 (Washington, D.C.: U.S. Government Printing Office, 1991), Table 1.

Table 6.11 Industrial Distribution of Hispanic-Owned Businesses, 1987

Ethnicity	Total, All Industries	Agriculture	Mining	Construction	Manufacturing	Industry Division — Transportation, Communications, Public Utilities	Wholesale Trade	Retail Trade	Finance, Insurance, Real Estate	Services	Unclassified
Mexican											
Number	229,706	11,991	578	34,143	5,969	13,131	4,467	40,900	10,271	95,683	12,573
Percent	100.00	5.22	0.25	14.86	2.60	5.72	1.94	17.81	4.47	41.65	5.47
Puerto Rican											
Number	27,697	506	34	2,671	662	2,131	650	5,044	1,758	12,508	1,733
Percent	100.00	1.83	0.12	9.64	2.39	7.69	2.35	18.21	6.35	45.16	6.26
Cuban											
Number	61,470	1,550	33	7,336	1,545	4,545	2,376	8,940	4,077	27,033	4,035
Percent	100.00	2.52	0.05	11.93	2.51	7.39	3.87	14.54	6.63	43.98	6.56
Other Central or South American											
Number	66,356	1,281	58	6,618	1,794	5,468	1,720	9,504	3,309	32,004	4,600
Percent	100.00	1.93	0.09	9.97	2.70	8.24	2.59	14.32	4.99	48.23	6.93
European Spanish											
Number	24,755	706	89	3,030	753	1,073	651	3,571	2,021	11,577	1,284
Percent	100.00	2.85	0.36	12.24	3.04	4.33	2.63	14.43	8.16	46.77	5.19
Other Hispanic											
Number	12,389	331	37	1,718	367	607	290	1,952	670	5,567	850
Percent	100.00	2.67	0.30	13.87	2.96	4.90	2.34	15.76	5.41	44.94	6.86
Total											
Number	422,373	16,365	829	55,516	11,090	26,955	10,154	69,911	22,106	184,372	25,075
Percent	100.00	3.87	0.20	13.14	2.63	6.38	2.40	16.55	5.23	43.65	5.94

Source: Adapted by the U.S. Small Business Administration, Office of Advocacy, from data published in: U.S. Department of Commerce, Bureau of the Census, 1987 *Survey of Minority-Owned Business Enterprises*, vol. 2, *Hispanic*, MB87-2 (Washington, D.C.: U.S. Government Printing Office, 1991), Table 2.

Table 6.12 Industrial Distribution of Receipts of Hispanic-Owned Businesses, 1987

Ethnicity	Total, All Industries	Agriculture	Mining	Construction	Manufacturing	Transportation, Communications, Public Utilities	Wholesale Trade	Retail Trade	Finance, Insurance, Real Estate	Services	Unclassified
Mexican											
Receipts[1]	11,835,080	536,546	22,556	1,929,246	576,508	669,222	835,716	3,793,339	301,681	2,782,169	388,097
Percent	100.00	4.53	0.19	16.30	4.87	5.65	7.06	32.05	2.55	23.51	3.28
Puerto Rican											
Receipts[1]	1,447,680	19,841	1,479	152,982	120,443	110,127	92,259	452,868	55,465	397,097	45,119
Percent	100.00	1.37	0.10	10.57	8.32	7.61	6.37	31.28	3.83	27.43	3.12
Cuban											
receipts[1]	5,481,974	50,608	404	667,621	393,819	248,410	969,712	1,621,807	275,026	1,120,069	134,498
percent	100.00	0.92	0.01	12.18	7.18	4.53	17.69	29.58	5.02	20.43	2.45
Other Central or South American											
Receipts[1]	3,202,238	38,396	1,098	288,343	170,141	246,841	287,656	910,552	115,681	1,018,906	124,624
Percent	100.00	1.20	0.03	9.00	5.31	7.71	8.98	28.43	3.61	31.82	3.89
European Spanish											
Receipts[1]	2,054,537	36,964	2,910	268,992	151,016	79,050	187,654	680,111	100,022	509,688	38,130
Percent	100.00	1.80	0.14	13.09	7.35	3.85	9.13	33.10	4.87	24.81	1.86
Other Hispanic											
Receipts[1]	710,091	12,582	1,389	131,524	37,986	27,331	72,419	185,173	16,407	203,477	21,803
Percent	100.00	1.77	0.20	18.52	5.35	3.85	10.20	26.08	2.31	28.66	3.07
Total											
Receipts[1]	24,731,600	694,937	29,836	3,438,708	1,449,913	1,380,981	2,445,416	7,643,850	864,282	6,031,406	752,271
Percent	100.00	2.81	0.12	13.90	5.86	5.58	9.89	30.91	3.49	24.39	3.04

[1]Figures for receipts represent thousands of dollars.

Source: Adapted by the U.S. Small Business Administration, Office of Advocacy, from data published in: U.S. Department of Commerce, Bureau of the Census, 1987 Survey of Minority-Owned Business Enterprises, vol. 2, Hispanic, MBB7-2 (Washington, D.C.: U.S. Government Printing Office, 1991), Table 2.

Table 6.13 Number of Businesses Owned by Asian Americans, American Indians, and Other Minorities, by SBA Region and State, 1982 and 1987

	Number of Firms		Percent Change, 1982-1987	Rank
	1982	1987		
U.S. Total	201,264	376,711	87.2	
Region I	**3,294**	**7,116**	**116.0**	
Connecticut	953	2,051	115.2	10
Maine	126	233	84.9	24
Massachusetts	1,774	3,916	120.7	9
New Hampshire	141	333	136.2	5
Rhode Island	244	472	93.4	18
Vermont	56	111	98.2	13
Region II	**21,098**	**48,922**	**131.9**	
New Jersey	4,737	12,665	167.4	1
New York	16,361	36,257	121.6	7
Region III	**12,671**	**25,143**	**98.4**	
Delaware	247	479	93.9	16
District of Columbia	896	807	-9.9	51
Maryland	4,098	7,954	94.1	15
Pennsylvania	3,923	7,189	83.3	26
Virginia	3,185	8,163	156.3	3
West Virginia	322	551	71.1	32
Region IV	**10,178**	**22,663**	**122.7**	
Alabama	496	1,007	103.0	11
Florida	3,413	8,902	160.8	2
Georgia	1,663	4,221	153.8	4
Kentucky	488	899	84.2	25
Mississippi	608	1,178	93.8	17
North Carolina	2,154	3,827	77.7	29
South Carolina	501	965	92.6	20
Tennessee	855	1,664	94.6	14
Region V	**16,687**	**28,895**	**73.2**	
Illinois	8,152	14,872	82.4	27
Indiana	1,095	1,808	65.1	35
Michigan	2,864	4,729	65.1	34
Minnesota	1,151	2,024	75.8	30
Ohio	2,540	4,011	57.9	38
Wisconsin	885	1,451	64.0	36
Region VI	**15,289**	**32,054**	**109.7**	
Arkansas	396	658	66.2	33
Louisiana	1,269	2,808	121.3	8
New Mexico	1,068	2,155	101.8	12
Oklahoma	2,462	3,751	52.4	43
Texas	10,094	22,682	124.7	6
Region VII	**2,572**	**4,627**	**79.9**	
Iowa	381	617	61.9	37
Kansas	754	1,366	81.2	28
Missouri	1,142	2,193	92.0	21
Nebraska	295	451	52.9	42

Table 6.13 Number of Businesses Owned by Asian Americans, American Indians, and Other Minorities, by SBA Region and State, 1982 and 1987--Continued

	Number of Firms		Percent Change,	Rank
	1982	1987	1982-1987	
Region VIII	**3,752**	**6,331**	**68.7**	
Colorado	1,889	3,543	87.6	23
Montana	394	612	55.3	41
North Dakota	210	329	56.7	39
South Dakota	278	375	34.9	44
Utah	796	1,239	55.7	40
Wyoming	185	233	25.9	48
Region IX	**104,268**	**183,832**	**76.3**	
Arizona	1,985	3,398	71.2	31
California	77,225	147,633	91.2	22
Hawaii	24,335	31,406	29.1	46
Nevada	723	1,395	92.9	19
Region X	**11,452**	**17,128**	**25.7**	
Alaska	3,939	5,034	17.1	49
Idaho	386	513	11.9	50
Oregon	2,071	3,340	31.7	45
Washington	5,056	8,241	26.2	47

Source: Adapted by the U.S. Small Business Administration, Office of Advocacy, from data published in: U.S. Department of Commerce, Bureau of the Census, <u>1987 Survey of Minority-Owned Business Enter-prises</u>, vol. 3, <u>Asian Americans, American Indians, and Other Minorities</u>, MB87-3 (Washington, D.C.: U.S. Government Printing Office, 1991), table 3.

Table 6.14 Receipts of Businesses Owned by Asian Americans, American Indians, and Other Minorities, by SBA Region and State, 1982 and 1987

	Receipts (Thousands of Dollars)		Percent Change, 1982-1987	Rank
	1982	1987		
U.S. Total	13,148,315	34,035,605	158.9	
Region I	89,166	643,556	621.8	
Connecticut	49,251	224,789	356.4	3
Maine	11,131	26,742	140.2	23
Massachusetts	NA	296,848	NA	NA
New Hampshire	8,223	41,518	404.9	2
Rhode Island	18,451	41,035	122.4	24
Vermont	2,110	12,624	498.3	1
Region II	999,541	4,427,906	343.0	
New Jersey	NA	1,210,068	NA	NA
New York	999,541	3,217,838	221.9	8
Region III	713,974	2,507,510	251.2	
Delaware	14,855	44,713	201.0	10
District of Columbia	NA	133,411	NA	NA
Maryland	264,731	711,101	168.6	17
Pennsylvania	241,848	931,479	285.2	5
Virginia	165,886	610,547	268.1	7
West Virginia	26,654	76,259	186.1	11
Region IV	499,462	2,408,748	382.3	
Alabama	35,209	130,824	271.6	6
Florida	NA	1,001,651	NA	NA
Georgia	121,340	469,069	286.6	4
Kentucky	35,835	97,361	171.7	14
Mississippi	79,733	141,054	76.9	32
North Carolina	120,401	300,323	149.4	19
South Carolina	32,470	87,724	170.2	16
Tennessee	74,474	180,742	142.7	21
Region V	1,010,888	2,790,298	176.0	
Illinois	512,759	1,444,913	181.8	12
Indiana	76,987	208,706	171.1	15
Michigan	161,907	414,413	156.0	18
Minnesota	54,086	172,007	218.0	9
Ohio	140,853	394,959	180.4	13
Wisconsin	64,296	155,300	141.5	22
Region VI	127,887	2,309,566	1705.9	
Arkansas	38,597	56,205	45.6	33
Louisiana	89,290	178,625	100.1	26
New Mexico	NA	104,085	NA	NA
Oklahoma	NA	155,468	NA	NA
Texas	NA	1,815,183	NA	NA
Region VII	86,318	339,298	293.1	
Iowa	28,927	55,233	90.9	29
Kansas	41,330	85,916	107.9	25
Missouri	NA	166,762	NA	NA
Nebraska	16,061	31,387	95.4	27

Table 6.14 Receipts of Businesses Owned by Asian Americans, American Indians, and Other
Minorities, by SBA Region and State, 1982 and 1987--Continued

	Receipts (Thousands of Dollars)		Percent Change, 1982-1987	Rank
	1982	1987		
Region VIII	110,001	390,608	255.1	
Colorado	NA	229,959	NA	NA
Montana	24,499	29,827	21.7	36
North Dakota	19,963	28,211	41.3	34
South Dakota	NA	16,880	NA	NA
Utah	52,165	70,851	35.8	35
Wyoming	13,374	14,880	11.3	37
Region IX	7,060,113	16,840,837	138.5	
Arizona	165,110	303,385	83.7	30
California	5,974,854	14,782,556	147.4	20
Hawaii	868,482	1,662,269	91.4	28
Nevada	51,667	92,627	79.3	31
Region X	23,626	1,377,278	25.7	
Alaska	NA	196,104	17.1	NA
Idaho	23,626	37,636	11.9	38
Oregon	NA	351,150	31.7	NA
Washington	NA	792,388	26.2	NA

NA = Data not available because of public disclosure restrictions.

Source: Adapted by the U.S. Small Business Administration, Office of Advocacy, from data
published in: U.S. Department of Commerce, Bureau of the Census, 1987 Survey of Minority-
Owned Business Enterprises, vol. 3, Asian Americans, American Indians, and Other Minorities,
MB87-3 (Washington, D.C.: U.S. Government Printing Office, 1991), Table 3.

Table 6.15 Black-Owned Businesses by SBA Region and State, 1982 and 1987

	Number of Firms		Percent Change, 1982-1987	Rank
	1982	1987		
U.S. Total	308,260	424,165	37.60	
Region I	5,815	9,769	68.00	
Connecticut	2,455	4,061	65.42	4
Maine	109	131	20.18	43
Massachusetts	2,782	4,761	71.14	3
New Hampshire	123	229	86.18	1
Rhode Island	283	489	72.79	2
Vermont	63	98	55.56	11
Region II	32,165	50,845	58.08	
New Jersey	9,121	14,556	59.59	6
New York	23,044	36,289	57.48	9
Region III	46,252	62,588	35.32	
Delaware	982	1,399	42.46	17
District of Columbia	8,179	8,275	1.17	50
Maryland	13,776	21,678	57.36	10
Pennsylvania	9,501	11,728	23.44	37
Virginia	13,192	18,781	42.37	18
West Virginia	622	727	16.88	46
Region IV	74,832	113,025	51.04	
Alabama	6,806	10,085	48.18	13
Florida	15,596	25,527	63.68	5
Georgia	13,490	21,283	57.77	7
Kentucky	2,814	3,738	32.84	24
Mississippi	6,464	9,667	49.55	12
North Carolina	13,333	19,487	46.16	15
South Carolina	9,129	12,815	40.38	20
Tennessee	7,200	10,423	44.76	16
Region V	46,019	58,398	26.90	
Illinois	14,785	19,011	28.58	31
Indiana	5,011	5,867	17.08	45
Michigan	10,947	13,708	25.22	34
Minnesota	1,042	1,448	38.96	22
Ohio	12,390	15,983	29.00	30
Wisconsin	1,844	2,381	29.12	29
Region VI	46,366	59,496	28.32	
Arkansas	3,323	4,392	32.17	26
Louisiana	12,359	15,331	24.05	35
New Mexico	486	587	20.78	42
Oklahoma	2,837	3,461	22.00	41
Texas	27,361	35,725	30.57	28
Region VII	8,970	11,721	30.67	
Iowa	603	703	16.58	47
Kansas	1,903	2,323	22.07	40
Missouri	5,782	7,832	35.45	23
Nebraska	682	863	26.54	32

Table 6.15   Black-Owned Businesses by SBA Region and State, 1982 and 1987--Continued

| | Number of Firms | | Percent Change, | Rank |
	1982	1987	1982-1987	
Region VIII	2,577	3,351	30.03	
Colorado	2,163	2,871	32.73	25
Montana	55	77	40.00	21
North Dakota	54	57	5.56	49
South Dakota	51	63	23.53	36
Utah	164	202	23.17	38
Wyoming	90	81	-10.00	51
Region IX	41,057	50,940	24.07	
Arizona	1,274	1,811	42.15	19
California	38,876	47,728	22.77	39
Hawaii	271	399	47.23	14
Nevada	636	1,002	57.55	8
Region X	3,207	4,032	25.72	
Alaska	433	507	17.09	44
Idaho	84	94	11.90	48
Oregon	644	848	31.68	27
Washington	2,046	2,583	26.25	33

Source: Adapted by the U.S. Small Business Administration, Office of Advocacy, from data published in: U.S. Department of Commerce, Bureau of the Census, 1987 Survey of Minority-Owned Business Enterprises, vol. 1, Black, MB87-1 (Washington, D.C.: U.S. Government Printing Office, 1991), Table 2.

Table 6.16 Receipts of Black-Owned Businesses by SBA Region and State, 1982 and 1987

	Receipts (Thousands of Dollars)		Percent Change, 1982-1987	Rank
	1982	1987		
U.S. Total	9,619,055	19,762,876	105.5	
Region I	163,757	538,904	NA	
Massachusetts	83,143	251,946	203.0	2
Rhode Island	NA	18,209	NA	NA
New Hampshire	NA	31,198	NA	NA
Maine	3,315	5,151	55.4	31
Connecticut	77,299	225,718	192.0	3
Vermont	NA	6,682	NA	NA
Region II	1,088,357	2,881,652	164.8	
New Jersey	430,280	995,614	131.4	11
New York	658,077	1,886,038	186.6	5
Region III	1,212,934	2,806,273	NA	
Delaware	34,235	77,701	127.0	14
Maryland	328,093	719,715	119.4	16
Virginia	325,125	810,569	149.3	10
Pennsylvania	324,068	747,417	130.6	12
District of Columbia	201,413	411,941	104.5	23
West Virginia	NA	38,930	NA	NA
Region IV	2,777,442	5,059,865	NA	
North Carolina	354,998	746,112	110.2	21
Florida	571,039	1,211,648	112.2	18
Georgia	456,940	1,179,730	158.2	7
South Carolina	NA	444,201	NA	NA
Alabama	206,008	439,966	113.6	17
Tennessee	230,081	386,078	67.8	29
Mississippi	203,889	531,929	160.9	6
Kentucky	754,487	120,201	-84.1	38
Region V	1,411,824	3,092,458	NA	
Illinois	631,622	1,100,204	74.2	27
Wisconsin	82,840	190,696	130.2	13
Minnesota	38,607	124,915	223.6	1
Michigan	332,477	701,335	110.9	19
Indiana	NA	349,643	NA	NA
Ohio	326,278	625,665	91.8	24
Region VI	1,336,174	1,951,194	NA	
New Mexico	14,495	27,133	87.2	25
Arkansas	96,209	214,596	123.1	15
Texas	790,142	1,084,014	37.2	33
Oklahoma	NA	93,903	NA	NA
Louisiana	435,328	531,548	22.1	
Region VII	254,898	626,163	NA	
Missouri	194,097	336,094	73.2	28
Iowa	NA	44,795	NA	NA
Kansas	60,801	154,448	154.0	8
Nebraska	NA	90,826	NA	NA
Region VIII	95,971	130,959	36.5	
Colorado	68,571	105,849	54.4	32
Utah	10,137	8,615	-15.0	37
South Dakota	2,653	4,832	82.1	26
Montana	2,755	6,944	152.1	9
North Dakota	8,781	1,207	-86.3	39
Wyoming	3,074	3,512	14.2	36

Table 6.16 Receipts of Black-Owned Businesses by SBA Region and State, 1982 and 1987--Continued

| | Receipts (Thousands of Dollars) | | Percent Change, 1982-1987 | Rank |
	1982	1987		
Region IX	1,182,483	2,506,381	NA	
Nevada	31,498	38,608	22.6	34
Arizona	NA	91,439	NA	NA
California	1,145,128	2,364,024	106.4	22
Hawaii	5,857	12,310	110.2	20
Region X	63,835	229,027	NA	
Oregon	NA	34,136	NA	NA
Washington	60,904	175,671	188.4	4
Alaska	NA	14,444	NA	NA
Idaho	2,931	4,776	62.9	30

NA = Data not available because of public disclosure restrictions.

Source: Adapted by the U.S. Small Business Administration, Office of Advocacy, from data published in: U.S. Department of Commerce, Bureau of the Census, 1987 Survey of Minority-Owned Business Enterprises, vol. 1, Black, MB87-1 (Washington, D.C.: U.S. Government Printing Office, 1991), Table 2.

Table 6.17 Hispanic-Owned Businesses by SBA Region and State, 1982 and 1987

	Number of Firms		Percent Change,	
	1982	1987	1982-1987	Rank
U.S. Total	233,975	422,373	80.5	
Region I	3,048	5,798	90.2	
Connecticut	1,081	2,235	106.8	5
Maine	90	139	54.4	37
Massachusetts	1,481	2,636	78.0	19
New Hampshire	98	244	149.0	1
Rhode Island	222	426	91.9	11
Vermont	76	118	55.3	36
Region II	20,143	40,348	100.3	
New Jersey	6,307	12,094	91.8	12
New York	13,836	28,254	104.2	6
Region III	4,862	9,420	93.7	
Delaware	102	184	80.4	17
District of Columbia	409	762	86.3	14
Maryland	1,391	2,931	110.7	4
Pennsylvania	1,641	2,650	61.5	30
Virginia	1,172	2,716	131.7	2
West Virginia	147	177	20.4	49
Region IV	34,984	69,273	98.0	
Alabama	250	397	58.8	32
Florida	32,404	64,413	98.8	8
Georgia	863	1,931	123.8	3
Kentucky	231	359	55.4	35
Mississippi	225	308	36.9	44
North Carolina	463	918	98.3	9
South Carolina	237	393	65.8	24
Tennessee	311	554	78.1	18
Region V	9,780	17,351	77.4	
Illinois	4,929	9,636	95.5	10
Indiana	871	1,427	63.8	27
Michigan	1,616	2,654	64.2	26
Minnesota	447	751	68.0	23
Ohio	1,350	1,989	47.3	40
Wisconsin	567	894	57.7	33
Region VI	70,439	113,590	61.3	
Arkansas	189	324	71.4	22
Louisiana	1,997	2,697	35.1	45
New Mexico	8,662	14,299	65.1	24
Oklahoma	968	1,516	56.6	34
Texas	58,623	94,754	61.6	29
Region VII	2,540	3,882	52.8	
Iowa	335	475	41.8	43
Kansas	1,038	1,541	48.5	39
Missouri	701	1,247	77.9	20
Nebraska	466	619	32.8	46

Table 6.17 Hispanic-Owned Businesses by SBA Region and State, 1982 and 1987--Continued

| | Number of Firms | | Percent Change, | Rank |
	1982	1987	1982-1987	
Region VIII	6,812	11,901	74.7	
Colorado	5,364	9,516	77.4	21
Montana	202	304	50.5	38
North Dakota	55	88	60.0	31
South Dakota	74	109	47.3	41
Utah	717	1,300	81.3	16
Wyoming	400	584	46.0	42
Region IX	77,838	145,050	86.3	
Arizona	6,036	9,845	63.1	28
California	70,256	132,212	88.2	13
Hawaii	662	1,226	85.2	15
Nevada	884	1,767	99.9	7
Region X	3,529	5,760	25.7	
Alaska	327	502	17.1	50
Idaho	523	974	11.9	51
Oregon	1,022	1,598	31.7	47
Washington	1,657	2,686	26.2	48

Source: Adapted by the U.S. Small Business Administration, Office of Advocacy, from data published in: U.S. Department of Commerce, Bureau of the Census, 1987 Survey of Minority-Owned Business Enterprises, vol. 2, Hispanic, MB87-2 (Washington, D.C.: U.S. Government Printing Office, 1991), Table 3.

Table 6.18 Receipts of Hispanic-Owned Businesses by SBA Region and State, 1982 and 1987

	Receipts (Thousands of Dollars)		Percent Change, 1982-1987	Rank
	1982	1987		
U.S. Total	11,759,133	24,731,600	110.3	
Region I	100,554	420,222	317.9	
Connecticut	73,479	175,520	138.9	11
Maine	4,361	12,061	176.6	8
Massachusetts	NA	173,969	NA	41
New Hampshire	4,656	12,818	175.3	9
Rhode Island	14,139	40,471	186.2	7
Vermont	3,919	5,383	37.4	29
Region II	1,199,459	2,457,805	104.9	
New Jersey	335,849	902,004	168.6	10
New York	863,610	1,555,801	80.2	22
Region III	139,487	657,331	371.2	
Delaware	4,797	6,230	29.9	31
District of Columbia	17,843	63,948	258.4	1
Maryland	58,620	185,308	216.1	4
Pennsylvania	NA	247,081	NA	50
Virginia	44,872	140,917	214.0	5
West Virginia	13,355	13,847	3.7	39
Region IV	1,774,154	5,297,548	198.6	
Alabama	14,688	30,006	104.3	16
Florida	1,728,005	4,949,151	186.4	6
Georgia	NA	145,252	NA	47
Kentucky	10,891	16,562	52.1	26
Mississippi	11,747	12,490	6.3	38
North Carolina	NA	92,903	NA	48
South Carolina	8,823	15,997	81.3	21
Tennessee	NA	35,187	NA	49
Region V	419,081	1,115,202	166.1	
Illinois	269,062	588,646	118.8	13
Indiana	50,236	106,111	111.2	15
Michigan	65,631	126,046	92.1	20
Minnesota	13,528	29,061	114.8	14
Ohio	NA	191,797	NA	45
Wisconsin	20,624	73,541	256.6	2
Region VI	3,295,934	5,010,474	52.0	
Arkansas	9,657	13,808	43.0	28
Louisiana	125,534	136,083	8.4	36
New Mexico	417,180	702,098	68.3	23
Oklahoma	NA	50,409	NA	51
Texas	2,743,563	4,108,076	49.7	27
Region VII	15,563	151,553	873.8	
Iowa	NA	20,210	NA	46
Kansas	NA	62,275	NA	44
Missouri	NA	49,677	NA	40
Nebraska	15,563	19,391	24.6	33

Table 6.18 Receipts of Hispanic-Owned Businesses by SBA Region and State, 1982 and 1987--Continued

	Receipts (Thousands of Dollars)		Percent Change,	
	1982	1987	1982-1987	Rank
Region VIII	228,655	479,937	109.9	
Colorado	199,168	394,410	98.0	17
Montana	5,202	10,107	94.3	19
North Dakota	1,382	2,167	56.8	25
South Dakota	2,701	4,262	57.8	24
Utah	NA	47,255	NA	43
Wyoming	20,202	21,736	7.6	37
Region IX	3,932,289	8,832,684	124.6	
Arizona	261,139	513,125	96.5	18
California	3,653,237	8,119,853	122.3	12
Hawaii	17,913	58,098	224.3	3
Nevada	NA	141,608	NA	42
Region X	41,397	308,844	25.7	
Alaska	NA	27,412	17.1	34
Idaho	NA	30,594	11.9	35
Oregon	41,397	109,642	31.7	30
Washington	NA	141,196	26.2	32

NA = Data not available because of public disclosure restrictions.

Source: Adapted by the U.S. Small Business Administration, Office of Advocacy, from data published in: U.S. Department of Commerce, Bureau of the Census, <u>1987 Survey of Minority-Owned Business Enterprises</u>, vol. 2, <u>Hispanic</u>, MB87-2 (Washington, D.C.: U.S. Government Printing Office, 1991), Table 3.

Table 6.19 Number and Receipts of Businesses with Paid Employees Owned by Asian Americans, American Indians, and Other Minorities, by Industry, 1982 and 1987

	Number of Firms 1982	1987	Percent Change, 1982-1987	Receipts (Thousands of Dollars) 1982	1987	Percent Change, 1982-1987
Total, All Industries	43,323	96,457	122.6	8,900,741	25,104,127	182.0
Agriculture, Forestry, Fishing	622	2,131	242.6	71,096	241,576	238.8
Mining	35	27	-22.9	16,263	12,450	-23.4
Construction	1,137	4,165	266.3	222,482	960,220	331.6
Manufacturing	1,079	3,849	256.7	232,293	1,382,676	495.2
Transportation, Communications, Public Utilities	488	1,315	169.5	120,459	455,617	278.2
Wholesale Trade	800	2,715	239.4	618,906	3,363,504	443.5
Retail Trade	18,576	38,236	105.8	4,621,232	10,823,873	134.2
Finance, Insurance, Real Estate	1,259	2,629	108.8	242,170	472,737	95.2
Services	18,091	39,249	117.0	2,550,358	7,070,672	177.2
Unclassified	1,236	2,141	73.2	205,482	320,802	56.1

Source: Adapted by the U.S. Small Business Administration, Office of Advocacy, from data published in: U.S. Department of Commerce, Bureau of the Census, 1987 Survey of Minority-Owned Business Enterprises, vol. 3, Asian Americans, American Indians, and Other Minorities, MB87-3 (Washington, D.C.: U.S. Government Printing Office, 1991), Table 1.

Table 6.20 Number and Receipts of Black-Owned Businesses with Paid Employees, by Industry, 1982 and 1987

	Number of Firms		Percent Change,	Receipts (Thousands of Dollars)		Percent Change,
	1982	1987	1982-1987	1982	1987	1982-1987
Total, All Industries	37,841	70,815	87.1	5,704,545	14,130,420	147.7
Agriculture, Forestry, Fishing	750	1,662	121.6	71,735	144,276	101.1
Mining	41	48	17.1	NA	46,013	NA
Construction	4,073	11,081	172.1	491,017	1,668,952	239.9
Manufacturing	976	2,612	167.6	299,822	927,105	209.2
Transportation, Communications, Public Utilities	2,215	4,987	125.1	262,764	786,091	199.2
Wholesale Trade	554	1,256	126.7	380,709	1,169,608	207.2
Retail Trade	10,121	14,293	41.2	2,396,824	4,861,485	102.8
Finance, Insurance, Real Estate	1,014	2,514	147.9	147,321	464,389	215.2
Services	16,693	29,963	79.5	1,518,613	3,888,212	156.0
Unclassified	1,404	2,399	70.9	NA	174,289	NA

NA = Data not available because of public disclosure restrictions.

Source: Adapted by the U.S. Small Business Administration, Office of Advocacy, from data published in: U.S. Department of Commerce, Bureau of the Census, 1987 Survey of Minority-Owned Business Enterprises, vol. 1, Black, MB87-1 (Washington, D.C.: U.S. Government Printing Office, 1991), Table 1.

Table 6.21 Number and Receipts of Hispanic-Owned Businesses with Paid Employees, by Industry, 1982 and 1987

	Number of Firms 1982	Number of Firms 1987	Percent Change, 1982-1987	Receipts (Thousands of Dollars) 1982	Receipts (Thousands of Dollars) 1987	Percent Change, 1982-1987
Total, All Industries	39,272	82,908	111.1	7,435,664	17,729,432	138.4
Agriculture, Forestry, Fishing	752	3,331	343.0	NA	479,658	NA
Mining	55	72	30.9	20,368	18,498	-9.2
Construction	5,060	14,717	190.8	756,100	2,646,244	250.0
Manufacturing	1,305	3,760	188.1	412,021	1,308,124	217.5
Transportation, Communications, Public Utilities	1,340	3,989	197.7	259,048	725,484	180.1
Wholesale Trade	786	2,309	193.8	635,154	1,991,736	213.6
Retail Trade	13,169	20,348	54.5	3,154,389	6,095,890	93.3
Finance, Insurance, Real Estate	900	2,236	148.4	143,140	433,851	203.1
Services	14,521	29,750	104.9	1,769,648	3,774,117	113.3
Unclassified	1,384	2,396	73.1	NA	255,830	NA

NA = Data not available because of public disclosure restrictions.

Source: Adapted by the U.S. Small Business Administration, Office of Advocacy, from data published in: U.S. Department of Commerce, Bureau of the Census, <u>1987 Survey of Minority-Owned Business Enterprises</u>, vol. 2, <u>Hispanic</u>, MB87-2 (Washington, D.C.: U.S. Government Printing Office, 1991), Table 1.

7 Health Insurance Availability, Eligibility, and Coverage in Small and Large Firms

Introduction

Employee benefits, including health insurance, are a vital part of the package small firms offer to hire and retain productive workers. Small firms are at the center of the debate on how to provide health care for America's uninsured: about three fourths of uninsured private wage-and-salary workers are in small firms. Numerous reasons exist for the disparity in health care availability, eligibility, and coverage of workers in small and large firms. Characteristics of the firms, worker characteristics, and factors related to the health delivery system are among these reasons.

Health insurance availability refers to whether or not a firm offers its workers a health insurance plan. Eligibility refers to the ability of a firm's workers to participate in their employer's health insurance plan. Federal nondiscrimination rules under the Tax Reform Act of 1986 allow employers to establish different health benefits for various groups of employees. Employees may be excluded from health plans for varying reasons. Even if insurance is offered, and workers are eligible, individuals have a perfect right not to elect it and therefore not to be covered by their employer's health insurance plan.

Small firms tend to hire more younger and older workers, minimum wage workers, and minorities. These groups may be especially difficult or expensive to insure. Also, small businesses experience higher turnover rates and hire more part-time and seasonal workers, all increasing the paperwork and administrative costs of providing health care. The fact that insurance premiums are the same for both full- and part-time workers adds expense for small firms employing more part-time workers. In addition, many workers are covered by a spouse in another firm and do not elect coverage from their firm.

Data Sources

Data from the Current Population Survey (CPS) conducted by the Bureau of the Census provide an opportunity to analyze changes in health insurance plan availability, eligibility, and coverage over the 10-year period between 1979 and 1988. The CPS household survey is conducted on a monthly basis; the May surveys for the three years 1979, 1983, and 1988 permit an analysis of health insurance change over two different segments: 1979 to 1983, a period which began with an economic expansion and ended with a severe recession; and 1983 to 1988, a period of extended economic growth. These data by size of firm indicate the availability, eligibility, and coverage of wage-and-salary workers by an employer- or union-provided health plan. The May 1988 CPS employee benefits survey permitted analysis for the first time of health insurance in very small firms (those with less than 10 employees). The May 1988 CPS subdivides the smallest firm size category into two categories—firms with 1 to 9 employees and firms with 10 to 24 employees. The reasons workers are not covered by employer-provided health plans, when offered, and the relationship between worker characteristics and the availability and coverage of health plans can also be analyzed.

Highlights

• After remaining the same in 1979 and 1983, the proportion of workers covered by an employer- or union-sponsored health plan declined slightly between 1983 and 1988—from 67.2 percent to 66.8 percent.

• Health insurance coverage in small firms has slightly increased between 1979 and 1988 (36.9 percent in 1979 to 39.2 percent in 1988). Coverage of workers in large firms declined during this period (84.2 percent in 1979 to 79.3 percent in 1988).

• In 1988, only 39.2 percent of all workers in firms with fewer than 25 employees were covered, compared with over 79 percent of workers in firms with 100 or more employees. This fell from 43.2 percent between 1983 and 1988; decreases occurred across all firm sizes.

• The availability of employer-provided health insurance increases with firm size. Eighty-one percent of all workers were offered health insurance, 42 percent for firms with under 10 employees, compared to 94 percent for firms with over 100 employees.

• Workers in professional or managerial professions, and those in the mining; manufacturing; transportation, communications, and public utilities; or the finance, insurance, and real estate industries are more likely to be offered health insurance plans than workers in service occupations and those in the construction, retail trade, and service industries.

• Employees in the smallest firms—those with less than 10 employees—are significantly less likely to be offered or covered by an employer- or union-provided pension plan than workers in firms with from 10 to 24 employees. Only 12 percent of workers were offered plans and 8.5 percent were covered by a plan in the smallest firm size category, compared with 25.7 and 18.7 percent, respectively, in the next firm size category.

• The single most important reason for an employee's not having coverage in a firm that offers it is ineligibility. Men cite ineligibility as the main reason for not being covered and women most often cite the fact that they are covered through a spouse's employer.

• Workers are more likely to be ineligible for an employer-sponsored health plan if they are young, part-time, and have been with their employer for less than one year.

• Younger workers place less emphasis on health insurance than older workers, citing good health and the preference for higher wages as reasons for declining coverage.

• Workers in small firms with fewer than 500 employees are more likely than workers in large firms with 500 employees or more to have an individual health plan: 46.1 percent versus 37.5 percent.

• Employers have become less likely to pay all of employee health plan costs (46.7 percent in 1983 compared with 40.8 percent in 1988).

• Workers in small firms that sponsor health insurance are more likely to have their employer pay all of the health plan costs than workers in larger firms.

• Employers appear less likely to pay all costs for family health insurance plans (42 percent of workers in small firms say their employer pays all costs for family coverage compared to 36.1 percent for workers in large firms).

Chapter 7 Tables

Table 7.1 Group Health Insurance Coverage of Wage-and-Salary Workers by Employment Size of Firm, 1979, 1983, and 1988 (Percent)

| | All Firms | Employment Size of Firm | | | | | | |
		1-24	25-99	100-499	500+	Under 100	100+	Under 500
Included in Employer's Health Plan[*]								
1979	67.2	36.3	65.0	76.8	86.4	45.8	84.2	52.7
1983	67.2	38.7	65.4	75.2	85.4	47.2	82.9	53.8
1988	66.8	39.2	65.9	74.4	80.8	48.6	79.3	55.0

[*]Whether or not health insurance coverage is offered.

Source: U.S. Small Business Administration, Office of Advocacy. Tabulations by Sheldon Haber of unpublished data from the U.S. Department of Commerce, Bureau of the Census, <u>Current Population Survey</u>, May 1979, May 1983, and May 1988.

Table 7.2 Group Health Insurance Availability, Eligibility and Coverage of Wage-and-Salary Workers by Employment Size of Firm, 1988 (Percent)

	All Firms	Employment Size of Firm						
		1-24	25-99	100-499	500+	Under 100	100+	Under 500
Offered Health Insurance by Employer	81.0	51.2	83.1	91.9	94.5	62.4	93.9	69.7
Eligible for Employer's Health Plan	93.4	94.2	93.0	93.0	93.3	93.6	93.3	93.4
Included in Employer's Health Plan (Whether or not offered)	66.8	39.2	65.9	74.4	80.8	48.6	79.3	55.0
Included in Employer's Health Plan (If offered)	82.4	76.8	79.4	81.0	85.5	78.0	84.5	79.0

Source: U.S. Small Business Administration, Office of Advocacy, Tabulations by Sheldon Haber of unpublished data from the U.S. Department of Commerce, Bureau of the Census, <u>Current Population Survey</u>, May 1988.

Table 7.3 Group Health Insurance Availability, Eligibility and Coverage of Wage-and-Salary Workers in Very Small Firms by Employment Size of Firm, 1988 (Percent)

	All Firms	Employment Size of Firm					
		1-9	10-24	25-49	50-99	Under 100	100+
Offered Health Insurance by Employer	81.0	42.2	65.7	79.4	87.9	62.4	93.9
Eligible for Employer's Health Plan	93.4	95.0	93.3	92.7	93.3	93.6	93.3
Included in Employer's Health Plan (Whether or not offered)	66.8	32.8	50.2	61.4	71.8	48.6	79.3
Included in Employer's Health Plan (If offered)	82.4	77.2	76.4	77.4	81.7	78.0	84.5

Source: U.S. Small Business Administration, Office of Advocacy, Tabulations by Sheldon Haber of unpublished data from the U.S. Department of Commerce, Bureau of the Census, Current Population Survey, May 1988.

Table 7.4 Demographic Characteristics of Wage-and-Salary Workers Offered Employer-Provided Group Health Insurance by Size of Firm, 1988 (Percent)

	All Firms	Employment Size of Firm						
		1-24	25-99	100-499	500+	Under 100	100+	Under 500
All Workers	**81.0**	**51.2**	**83.1**	**91.9**	**94.5**	**62.4**	**93.9**	**69.7**
Age								
16-24	67.6	36.6	73.7	84.7	84.4	48.9	84.5	56.2
25-44	85.4	58.2	85.0	94.1	96.9	68.1	96.2	75.1
45-64	82.3	50.5	86.5	91.4	96.1	62.9	95.1	70.1
65+	65.9	43.8	86.1*	93.6*	84.1	54.2	87.9	60.5
Gender								
Men	83.2	54.9	85.4	92.8	95.9	65.9	95.2	72.4
Women	78.2	46.5	79.9	90.9	92.8	57.9	92.3	66.3
Marital Status								
Married, Spouse Present	84.0	54.8	87.3	92.7	96.5	66.2	95.6	73.0
Other	76.7	46.1	77.4	90.8	91.5	57.1	91.3	65.1
Race								
White	81.5	52.5	84.4	92.8	95.0	63.5	94.5	70.6
Black	78.1	30.3	74.2	87.2	91.0	47.2	90.2	61.0
Other	75.7	46.8	67.9	78.6*	93.6	56.6	90.5	61.4
Origin								
Hispanic	68.8	34.5	65.5	88.4	91.2	45.1	90.6	53.8
Non-Hispanic	81.9	52.5	84.4	92.1	94.7	63.8	94.1	70.9
Years of Education								
< 12	65.8	30.1	70.0	89.4	85.4	44.3	85.1	53.3
12-15	81.5	51.8	83.0	92.8	95.2	62.4	94.7	69.9
≥ 16	90.8	69.8	95.0	94.6	97.8	79.4	97.1	83.7
Region								
Northeast	84.2	56.9	85.8	94.2	95.5	67.9	95.1	75.2
Midwest	82.5	52.0	83.2	91.3	95.2	63.2	94.3	70.8
South	79.6	48.1	82.9	92.7	94.0	59.4	93.7	67.3
West	78.2	50.0	80.6	88.4	93.6	60.8	92.4	66.7
Area								
Metropolitan	82.3	53.9	83.2	91.9	94.5	64.5	93.9	71.4
Non-Metropolitan	75.7	41.7	82.9	92.0	94.7	54.6	94.0	63.3
Central City	80.2	51.9	79.2	90.8	93.3	62.1	92.7	69.2
Non-Central City	83.4	55.0	85.6	92.5	95.1	65.9	94.6	72.7

*Less than 50 observations.

Source: U.S. Small Business Administration, Office of Advocacy. Tabulations by Sheldon Haber of unpublished data from the U.S. Department of Commerce, Bureau of the Census, Current Population Survey, May 1988.

Table 7.5 Demographic Characteristics of Wage-and-Salary Workers Offered Employer-Provided Group Health Insurance in Very Small Firms by Employment Size of Firm, 1988 (Percent)

	All Firms	Employment Size of Firm					
		1-9	10-24	25-49	50-99	Under 100	100+
All Workers	81.0	42.2	65.7	79.4	87.9	62.4	93.9
Age							
16-24	67.6	29.7	47.7	66.6	83.5	48.9	84.5
25-44	85.4	48.4	72.9	82.3	88.7	68.1	96.2
45-64	82.3	43.3	64.3	84.4	89.0	62.9	95.1
65+	65.9	28.5*	81.9*	78.5*	93.3*	54.2	87.9
Gender							
Men	83.2	45.5	69.7	82.2	89.7	65.9	95.2
Women	78.2	38.3	60.7	75.6	85.4	57.9	92.3
Marital Status							
Married, Spouse Present	84.0	45.9	69.5	86.2	88.8	66.2	95.6
Other	76.7	37.2	60.6	70.2	86.7	57.1	91.3
Race							
White	81.5	43.4	67.7	81.5	88.3	63.5	94.7
Black	78.1	25.6*	37.4*	66.4*	82.5*	47.2	90.2
Other	75.7	36.3*	62.0*	59.9*	89.0*	56.7	90.5
Origin							
Hispanic	68.8	29.1*	41.4*	65.9	64.7*	45.1	90.6
NonHispanic	81.9	43.2	68.1	80.7	89.3	63.8	94.1
Years of Education							
< 12	65.8	25.6	38.1	64.0	79.3	44.3	85.1
12-15	81.5	41.6	68.8	79.3	87.6	62.4	94.7
≥ 16	90.8	62.6	80.2	94.1	96.2	79.4	97.1
Region							
Northeast	84.2	48.8	71.4	82.7	90.1	67.9	95.1
Midwest	82.5	41.3	68.0	79.3	88.0	63.2	94.3
South	79.6	39.8	63.2	80.5	85.9	59.4	93.7
West	78.2	41.1	62.5	74.8	88.5	60.8	92.4
Area							
Metropolitan	82.3	44.9	67.9	79.3	88.5	64.5	93.9
Non-Metropolitan	75.7	33.7	57.3	80.3	85.6	54.6	94.0
Central City	80.2	42.8	66.3	75.2	85.3	65.5	93.2
Non-Central City	83.4	46.1	68.8	81.9	90.3	67.0	94.9

*Less than 50 observations.

Source: U.S. Small Business Administration, Office of Advocacy. Tabulations by Sheldon Haber of unpublished data from the U.S. Department of Commerce, Bureau of the Census, <u>Current Population Survey</u>, May 1988.

Table 7.6 Economic Characteristics of Wage-and-Salary Workers Offered Employer-Provided Group Health Insurance by Employment Size of Firm, 1988 (Percent)

	All Firms	Employment Size of Firm						
		1-24	25-99	100-499	500+	Under 100	100+	Under 500
All Workers	81.0	51.2	83.1	91.9	94.5	62.4	93.9	69.7
Union Contract								
Covered	94.2	72.1	87.1	92.2	97.1	81.6	96.3	86.8
Not Covered	80.4	49.8	83.2	92.1	94.2	62.1	93.7	70.0
Tenure								
Less than 1 Year Employment	68.3	38.7	75.2	85.9	86.5	50.4	86.3	57.4
1 Year or More Employment	84.8	55.9	85.6	93.7	96.6	66.7	96.0	73.9
Major Occupation								
Managerial/Prof.	88.1	63.5	91.9	96.6	97.3	74.3	97.2	80.2
Technical, Sales	82.9	56.6	87.6	93.5	93.8	66.8	93.7	73.1
Services	57.8	24.8	58.0	80.0	80.7	35.8	80.5	44.6
Precision Production/ Craft	80.5	51.5	83.3	92.4	97.8	61.2	96.6	67.5
Operators, Fabricators and Laborers	83.1	45.5	80.6	89.4	96.0	60.4	94.4	69.8
Farmers, Forestry and Fishing	55.8	15.6*	78.9*	91.0*	100.0*	36.4	95.2	47.7
Major Industry								
Mining	96.4	90.0*	91.9*	95.1*	99.2	90.9	98.3	92.5
Construction	64.4	48.3	83.8	85.1	86.1	57.6	85.6	61.8
Manufacturing, Durable	94.7	71.6	89.7	95.8	99.3	81.5	98.7	86.9
Manufacturing, NonDurable	91.2	65.0	75.4	95.6	97.9	70.2	97.4	80.9
Transportation, Communications and Public Utilities	90.8	52.3	91.3	93.9	98.3	69.4	97.7	76.4
Wholesale Trade	87.4	71.1	90.0	93.6	98.4	79.5	96.8	82.6
Retail Trade	67.1	37.3	70.7	85.6	85.7	47.0	85.7	52.7
Finance, Insurance and Real Estate	90.0	67.7	93.3	94.7	96.7	77.1	96.3	82.3
Miscellaneous Services	75.8	49.6	83.8	90.7	91.8	60.2	91.5	67.7
Industry								
Goods Producing	87.8	57.9	84.2	93.8	98.3	68.7	97.3	76.5
Service Producing	77.7	49.0	82.6	90.8	92.3	60.0	91.9	66.9
Usual Hours Worked/Week								
1-20	51.3	25.1	61.0	79.4	75.5	32.9	76.4	39.7
21-34	63.3	31.0	73.4	74.4	84.9	42.0	82.5	48.6
35+	87.0	58.8	86.1	94.2	96.7	70.2	96.1	77.3
Wage Level								
Less than $5/hr.	57.1	25.7	65.1	79.5	79.9	37.4	79.8	44.9
5.01 to $10/hr.	84.6	58.9	86.4	93.8	96.4	69.2	95.7	76.0
10.01/hr. and over	93.9	72.2	92.7	95.9	98.2	82.3	97.8	87.0

*Less than 50 observations.

Source: U.S. Small Business Administration, Office of Advocacy. Tabulations by Sheldon Haber of unpublished data from the U.S. Department of Commerce, Bureau of the Census, <u>Current Population Survey</u>, May 1988.

Table 7.7 Economic Characteristics of Wage-and-Salary Workers Offered Employer-Provided Group Health Insurance in Very Small Firms by Employment Size of Firm, 1988 (Percent)

Major Industry	All Firms	Employment Size of Firm				Under 100	100+
		1-9	10-24	25-49	50-99		
All Workers	81.0	42.2	65.7	79.4	87.9	62.4	92.9
Union Contract							
Covered	94.2	61.1*	78.2	87.1	87.2	81.6	96.3
Not Covered	80.4	40.2	65.0	79.1	88.4	62.1	93.7
Tenure							
Less than 1 year employment	68.3	30.0	54.4	67.3	84.3	50.4	86.3
1 year or more employment	84.8	47.0	69.5	82.9	89.2	66.7	96.0
Major Occupation							
Managerial/Prof.	88.1	53.9	77.4	90.3	94.1	74.3	97.2
Technical, Sales	82.9	47.5	72.6	86.0	89.6	66.8	93.7
Services	57.8	20.4	31.6	46.8	72.9	35.8	80.5
Precision Production/ Craft	80.5	40.7	69.6	77.3	90.9	61.2	96.6
Operators, Fabricators and Laborers	83.1	37.1	58.8	77.5	84.5	60.4	94.4
Farmers, Forestry and Fishing	55.8	13.3	47.4	76.1	88.0	36.4	95.2
Major Industry							
Mining	96.4	95.5	78.0	89.4	100.0	90.9	98.3
Construction	64.4	41.4	61.0	84.5	82.9	57.6	85.6
Manufacturing, Durable	94.7	55.9	82.1	85.4	93.3	81.5	98.7
Manufacturing, NonDurable	91.2	54.8	75.1	68.2	84.8	70.2	97.4
Transportation, Communications and Public Utilities	90.8	35.2	74.7	92.5	89.5	69.4	97.7
Wholesale Trade	87.4	64.2	79.5	89.1	91.2	79.5	96.8
Retail Trade	67.1	31.2	47.4	63.7	82.6	47.0	85.7
Finance, Insurance and Real Estate	90.0	60.5	79.7	92.3	94.4	77.1	96.3
Miscellaneous Services	75.8	40.9	68.1	81.6	86.6	60.2	91.5
Industry							
Goods Producing	87.8	47.4	71.3	80.3	88.8	68.7	97.3
Service Producing	77.7	40.8	63.5	79.1	87.4	60.0	91.9
Usual Hours Worked/Week							
1-20	51.3	19.4	39.2	50.4	75.9*	32.9	76.4
21-34	63.3	27.0	39.4	73.4	73.3	42.0	58.0
35+	87.0	48.5	72.3	82.7	90.2	70.2	96.1
Wage Level							
Less than $5/hr.	57.1	20.7	35.7	59.3	74.0	37.4	79.8
5.01 to $10/hr.	84.6	48.4	73.9	82.6	91.4	69.2	95.7
10.01/hr. and over	93.9	62.0	83.7	92.2	93.3	82.3	97.8

*Less than 50 observations

Source: U.S. Small Business Administration, Office of Advocacy. Tabulations by Sheldon Haber of unpublished data from the U.S. Department of Commerce, Bureau of the Census, Current Population Survey, May 1988.

Table 7.8 Demographic Characteristics of Wage-and-Salary Workers Eligible for Employer-Provided Group Health Insurance by Employment Size of Firm, 1988 (Percent)

| | All Firms | Employment Size of Firm | | | | | | |
		1-24	25-99	100-499	500+	Under 100	Under 100+	Under 500
All Workers	93.4	94.2	93.0	93.0	93.3	93.6	93.3	93.4
Age								
16-24	79.4	85.7	82.3	80.2	76.1	84.0	77.1	82.8
25-44	95.8	96.1	95.1	94.3	96.2	95.6	95.8	95.2
45-64	96.7	95.8	96.3	97.7*	96.8	96.0	97.0	96.6
65+	88.0	90.6	88.5*	98.1*	78.1	89.8	85.9	91.8
Gender								
Men	94.8	95.5	94.7	94.3	94.8	95.1	94.7	94.9
Women	91.4	92.3	90.5	91.6	91.3	91.4	91.4	91.5
Marital Status								
Married, Spouse Present	96.1	96.0	96.0	95.2	96.4	96.0	96.2	95.8
Other	88.9	91.2	88.4	89.7	88.1	89.9	88.5	89.8
Race								
White	93.4	94.1	92.9	93.3	93.4	93.6	93.4	93.5
Black	92.4	96.5	96.7	92.0	91.5	96.6	91.6	94.4
Other	94.5	95.3	88.0	88.6*	97.9	91.2	96.2	90.5
Origin								
Hispanic	89.6	92.2	91.8	84.8	89.5	92.1	88.4	89.4
Non-Hispanic	93.6	94.3	93.0	93.5	93.5	93.7	93.5	93.7
Years of Education								
< 12	87.0	94.2	89.4	85.5	84.8	91.5	85.0	89.4
12-15	93.2	93.1	92.1	93.7	93.3	92.7	93.4	93.0
≥ 16	97.2	97.1	97.5	95.7	97.5	97.3	97.2	96.8
Region								
Northeast	94.1	95.7	91.8	94.4	94.2	93.8	94.3	94.0
Midwest	93.4	92.5	93.4	91.8	94.1	92.9	93.6	92.6
South	93.2	95.1	93.2	92.2	92.8	94.3	92.6	93.6
West	92.9	93.1	93.3	94.4	92.3	93.2	92.7	93.6
Area								
Metropolitan	93.6	94.5	93.0	93.4	93.5	93.8	93.5	93.6
Non-Metropolitan	92.4	93.1	93.0	91.5	92.2	93.0	92.0	92.5
Central City	92.0	94.0	91.3	91.4	91.8	92.7	91.7	92.3
Non Central City	94.4	94.7	93.9	94.5	94.4	94.3	94.5	94.4

*Less than 50 observations.

Source: U.S. Small Business Administration, Office of Advocacy. Tabulations by Sheldon Haber of unpublished data from the U.S. Department of Commerce, Bureau of the Census, Current Population Survey, May 1988.

Table 7.9 Demographic Characteristics of Wage-and-Salary Workers Eligible for Employer-Provided Group Health Insurance in Very Small Firms by Employment Size of Firm, 1988 (Percent)

	All Firms	Employment Size of Firm					
		1-9	10-24	25-49	50-99	Under 100	100+
All Workers	93.4	95.0	93.3	92.7	93.3	93.6	93.3
Age							
16-24	79.4	88.2	83.1	79.0	85.9	84.0	77.1
25-44	95.8	96.8	95.4	96.0	93.9	95.6	95.8
45-64	96.7	96.4	95.0	95.8	96.8	96.0	97.0
65+	88.0	85.9*	94.6*	76.2*	98.5*	89.5	85.9
Gender							
Men	94.8	96.2	94.8	94.0	95.5	95.1	94.7
Women	91.4	93.4	91.1	90.7	90.3	91.4	91.4
Marital Status							
Married, Spouse Present	96.1	96.4	95.7	95.8	96.2	96.0	96.2
Other	88.9	92.8	89.7	87.4	89.4	89.9	88.5
Race							
White	93.4	94.9*	93.2	92.4*	93.5	93.6	93.4
Black	92.4	98.5*	94.5*	100.0*	93.9*	96.6	91.6
Other	94.5	94.6*	96.0*	89.4*	85.4*	91.2	96.2
Origin							
Hispanic	89.6	94.0*	90.7*	87.2*	100.0*	92.1	88.4
NonHispanic	93.6	95.1	93.5	93.1	93.0	93.7	93.5
Years of Education							
< 12	87.0	94.8	93.4	89.2	89.5	91.5	85.0
12-15	93.2	94.3	91.9	91.7	92.6	92.7	93.4
≥ 16	97.2	97.0	97.3	97.1	97.9	97.3	97.2
Region							
Northeast	94.1	95.8	95.7	89.4	94.8	93.8	94.3
Midwest	93.4	93.9	91.2	93.2	93.7	92.9	93.6
South	93.2	94.4	96.0	93.2	93.3	94.3	92.6
West	92.9	96.6	89.9	95.1	91.3	93.2	92.7
Area							
Metropolitan	93.6	95.4	93.5	92.7	93.3	93.8	93.5
Non-Metropolitan	92.4	93.3	92.8	92.8	93.2	93.0	92.0
Central City	92.0	95.0	93.0	89.8	93.4	92.7	91.7
Non-Central City	94.4	95.7	93.8	94.4	93.3	94.3	94.5

*Less than 50 observations.

Source: U.S. Small Business Administration, Office of Advocacy. Tabulations by Sheldon Haber of unpublished data from the U.S. Department of Commerce, Bureau of the Census, <u>Current Population Survey</u>, May 1988.

Table 7.10 Economic Characteristics of Wage-and-Salary Workers Eligible for Employer-Provided Group Health Insurance by Employment Size of Firm, 1988 (Percent)

	All Firms	Employment Size of Firm						
		1-24	25-99	100-499	500+	Under 100	100+	Under 500
All Workers	93.4	94.2	93.0	93.0	93.3	93.6	93.3	93.4
Union Contract								
Covered	96.6	97.6	96.5	98.5	97.6	96.8	97.7	97.7
Not Covered	92.5	93.5	92.5	92.3	92.4	93.0	92.3	92.8
Tenure								
Less than 1 Year Employment	77.4	85.4	79.9	77.1	73.4	82.7	74.3	81.1
1 Year or More Employment	96.7	96.4	96.5	96.5	96.9	96.5	96.8	96.5
Major Occupation								
Managerial/Prof.	97.4	97.4	97.5	96.6	97.7	97.4	97.5	97.2
Technical, Sales	91.4	93.1	89.8	91.4	91.2	91.7	91.2	91.6
Services	82.0	84.8	86.4	79.5	80.5	85.7	80.2	83.5
Precision Production/Craft	97.5	94.7	97.7	97.7	98.5	95.9	98.3	96.4
Operators, Fabricators and Laborers	93.1	95.0	92.1	94.4	92.7	93.4	93.1	93.8
Farmers, Forestry and Fishing	74.7	78.9*	72.9*	71.8*	77.4*	74.6*	74.7*	73.6
Major Industry								
Mining	98.8	100.0*	90.4*	100.0*	99.8	95.7*	99.8	97.4
Construction	95.7	93.3	97.2	98.2	97.0	94.8	97.7	95.5
Manufacturing, Durable	97.0	94.9	94.5	97.0	97.7	94.7	97.6	95.7
Manufacturing, NonDurable	96.3	93.3	95.1	95.6	97.0	94.7	97.6	95.7
Transportation, Communications and Public Utilities	96.4	96.2	95.4	95.0	96.8	95.7	96.5	95.4
Wholesale Trade	97.2	98.6	94.7	97.3	98.0	96.6	97.8	96.8
Retail Trade	85.6	94.9	91.5	86.8	80.6	93.4	81.6	91.3
Finance, Insurance and Real Estate	94.4	92.6	95.3	96.0	94.2	93.8	94.6	94.6
Miscellaneous Services	91.4	93.2	89.4	88.7	92.5	91.6	91.3	90.7
Industry								
Goods Producing	96.6	94.0	95.3	96.8	97.5	94.6	97.3	95.5
Service Producing	91.6	94.3	91.9	90.8	90.6	93.2	90.7	92.5
Usual Hours Worked/Week								
1-20	59.8	78.3	66.7*	51.0*	52.0	73.5	51.8	67.0
21-34	73.6	85.0	73.2	76.2	69.5	79.6	70.8	78.5
35+	96.4	95.7	95.5	96.2*	96.9	95.6	96.7	95.8
Wage Level								
Less than $5/hr.	74.7	80.0	80.0	74.3	71.3	79.9	72.0	78.1
5.01 to $10/hr.	94.2	95.5	93.2	94.8	93.7	94.4	94.0	94.5
10.01/hr. and over	98.7	97.7	98.8	98.4	98.8	98.3	98.7	98.4

*Less than 50 observations.

Source: U.S. Small Business Administration, Office of Advocacy. Tabulations by Sheldon Haber of unpublished data from the U.S. Department of Commerce, Bureau of the Census, Current Population Survey, May 1988.

Table 7.11 Economic Characteristics of Wage-and-Salary Workers Eligible for Employer-Provided Group Health Insurance in Very Small Firms by Employment Size of Firm, 1988 (Percent)

Major Industry	All Firms	Employment Size of Firm					
		1-9	10-24	25-49	50-99	Under 100	100+
All Workers	93.4	95.0	93.3	92.7	93.3	93.6	93.3
Union Contract							
Covered	97.6	96.0*	98.3*	94.1	99.4	96.8	97.7
Not Covered	92.5	93.9	93.0	92.3	92.7	93.0	92.3
Tenure							
Less than 1 year employment	77.4	89.9	81.0	79.5	80.2	82.7	74.3
1 year or more employment	96.7	96.4	96.4	96.0	97.3	96.5	96.8
Major Occupation							
Managerial/Prof.	97.4	97.4	97.4	97.9	96.9	97.4	97.5
Technical, Sales	91.4	93.6	92.7	87.3	92.8	91.7	91.2
Services	82.0	86.8	82.7	91.9	81.8	85.7	80.2
Precision Production/ Craft	97.5	96.0	93.4	96.2	99.2	95.9	98.3
Operators, Fabricators and Laborers	93.1	98.6	91.4	92.7	91.5	93.4	93.1
Farmers, Forestry and Fishing	74.7	77.3*	85.0*	78.3*	58.3*	74.6	74.7
Major Industry							
Mining	98.8	100.0*	100.0*	87.1*	100.0*	95.7	99.8
Construction	95.7	95.9	89.8	97.2	97.2	94.8	97.7
Manufacturing, Durable	97.0	98.3	93.3	94.5	94.6	94.7	97.6
Manufacturing, NonDurable	96.3	95.5*	91.8	94.8	95.4	94.3	96.7
Transportation, Communications and Public Utilities	96.4	96.4*	96.0	93.4	98.3	95.7	96.5
Wholesale Trade	97.2	97.3	99.8	97.7	90.8	96.6	97.8
Retail Trade	85.6	95.3	94.5	89.8	93.7	93.4	81.6
Finance, Insurance and Real Estate	94.4	93.1	91.9	93.5	97.2	93.8	94.6
Miscellaneous Services	91.4	93.8	92.5	89.7	89.1	91.6	91.3
Industry							
Goods Producing	96.6	96.5	91.7	95.2	95.4	94.6	97.3
Service Producing	91.6	94.5	94.1	91.6	92.2	93.2	90.7
Usual Hours Worked/Week							
1-20	59.8	80.6	75.5	68.5*	65.2*	73.5	51.8
21-34	73.6	85.0	85.0	74.1	71.8*	79.6	70.8
35+	96.4	96.2	95.2	95.0	96.2	95.6	96.7
Wage Level							
Less than $5/hr.	74.7	82.3	77.3	78.6	81.1	79.9	72.0
5.01 to $10/hr.	94.2	95.7	95.4	93.2	93.2	94.4	94.0
10.01/hr. and over	98.7	98.2	97.3	98.5	99.2	98.3	98.7

*Less than 50 observations.

Source: U.S. Small Business Administration, Office of Advocacy. Tabulations by Sheldon Haber of unpublished data from the U.S. Department of Commerce, Bureau of the Census, Current Population Survey, May 1988.

Table 7.12 Demographic Characteristics of Wage-and-Salary Workers Covered by Employer-Provided Group Health Insurance, if Offered, by Employment Size of Firm, 1988 (Percent)

	All Firms	Employment Size of Firm						
		1-24	25-99	100-499	500+	Under 100	100+	Under 500
All Workers	82.4	76.8	79.4	81.0	85.5	78.0	84.5	79.0
Age								
16-24	63.4	63.3	63.3	68.8	61.8	63.3	63.4	65.0
25-44	85.6	79.3	82.3	82.5	89.2	80.7	87.7	81.3
45-64	87.8	80.5	85.1	86.3	91.0	82.7	90.0	83.9
65+	69.2	71.7	73.2*	64.2*	66.5*	72.3	65.6	70.3
Gender								
Men	88.1	84.3	87.3	86.3	90.0	85.7	89.2	85.9
Women	74.8	66.0	67.8	74.5	79.4	66.9	78.2	69.5
Marital Status								
Married, Spouse Present	83.9	75.8	79.9	80.6	88.5	77.7	86.7	78.6
Other	80.0	78.6	78.5	81.6	80.5	78.5	80.8	79.6
Race								
White	82.3	76.1	79.2	81.5	85.6	77.5	84.7	78.8
Black	83.6	96.5	89.9	76.6	83.1	92.5	81.8	84.6
Other	82.6	77.3*	65.9*	79.3*	90.4	70.9	88.4	73.2
Origin								
Hispanic	82.1	76.5	78.5	82.2	84.8	77.5	84.2	79.0
Non-Hispanic	82.5	76.9	79.4	80.9	85.5	78.0	84.5	79.0
Years of Education								
< 12	72.5	74.2	73.3	68.1	73.3	73.7	72.0	71.7
12-15	81.7	74.0	78.1	81.6	85.2	75.9	84.4	77.7
≥ 16	89.5	85.4	86.6	87.2	92.3	86.0	91.2	86.4
Region								
Northeast	83.8	79.9	80.8	83.0	86.3	80.3	85.5	81.2
Midwest	82.2	73.8	78.6	80.0	86.0	76.1	84.7	77.4
South	81.8	78.2	78.2	79.1	84.7	78.2	83.5	78.5
West	82.3	74.8	80.5	83.3	85.3	77.5	84.8	79.1
Area								
Metropolitan	82.8	77.0	79.9	82.1	85.6	78.4	84.9	79.6
Non-Metropolitan	80.6	76.0	77.0	76.6	84.7	76.5	82.6	76.5
Central City	81.0	74.7	78.6	80.8	83.7	76.6	83.1	78.0
Non Central City	83.8	78.3	80.6	82.7	86.6	79.3	85.8	80.4

*Less than 50 observations.

Source: U.S. Small Business Administration, Office of Advocacy. Tabulations by Sheldon Haber of unpublished data from the U.S. Department of Commerce, Bureau of the Census, Current Population Survey, May 1988.

Table 7.13 Demographic Characteristics of Wage-and-Salary Workers Covered by Employer-Provided Group Health Insurance, if Offered, in Very Small Firms by Employment Size of Firm, 1988 (Percent)

	All Firms	Employment Size of Firm					
		1-9	10-24	25-49	50-99	Under 100	100+
All Workers	82.4	77.2	76.4	77.4	81.7	78.0	84.5
Age							
16-24	63.4	65.8	60.8	57.7	69.4	63.3	63.4
25-44	85.6	79.0	79.6	81.3	83.5	80.7	87.7
45-64	87.8	81.6	79.1	84.3	86.0	82.7	90.0
65+	69.2	63.9˙	78.4˙	52.1˙	90.4˙	72.3	63.6
Gender							
Men	88.1	85.2	83.3	85.8	89.2	85.7	89.2
Women	74.8	65.9	66.1	64.8	71.3	66.9	78.2
Marital Status							
Married, Spouse Present	83.9	76.3	75.2	78.4	81.9	77.7	86.7
Other	80.0	78.8	78.4	75.6	81.5	78.5	80.8
Race							
White	82.3	76.5	75.8	77.2	81.5	77.5	84.2
Black	83.6	98.5˙	94.5˙	90.0˙	89.8˙	92.5	81.8
Other	82.6	77.6˙	77.1˙	65.0˙	67.4˙	70.9	88.4
Origin							
Hispanic	82.1	65.4˙	86.3˙	75.8˙	83.6˙	77.5	84.2
NonHispanic	82.5	77.8	75.8	77.5	81.6	78.0	84.5
Years of Education							
< 12	72.5	73.7	74.8	71.3	75.7	73.7	72.0
12-15	81.7	73.7	74.4	75.7	80.7	75.9	84.4
≥ 16	89.5	87.5	83.0	85.1	88.7	86.0	91.2
Region							
Northeast	83.8	78.9	81.1	79.8	82.0	80.3	85.5
Midwest	82.2	75.9	71.9	74.4	83.2	76.1	84.7
South	81.8	77.7	78.8	75.2	81.7	78.2	83.5
West	82.3	75.8	73.9	81.1	79.7	77.5	84.8
Area							
Metropolitan	82.8	77.1	76.9	78.3	81.8	78.4	84.9
Non-Metropolitan	80.6	77.6	74.1	72.8	81.2	76.5	82.6
Central City	81.0	72.9	76.6	76.4	81.7	76.6	83.1
Non-Central City	83.8	79.4	77.1	79.5	81.9	79.3	85.8

*Less than 50 observations.

Source: U.S. Small Business Administration, Office of Advocacy. Tabulations by Sheldon Haber of unpublished data from the U.S. Department of Commerce, Bureau of the Census, <u>Current Population Survey</u>, May 1988.

Table 7.14 Economic Characteristics of Wage-and-Salary Workers Covered by Employer-Provided Group Health Insurance, if Offered, by Employment Size of Firm, 1988 (Percent)

	All Firms	Employment Size of Firm						
		1-24	25-99	100-499	500+	Under 100	100+	Under 500
All Workers	82.4	76.8	79.4	81.0	85.5	78.0	84.5	79.0
Union Contract								
Covered	94.3	89.3*	92.0*	93.6	95.0	91.1	94.8	92.4
Not Covered	80.0	73.2	77.9	79.2	83.1	75.5	82.2	76.7
Tenure								
Less than 1 Year Employment	59.4	58.5	59.2	62.8	58.7	58.8	59.7	60.0
1 Year or More Employment	87.4	81.7	84.8	84.7	90.4	83.2	89.2	83.7
Major Occupation								
Managerial/Prof.	89.0	84.7	85.4	86.4	92.5	85.0	91.0	85.5
Technical, Sales	77.8	71.5	75.0	79.1	80.4	73.0	80.1	74.8
Services	59.1	54.6	62.1	54.2	61.1	58.7	59.4	57.1
Precision Production/Craft	91.1	82.4	90.5	88.1	95.4	85.8	93.9	86.4
Operators, Fabricators and Laborers	85.0	80.2	78.2	84.8	87.5	79.0	86.9	81.4
Farmers, Forestry and Fishing	64.0	47.5*	67.4*	54.3*	77.4*	61.7*	65.9*	58.9*
Major Industry								
Mining	95.8	93.8*	74.3*	97.7*	99.8	85.0*	99.3	89.9*
Construction	84.5	76.9	90.4	88.4	90.8	82.1	89.5	83.4
Manufacturing, Durable	93.7	88.0	86.7	92.9	95.8	87.2	95.3	89.6
Manufacturing, NonDurable	90.4	83.6	82.8	83.8	94.2	83.2	92.0	83.5
Transportation, Communications and Public Utilities	91.3	81.8	84.3	88.2	93.9	83.3	93.2	85.0
Wholesale Trade	87.6	83.6	84.8	90.6	91.1	84.2	90.9	85.8
Retail Trade	66.1	74.6	68.4	67.2	62.3	71.8	63.1	70.7
Finance, Insurance and Real Estate	83.4	72.3	84.3	86.2	85.5	77.6	85.7	80.5
Miscellaneous Services	75.6	72.7	73.3	71.8	79.9	73.0	77.3	72.6
Industry								
Goods Producing	91.4	82.1	86.5	88.9	95.2	84.3	93.8	86.1
Service Producing	77.5	74.8	76.0	76.3	79.3	75.3	78.6	75.6
Usual Hours Worked/Week								
1-20	25.2	33.4	31.7*	17.5*	21.8	32.7	20.8	28.3
21-34	44.7	48.5	39.7*	48.4	43.8	44.5	44.8	45.7
35+	87.9	79.5	84.3	86.4	91.4	82.0	90.3	83.6
Wage Level								
Less than $5/hr.	50.6	50.2	52.9	54.6	48.5	51.6	50.0	52.6
5.01 to $10/hr.	81.7	74.7	78.8	81.8	85.3	76.6	84.4	78.4
10.01/hr. and over	93.5	86.0	92.7	90.9	95.4	89.7	94.6	90.2

*Less than 50 observations.

Source: U.S. Small Business Administration, Office of Advocacy. Tabulations by Sheldon Haber of unpublished data from the U.S. Department of Commerce, Bureau of the Census, <u>Current Population Survey</u>, May 1988.

Table 7.15 Economic Characteristics of Wage-and-Salary Workers Covered by Employer-Provided Group Health Insurance, if Offered, in Very Small Firms by Employment Size of Firm, 1988 (Percent)

	All Firms	Employment Size of Firm					
		1-9	10-24	25-49	50-99	Under 100	100+
All Workers	82.4	77.2	76.4	77.4	81.7	78.0	84.5
Union Contract							
Covered	94.3	72.9*	96.4*	86.9	98.5	91.1	94.8
Not Covered	80.0	72.6	73.7	75.8	80.3	75.5	82.2
Tenure							
Less than 1 year employment	59.4	62.1	54.9	55.4	62.6	58.8	59.7
1 year or more employment	87.4	81.4	82.1	82.5	87.6	83.2	89.2
Major Occupation							
Managerial/Prof.	89.0	87.7	81.7	84.0	87.3	85.0	91.0
Technical, Sales	77.8	71.6	71.4	71.6	79.1	73.0	80.1
Services	59.1	52.6*	56.7	62.9	61.5	58.7	59.4
Precision Production/ Craft	91.1	80.8	84.0	88.3	92.9	85.8	93.9
Operators, Fabricators and Laborers	85.0	81.8	78.5	75.5	81.2	79.0	86.9
Farmers, Forestry and Fishing	64.0	37.8*	85.0*	70.7*	58.3*	61.7*	65.9*
Major Industry							
Mining	95.8	91.5*	100.0*	65.2*	100.0*	85.0	99.3
Construction	84.5	80.6	72.2	88.5	93.6	82.1	89.5
Manufacturing, Durable	93.7	92.5	85.9	84.3	88.6	87.2	95.3
Manufacturing, NonDurable	90.4	82.4*	84.5	78.3	87.4	83.2	92.0
Transportation, Communications and Public Utilities	91.3	77.7*	84.4	79.7	91.5*	83.3	93.2
Wholesale Trade	87.6	77.2	89.8	86.1	83.1	84.2	90.9
Retail Trade	66.1	76.8	72.0	69.9	66.3	71.8	63.1
Finance, Insurance and Real Estate	83.4	72.7	71.7	79.6	88.9	77.6	85.7
Miscellaneous Services	75.6	74.0	71.1	71.3	75.8	73.0	77.3
Industry							
Goods Producing	91.4	83.9	80.6	83.6	89.6	84.3	93.8
Service Producing	77.5	75.0	74.6	74.7	77.6	75.3	78.6
Usual Hours Worked/Week							
1-20	25.2	38.0*	27.9*	22.8*	40.1*	32.7	20.8
21-34	44.7	49.9*	46.5*	42.2*	35.8*	44.5	44.8
35+	87.9	78.5	80.5	82.1	86.9	82.0	90.3
Wage Level							
Less than $5/hr.	50.6	52.0	48.1	47.9	59.1	51.6	50.0
5.01 to $10/hr.	81.7	73.6	75.8	76.1	81.8	76.6	84.4
10.01/hr. and over	93.5	84.7	87.1	92.7	92.7	89.7	94.6

*Less than 50 observations
Source: U.S. Small Business Administration, Office of Advocacy. Tabulations by Sheldon Haber of unpublished data from the U.S. Department of Commerce, Bureau of the Census, <u>Current Population Survey</u>, May 1988.

Table 7.16 Reasons Wage-and-Salary Workers Are Not Covered by a Health Insurance Plan If Offered by Employer, by Employment Size of Firm, 1988 (Percent)

| | | Employment Size of Firm | | | | | | |
Reason	All Firms	1-24	25-99	100-499	500+	Under 100	100+	Under 500
Ineligible	39.3	26.0	35.4	38.6	47.8	30.1	45.3	32.6
Covered Through Spouse's Employer	32.0	39.5	36.4	31.7	26.6	38.1	28.0	36.2
Have Other Health Insurance	19.5	21.6	17.2	21.3	18.7	19.6	19.4	20.1
Costs Too Much	8.1	8.4*	10.6*	10.7*	6.0	9.4	7.3	9.8
Don't Need Any Health Insurance	1.3	1.0*	1.3*	0.7*	1.8*	1.1*	1.5*	1.0*
Other Reason	6.4	9.6*	6.2*	3.5*	6.0	8.1	5.4	6.8

*Less than 50 observations.

Source: U.S. Small Business Administration, Office of Advocacy. Tabulations by Sheldon Haber of unpublished data from the U.S. Department of Commerce, Bureau of the Census, Current Population Survey, May 1988.

Table 7.17 Reasons Wage-and-Salary Workers Are Not covered by a Health Insurance Plan If Offered by Employer, in Very Small Firms by Employment Size of Firm, 1988 (Percent)

Reason	All Firms	Employment Size of Firm					
		1-9	10-24	25-49	50-99	Under 100	100+
Ineligible	39.3	22.9	29.1	33.8	37.6	30.1	45.3
Covered Through Spouse's Employer	32.0	39.5	39.0	37.7	34.5	38.1	28.0
Have Other Health Insurance	19.5	20.3	22.9	17.1˙	17.2˙	19.6	19.4
Costs Too Much	8.1	9.4˙	7.3˙	11.1˙	9.9˙	9.4	7.3
Don't Need Any Health Insurance	1.3	0.9˙	1.0˙	1.3˙	1.4˙	1.1˙	1.5˙
Other Reason	6.4	13.0˙	6.2˙	7.1˙	4.9˙	8.1	5.4

˙Less than 50 observations.

Source: U.S. Small Business Administration, Office of Advocacy. Tabulations by Sheldon Haber of unpublished data from the U.S. Department of Commerce, Bureau of the Census, Current Population Survey, May 1988.

Table 7.18 Type of Employer-Sponsored Health Plan Provided Wage-and-Salary Workers by Employment Size of Firm, 1988 (Percent)

Plan Type	All Firms	Employment Size of Firm						
		1-24	25-99	100-499	500+	Under 100	100+	Under 500
Individual Plan	41.4	45.2	47.4	45.8	37.5	46.2	39.2	46.1
Family Plan	58.6	54.8	52.6	54.2	62.5	53.8	60.8	53.9
Total	100.0	100.0	100.0	100.0	100.0	100.0	100.0	100.0

Source: U.S. Small Business Administration, Office of Advocacy. Tabulations by Sheldon Haber of unpublished data from the U.S. Department of Commerce, Bureau of the Census, Current Population Survey, May 1988.

Table 7.19 Type of Employer-Sponsored Health Plan Provided Wage-and-Salary Workers in Very Small Firms by Employment Size of Firm, 1988 (Percent)

Plan Type	All Firms	Employment Size of Firm					
		1-9	10-24	25-49	50-99	Under 100	100+
Individual Plan	41.4	43.5	47.1	46.4	48.6	46.2	39.2
Family Plan	58.6	56.5	52.9	53.6	51.4	53.8	60.8
Total	100.0	100.0	100.0	100.0	100.0	100.0	100.0

Source: U.S. Small Business Administration, Office of Advocacy, Tabulations by Sheldon Haber of unpublished data from the U.S. Department of Commerce, Bureau of the Census, Current Population Survey, May 1988.

Table 7.20 Employer Payments for Health Plans of Wage-and-Salary Workers by Employment Size of Firm, 1988 (Percent)

Employer Contribution	All Firms	Employment Size of Firm						
		1-24	25-99	100-499	500+	Under 100	100+	Under 500
All Health Plans								
Pays All	40.8	52.0	43.8	38.6	37.3	48.3	37.6	45.1
Pays Part	54.6	41.4	51.1	56.0	59.1	45.8	58.4	49.2
Pays None	4.6	6.6	5.1	5.4	3.6	5.9	4.0	5.7
Total	100.0	100.0	100.0	100.0	100.0	100.0	100.0	100.0
Individual Plan								
Pays All	44.0	51.8	46.6	47.5	39.3	49.4	41.3	48.8
Pays Part	51.0	42.1	46.9	47.3	56.7	44.3	54.4	45.3
Pays None	5.0	6.1	6.5*	5.2*	4.0	6.3	4.3	5.9
Total	100.0	100.0	100.0	100.0	100.0	100.0	100.0	100.0
Family Plan								
Pays All	38.5	52.3	41.3	31.1	36.1	47.3	35.2	42.0
Pays Part	57.2	40.8	54.8	63.4	60.5	47.1	61.0	52.4
Pays None	4.3	6.9	3.9*	5.5*	3.4	5.6	3.8	5.6
Total	100.0	100.0	100.0	100.0	100.0	100.0	100.0	100.0

*Less than 50 observations.

Source: U.S. Small Business Administration, Office of Advocacy, Tabulations by Sheldon Haber of unpublished data from the U.S. Department of Commerce, Bureau of the Census, Current Population Survey, May 1988.

Table 7.21 Employer Payments for Health Plans of Wage-and-Salary Workers in Very Small Firms by Employment Size of Firm, 1988 (Percent)

Employer Contribution	All Firms	Employment Size of Firm					
		1-9	10-24	25-49	50-99	Under 100	100+
All Health Plans							
Pays All	40.8	55.0	48.9	45.9	41.3	48.3	37.6
Pays Part	54.6	37.7	45.4	49.1	53.4	45.8	58.4
Pays None	4.6	7.3	5.7˙	5.0˙	5.3˙	5.9	4.0
Total	100.0	100.0	100.0	100.0	100.0	100.0	100.0
Individual Plan							
Pays All	44.0	53.2	50.4	49.9	42.9	49.4	41.3
Pays Part	51.0	38.7	45.5	43.6	50.6	44.3	54.4
Pays None	5.0	8.1˙	4.1˙	6.5˙	6.5˙	6.3	4.3
Total	100.0	100.0	100.0	100.0	100.0	100.0	100.0
Family Plan							
Pays All	38.5	56.3	47.6	42.4	39.8	47.3	35.2
Pays Part	57.2	36.9	45.4	53.9	56.0	47.1	61.0
Pays None	4.3	6.8˙	7.0˙	3.7˙	4.2˙	5.6	3.8
Total	100.0	100.0	100.0	100.0	100.0	100.0	100.0

˙Less than 50 observations.

Source: U.S. Small Business Administration, Office of Advocacy, Tabulations by Sheldon Haber of unpublished data from the U.S. Department of Commerce, Bureau of the Census, Current Population Survey, May 1988.

8 Pension Availability and Coverage in Small and Large Firms

Introduction

Employee benefits, including retirement benefits, are a vital part of the package small firms offer to hire and retain productive workers. Dramatic changes are taking place which will affect the prospects of small businesses offering retirement benefits between now and the year 2000. The average age of the work force will increase and growth in the labor force will continue to slow. Changes in the work force will challenge the continued effectiveness of the current retirement system, built on assumptions of long service to one employer. The issue of benefit "portability," or transferability, will become especially important.

This chapter presents data on changes in pension availability and coverage for workers in small and large firms over a 10-year period between 1979 and 1988. In addition, this chapter presents data for two segments of the 10-year period: 1979–1983, a period of two recessions; and 1983–1988, a period of the longest peacetime expansion in U.S. history.

Data Sources

Data from the Current Population Survey (CPS) conducted by the Bureau of the Census provide an opportunity to analyze changes in pension availability and coverage over the 10-year period between 1979 and 1988. The CPS household survey is conducted on a monthly basis; the May surveys for the three years 1979, 1983, and 1988 permit an analysis of pension change over two different segments—1979-1983, a period which began with an economic expansion and ended with a severe recession, and 1983-1988, a period of extended economic growth. These data by size of firm indicate the availability and coverage of wage-and-salary workers by an employer-provided pension, profit-sharing, or stock plan. The May 1988 CPS employee benefits survey permitted analysis for the first time of pensions in very small firms (that is, those with less than 10 employees). The May 1988 CPS subdivides the smallest firm size category into two categories: firms with 1 to 9 employees and firms with 10 to 24 employees. The reasons workers are not covered by employer-provided retirement plans, when offered, and the relationship between worker characteristics and the availability and coverage of retirement plans can also be analyzed.

Highlights

- After declining between 1979 and 1983 from 60.0 percent to 56.4 percent, the proportion of workers employed by firms offering an employer- or union-sponsored pension plan rebounded slightly between 1983 and 1988—from 56.4 percent to 57.6 percent.
- Actual retirement plan coverage declined from 48.3 to 45.6 percent between 1979 and 1983, and continued to decline to 43.2 percent between 1983 and 1988; decreases occurred across all firm sizes.
- Between 1983 and 1988, coverage in small firms (those with fewer than 500 workers) declined proportionately less, from 26.2 to 24.9 percent, compared with a drop from 72.1 to 65.0 percent in large firms.
- Retirement plan coverage increases with firm size. In 1988, pension coverage ranged from 13 percent of workers in small firms (with fewer than 25 employees) to 65 percent in large firms (with 500 or more employees).
- Employees in the smallest firms (those with less than 10 employees) are significantly less likely to be offered or covered by an employer- or union-provided pension plan than workers in firms with from 10 to 24 employees. Only 12 percent of workers were offered plans and 8.5 percent were covered by a plan in the smallest firm size category, compared with 25.7 and 18.7 percent, respectively, in the next firm size category.
- Workers more likely to be employed in small firms—and therefore more likely to be working for firms which do not offer pension plans—include younger and older workers, minorities (particularly Hispanics), less educated workers (especially with less than 12 years of schooling), and single workers.
- The most common reason given by employees in 1988 for their ineligibility for pension coverage was that they were new employees. Almost half—over 44 percent—of all ineligible workers cite this as the reason.
- Workers in small firms that offered retirement plans were more likely to be covered by profit-sharing or stock plans than workers in large firms—69 versus 61 percent.
- Workers in small firms (those with less than 500 employees) were almost twice as likely as workers in large firms to have a de-

fined contribution plan, where benefits are based on contributions.

• Almost 55 percent of workers in small firms (with less than 500 employees) would be eligible for a lump-sum payment compared with 45 percent of workers in large firms.

• Workers in small firms are much less likely than their counterparts in large firms to work for an employer who offers a 401(k) plan. Only 12 percent of workers in firms with fewer than 500 workers are offered a 401(k) plan, compared with over 43 percent in large firms.

Chapter 8 Tables

Table 8.1 Pension Availability and Coverage of Wage-and-Salary Workers by Employment
Size of firm, 1979, 1983, and 1988 (Percent)

	All Firms	Employment Size of Firm						
		1-24	25-99	100-499	500+	Under 100	100+	Under 500
Employer or Union Offers Pension Plan								
1979	60.0	20.2	46.2	70.0	88.6	28.7	84.5	37.8
1983	56.4	18.7	40.7	63.6	86.2	25.5	80.6	34.3
1988	57.6	17.0	44.2	62.9	84.0	26.3	79.2	35.3
Covered by Employer or Union Pension Plan								
1979	48.3	14.9	34.5	53.6	74.2	21.3	69.6	28.3
1983	45.6	14.4	30.8	48.6	72.1	19.5	66.4	26.2
1988	43.2	12.3	30.4	45.4	65.0	18.5	60.6	24.9

Source: U.S. Small Business Administration, Office of Advocacy. Tabulations by Sheldon
Haber of unpublished data from the U.S. Department of Commerce, Bureau of the Census, Current
Population Survey, May 1979, May 1983, and May 1988.

Table 8.2 Pension Availability and Coverage of Wage-and-Salary Workers by Employment Size of Firm, 1988 (Percent)

	All Firms	Employment Size of Firm					
		1-9	10-24	25-49	50-99	Under 100	100+
Employer or Union Offers Pension Plan	57.6	12.0	25.7	39.6	50.2	26.3	79.2
Covered by Employer or Union Pension Plan	43.2	8.5	18.7	26.9	35.1	18.5	60.6

Source: U.S. Small Business Administration, Office of Advocacy. Tabulations by Sheldon Haber of unpublished data from the U.S. Department of Commerce, Bureau of the Census, Current Population Survey, May 1988.

Table 8.3 Demographic Characteristics of Wage-and-Salary Workers Offered an Employer or Union Pension Plan by Employment Size of Firm, 1988 (Percent)

	All Firms	Employment Size of Firm						
		1-24	25-99	100-499	500+	Under 100	100+	Under 500
Total	57.6	17.0	44.2	62.9	84.0	26.3	79.2	35.3
Age								
16-24	43.1	10.5	32.5	59.1	69.4	17.5	67.1	25.6
25-44	61.0	18.7	45.8	63.8	86.2	28.5	81.1	37.9
45-64	61.5	19.5	48.9	63.9	88.1	29.4	82.9	37.9
65+	39.2	15.2*	54.8*	51.5	73.7	25.2	66.3	29.1
Gender								
Men	59.6	18.0	46.3	64.3	86.2	27.9	81.5	36.6
Women	55.0	15.8	41.2	61.1	81.0	24.3	76.3	33.5
Marital Status								
Married, Spouse Present	60.9	20.1	49.5	62.5	86.3	30.2	81.0	38.4
Other	52.4	12.7	36.8	63.4	80.2	21.0	76.4	30.7
Race								
White	57.6	17.5	45.9	63.8	84.5	27.0	79.8	35.8
Black	59.3	11.9*	32.2*	55.4	79.8	19.7	74.9	31.8
Other	52.6	58.4*	25.7*	58.4	84.2*	18.1	79.3	26.1
Origin								
Hispanic	43.5	8.3*	31.0*	59.4	72.0	15.8	69.1	24.5
Non-Hispanic	58.5	17.7	45.2	63.1	84.7	27.2	79.8	36.1
Years of Education								
< 12	41.5	8.3	32.1	51.8	69.5	16.4	64.9	24.1
12-15	57.5	16.5	44.1	63.1	84.2	25.7	79.5	34.7
≥ 16	69.2	27.9	54.7	70.1	91.2	38.0	86.7	46.8
Region								
Northeast	61.8	19.4	46.8	70.1	88.7	29.6	83.9	40.6
Midwest	62.1	20.8	46.4	68.6	85.3	29.9	81.7	40.2
South	53.5	13.0	41.3	57.1	80.9	21.9	75.8	30.0
West	53.9	54.7	82.4	54.7	82.4	26.2	76.4	32.2
Area								
Metropolitan	59.1	17.7	44.6	64.0	84.6	27.1	80.1	36.3
Non-Metropolitan	50.9	14.8	42.6	58.2	80.7	23.4	74.8	31.4
Central City	56.8	17.3	42.5	63.3	81.8	26.3	77.7	35.4
Non-Central City	60.4	17.9	45.8	64.4	86.1	27.6	81.5	36.7

*Less than 50 observations.

Source: U.S. Small Business Administration, Office of Advocacy. Tabulations by Sheldon Haber of unpublished data from the U.S. Department of Commerce, Bureau of the Census, Current Population Survey, May 1988.

Table 8.4 Demographic Characteristics of Wage-and-Salary Workers Offered an Employer or Union Pension Plan by Employment Size of Firm, 1988 (Percent)

	All Firms	Employment Size of Firm					
		1-9	10-24	25-49	50-99	Under 100	100+
Total	57.6	12.6	25.8	40.6	50.6	26.3	79.2
Age							
16-24	43.1	6.3	18.1	23.0	46.4	17.5	67.1
25-44	61.0	12.7	28.1	42.1	50.8	28.5	81.1
45-64	61.5	15.9	26.5	47.3	50.9	29.4	82.9
65+	39.2	9.5	28.4	51.3	58.2	25.2	66.3
Gender							
Men	59.6	12.5	27.2	43.0	50.8	27.9	81.5
Women	55.0	11.4	23.7	34.8	49.5	24.3	76.3
Marital Status							
Married, Spouse Present	60.9	15.4	28.1	46.6	53.3	30.2	81.0
Other	52.4	7.2	22.3	29.8	46.0	21.0	76.4
Race							
White	57.6	12.2	26.7	41.5	51.7	27.0	79.8
Black	59.3	8.6	16.9	25.8	39.6	19.7	74.9
Other	57.6	12.7	9.9	23.2	31.7	18.1	79.3
Origin							
Hispanic	43.5	5.4*	11.9*	28.2*	40.0*	15.8	69.1
NonHispanic	58.5	12.4	27.0	40.7	50.9	27.2	79.8
Years of Education							
< 12	41.5	5.9	12.6	28.4	37.9	16.4	64.9
12-15	57.5	11.2	25.5	38.8	51.0	25.7	79.5
≥ 16	69.2	21.3	37.8	52.2	57.9	38.0	86.7
Region							
Northeast	61.8	13.7	29.9	44.5	50.1	29.6	83.9
Midwest	62.1	14.2	30.9	44.8	52.0	29.9	81.7
South	53.5	9.4	19.8	37.0	46.7	21.9	75.8
West	53.9	12.4	25.0	35.5	53.6	26.2	76.4
Area							
Metropolitan	59.1	12.3	26.3	39.7	51.2	27.1	80.1
Non-Metropolitan	50.9	10.8	23.0	38.8	46.6	23.4	74.8
Central City	56.8	11.5	26.6	36.5	51.6	26.3	77.7
Non-Central City	60.4	12.8	26.2	41.7	51.0	27.6	81.5

*Less than 50 observations.

Source: U.S. Small Business Administration, Office of Advocacy. Tabulations by Sheldon Haber of unpublished data from the U.S. Department of Commerce, Bureau of the Census, Current Population Survey, May 1988.

Table 8.5 Economic Characteristics of Wage-and-Salary Workers Offered an Employer or Union Pension Plan by Employment Size of Firm, 1988 (Percent)

	All Firms	Employment Size of Firm						
		1-24	25-99	100-499	500+	Under 100	100+	Under 500
Total	57.6	17.0	44.2	62.9	84.0	26.3	79.2	35.3
Union Contract								
Covered	89.1	66.3	77.1	80.0	94.0	73.1	91.8	76.4
Not Covered	54.8	16.0	40.9	60.2	81.7	25.0	76.6	33.7
Tenure								
Less than 1 Year Employment	42.0	10.8	35.2	56.4	70.0	18.4	66.8	25.3
1 Year or More Employment	61.7	19.5	46.9	64.0	86.9	29.3	81.8	38.9
Major Occupation								
Managerial/Prof.	64.1	24.4	51.3	68.5	88.0	34.4	83.4	43.4
Technical, Sales	59.2	17.4	50.6	64.0	84.8	28.0	80.5	36.4
Services	33.2	7.4	20.1	44.3	61.1	11.4	56.8	17.7
Precision Production/Craft	58.3	17.3	45.8	67.3	89.4	26.0	84.9	34.2
Operators, Fabricators and Laborers	59.9	14.0	60.2	60.2	83.1	24.0	77.7	64.3
Farmers, Forestry and Fishing	31.9	5.1	33.5	62.3*	85.8	14.0	74.1	22.8
Major Industry								
Mining	70.2	26.9*	26.9	46.9	95.8	26.9	85.0	34.7
Construction	35.4	17.9	42.6	62.2	80.0	24.3	70.4	29.8
Manufacturing, Durable	75.1	18.4	46.9	65.0	91.6	34.2	86.8	46.0
Manufacturing, NonDurable	72.5	23.2	8.7	64.0	88.5	35.6	83.1	47.9
Transportation, Communications and Public Utilities	71.4	13.2	45.3	65.4	89.1	26.8	86.3	36.9
Wholesale Trade	55.7	22.4	51.1	75.6	83.0	34.7	80.5	43.8
Retail Trade	39.7	8.3	27.7	46.2	68.9	13.7	65.4	18.1
Finance, Insurance and Real Estate	72.9	23.9	69.7	78.4	90.7	40.8	88.4	51.5
Miscellaneous Services	50.1	20.2	44.1	60.8	79.0	27.4	73.0	35.5
Industry								
Goods Producing	66.5	19.2	45.7	63.7	90.1	29.9	84.3	40.4
Service Producing	53.1	16.3	43.5	62.4	80.2	25.0	76.1	33.1
Usual Hours Worked/Week								
1-20	34.5	9.0	29.7	60.5	67.0	13.6	65.6	19.7
21-34	42.4	9.2	37.1	45.4	73.6	16.2	67.3	21.7
35+	63.6	20.7	45.9	64.3	86.2	31.1	81.2	40.8
Wage Level								
Less than $5/hr.	31.8	6.5	27.9	42.4	59.2	12.6	55.0	17.7
5.01 to $10/hr.	56.6	20.3	42.1	62.9	82.9	28.3	77.4	37.7
10.01/hr. and over	77.7	29.1	57.7	72.1	92.7	43.1	89.1	53.2

*Less than 50 observations.

Source: U.S. Small Business Administration, Office of Advocacy. Tabulations by Sheldon Haber of unpublished data from the U.S. Department of Commerce, Bureau of the Census, Current Population Survey, May 1988.

Table 8.6 Economic Characteristics of Wage-and-Salary Workers Offered an Employer or Union Pension Plan by Employment Size of Firm, 1988 (Percent)

	All Firms	Employment Size of Firm					
		1-9	10-24	25-49	50-99	Under 100	100+
Total	57.6	12.6	25.8	40.6	50.6	26.3	79.2
Union Contract							
Covered	89.1	56.7	71.1	77.0	77.2	73.1	91.8
Not Covered	54.8	11.3	23.6	35.3	48.1	25.0	76.6
Tenure							
Less than 1 year employment	42.0	6.2	19.9	26.8	45.5	18.4	66.8
1 year or more employment	61.7	14.3	27.7	43.3	51.8	29.3	81.8
Major Occupation							
Managerial/Prof.	64.1	19.9	30.9	46.5	57.8	34.4	83.4
Technical, Sales	59.2	12.1	27.1	46.3	56.1	28.0	80.5
Services	33.2	5.7	10.1	11.6	32.5	11.4	56.8
Precision Production/Craft	58.3	10.2	29.8	45.5	46.2	26.0	84.9
Operators, Fabricators and Laborers	59.9	8.2	23.8	34.1	43.8	24.0	77.7
Farmers, Forestry and Fishing	31.9	4.8	13.2	28.3	50.1	14.0	74.1
Major Industry							
Mining	70.2	24.1*	33.1*	28.7*	19.5*	26.9	85.0
Construction	35.4	11.4	30.7	44.8	39.2*	24.3	70.4
Manufacturing, Durable	75.1	9.6*	24.7*	47.9	46.1	34.2	86.8
Manufacturing, NonDurable	72.5	11.7*	34.6*	40.2*	58.8	35.6	83.1
Transportation, Communications and Public Utilities	71.4	5.0*	23.7*	38.5*	55.3*	26.8	86.3
Wholesale Trade	55.7	14.3*	32.4*	45.5	59.5*	34.7	80.5
Retail Trade	39.7	6.6*	11.4	22.5	36.3	13.7	82.9
Finance, Insurance and Real Estate	72.9	15.6*	40.2	62.4	78.0	40.8	88.4
Miscellaneous Services	50.1	14.4	39.9	63.1	76.5	27.4	73.0
Industry							
Goods Producing	66.5	11.4	29.6	44.2	47.4	29.9	84.3
Service Producing	53.1	12.1	24.1	37.6	51.7	25.0	76.1
Usual Hours Worked/Week							
1-20	34.5	8.1*	11.4*	23.3*	38.6*	13.6	65.6
21-34	42.4	7.1*	13.9*	30.0*	47.8*	16.2	67.3
35+	63.6	14.1	29.5	41.2	51.8	31.1	81.2
Wage Level							
Less than $5/hr.	31.8	5.8*	8.1	21.7	37.7	12.6	55.0
5.01 to $10/hr.	56.6	14.3	29.0	36.3	49.6	28.3	77.4
10.01/hr. and over	77.7	19.7	40.0	56.5	72.1	43.1	89.1

*Less than 50 observations

Source: U.S. Small Business Administration, Office of Advocacy. Tabulations by Sheldon Haber of unpublished data from the U.S. Department of Commerce, Bureau of the Census, Current Population Survey, May 1988.

Table 8.7 Reasons for Ineligibility of Wage-and-Salary Workers for Employer or Union Pension Plan by Employment Size of Firm, 1988 (Percent)

	All Firms	Employment Size of Firm						
		1-24	25-99	100-499	500+	Under 100	100+	Under 500
Job Not Covered	9.7	10.7	12.6	9.4	8.9	11.9	9.0	10.9
Part-time/Seasonal	21.5	23.5	19.9	20.2	21.9	21.3	21.6	20.8
New Employee	44.4	47.6	46.5	43.4	43.8	46.9	43.7	45.4
Too Young	2.9	1.5	2.1	2.0	3.4	1.9	3.1	1.9
Too Old	0.8	1.3	0.9	2.1	0.3	1.1	0.7	1.5
Choose Not to Belong	22.0	14.8	19.2	19.9	24.2	17.6	23.3	18.5
Other	5.4	5.7	3.2	6.3	5.6	4.1	5.8	5.0

Sources: U.S. Small Business Administration, Office of Advocacy. Tabulations by Sheldon Haber of unpublished data from the U.S. Department of Commerce, Bureau of the Census, Current Population Survey, May 1988.

Table 8.8 Reasons for Ineligibility of Wage-and-Salary Workers for Employer or
Union Pension Plan in Very Small Firm by Employment Size of Firm, 1988 (Percent)

	All Firms	Employment Size of Firm					
		1-9	10-24	25-49	50-99	Under 100	100+
Job Not Covered	9.7	8.1	12.9	11.9	13.4	11.9	9.0
Part-time/Seasonal	21.5	27.9	19.7	20.6	19.3	21.3	21.6
New Employee	44.4	49.8	45.7	43.5	49.7	46.9	43.7
Too Young	2.9	*	2.7	1.9	2.4	1.9	3.1
Too Old	0.8	1.5	1.2	1.2	0.6	1.1	0.7
Choose Not to Belong	22.0	11.1	18.0	21.9	16.4	17.6	23.3
Other	5.4	6.8	4.8	4.3	2.0	4.1	5.8

*Data not available.

Sources: U.S. Small Business Administration, Office of Advocacy. Tabulations
by Sheldon Haber of unpublished data from the U.S. Department of Commerce,
Bureau of the Census, Current Population Survey, May 1988.

Table 8.9 Availability and Coverage by Employer- or Union-Provided Pension, Profit-Sharing or Stock Plan[1] of Wage-and-Salary Workers by Employment Size of Firm, 1988 (Percent)

	All Firms	Employment Size of Firm						
		1-24	25-99	100-499	500+	Under 100	100+	Under 500
Employer Offers								
Pension Plan	57.6	17.0	44.2	62.9	84.0	26.3	79.2	35.3
Profit-Sharing or Stock Plan	3.8	2.2	4.9	5.4	4.0	3.1	4.3	3.7
Retirement Plan[2]	59.7	18.7	47.2	65.9	86.1	28.6	81.5	37.7
Covered by Employer if Offered								
Pension Plan	76.1	74.5	70.0	73.4	77.8	71.9	77.1	72.6
Profit-Sharing or or Stock Plan	65.0	72.2	66.3	69.3	60.6	69.0	63.0	69.1
Retirement Plan[2]	75.4	74.3	69.6	73.1	77.0	71.6	76.3	72.2

[1]Assumes that stock or profit-sharing plans are not offered if a pension plan is offered.
[2]Includes pension or profit-sharing or stock plan.

Source: U.S. Small Business Administration, Office of Advocacy. Tabulations by Sheldon Haber of unpublished data from the U.S. Department of Commerce, Bureau of the Census, <u>Current Population Survey</u>, May 1988.

Table 8.10 Availability and Coverage by Employer- or Union-Provided Pension, Profit-Sharing or Stock Plan[1] of Wage-and-Salary Workers in Very Small Firms by Employment Size of Firm, 1988 (Percent)

| | All Firms | Employment Size of Firm | | | | | |
		1-9	10-24	25-49	50-99	Under 100	100+
Employer Offers							
Pension Plan	57.6	12.0	25.7	39.6	50.2	26.3	79.2
Profit-Sharing or Stock Plan	3.8	1.7	3.0	3.3	7.0	3.1	4.3
Retirement Plan[2]	59.7	13.4	27.7	41.3	55.0	28.6	81.5
Covered by Employer if Offered							
Pension Plan	76.1	73.2	75.7	69.2	70.8	71.9	77.1
Profit-Sharing or or Stock Plan	65.0	72.8	71.7	62.3	68.8	69.0	63.0
Retirement Plan[2]	75.4	73.1	75.2	68.6	70.5	71.6	76.3

[1]Assumes that stock or profit-sharing plans are not offered if a pension plan is offered.
[2]Includes pension or profit-sharing or stock plan.

Source: U.S. Small Business Administration, Office of Advocacy. Tabulations by Sheldon Haber of unpublished data from the U.S. Department of Commerce, Bureau of the Census, Current Population Survey, May 1988.

Table 8.11 Type of Pension Plan Provided to Wage-and-Salary Workers by Firm Size, 1988 (Percent)

	All Firms	Employment Size of Firm						
		1-24	25-99	100-499	500+	Under 100	100+	Under 500
Defined Benefit Plan[1]	73.4	57.4	60.2	63.8	79.3	59.0	76.7	61.1
Defined Contribution Plan[2]	23.8	35.8	37.0	32.2	18.5	36.5	20.9	34.7
Other	2.8	6.8	2.8	3.8	2.2	4.5	2.4	4.2
Total	100.0	100.0	100.0	100.0	100.0	100.0	100.0	100.0

[1]Based on years of service and earnings.
[2]Based on contributions.

Source: U.S. Small Business Administration, Office of Advocacy. Tabulations by Sheldon Haber of unpublished data from the U.S. Department of Commerce, Bureau of the Census, <u>Current Population Survey</u>, May 1988.

Table 8.12 Type of Pension Plan Provided to Wage-and-Salary Workers in Very Small Firms by Firm Size, 1988 (Percent)

	All Firms	Employment Size of Firm					
		1-9	10-24	25-49	50-99	Under 100	100+
Defined Benefit Plan[1]	73.4	56.0	58.7	59.4	60.9	59.0	76.7
Defined Contribution Plan[2]	23.8	34.9	36.4	38.3	35.8	36.5	20.9
Other	2.8	9.1	4.9	2.3	3.3	4.5	2.4
Total	100.0	100.0	100.0	100.0	100.0	100.0	100.0

[1]Based on years of service and earnings.
[2]Based on contributions.

Source: U.S. Small Business Administration, Office of Advocacy. Tabulations by Sheldon Haber of unpublished data from the U.S. Department of Commerce, Bureau of the Census, Current Population Survey, May 1988.

Table 8.13 Vesting Status, Years in Plan, and Lump Sum Eligibility of Wage-and-Salary Workers in Retirement Plans by Employment Size of Firm, 1988 (Percent)

	All Firms	Employment Size of Firm						
		1-24	25-99	100-499	500+	Under 100	100+	Under 500
Vested	71.4	75.2	72.2	69.1	71.3	73.5	70.9	71.6
Not Vested	28.6	24.8	27.8	30.9	28.7	26.5	29.1	28.4
Total	100.0	100.0	100.0	100.0	100.0	100.0	100.0	100.0
Years in Retirement Plan								
< 5 Years	40.7	49.7	51.7	51.4	35.7	50.8	38.4	51.0
5-9 Years	22.3	25.5	22.8	21.6	22.0	24.0	21.9	23.0
≥ 10 Years	37.0	24.8	25.5	26.0	42.3	25.2	39.7	26.0
Total	100.0	100.0	100.0	100.0	100.0	100.0	100.0	100.0
Eligible for Lump Sum Payment								
Yes	48.2	58.4	57.8	49.8	45.0	58.0	45.8	54.4
No	51.8	41.6	42.2	50.2	55.0	42.0	54.2	45.6
Total	100.0	100.0	100.0	100.0	100.0	100.0	100.0	100.0

Source: U.S. Small Business Administration, Office of Advocacy. Tabulations by Sheldon Haber of unpublished data from the U.S. Department of Commerce, Bureau of the Census, Current Population Survey, May 1988.

Table 8.14 Vesting Status, Years in Plan, and Lump Sum Eligibility of Wage-and-Salary Workers in Retirement Plans in Very Small Firms by Employment Size of Firm, 1988 (Percent)

| | All Firms | Employment Size of Firm | | | | | |
		1-9	10-24	25-49	50-99	Under 100	100+
Vested	71.4	80.5	71.1	69.3	74.9	73.5	70.9
Not Vested	28.6	19.5	28.9	30.7	25.1	26.5	29.1
Total	100.0	100.0	100.0	100.0	100.0	100.0	100.0
Years in Retirement Plan							
< 5 years	40.7	45.3	53.2	50.4	53.0	50.8	38.4
5-9 years	22.3	27.1	24.3	25.0	20.6	24.0	21.9
≥ 10 years	37.0	27.6	22.5	24.6	26.4	25.2	39.7
Total	100.0	100.0	100.0	100.0	100.0	100.0	100.0
Eligible for Lump Sum Payment							
Yes	48.2	60.6	56.6	59.4	56.2	58.0	45.8
No	51.8	39.4	43.4	40.6	43.8	42.0	54.2
Total	100.0	100.0	100.0	100.0	100.0	100.0	100.0

Source: U.S. Small Business Administration, Office of Advocacy. Tabulations by Sheldon Haber of unpublished data from the U.S. Department of Commerce, Bureau of the Census, Current Population Survey, May 1988.

Table 8.15 Wage-and-Salary Workers Who Contributed to an Individual Retirement Account (IRA) in the Previous Year by Employment Size of Firm, 1988 (Percent)

	All Firms	Employment Size of Firm						
		1-24	25-99	100-499	500+	Under 100	100+	Under 500
IRA Contributed	12.5	13.6	12.9	13.0	11.9	13.2	11.6	13.4
Did Not Contribute	87.5	86.4	87.1	87.0	88.1	86.8	88.4	86.6
Total	100.0	100.0	100.0	100.0	100.0	100.0	100.0	100.0

Source: U.S. Small Business Administration, Office of Advocacy. Tabulations by Sheldon Haber of unpublished data from the U.S. Department of Commerce, Bureau of the Census, Current Population Survey, May 1988.

Table 8.16 Wage-and-Salary Workers Who Contributed to an Individual Retirement Account (IRA) in the Previous Year in Very Small Firms by Employment Size of Firm, 1988 (Percent)

| | All Firms | Employment Size of Firm | | | | | |
		1-9	10-24	25-49	50-99	Under 100	100+
IRA Contributed	12.5	13.9	13.1	12.9	12.9	13.2	11.6
Did Not Contribute	87.5	86.1	86.9	87.1	87.1	86.8	88.4
Total	100.0	100.0	100.0	100.0	100.0	100.0	100.0

Source: U.S. Small Business Administration, Office of Advocacy. Tabulations by Sheldon Haber of unpublished data from the U.S. Department of Commerce, Bureau of the Census, Current Population Survey, May 1988.

Table 8.17 Availability and Employer/Employee Contribution to Employer-Sponsored 401(k) Plans for Wage-and-Salary Workers by Employment Size of Firm, 1988 (Percent)

	All Firms	Employment Size of Firm						
		1-24	25-99	100-499	500+	Under 100	100+	Under 500
Offers 401(k) Plan	26.3	4.7	14.5	24.2	43.5	8.1	39.1	12.1
Does Not Offer 401(k) Plan	73.7	95.3	85.5	75.8	56.5	91.9	60.9	87.9
Total	100.0	100.0	100.0	100.0	100.0	100.0	100.0	100.0
Employer Contributes to 401(k)								
Yes	82.2	68.2	73.5	79.7	84.5	71.3	83.9	75.3
No	17.8	31.8*	26.5	20.3	15.5	28.7	16.1	24.7
Total	100.0	100.0	100.0	100.0	100.0	100.0	100.0	100.0
Percent of Gross Pay Worker Contributes to 401(k) Plan								
< 5%	29.9	24.5*	36.6	35.6	28.8	31.8	29.7	33.6
5-9%	47.4	35.2*	39.2	42.5	49.7	37.6	48.8	39.9
≥ 10%	22.7	40.3*	24.2*	21.9	21.5	30.6	21.5	26.5
Total	100.0	100.0	100.0	100.0	100.0	100.0	100.0	100.0

*Less than 50 observations.

Source: U.S. Small Business Administration, Office of Advocacy. Tabulations by Sheldon Haber of unpublished data from the U.S. Department of Commerce, Bureau of the Census, <u>Current Population Survey</u>, May 1988.

Table 8.18 Availability and Employer/Employee Contribution to Employer-Sponsored 401(k) Plans for Wage-and-Salary Workers in Very Small Firms by Employment Size of Firm, 1988 (Percent)

	All Firms	Employment Size of Firm					
		1-9	10-24	25-49	50-99	Under 100	100+
Offers 401(k) Plan	26.3	3.0	7.6	13.1	16.4	8.1	39.1
Does Not Offer 401(k) Plan	73.7	97.0	92.4	86.9	83.6	91.9	60.9
Total	100.0	100.0	100.0	100.0	100.0	100.0	100.0
Employer Contributes to 401(k)							
Yes	82.2	65.4*	69.7	68.5	78.4	71.3	83.9
No	17.8	34.6	30.3	31.5	21.6	28.7	16.1
Total	100.0	100.0	100.0	100.0	100.0	100.0	100.0
Percent of Gross Pay Worker Contributes to 401(k) Plan							
< 5%	29.9	28.8*	22.0*	34.5*	38.4*	31.8	29.7
5-9%	47.4	22.2*	42.5*	32.1*	45.6*	37.6	48.8
≥ 10%	22.7	49.0*	35.5*	33.4*	16.1*	30.6	21.5
Total	100.0	100.0	100.0	100.0	100.0	100.0	100.0

*Less than 50 observations.

Source: U.S. Small Business Administration, Office of Advocacy. Tabulations by Sheldon Haber of unpublished data from the U.S. Department of Commerce, Bureau of the Census, Current Population Survey, May 1988.

9 Financial Data on Small Business

Introduction

Comprehensive data on small firm financing has generally remained elusive for many years, because of the expense and difficulty of collecting it as well as its generally confidential nature.[1] Generically, there are at least three categories of small firms to consider when studying small firm financing. The first category consists of very small firms, most of which do not borrow.[2] Data is not generally available—with the exceptions noted below—to describe the exact funding sources of these businesses because of many reasons, such as the intermingling of personal and business finances, lack of recordkeeping, etc.

The second category of small firms includes four to five million small firms which have employees. They are often referred to as "traditional small businesses." These firms provide goods and services to consumers and businesses in local markets.

Finally, there are some half million dynamic small "enterprises" which were formed to serve regional, national, or even international markets. Generally, these firms are financed by a combination of equity and debt instruments, including bank loans, loans from finance companies and leasing firms, debt and/or equity financing by private investors, government loan guarantees, and, for a very small number of small firms, financing from venture capital companies and the public markets.

1 An excellent reference guide to the many sources of data available for the study of small firm finances is found in Charles Ou, "Available Financial Data Bases for Research on Small Firms," in Rassoul Yazdipour, ed., *Advances in Small Business Finance* (Boston, Mass.: Kluwer, 1991), 169–179.

2 For startup financing by owners of business, see "Summary of Findings" in U.S. Department of Commerce, Bureau of the Census, *Characteristics of Business Owners: 1987,* CBO87-1 (Washington, D.C.: U. S. Government Printing Office, 1992) 5–7.

Data Sources For Small Firms

Aggregate financial data for some segments of the small business sector is available in the *Flow of Funds* statistics published by the Board of Governors of the Federal Reserve System.[3] The flow of funds accounts for the nonfarm, noncorporate sector contain annual and quarterly estimates of income, savings, investment in physical and financial assets, and changes in major liabilities for the sector.[4] The flow of funds accounts for the nonfinancial corporate sector, however, do not allow for the separation of small corporations from large corporations and are thus not very useful (Tables 9.1 through 9.4).

The most comprehensive financial data describing the small business sector is collected and published by the Internal Revenue Service (IRS) of the U.S. Department of the Treasury. The Statistics of Income Division of the IRS annually processes representative samples of tax returns filed by American businesses for estimates of statistics of income for corporations, partnerships, and sole proprietorships. Both balance sheet information (on assets, liabilities, and equity) and income statement information (for revenues and cost of operations) are available for corporations and partnerships. Only income statement data are available for sole proprietorships.[5] Two major deficiencies of this data source are (1) the data are not current, that is, there is usually a two- to three-year time lag in reporting the information, and (2) no information is available on financing from different sources or suppliers (Tables 9.5 through 9.13).

Debt and Equity Financing Data from Suppliers

Small business financing data are also available from suppliers— loans from banks and finance companies, and equity investments from venture capital companies. The majority of data on lending by financial institutions is collected by the Federal Reserve Board.[6] The Federal Reserve Board also collects information on the terms of bank lending for small-size loans. Again, these data do not allow for

3   The Board of Governors of the Federal Reserve System, *Flow of Funds Accounts* (various issues) and ibid., *Balance Sheets of the U.S. Economy* (various issues).

4   The nonfarm, noncorporate sector includes sole proprietorships, partnerships, and the nonprofit sector.

5   See *SOI Bulletin* (various issues). For corporations, aggregate data from the IRS are generally available for firms by 12 asset size classes, by which small firms can be defined in many ways, such as those with assets of less than $25 million, or those with assets $10 million or less.

6   *Federal Reserve Bulletin* and various statistical releases published by the Board.

break-out by the size of business.

Tables 9.14 through 9.17 only reflect the commercial lending market for small firms. Financing provided by venture capital companies and by the public equity market are provided in Tables 9.18 through 9.21.

The National Survey of Small Business Finances

Congress has always been concerned with access to capital by both large and small firms. After the deregulation of the banking system during the 1980s, Congress wanted to make certain that small firms were not having a more difficult time obtaining funds post-deregulation or were not paying excessively high interest rates to obtain funds. Because such detailed information was not being collected by any branch of the federal government, the Federal Reserve Board and the U.S. Small Business Administration conducted a survey to study the sources and uses of funds by small firms.

During the fall of 1989, after extensive pretests, detailed questionnaires were sent to a sample of more than 6,000 randomly selected companies with fewer than 500 employees. The firms, which were drawn from a Dun and Bradstreet Corporation data base, were asked very detailed questions about their recent borrowing practices, as well as about the sources and uses of funds in their companies (Tables 9.22 through 9.23).

Summary

With the exception of summary data from the IRS and the Federal Reserve Board, most data on small firm financing is collected infrequently, and microdata is difficult to obtain because of the confidential nature of much of the information. However, significant strides have been made in recent years through such recent studies as the National Survey of Small Firm Finances sponsored by the Federal Reserve Board and the Small Business Administration. In the future, much more indirect information about small firm financing will be able to be derived by implication from the revised call reports that are submitted by banks to federal financial regulatory authorities. Beginning in the second quarter of 1993, banks were required to classify the commercial and industrial loans they report in the call reports by the size of the loan. Unfortunately, no information on the size of the companies receiving financing will be collected.

Historically, some of the data gaps in small firm financing have been provided by the private sector, particularly the Dun and Bradstreet Corporation and Robert Morris Associates. The Dun's Financial Profile (DFP) series provides income statement and balance sheet information for about 4 million firms. The user fees associated with such data sets, however, can be very expensive.

Finally, most of the available data on small firm financing is for small corporations that operate full-time. Much less information—with the exception of IRS summary data—is available for small sole proprietorship and partnership businesses.

Chapter 9 Tables

Table 9.1 Major Sources of Business Financing, 1990[1] (Billions of Dollars)

	All Business	Small Business
Total Assets[1]	10,818	4,515
Total Debt[2]	4,894	2,086
Total Net Worth[2]	5,620	2,340
Other Debt and Net Worth Estimates[3]		
Commercial Mortgages	624	434[4]
Commercial and Industrial Loans by Banks[5]	648	331
Trade Credit[6]	753	217
Finance Company Receivables from Businesses	294	NA
Initial Public Offerings of Common Stock[7]	47	26
Venture Capital Pool	33	33

NA = Not available.

[1]All estimates are stock estimates valued at the end of 1990, unless otherwise noted. Small business includes all noncorporate business and small corporations with assets under $25 million.

[2]Estimates by the Federal Reserve Board for nonfarm, nonfinancial corporations and nonfarm, noncorporate businesses. Total assets and debt for small corporations were estimated by applying 17.5 percent and 19.0 percent respectively to that of all corporations. Net worth is treated as a residual. (These ratios were estimated by using corporate tax return data published by Internal Revenue Service of the U.S. Department of Treasury).

[3]These estimates are obtained from sources using different methodologies. They are not strictly comparable and should not be summed for a total.

[4]For nonfarm, noncorporate business only. Major revisions have been made in the data.

[5]Total commercial and industrial loans outstanding of banks other than large weekly reporting banks are used as a proxy for loans to small businesses.

[6]Totals for small business estimated by applying 20 percent to trade credit for all nonfinancial corporations for small corporation share.

[7]The total estimated cumulative value of initial public offerings of common stock for the period 1976-1987.

Source: Board of Governors of the Federal Reserve System, Balance Sheets for the U.S. Economy 1960-1991 (Washington, D.C.: Board of Governors of the Federal Reserve System, September 1992); U.S. Securities and Exchange Commission, Directorate of Economic and Policy Analysis, Small Business Financing Trends (Washington, D.C.: U.S. Securities and Exchange Commission, September 1988).

Table 9.2 Credit Borrowing by Borrowing Sector, 1980-1992 (Billions of Dollars)[1]

Sector	1980	1981	1982	1983	1984	1985	1986	1987	1988	1989	1990	1991	1992[2]
Total	337.1	384.9	406.2	553.3	765.4	903.1	893.8	721.2	775.8	740.8	665.0	452.7	527.5
Government													
Federal	77.4	85.5	161.3	185.2	197.2	225.7	216.0	143.9	155.1	146.4	246.9	278.2	304.7
State and Local	10.9	16.3	30.4	34.6	35.7	134.0[3]	59.2	83.0	48.9	63.2	48.3	38.5	53.2
Business													
Farm	15.8	16.3	6.7	3.9	-0.4	-14.5	-16.3	-10.6	-7.5	1.6	2.5	0.9	2.6
Nonfarm Noncorporate	55.8	44.4	69.8	83.9	123.2	130.0	100.7	65.3	61.8	50.4	26.7	-23.6	-45.9
Nonfinancial Corporate	66.2	111.3	52.1	60.1	177.8	143.0	214.8	143.1	198.8	173.6	86.4	0.6	43.4
Households	111.2	111.1	85.9	185.7	232.7	284.9	319.4	296.4	318.6	305.6	254.2	158.0	169.5

[1]Excluding equity, foreign sector, and borrowing by financial institutions.

[2]Average of first three quarters of 1992. Annual rates.

[3]Probably the result of a large increase in borrowing in the municipal bond market before the enactment of the Tax Reform Act of 1986.

Source: Board of Governors of the Federal Reserve System, Flow of Funds Accounts, Flows and Outstandings, Third Quarter 1992, Annual Revisions (December 1992).

Table 9.3 Major Sources and Uses of Funds by Nonfarm, Nonfinancial Corporate Businesses, 1980-1992 (Billions of Dollars)

	1980	1981	1982	1983	1984	1985	1986	1987	1988	1989	1990	1991	1992[1]
Before-Tax Profit	181.1	180.9	133.0	156.0	189.0	165.5	149.0	212.1	256.1	232.4	232.1	206.2	243.6
Domestic Undistributed Profit	69.2	64.2	30.6	30.5	46.4	21.7	-2.1	41.3	73.6	32.2	22.0	8.9	35.2
Depreciation with Capital Consumption Adjustment	154.8	186.2	215.1	251.5	274.2	310.1	312.8	324.3	338.1	352.5	354.0	356.3	383.6
Total Internal Funds, on Book Basis	224.0	250.3	245.7	282.0	320.7	331.9	310.8	365.6	411.7	384.6	376.0	365.1	418.8
Net Increase in Liability	130.6	143.1	69.1	131.0	156.8	113.9	179.2	164.8	184.4	132.3	103.9	27.5	106.4
Funds Raised in Debt Market	66.2	111.3	52.1	60.1	177.0	143.0	214.8	143.1	198.8	173.6	86.4	0.4	43.4
Net New Equity Issues	10.4	-13.5	1.9	20.0	-79.0	-84.5	-85.0	-75.5	-129.5	-124.2	-63.0	18.3	31.0
Capital Expenditures	255.8	313.0	285.3	300.1	398.5	374.9	351.9	365.1	394.4	406.0	395.1	363.9	381.3
Net Financial Investment	-33.5	-47.2	-21.5	-10.6	-53.0	-30.9	-28.8	-56.4	-24.6	-26.1	-16.6	36.6	52.5

[1]Average of first three quarters of 1992. Annual rates.

Source: Board of Governors of the Federal Reserve System, Flow of Funds Accounts, Flows and Outstandings, Third Quarter 1992 Annual Revisions (December 1992).

Table 9.4 Major Sources and Uses of Funds by Nonfarm Noncorporate Businesses, 1980-1992 (Billions of Dollars)

	1980	1981	1982	1983	1984	1985	1986	1987	1988	1989	1990	1991	1992[1]
Net Income	176.0	182.3	183.5	213.4	248.2	273.6	292.0	307.9	325.6	339.9	360.2	370.6	374.0
Gross Investment	48.7	56.7	63.1	65.2	68.4	72.7	77.1	81.5	87.2	94.6	98.8	101.7	103.2
Fixed Capital Expenditures	63.6	72.2	70.6	69.9	85.1	95.9	97.4	96.7	100.5	104.1	96.8	77.1	82.3
Changes in Inventories	-.2	0.8	-1.0	0.5	3.0	0.9	0.5	1.6	1.3	1.6	0.2	-.5	0.1
Net Financial Investments	-14.7	-16.3	-6.4	-5.1	-19.8	-24.2	-20.8	-16.8	-14.6	-11.1	1.8	25.1	20.85
Net Increase in Credit Market Debt	55.8	44.4	69.8	83.9	123.2	130.0	100.7	65.3	61.8	50.4	26.7	-23.6	-45.9
Mortgages	45.7	23.3	75.0	73.0	88.2	111.0	76.3	40.7	38.0	35.6	15.5	-8.4	-37.2
Net Investment by Proprietors	-42.1	-37.5	-74.6	-62.2	-82.5	-83.0	-51.0	-51.1	-22.5	-33.0	-31.1	1.9	9.9

[1]Average of three quarters. Annual rates.

Source: Board of Governors of the Federal Reserve System, Flow of Funds Accounts, Flows and Outstandings Second Quarter 1992, Annual Revisions (August 1992).

Table 9.5 Number of Businesses, Business Receipts, and Net Income for U.S. Businesses, by Company Organization, 1980-1990

	1980	1985	1987	1988	1989	1990
Sole Proprietorships						
Number (Thousands)	8,932	11,929	13,091	13,679	14,298	14,783
Receipts (Millions of Dollars)	411,206	540,045	610,823	671,670	692,811	730,606
Net Income (Millions of Dollars)	54,947	78,773	105,461	126,323	132,738	141,430
Partnerships						
Number (Thousands)	1,380	1,714	1,648	1,654	1,635	1,554
Receipts (Millions of Dollars)	271,109	302,733	411,457	463,956	464,952	483,418
Net Income (Millions of Dollars)	8,249	-8,884	-5,419	14,493	14,099	16,610
Corporations						
Number (Thousands)	2,711	3,277	3,612	3,563	3,628	3,717
Receipts (Millions of Dollars)	5,731,616	7,369,539	8,414,538	8,949,846	9,427,278	9,860,442
Net income (Millions of Dollars)	239,007	240,119	328,224	412,983	389,011	370,863
All Businesses						
Number (Thousands)	13,023	16,920	18,351	18,896	19,561	20,054
Receipts (Millions of Dollars)	6,413,931	8,212,317	9,436,818	10,085,472	10,585,041	11,074,466
Net Income (Millions of Dollars)	302,203	310,008	428,266	553,799	535,848	528,908

Sources: U.S. Department of Treasury, Internal Revenue Services, SOI Bulletin (various issues).

Table 9.6   Balance Sheet and Income Statements for U.S. Corporations by Asset Size of Corporation: Agriculture, 1989 (Thousands of Dollars)

Item	Total	Zero Assets	Zero to Under 100	100 to Under 250	250 to Under 500	500 to Under 1,000	1,000 to Under 5,000	5,000 to Under 10,000	10,000 to Under 25,000	25,000 to Under 50,000	50,000 to Under 100,000	100,000 to Under 250,000	250,000 or More
Number of Returns	123,195	7,166	48,769	23,770	19,333	14,152	8,841	695	272	101	52	35	7
Total Assets	63,413,253	0	1,657,774	3,845,494	6,959,467	10,060,419	16,067,836	4,781,626	4,024,387	3,553,453	3,612,621	5,710,858	3,139,317
Cash	4,779,025	0	304,028	584,901	780,653	855,485	947,222	401,068	231,536	161,997	188,713	183,167	140,254
Notes and Accounts Receivable	6,297,908	0	95,800	310,978	501,803	644,142	1,467,548	609,599	500,461	524,552	492,955	797,398	352,671
Less: Allowance for Bad Debts	82,188	0	0	332	1,484	1,136	35,029	3,056	4,342	10,893	9,516	14,024	2,375
Inventories	7,188,371	0	63,445	180,607	317,300	799,784	1,604,763	694,520	460,687	679,234	582,326	1,087,991	717,712
Invest in Government Obligations: Total	219,410	0	22	823	41,594	11,396	112,769	12,218	28,699	0	7,496	804	3,589
Other Current Assets	2,142,089	0	36,298	117,146	162,360	275,206	319,320	208,883	140,746	294,396	180,831	329,723	77,179
Loans to Stockholders	1,658,414	0	116,830	200,378	397,040	333,621	376,351	66,652	32,667	56,650	47,745	4,496	25,983
Mortgage and Real Estate Loans	725,242	0	32,077	25,114	75,150	125,744	246,491	50,620	113,344	9,009	32,832	14,861	0
Other Investments	5,397,186	0	86,161	141,418	446,630	467,756	1,064,508	345,726	445,053	308,635	485,199	893,406	712,693
Depreciable Assets	44,390,053	0	2,467,746	4,319,148	6,624,975	7,516,279	10,799,498	2,679,686	2,316,012	1,927,841	1,648,324	2,438,351	1,652,193
Less: Accumulated Depreciation	27,177,737	0	1,864,732	2,932,064	4,506,495	5,123,872	6,817,253	1,434,672	1,067,468	816,960	771,413	967,272	875,538
Depletable Assets	963,319	0	15,160	47,211	23,243	37,970	48,587	79,626	106,167	139,250	30,649	339,914	95,541
Less: Accumulated Depletion	417,426	0	9,448	680	18,036	16,075	24,064	43,339	79,340	125,252	980	35,037	65,174
Land	14,095,183	0	203,408	710,184	1,815,969	3,489,333	5,068,617	945,768	662,710	271,847	427,039	365,990	134,317
Intangible Assets (Amortizable)	266,701	0	19,439	13,367	23,588	18,859	46,629	21,587	23,583	15,990	43,987	36,262	3,411
Less: Accumulated Amortization	105,113	0	11,482	8,991	12,651	9,657	7,412	6,483	5,185	4,567	13,642	24,279	765
Other Assets	2,913,695	0	103,020	136,285	257,859	625,420	846,322	153,224	102,398	121,721	226,872	258,973	81,602
Total Liabilities	63,413,253	0	1,657,774	3,845,494	6,959,467	10,060,419	16,067,836	4,781,626	4,024,387	3,553,453	3,612,621	5,710,858	3,139,317
Accounts Payable	3,678,290	0	127,429	161,475	314,839	253,181	901,210	439,772	250,762	298,316	404,452	325,000	201,854
Mort, Notes, and Bonds under 1 Year	9,540,479	0	397,950	727,403	818,847	1,303,130	2,414,025	736,597	674,122	484,871	567,731	1,161,720	254,084
Other Current Liabilities	2,863,450	0	70,416	116,039	157,047	293,291	623,599	206,926	262,059	250,330	352,269	345,859	185,616
Loans from Stockholders	6,298,333	0	746,229	998,313	1,071,575	912,682	1,186,276	621,335	402,216	111,281	141,408	68,291	38,727
Mort, Notes, Bonds 1 Year or More	16,694,788	0	472,289	980,489	1,976,235	2,515,502	4,689,199	1,398,092	1,210,442	869,672	802,566	1,296,192	484,112
Other Liabilities	3,240,782	0	124,393	203,524	192,806	250,111	841,039	203,283	175,102	358,771	248,014	384,912	258,826
Capital Stock	8,296,573	0	555,527	899,865	1,457,508	1,848,496	2,201,614	403,930	250,229	134,356	235,161	291,065	112,823
Paid-in or Capital Surplus	8,400,456	0	230,125	430,990	552,574	1,273,033	1,630,543	691,325	919,916	609,492	801,857	1,132,261	128,342

Table 9.6 Balance Sheet and Income Statements for U.S. Corporations by Asset Size of Corporation: Agriculture, 1989 (Thousands of Dollars)--Continued

Item	Total	Zero Assets	Zero to Under 100	100 to Under 250	250 to Under 500	500 to Under 1,000	1,000 to Under 5,000	5,000 to Under 10,000	10,000 to Under 25,000	25,000 to Under 50,000	50,000 to Under 100,000	100,000 to Under 250,000	250,000 or More
Retained Earnings, Appropriated	98,408	0	0	38	0	45,728	43,316	94	8,446	0	0	785	0
Retained Earnings, Unappropriated	6,583,753	0	-288,233	260,217	687,311	1,539,748	1,310,206	263,826	111,519	319,200	78,020	805,275	1,496,664
Other Retained Earnings (1120S)	-875,555	0	-697,054	-776,128	-192,980	27,570	665,404	-41,867	-83,862	157,560	49,520	16,282	0
Less: Cost of Treasury Stock	1,406,506	0	81,295	156,729	76,296	202,055	438,594	141,687	62,564	40,395	68,376	116,783	21,731
Total Receipts	86,627,044	809,903	6,464,730	7,260,859	12,985,250	10,370,555	18,412,545	5,413,534	5,715,845	4,526,997	4,975,205	5,605,014	4,086,606
Business Receipts	81,159,501	684,163	6,068,061	6,738,719	12,407,758	9,561,679	17,134,135	5,065,482	5,427,071	4,316,259	4,614,551	5,311,948	3,829,673
Total Deductions	85,065,088	794,938	6,410,783	7,143,373	12,893,774	10,077,534	18,210,912	5,386,529	5,740,920	4,406,083	4,817,796	5,478,384	3,704,062
Cost of Sales and Operations	57,275,674	356,599	2,912,960	3,818,959	9,419,039	6,191,677	12,540,749	3,740,906	4,345,495	3,509,415	3,820,273	4,381,879	2,237,721
Net Income (Less Deficit), Total	1,550,580	13,784	53,947	114,858	90,366	286,709	195,485	26,948	-25,679	122,651	155,779	124,879	390,852

Source: Department of Treasury, Internal Revenue Service, Publication No. 1053, <u>Corporation Income Tax Returns, Sourcebook</u>, 1989.

Table 9.7 Balance Sheet and Income Statements for U.S. Corporations by Asset Size of Corporation: Mining, 1989 (Thousands of Dollars)

Item	Total	Zero Assets	Zero to Under 100	100 to Under 250	250 to Under 500	500 to Under 1,000	1,000 to Under 5,000	5,000 to Under 10,000	10,000 to Under 25,000	25,000 to Under 50,000	50,000 to Under 100,000	100,000 to Under 250,000	250,000 or More
Number of Returns	41,631	3,160	19,594	7,119	4,132	3,095	2,878	751	441	177	123	74	87
Total Assets	2.4E+08	0	573,298	1,086,323	1,473,467	10,060,419	16,067,836	4,781,626	4,024,387	3,553,453	3,612,621	5,710,858	3,139,317
Cash	8,723,259	0	304,028	584,901	780,653	855,485	947,222	401,068	231,536	161,997	188,713	183,167	140,254
Notes and Accounts Receivable	20,048,765	0	95,800	310,978	501,803	644,142	1,467,548	609,599	500,461	524,552	492,955	797,398	352,671
Less: Allowance for Bad Debts	283,713	0	0	332	1,484	1,136	35,029	3,056	4,342	10,893	9,516	14,024	2,375
Inventories	6,342,748	0	63,445	180,607	317,300	799,784	1,604,763	694,520	460,687	679,234	582,326	1,087,991	717,712
Invest in Government Obligations: Total	677,658	0	22	823	41,594	11,396	112,769	12,218	28,699	0	7,496	804	3,589
Other Current Assets	6,450,851	0	36,298	117,146	162,360	275,206	319,320	208,883	140,746	294,396	180,831	329,723	77,179
Loans to Stockholders	1,909,458	0	116,830	200,378	397,040	333,621	376,351	66,652	32,667	56,650	47,745	4,496	25,983
Mortgage and Real Estate Loans	419,643	0	32,077	25,114	75,150	125,744	246,491	50,620	113,344	9,009	32,832	14,861	0
Other Investments	1.0E+08	0	86,161	141,418	446,630	467,756	1,064,508	345,726	445,053	308,635	485,199	893,406	712,693
Depreciable Assets	1.0E+08	0	2,467,746	4,319,148	6,624,975	7,516,279	10,799,498	2,679,686	2,316,012	1,927,841	1,648,324	2,438,351	1,652,193
Less: Accumulated Depreciation	50,503,967	0	1,864,732	2,932,064	4,506,495	5,123,872	6,817,253	1,434,672	1,067,468	816,960	771,413	967,272	875,538
Depletable Assets	38,811,954	0	15,160	47,211	23,243	37,970	48,587	79,626	106,167	139,250	30,649	339,914	95,541
Less: Accumulated Depletion	417,426	0	9,448	680	18,036	16,075	24,064	43,339	79,340	125,252	980	35,037	65,174
Land	14,095,183	0	203,408	710,184	1,815,969	3,489,333	5,068,617	945,768	662,710	271,847	427,039	365,990	134,317
Intangible Assets (Amortizable)	266,701	0	19,439	13,367	23,588	18,859	46,629	21,587	23,583	15,990	43,987	36,262	3,411
Less: Accumulated Amortization	105,113	0	11,482	8,991	12,651	9,657	7,412	6,483	5,185	4,567	13,642	24,279	765
Other Assets	2,913,695	0	103,020	136,285	257,859	625,420	846,322	153,224	102,398	121,721	226,872	258,973	81,602
Total Liabilities	63,413,253	0	1,657,774	3,845,494	6,959,467	10,060,419	16,067,836	4,781,626	4,024,387	3,553,453	3,612,621	5,710,858	3,139,317
Accounts Payable	3,678,290	0	127,429	161,475	314,839	253,181	901,210	439,772	250,762	298,316	404,452	325,000	201,854
Mort, Notes, and Bonds under 1 Year	9,540,479	0	397,950	727,403	818,847	1,303,130	2,414,025	736,597	674,122	484,871	567,731	1,161,720	254,084
Other Current Liabilities	2,863,450	0	70,416	116,039	157,047	293,291	623,599	206,926	262,059	250,330	352,269	345,859	185,616
Loans from Stockholders	6,298,333	0	746,229	998,313	1,071,575	912,682	1,186,276	621,335	402,216	111,281	141,408	68,291	38,727
Mort, Notes, Bonds 1 Year or More	16,694,788	0	472,289	980,489	1,976,235	2,515,502	4,689,199	1,398,092	1,210,442	869,672	802,566	1,296,192	484,112
Other Liabilities	3,240,782	0	124,393	203,524	192,806	250,111	841,039	203,283	175,102	358,771	248,014	384,912	258,826
Capital Stock	8,296,573	0	555,527	899,865	1,457,508	1,848,496	2,201,614	403,930	156,229	134,356	235,161	291,065	112,823
Paid-in or Capital Surplus	8,400,456	0	230,125	430,990	552,574	1,273,033	1,630,543	691,325	919,916	609,492	801,857	1,132,261	128,342
Retained Earnings, Appropriated	98,408	0	0	38	0	45,728	43,316	94	8,446	0	0	785	0
Retained Earnings, Unappropriated	6,583,753	0	-288,233	260,217	687,311	1,539,748	1,310,206	263,826	111,519	319,200	78,020	805,275	1,496,664

Table 9.7 Balance Sheet and Income Statements for U.S. Corporations by Asset Size of Corporation: Mining, 1989 (Thousands of Dollars)--Continued

Item	Total	Zero Assets	Zero to Under 100	100 to Under 250	250 to Under 500	500 to Under 1,000	1,000 to Under 5,000	5,000 to Under 10,000	10,000 to Under 25,000	25,000 to Under 50,000	50,000 to Under 100,000	100,000 to Under 250,000	250,000 or More
Other Retained Earnings (1120S)	-875,555	0	-697,054	-776,128	-192,980	27,570	665,404	-41,867	-83,862	157,560	49,520	16,282	0
Less: Cost of Treasury Stock	1,406,506	0	81,295	156,729	76,296	202,055	438,594	141,687	62,564	40,395	68,376	116,783	21,731
Total Receipts	86,627,044	809,903	6,464,730	7,260,859	12,985,250	10,370,555	18,412,545	5,413,534	5,715,845	4,526,997	4,975,205	5,605,014	4,086,606
Business Receipts	81,159,501	684,163	6,068,061	6,738,719	12,407,758	9,561,679	17,134,135	5,065,482	5,427,071	4,316,259	4,614,551	5,311,948	3,829,673
Total Deductions	85,065,088	794,938	6,410,783	7,143,373	12,893,774	10,077,534	18,210,912	5,386,529	5,740,920	4,406,083	4,817,796	5,478,384	3,704,062
Cost of Sales and Operations	57,275,674	356,599	2,912,960	3,818,959	9,419,039	6,191,677	12,540,749	3,740,906	4,345,495	3,509,415	3,820,273	4,381,879	2,237,721
Net Income (Less Deficit), Total	1,550,580	13,784	53,947	114,858	90,366	286,709	195,485	26,948	-25,679	122,651	155,779	124,879	390,852

Source: Department of Treasury, Internal Revenue Service, Publication No. 1053, Corporation Income Tax Returns, Sourcebook, 1989.

Table 9.8 Balance Sheet and Income Statements for U.S. Corporations by Asset Size of Corporation: Construction, 1989 (Thousands of Dollars)

Item	Total	Zero Assets	Zero to Under 100	100 to Under 250	250 to Under 500	500 to Under 1,000	1,000 to Under 5,000	5,000 to Under 10,000	10,000 to Under 25,000	25,000 to Under 50,000	50,000 to Under 100,000	100,000 to Under 250,000	250,000 or More
Number of Returns	393,103	16,283	206,748	62,853	44,244	28,114	29,299	3,381	1,522	367	163	86	43
Total Assets	2.5E+08	0	6,266,876	10,397,585	15,793,726	20,315,897	60,198,802	23,574,640	22,378,699	12,381,829	11,030,572	15,204,873	52,167,712
Cash	25,378,919	0	1,379,750	1,866,668	2,452,107	2,725,883	7,006,723	2,761,915	2,410,110	1,038,292	991,653	1,005,857	1,739,961
Notes and Accounts Receivable	67,626,809	0	936,352	2,344,185	4,068,648	5,809,011	18,335,931	7,858,694	7,270,535	3,824,512	3,070,121	4,511,045	9,597,776
Less: Allowance for Bad Debts	433,252	0	2,611	7,146	15,442	17,531	101,539	41,565	57,911	21,383	16,659	51,077	100,388
Inventories	34,156,301	0	403,094	1,181,380	2,233,896	3,320,221	10,866,965	3,769,988	3,269,698	1,935,776	1,345,941	2,104,551	3,724,792
Invest in Government Obligations: Total	1,083,195	0	4,108	579	1,393	1,265	236,147	61,413	115,999	225,087	84,750	25,669	326,786
Other Current Assets	25,708,733	0	325,702	664,356	1,275,715	1,862,398	6,841,809	3,298,743	3,055,436	1,490,855	1,644,967	1,836,646	3,412,106
Loans to Stockholders	4,327,195	0	645,501	676,069	666,426	447,136	839,174	335,005	115,673	79,700	120,912	39,546	362,054
Mortgage and Real Estate Loans	8,954,681	0	18,653	102,171	282,455	178,656	602,344	151,451	169,052	122,997	100,792	253,249	6,972,861
Other Investments	25,544,181	0	56,602	315,450	426,334	728,745	2,531,929	1,067,737	1,373,104	904,338	1,038,262	1,381,598	15,720,084
Depreciable Assets	91,446,213	0	6,475,841	7,235,338	9,751,981	10,249,548	22,589,115	7,326,238	7,442,628	4,078,824	3,504,482	3,544,935	9,247,284
Less: Accumulated Depreciation	54,107,667	0	4,333,705	4,643,501	6,245,955	6,469,459	13,502,192	4,486,299	4,142,309	2,252,026	1,798,902	1,409,628	4,823,692
Depletable Assets	423,325	0	1,235	0	14,223	15,019	54,658	8,115	31,696	13,272	86,904	70,707	127,497
Less: Accumulated Depletion	98,482	0	0	0	4,294	4,428	10,359	3,585	12,058	1,871	46,873	7,606	7,406
Land	7,610,023	0	143,378	354,718	457,054	777,766	2,138,585	914,300	603,908	449,920	335,935	421,876	1,012,584
Intangible Assets (Amortizable)	1,952,981	0	155,216	85,350	100,789	69,057	191,555	39,772	89,014	72,340	73,208	524,632	552,047
Less: Accumulated Amortization	546,927	0	89,135	47,333	47,231	15,725	82,306	19,213	25,703	13,035	11,970	53,554	141,722
Other Assets	9,878,660	0	146,894	267,424	362,033	605,421	1,598,137	498,359	570,905	338,897	470,303	976,364	4,043,924
Total Liabilities	2.5E+08	0	6,266,876	10,397,585	15,793,726	20,315,897	60,198,802	23,574,640	22,378,699	12,381,829	11,030,572	15,204,873	52,167,712
Accounts Payable	44,408,823	0	1,154,034	1,602,147	2,405,335	3,497,368	12,049,817	5,166,235	4,957,027	2,745,900	2,131,666	3,160,585	5,538,709
Mort, Notes, and Bonds Under 1 Year	32,377,329	0	1,360,213	1,509,094	2,484,166	3,345,365	10,056,431	2,913,786	3,038,468	1,431,434	1,254,144	1,512,388	3,471,840
Other Current Liabilities	36,108,584	0	904,393	931,778	1,610,764	2,296,065	9,034,046	4,464,455	3,776,513	1,778,662	1,861,053	2,530,393	6,920,461
Loans from Stockholders	9,696,987	0	1,845,764	1,028,335	1,093,232	1,339,228	2,704,973	509,220	373,862	298,947	141,680	149,060	212,686
Mort, Notes, Bonds, 1 Year or More	45,173,077	0	1,447,901	1,667,781	2,749,708	2,772,394	7,500,887	2,863,328	3,006,370	1,820,233	1,931,123	3,087,908	16,325,443
Other Liabilities	15,222,959	0	163,426	201,213	325,338	467,026	2,275,003	1,050,764	1,257,818	1,193,111	802,181	1,249,198	6,237,880
Capital Stock	8,108,527	0	850,342	708,083	783,486	820,489	1,475,400	381,906	530,706	387,203	398,205	530,829	1,241,878
Paid-in or Capital Surplus	17,664,227	0	1,022,518	654,669	475,347	758,760	1,705,980	599,401	825,332	523,016	768,795	1,290,607	9,039,804
Retained Earnings, Appropriated	225,382	0	2,437	22,740	23	25,393	45,122	12,492	8,010	2,397	7,143	4	99,621
Retained Earnings, Unappropriated	29,002,201	0	-1,799,530	1,972,092	3,232,752	4,289,989	8,944,534	3,032,657	2,577,983	1,263,013	1,156,673	1,242,487	3,089,550

Table 9.8 Balance Sheet and Income Statements for U.S. Corporations by Asset Size of Corporation: Construction, 1989 (Thousands of Dollars)--Continued

Item	Total	Zero Assets	Zero to Under 100	100 to Under 250	250 to Under 500	500 to Under 1,000	1,000 to Under 5,000	5,000 to Under 10,000	10,000 to Under 25,000	25,000 to Under 50,000	50,000 to Under 100,000	100,000 to Under 250,000	250,000 or More
Other Retained Earnings (1120S)	15,728,949	0	-516,088	285,912	963,948	1,307,855	5,476,612	2,981,926	2,369,619	1,061,611	699,578	576,325	521,649
Less: Cost of Treasury Stock	4,005,832	0	168,536	186,259	330,375	604,035	1,070,004	401,531	343,008	123,698	121,669	124,909	531,808
Total Receipts	5.2E+08	6,804,751	46,246,628	40,049,160	46,720,512	49,264,081	1.3E+08	44,750,638	44,835,991	22,038,672	17,760,517	23,396,322	44,950,907
Business Receipts	5.0E+08	6,506,984	45,763,028	39,696,621	46,130,591	48,512,243	1.3E+08	43,744,529	43,770,296	21,418,895	17,217,471	22,565,796	41,231,048
Total Deductions	5.1E+08	6,815,479	45,777,529	39,530,576	46,359,904	48,792,192	1.3E+08	43,571,681	43,614,770	21,520,971	17,261,292	22,944,648	44,314,921
Cost of Sales and Operations	3.9E+08	5,007,405	28,105,143	26,757,194	33,444,528	36,218,776	1.0E+08	36,623,004	37,746,385	18,304,827	14,842,560	19,873,548	33,187,451
Net Income (Less Deficit), Total	8,736,930	-10,111	469,100	517,224	360,491	469,861	2,366,449	1,173,328	1,211,840	508,032	491,744	438,784	740,188

Note: Figures that are too large to print are expressed in exponential notation (for example, 5.2E+08 equals 5,200,000,000.

Source: Department of Treasury, Internal Revenue Service, Publication No. 1053, Corporation Income Tax Returns, Sourcebook, 1989.

Table 9.9 Balance Sheet and Income Statements for U.S. Corporations by Asset Size of Corporation: Manufacturing, 1989 (Thousands of Dollars)

Item	Total	Zero Assets	Zero to Under 100	100 to Under 250	250 to Under 500	500 to Under 1,000	1,000 to Under 5,000	5,000 to Under 10,000	10,000 to Under 25,000	25,000 to Under 50,000	50,000 to Under 100,000	100,000 to Under 250,000	250,000 or More
Number of Returns	301,346	12,458	112,543	50,625	35,499	29,709	41,337	8,092	5,785	2,138	1,172	932	1,056
Total Assets	3.7E+09	0	3,793,707	8,422,156	12,821,086	21,198,804	91,182,187	56,979,354	90,151,423	74,583,175	82,846,065	1.5E+08	3.1E+09
Cash	90,661,255	0	609,950	1,379,766	1,643,436	2,533,067	8,361,583	4,203,983	6,074,324	4,457,069	5,063,534	7,305,707	49,028,836
Notes and Accounts Receivable	8.0E+08	0	760,687	2,038,832	3,256,257	5,961,796	25,024,434	14,898,480	21,854,138	17,357,790	17,848,066	30,452,029	6.6E+08
Less: Allowance for Bad Debts	14,375,829	0	909	60,693	36,247	53,698	380,556	324,609	489,835	434,379	504,486	868,198	11,222,220
Inventories	3.7E+08	0	594,797	1,447,095	2,586,685	4,628,770	22,421,897	13,844,764	22,577,935	16,299,946	17,025,924	26,449,793	2.5E+08
Invest in Government Obligations: Total	22,231,304	0	0	22,991	50,576	25,124	211,205	249,113	564,313	356,188	419,696	1,070,870	19,261,227
Other Current Assets	1.9E+08	0	109,214	356,615	424,487	708,515	3,405,566	2,291,377	3,932,871	3,515,103	3,677,621	6,837,416	1.7E+08
Loans to Stockholders	22,653,219	0	242,125	277,452	350,767	398,020	867,550	449,872	328,951	347,123	447,485	458,085	18,485,789
Mortgage and Real Estate Loans	37,569,333	0	15,777	26,000	40,874	75,364	211,949	100,784	135,452	75,298	96,299	311,233	36,480,303
Other Investments	8.9E+08	0	48,147	234,097	323,278	693,895	3,419,537	2,831,960	4,981,056	5,702,464	6,820,066	15,638,059	8.5E+08
Depreciable Assets	1.5E+09	0	3,327,321	6,873,178	10,446,333	14,802,655	55,425,204	32,806,858	48,520,550	37,333,795	38,810,183	66,279,030	1.2E+09
Less: Accumulated Depreciation	7.3E+08	0	2,180,630	4,643,676	7,072,501	9,550,529	32,997,448	17,871,270	24,820,925	17,640,474	17,030,187	28,155,387	5.7E+08
Depletable Assets	83,024,177	0	8,848	47,200	2,995	20,167	134,387	33,083	487,654	229,787	228,351	823,091	81,008,615
Less: Accumulated Depletion	34,889,862	0	7,375	41,924	990	10,906	14,852	3,832	220,344	82,521	40,127	266,677	34,200,313
Land	38,184,518	0	23,070	86,963	213,245	288,409	1,723,933	1,173,891	1,526,649	1,387,217	1,573,353	2,294,142	27,893,645
Intangible Assets (Amortizable)	2.5E+08	0	147,046	178,684	275,969	325,646	1,556,048	1,829,577	2,314,101	3,335,171	4,910,529	9,739,462	2.3E+08
Less: Accumulated Amortization	46,953,045	0	65,771	82,721	154,328	118,722	740,104	690,369	629,544	676,849	803,634	1,282,002	41,709,002
Other Assets	2.2E+08	0	161,410	279,775	464,888	457,263	2,109,622	1,275,995	2,754,895	2,766,192	4,028,946	8,795,975	2.0E+08
Total Liabilities	3.7E+09	0	3,793,707	8,422,156	12,821,086	21,198,804	91,182,187	56,979,354	90,151,423	74,583,175	82,846,065	1.5E+08	3.1E+09
Accounts Payable	3.3E+08	0	805,726	1,356,572	2,031,607	3,598,678	15,104,051	8,460,346	12,174,305	9,276,296	8,828,517	14,282,152	2.5E+08
Mort, Notes, and Bonds Under 1 Year	4.3E+08	0	556,497	942,570	1,596,910	2,258,140	12,037,468	8,393,779	12,393,890	8,127,028	8,448,799	11,903,361	3.6E+08
Other Current Liabilities	3.7E+08	0	514,009	890,976	1,083,380	1,789,418	7,802,774	4,963,892	7,953,534	6,649,086	7,597,619	14,192,456	3.2E+08
Loans from Stockholders	69,576,898	0	1,745,962	1,357,173	1,482,136	1,469,014	4,367,813	1,433,891	1,693,939	729,849	1,394,782	2,374,678	51,527,661
Mort, Notes, Bonds 1 Year or More	7.5E+08	0	997,414	1,444,682	2,641,612	4,010,898	15,423,120	9,970,282	16,554,658	16,858,485	18,976,405	38,503,368	6.2E+08
Other Liabilities	4.0E+08	0	139,219	111,449	322,768	586,523	2,350,506	1,710,824	3,179,996	3,578,419	4,119,807	8,816,889	3.7E+08
Capital Stock	1.6E+08	0	1,993,091	1,135,322	1,341,758	2,117,924	7,313,542	4,891,112	6,488,674	5,075,961	6,413,574	10,156,085	1.2E+08
Paid-in or Capital Surplus	6.0E+08	0	714,356	1,007,510	1,063,196	1,524,008	7,789,247	5,323,781	9,486,363	9,256,346	11,963,916	21,131,165	5.3E+08
Retained Earnings, Appropriated	7,073,835	0	3,073	9,464	27,517	12,281	176,586	117,641	84,244	72,745	77,356	136,949	6,355,978

Table 9.9 Balance Sheet and Income Statements for U.S. Corporations by Asset Size of Corporation: Manufacturing, 1989 (Thousands of Dollars)--Continued

Item	Total	Zero Assets	Zero to Under 100	100 to Under 250	250 to Under 500	500 to Under 1,000	1,000 to Under 5,000	5,000 to Under 10,000	10,000 to Under 25,000	25,000 to Under 50,000	50,000 to Under 100,000	100,000 to Under 250,000	250,000 or More
Retained Earnings, Unappropriated	6.5E+08	0	-1,937,066	565,229	1,506,934	3,350,900	10,085,157	4,940,261	9,713,900	10,381,561	11,541,582	23,667,162	5.8E+08
Other Retained Earnings (1120S)	47,432,250	0	-1,365,980	-14,786	149,948	1,517,017	11,700,721	8,073,680	12,362,289	5,930,029	4,979,848	3,366,770	732,715
Less: Cost of Treasury Stock	96,183,839	0	372,595	384,005	426,677	1,035,997	2,968,797	1,300,135	1,934,369	1,352,629	1,496,142	2,333,567	82,578,927
Total Receipts	3.5E+09	38,579,237	17,288,937	27,478,884	32,628,240	52,208,594	2.1E+08	1.1E+08	1.7E+08	1.2E+08	1.2E+08	1.9E+08	2.5E+09
Business Receipts	3.3E+09	34,487,774	16,980,488	27,114,470	32,192,798	51,284,170	2.0E+08	1.1E+08	1.6E+08	1.1E+08	1.1E+08	1.8E+08	2.2E+09
Total Deductions	3.4E+09	36,449,354	17,496,129	27,323,521	32,791,866	51,542,790	2.0E+08	1.1E+08	1.6E+08	1.1E+08	1.1E+08	1.8E+08	2.3E+09
Cost of Sales and Operations	2.3E+09	22,781,162	8,806,274	15,301,904	20,053,561	33,865,068	1.4E+08	80,646,961	1.2E+08	82,813,428	80,698,355	1.3E+08	1.5E+09
Net Income (Less Deficit), Total	1.8E+08	2,755,321	-207,191	154,861	-164,122	664,681	3,679,817	2,790,020	4,716,967	4,045,718	4,787,279	7,429,181	1.5E+08

Note: Figures that are too large to print are expressed in exponential notation (for example, 5.2E+08 equals 5,200,000,000.

Source: Department of Treasury, Internal Revenue Service, Publication No. 1053, Corporation Income Tax Returns, Sourcebook, 1989.

Table 9.10 Balance Sheet and Income Statements for U.S. Corporations by Asset Size of Corporation: Wholesale Trade, 1989 (Thousands of Dollars)

Item	Total	Zero Assets	Zero to Under 100	100 to Under 250	250 to Under 500	500 to Under 1,000	1,000 to Under 5,000	5,000 to Under 10,000	10,000 to Under 25,000	25,000 to Under 50,000	50,000 to Under 100,000	100,000 to Under 250,000	250,000 or More
Number of Returns	320,971	17,994	123,104	51,364	38,790	34,891	43,297	6,156	3,445	1,020	436	269	204
Total Assets	6.5E+08	0	4,131,265	8,595,526	13,826,858	24,820,114	91,557,445	42,443,060	52,385,411	34,594,493	30,501,989	42,190,978	3.1E+08
Cash	34,877,060	0	892,217	1,543,275	1,908,876	2,745,172	8,531,339	2,969,969	3,267,063	1,970,109	1,594,259	1,910,095	7,544,688
Notes and Accounts Receivable	1.8E+08	0	800,547	2,269,226	3,757,734	7,837,279	29,290,032	13,807,273	16,775,996	10,614,803	9,431,220	12,133,501	71,758,048
Less: Allowance for Bad Debts	3,394,896	0	1,915	13,497	29,675	73,083	382,142	259,132	399,028	262,588	284,655	371,748	1,317,434
Inventories	1.7E+08	0	918,623	2,242,018	4,315,525	7,796,782	31,124,173	14,362,101	16,947,043	10,582,709	9,517,805	10,779,520	62,069,070
Invest in Government Obligations: Total	40,205,214	0	847	2,862	33,153	48,430	239,506	53,093	188,584	140,392	87,211	210,397	39,200,738
Other Current Assets	48,779,606	0	143,559	344,072	423,322	757,878	2,919,978	1,550,078	2,183,700	1,756,057	1,608,033	2,658,710	34,434,219
Loans to Stockholders	4,047,667	0	251,685	366,383	388,296	404,809	1,017,757	296,582	246,021	131,004	91,438	138,601	715,089
Mortgage and Real Estate Loans	4,198,423	0	29,365	30,715	64,022	74,660	295,399	82,714	75,242	98,260	32,743	20,833	3,394,471
Other Investments	51,124,054	0	48,176	206,741	445,531	814,602	2,836,313	1,699,768	2,624,355	1,982,577	1,881,770	3,476,592	35,107,629
Depreciable Assets	1.5E+08	0	2,529,837	3,566,838	5,079,371	8,755,300	28,103,495	12,024,176	14,494,173	9,662,825	7,653,375	10,831,191	49,501,773
Less: Accumulated Depreciation	74,358,430	0	1,739,186	2,452,694	3,354,201	5,576,339	16,570,899	6,363,834	7,115,915	4,590,939	3,101,489	4,180,825	19,312,107
Depletable Assets	989,972	0	611	27,276	122	175	62,670	21,873	76,513	74,351	75,452	166,054	484,876
Less: Accumulated Depletion	417,848	0	122	18,501	122	75	24,179	3,353	46,392	36,103	27,890	81,742	179,371
Land	9,231,815	0	44,987	73,561	216,490	475,792	1,759,539	920,722	923,573	607,559	410,027	1,054,313	2,745,252
Intangible Assets (Amortizable)	15,333,441	0	82,199	162,664	288,692	416,554	1,148,271	630,097	1,084,846	1,004,784	716,958	1,981,067	7,817,309
Less: Accumulated Amortization	2,805,355	0	37,575	66,352	94,449	119,623	465,466	238,177	297,954	179,317	140,958	356,734	808,752
Other Assets	22,272,514	0	166,688	307,243	381,586	452,995	1,584,301	771,235	1,307,773	981,818	835,422	1,818,114	13,665,339
Total Liabilities	6.5E+08	0	4,131,265	8,595,526	13,826,858	24,820,114	91,557,445	42,443,060	52,385,411	34,594,493	30,501,989	42,190,978	3.1E+08
Accounts Payable	1.2E+08	0	1,061,280	2,205,758	3,615,036	6,451,873	24,531,888	11,026,661	12,559,091	7,731,904	6,778,459	8,050,443	38,225,280
Mort, Notes, and Bonds Under 1 Year	1.5E+08	0	672,903	921,795	1,484,702	2,784,255	13,620,518	7,685,142	10,610,467	6,788,124	6,422,692	8,589,764	86,090,226
Other Current Liabilities	96,112,309	0	472,047	628,008	904,855	1,646,409	6,889,545	3,280,967	4,027,167	3,053,934	2,354,922	3,149,731	69,704,724
Loans from Stockholders	18,001,311	0	1,728,017	1,240,876	1,526,981	1,898,002	3,977,004	1,096,425	1,078,633	570,010	534,783	592,269	3,758,312
Mort, Notes, Bonds 1 Year or More	86,719,489	0	866,282	1,480,474	1,944,379	3,182,983	10,455,906	4,915,768	7,201,256	5,686,581	5,181,621	8,433,867	37,370,372
Other Liabilities	21,644,354	0	119,335	136,915	204,807	298,207	1,462,129	542,397	1,170,048	1,333,315	913,803	1,985,591	13,477,808
Capital Stock	34,164,842	0	966,715	1,231,537	1,202,983	1,840,849	4,700,952	1,706,245	2,167,521	1,641,939	1,828,206	2,532,759	14,345,135
Paid-in or Capital Surplus	41,723,481	0	422,365	582,842	781,980	1,008,131	4,284,240	1,732,831	2,974,232	2,617,309	2,537,492	4,061,767	20,720,292
Retained Earnings, Appropriated	534,626	0	22	119	20,715	77,212	182,830	38,612	24,273	39,481	19,298	18,359	113,704

Table 9.10 Balance Sheet and Income Statements for U.S. Corporations by Asset Size of Corporation: Wholesale Trade, 1989 (Thousands of Dollars)[1]--Continued

Item	Total	Zero Assets	Zero to Under 100	100 to Under 250	250 to Under 500	500 to Under 1,000	1,000 to Under 5,000	5,000 to Under 10,000	10,000 to Under 25,000	25,000 to Under 50,000	50,000 to Under 100,000	100,000 to Under 250,000	250,000 or More
Retained Earnings, Unappropriated	64,069,949	0	-1,185,594	293,553	2,139,153	4,794,636	13,540,567	5,495,493	5,179,420	2,713,620	2,435,092	3,738,224	24,925,785
Other Retained Earnings (1120S)	30,999,361	0	-784,068	197,506	615,090	1,697,963	10,069,551	5,707,404	6,415,583	3,024,092	1,761,870	1,340,313	954,057
Less: Cost of Treasury Stock	9,309,768	0	208,039	323,855	613,824	860,405	2,157,686	784,885	1,022,281	605,816	266,249	302,107	2,164,623
Total Receipts	1.5E+09	27,270,106	24,131,241	37,737,744	50,235,029	87,652,516	2.9E+08	1.3E+08	1.5E+08	1.0E+08	81,103,787	1.1E+08	4.6E+08
Business Receipts	1.5E+09	26,631,650	23,578,740	37,175,787	49,288,120	86,198,591	2.9E+08	1.3E+08	1.4E+08	1.0E+08	79,602,346	1.1E+08	4.4E+08
Total Deductions	1.5E+09	27,121,001	24,385,694	37,503,662	49,944,527	86,955,407	2.9E+08	1.3E+08	1.4E+08	1.0E+08	80,030,899	1.1E+08	4.5E+08
Cost of Sales and Operations	1.3E+09	23,550,815	14,862,329	27,457,252	36,295,017	66,710,339	2.3E+08	1.1E+08	1.2E+08	86,658,875	67,701,372	91,245,020	3.9E+08
Net Income (Less Deficit), Total	18,764,751	226,389	-254,538	234,083	289,923	696,087	4,139,060	2,050,353	2,730,872	1,359,024	1,073,822	1,270,545	4,949,131

Note: Figures that are too large to print are expressed in exponential notation (for example, 5.2E+08 equals 5,200,000,000.

Source: Department of Treasury, Internal Revenue Service, Publication No. 1053, *Corporation Income Tax Returns, Sourcebook,* 1989.

Table 9.11 Balance Sheet and Income Statements for U.S. Corporations by Asset Size of Corporation: Retail Trade, 1989 (Thousands of Dollars)

Item	Total	Zero Assets	Zero to Under 100	100 to Under 250	250 to Under 500	500 to Under 1,000	1,000 to Under 5,000	5,000 to Under 10,000	10,000 to Under 25,000	25,000 to Under 50,000	50,000 to Under 100,000	100,000 to Under 250,000	250,000 or More
Number of Returns	689,305	36,584	314,620	154,255	79,995	48,597	46,355	5,314	2,275	603	291	213	203
Total Assets	7.4E+08	0	12,865,768	24,692,193	27,955,354	33,675,560	96,082,518	35,939,707	33,667,728	20,928,968	20,261,082	33,931,365	4.0E+08
Cash	35,472,489	0	1,781,723	3,031,334	3,205,477	4,032,426	7,722,566	2,091,424	2,050,646	1,210,944	1,109,295	1,678,219	7,558,436
Notes and Accounts Receivable	1.3E+08	0	1,021,856	2,865,337	3,642,328	4,776,881	13,382,845	5,550,430	5,234,675	3,101,017	3,159,671	4,210,832	82,329,622
Less: Allowance for Bad Debts	2,069,812	0	11,719	15,673	21,813	48,592	185,579	96,935	116,703	108,455	110,885	211,004	1,142,454
Inventories	2.0E+08	0	4,175,584	8,692,039	9,815,686	12,435,825	45,447,303	16,929,566	12,646,485	6,135,116	5,906,076	9,429,399	69,014,111
Invest in Government Obligations: Total	1,305,800	0	2,412	6,960	2,622	16,532	188,516	79,187	51,486	46,826	5,060	100,665	805,534
Other Current Assets	33,622,356	0	328,347	624,048	732,860	906,658	2,442,015	1,079,201	1,131,841	822,588	935,557	1,320,418	23,298,824
Loans to Stockholders	7,999,494	0	545,178	772,125	958,250	521,982	1,132,455	256,955	336,886	117,575	57,095	22,279	3,278,713
Mortgage and Real Estate Loans	2,401,600	0	63,605	154,253	178,049	171,171	439,082	50,323	62,082	155,238	104,407	71,438	951,953
Other Investments	65,044,011	0	128,235	496,728	836,585	1,266,354	2,987,452	1,083,290	1,441,040	1,214,202	860,003	2,230,242	52,499,879
Depreciable Assets	2.8E+08	0	10,361,073	13,850,265	15,029,548	15,925,140	34,799,680	12,601,703	14,333,110	9,390,865	9,346,673	15,361,851	1.3E+08
Less: Accumulated Depreciation	1.2E+08	0	6,943,773	8,323,129	8,827,901	9,048,008	18,287,936	6,022,801	6,454,445	3,761,951	3,484,823	5,438,544	43,472,743
Depletable Assets	428,952	0	45,948	61,933	37,811	34,073	28,303	7,522	17,092	82,411	29,982	21,781	62,097
Less: Accumulated Depletion	132,639	0	35,858	14,782	12,440	25,280	12,117	961	6,812	3,170	4,446	3,284	13,490
Land	22,587,449	0	163,103	426,717	756,253	984,646	2,590,283	1,065,504	1,296,477	1,033,425	733,901	1,250,056	12,287,085
Intangible Assets (Amortizable)	27,903,999	0	780,383	1,169,813	873,711	1,186,183	2,075,067	700,208	921,964	1,026,709	799,846	1,561,202	16,808,913
Less: Accumulated Amortization	5,158,995	0	401,715	487,474	367,653	409,453	739,404	179,704	279,697	184,328	150,224	275,404	1,633,938
Other Assets	43,335,322	0	860,394	1,374,469	1,090,236	904,600	2,005,088	693,935	984,293	646,082	886,243	2,566,720	31,323,262
Total Liabilities	7.4E+08	0	12,865,768	24,692,193	27,955,354	33,675,560	96,082,518	35,939,707	33,667,728	20,928,968	20,261,082	33,931,365	4.0E+08
Accounts Payable	1.1E+08	0	2,454,783	4,258,823	4,524,846	5,485,157	13,321,984	4,197,701	4,652,151	3,087,304	3,198,150	4,809,649	56,260,614
Mort, Notes, and Bonds Under 1 Year	1.1E+08	0	1,196,826	2,197,947	2,861,160	4,020,410	30,008,984	14,041,323	10,077,470	4,095,435	2,413,578	2,815,344	39,202,587
Other Current Liabilities	77,054,983	0	1,109,655	1,792,729	1,668,570	2,213,499	6,454,247	2,561,697	2,459,682	1,736,236	1,943,552	2,909,789	52,205,328
Loans from Stockholders	29,308,854	0	6,291,232	5,495,257	3,488,028	3,335,866	4,551,515	1,194,961	724,579	374,352	155,328	281,854	3,415,882
Mort, Notes, Bonds 1 Year or More	1.8E+08	0	2,903,313	5,614,537	5,788,550	6,711,419	15,975,431	5,817,247	6,615,115	5,318,155	5,660,565	10,456,744	1.1E+08
Other Liabilities	49,141,936	0	340,735	365,120	445,787	587,470	1,772,544	765,749	901,828	694,811	893,548	1,526,712	40,847,631
Capital Stock	32,604,939	0	3,275,557	3,000,810	2,589,244	2,364,552	5,188,529	1,384,370	1,180,589	921,693	882,152	1,538,223	10,279,219
Paid-in or Capital Surplus	65,340,036	0	1,543,624	1,938,696	1,358,193	2,514,156	3,806,648	1,506,305	2,008,536	1,901,359	1,953,048	4,596,294	42,213,176
Retained Earnings, Appropriated	701,805	0	8,067	31,554	46,648	98,858	129,313	3,732	6,922	6,342	8,960	168,611	192,797
Retained Earnings, Unappropriated	82,270,403	0	-19,112,486	2,534,841	5,235,551	6,701,695	10,356,789	1,932,802	2,736,607	1,295,551	1,831,025	4,423,285	47,134,741

Table 9.11 Balance Sheet and Income Statements for U.S. Corporations by Asset Size of Corporation: Retail Trade, 1989 (Thousands of Dollars)--Continued

Item	Total	Zero Assets	Zero to Under 100	100 to Under 250	250 to Under 500	500 to Under 1,000	1,000 to Under 5,000	5,000 to Under 10,000	10,000 to Under 25,000	25,000 to Under 50,000	50,000 to Under 100,000	100,000 to Under 250,000	250,000 or More
Other Retained Earnings (1120S)	13,059,245	0	-3,816,445	-1,507,736	878,298	555,586	6,388,436	3,007,066	2,701,790	1,757,898	1,538,563	886,352	669,435
Less: Cost of Treasury Stock	13,707,977	0	529,095	1,030,385	929,522	913,109	1,871,903	473,247	397,541	260,168	217,386	481,492	6,604,128
Total Receipts	1.6E+09	18,616,033	65,317,832	90,411,705	87,640,045	98,997,700	3.2E+08	1.3E+08	1.0E+08	52,433,947	46,335,729	73,653,386	5.5E+08
Business Receipts	1.6E+09	17,630,009	64,606,340	89,325,073	86,421,423	97,358,232	3.2E+08	1.3E+08	99,352,601	50,970,438	44,692,154	71,234,944	5.2E+08
Total Deductions	1.6E+09	18,933,481	65,883,135	90,492,403	87,016,711	98,448,571	3.2E+08	1.3E+08	1.0E+08	52,120,213	45,613,481	72,355,604	5.4E+08
Cost of Sales and Operations	1.1E+09	11,700,376	38,658,155	59,101,899	57,228,547	66,790,364	2.5E+08	1.0E+08	78,114,113	37,999,177	31,324,620	4,9369,451	3.5E+08
Net Income (Less Deficit), Total	17,358,958	-317,469	-566,347	-81,451	621,910	546,401	1,175,787	499,580	491,646	313,274	718,249	1,295,730	12,661,648

Note: Figures that are too large to print are expressed in exponential notation (for example, 5.2E+08 equals 5,200,000,000).

Source: Department of Treasury, Internal Revenue Service, Publication No. 1053, Corporation Income Tax Returns, Sourcebook, 1989.

Table 9.12 Balance Sheet and Income Statements for U.S. Corporations by Asset Size of Corporation: Finance, Insurance, and Real Estate 1989 (Thousands of Dollars)

Item	Total	Zero Assets	Zero to Under 100	100 to Under 250	250 to Under 500	500 to Under 1,000	1,000 to Under 5,000	5,000 to Under 10,000	10,000 to Under 25,000	25,000 to Under 50,000	50,000 to Under 100,000	100,000 to Under 250,000	250,000 or More
Number of Returns	592,832	44,686	266,308	93,168	63,486	44,202	48,421	8,170	7,886	5,235	4,460	3,521	3,290
Total Assets	1.0E+10	0	8,100,764	15,089,401	22,532,841	30,950,252	1.0E+08	57,271,704	1.3E+08	1.9E+08	3.2E+08	5.5E+08	8.5E+09
Cash	5.6E+08	0	2,394,254	3,122,266	3,312,307	3,715,192	8,639,245	4,249,787	8,972,007	11,386,178	17,340,995	25,498,285	4.7E+08
Notes and Accounts Receivable	2.7E+09	0	563,457	1,387,182	1,849,721	2,904,937	9,727,465	7,862,156	31,395,999	60,087,738	1.0E+08	1.5E+08	2.4E+09
Less: Allowance for Bad Debts	75,207,281	0	17,976	36,569	54,713	118,029	238,552	97,237	601,071	1,256,444	2,279,194	3,865,364	66,642,131
Inventories	33,865,422	0	95,313	295,439	481,315	1,551,125	5,260,967	2,383,363	3,016,370	2,457,273	2,649,156	3,775,921	11,899,179
Invest in Government Obligations: Total	8.5E+08	0	1,025	51,012	132,900	253,550	1,535,677	2,495,569	14,834,484	27,084,912	43,760,756	65,830,057	7.0E+08
Other Current Assets	6.2E+08	0	602,241	809,584	1,602,690	2,200,190	8,285,855	3,963,838	7,333,541	9,694,379	12,039,865	22,104,471	5.5E+08
Loans to Stockholders	28,341,043	0	576,963	863,106	1,042,675	864,102	1,651,705	585,628	809,915	746,093	902,790	2,564,537	17,733,530
Mortgage and Real Estate Loans	1.5E+09	0	115,143	513,053	1,014,932	1,043,964	3,395,746	2,248,909	5,799,258	15,991,845	42,430,959	1.0E+08	1.4E+09
Other Investments	2.5E+09	0	496,879	1,510,102	2,658,190	3,519,672	15,203,017	11,890,598	27,300,920	33,486,664	61,024,986	1.3E+08	2.2E+09
Depreciable Assets	3.5E+08	0	5,576,287	7,252,001	10,978,116	13,849,370	40,588,958	17,528,402	21,065,163	17,782,815	18,940,339	25,992,862	1.7E+08
Less: Accumulated Depreciation	1.1E+08	0	3,543,249	3,679,689	4,867,583	5,178,671	12,244,232	4,761,000	5,333,685	5,008,284	5,494,776	7,272,645	55,234,312
Depletable Assets	1,693,551	0	17,652	42,188	32,044	22,825	82,735	58,927	71,837	116,882	159,979	166,619	921,864
Less: Accumulated Depletion	520,890	0	12,618	6,715	13,653	6,982	11,464	21,938	19,126	51,186	58,245	34,092	284,872
Land	67,241,034	0	727,520	2,006,964	3,210,432	4,702,111	14,233,402	5,400,470	6,495,927	4,464,422	3,825,898	4,935,526	17,238,363
Intangible Assets (Amortizable)	41,522,318	0	221,158	398,373	307,005	478,676	1,413,833	869,432	1,069,654	1,243,668	2,266,316	3,279,469	29,974,733
Less: Accumulated Amortization	7,781,175	0	118,027	191,640	133,546	160,224	453,717	287,835	291,277	305,310	452,597	634,506	4,752,497
Other Assets	4.7E+08	0	401,944	711,137	910,992	1,120,378	4,613,722	2,254,370	3,966,985	4,278,696	6,131,426	11,860,012	4.4E+08
Total Liabilities	1.0E+10	0	8,100,764	15,089,401	22,532,841	30,950,252	1.0E+08	57,271,704	1.3E+08	1.9E+08	3.2E+08	5.5E+08	8.5E+09
Accounts Payable	3.3E+08	0	638,453	878,338	1,364,287	1,711,841	5,707,173	2,415,284	3,892,667	4,285,285	5,902,363	10,444,931	3.0E+08
Mort, Notes, and Bonds Under 1 Year	7.3E+08	0	739,039	1,002,418	2,011,062	2,801,930	12,780,240	6,607,723	9,878,253	8,748,480	13,968,096	18,976,509	6.5E+08
Other Current Liabilities	4.4E+09	0	974,970	1,049,136	1,393,004	1,503,083	6,967,063	8,062,464	48,549,607	1.0E+08	1.8E+08	3.0E+08	3.7E+09
Loans from Stockholders	68,318,967	0	2,963,514	2,719,421	3,522,926	3,609,888	9,348,380	3,441,423	3,473,492	2,561,206	2,087,044	3,211,372	31,380,302
Mort, Notes, Bonds 1 Year or More	7.3E+08	0	1,740,002	3,916,898	6,059,950	9,741,474	34,641,677	17,387,193	21,858,688	19,645,469	20,928,560	35,563,301	5.5E+08
Other Liabilities	1.7E+09	0	1,427,708	1,572,691	1,196,113	1,610,064	6,609,233	4,191,885	8,136,027	9,070,815	13,960,380	33,223,225	1.6E+09
Capital Stock	1.0E+09	0	2,254,946	2,389,776	3,223,631	3,698,295	10,536,690	5,904,734	9,231,054	9,965,441	14,598,407	43,055,606	9.2E+08
Paid-in or Capital Surplus	1.5E+09	0	2,199,512	2,220,674	3,104,949	3,941,548	17,064,699	10,268,798	21,377,362	27,703,457	52,951,844	1.0E+08	1.2E+09
Retained Earnings, Appropriated	62,529,905	0	84,659	97,340	116,747	215,458	407,084	153,452	361,382	610,195	1,350,303	2,419,482	56,713,804
Retained Earnings,													

Table 9.12 Balance Sheet and Income Statements for U.S. Corporations by Asset Size of Corporation: Finance, Insurance, and Real Estate 1989 (Thousands of Dollars)--Continued

Item	Total	Zero Assets	Zero to Under 100	100 to Under 250	250 to Under 500	500 to Under 1,000	1,000 to Under 5,000	5,000 to Under 10,000	10,000 to Under 25,000	25,000 to Under 50,000	50,000 to Under 100,000	100,000 to Under 250,000	250,000 or More
Unappropriated	3.2E+08	0	-1,834,751	511,134	857,708	2,723,222	1,383,167	-776,053	774,872	1,481,919	7,678,350	10,755,821	3.0E+08
Other Retained Earnings (1120S)	915,537	0	-2,667,484	-597,047	85,021	37,986	-181,157	125,553	1,372,557	509,452	546,664	1,050,486	633,507
Less: Cost of Treasury Stock	8.4E+08	0	419,807	671,378	402,557	644,536	2,939,335	510,752	692,456	915,301	3,477,712	10,976,183	8.2E+08
Total Receipts	1.9E+09	96,987,259	27,206,314	12,648,276	14,822,158	15,353,316	37,579,890	20,706,965	33,150,167	38,035,379	55,613,887	92,410,573	1.4E+09
Business Receipts	8.6E+08	8,807,634	24,933,381	10,824,776	11,805,838	12,367,470	28,961,102	15,083,968	22,080,540	21,011,066	27,544,282	42,838,327	6.3E+08
Total Deductions	1.7E+09	97,057,414	26,785,519	12,536,264	14,763,342	14,875,937	36,999,638	20,160,426	32,139,696	35,962,642	50,810,039	82,132,540	1.3E+09
Cost of Sales and Operations	4.9E+08	2,123,272	4,513,646	2,616,244	3,723,628	3,247,644	12,240,241	7,839,435	12,038,061	12,094,486	17,007,457	25,805,728	3.8E+08
Net Income (Less Deficit), Total	1.1E+08	161,229	384,112	107,483	51,194	455,642	509,138	462,758	728,434	1,487,061	3,595,164	7,939,473	93,025,662

Note: Figures that are too large to print are expressed in exponential notation (for example, 5.2E+08 equals 5,200,000,000.

Source: Department of Treasury, Internal Revenue Service, Publication No. 1053, <u>Corporation Income Tax Returns, Sourcebook</u>, 1989.

Table 9.13   Balance Sheet and Income Statements for U.S. Corporations by Asset Size of Corporation: Services, 1989 (Thousands of Dollars)

Item	Total	Zero Assets	Zero to Under 100	100 to Under 250	250 to Under 500	500 to Under 1,000	1,000 to Under 5,000	5,000 to Under 10,000	10,000 to Under 25,000	25,000 to Under 50,000	50,000 to Under 100,000	100,000 to Under 250,000	250,000 or More
Number of Returns	989,850	55,821	656,761	143,725	61,861	34,680	29,589	3,723	2,078	754	370	287	202
Total Assets	5.5E+08	0	18,158,965	22,713,534	21,370,885	24,526,726	59,934,141	25,759,292	32,123,666	25,957,529	25,949,956	50,140,287	2.5E+08
Cash	40,985,161	0	4,809,424	4,386,570	3,667,774	3,721,299	6,806,056	2,400,882	2,894,369	2,043,958	1,634,272	2,539,559	6,080,998
Notes and Accounts Receivable	98,252,929	0	1,887,910	3,386,306	3,647,786	4,808,293	13,257,038	5,848,045	7,105,187	5,682,063	5,231,879	10,014,410	37,384,012
Less: Allowance for Bad Debts	4,223,480	0	30,873	37,744	40,031	71,102	380,661	223,777	286,847	182,898	323,627	480,214	2,165,706
Inventories	23,060,757	0	836,015	1,166,642	1,166,371	1,245,861	3,321,861	1,254,287	1,484,738	1,071,883	1,077,810	2,132,347	8,302,940
Invest in Government Obligations: Total	1,766,833	0	21,672	64,127	8,110	46,034	220,794	123,307	183,039	166,045	79,879	231,299	622,528
Other Current Assets	34,394,791	0	834,170	1,396,706	1,172,500	1,152,693	3,250,493	1,509,232	2,231,760	1,763,727	1,430,188	4,192,517	15,460,805
Loans to Stockholders	7,723,755	0	1,403,943	1,480,768	942,271	817,901	1,269,063	422,211	158,110	380,104	178,812	359,394	311,179
Mortgage and Real Estate Loans	3,232,421	0	56,705	269,659	278,382	284,548	802,394	65,952	145,929	165,018	223,963	119,927	819,943
Other Investments	87,864,765	0	592,490	1,132,591	1,234,334	1,633,539	3,869,030	1,915,459	3,330,051	2,422,201	3,303,020	8,637,923	59,794,127
Depreciable Assets	2.9E+08	0	21,434,142	18,368,000	17,197,024	17,831,948	39,930,375	15,982,299	17,491,691	13,541,434	13,810,761	19,230,308	98,564,741
Less: Accumulated Depreciation	1.3E+08	0	15,204,202	11,081,553	10,077,577	9,820,559	19,009,839	6,742,949	6,922,239	5,085,122	5,666,683	6,424,695	32,485,830
Depletable Assets	256,381	0	72,257	33,532	21,374	7,396	27,908	6,016	2,104	4,615	1,587	40,941	38,652
Less: Accumulated Depletion	136,159	0	43,777	14,448	12,523	4,794	7,579	4,957	165	684	109	30,519	16,604
Land	17,050,619	0	206,365	569,654	687,722	1,330,872	2,612,342	960,955	1,302,336	917,123	927,509	1,512,880	6,022,861
Intangible Assets (Amortizable)	38,444,862	0	672,725	934,984	777,834	792,056	2,095,989	1,338,332	1,571,045	1,529,862	3,033,373	5,764,634	19,934,027
Less: Accumulated Amortization	8,423,961	0	334,215	374,867	330,874	334,448	769,181	456,952	441,746	345,538	971,894	1,415,667	2,648,578
Other Assets	46,098,598	0	938,661	1,007,395	975,025	1,066,567	2,575,897	1,305,752	1,784,689	1,776,212	1,794,448	3,660,850	29,213,102
Total Liabilities	5.5E+08	0	18,158,965	22,713,534	21,370,885	24,526,726	59,934,141	25,759,292	32,123,666	25,957,529	25,949,956	50,140,287	2.5E+08
Accounts Payable	47,273,741	0	1,900,906	2,369,334	2,168,964	2,772,574	7,201,590	3,004,093	3,185,089	2,254,389	1,965,852	4,079,361	16,371,588
Mort., Notes, and Bonds Under 1 Year	60,726,805	0	2,126,791	2,517,641	2,349,419	2,376,140	7,613,125	3,454,708	4,394,672	3,120,405	3,440,909	6,863,964	22,469,029
Other Current Liabilities	65,489,816	0	2,660,704	2,116,135	2,046,541	2,637,977	7,668,733	3,048,957	4,254,887	3,305,456	2,595,287	6,800,624	28,354,515
Loans from Stockholders	29,015,823	0	6,118,000	4,578,006	2,814,517	2,963,734	5,015,743	1,220,705	975,449	578,811	486,042	861,821	3,402,993
Mort., Notes, Bonds 1 Year or More	1.7E+08	0	3,932,140	5,181,961	5,206,760	6,575,036	17,348,830	7,439,925	10,124,586	8,814,002	9,393,953	17,777,528	81,666,147
Other Liabilities	43,789,868	0	1,138,848	669,800	699,408	1,048,724	2,943,764	1,652,264	1,910,273	1,687,648	2,311,793	4,058,260	25,669,086
Capital Stock	32,967,230	0	3,269,045	2,006,920	1,849,996	2,281,621	3,964,836	1,784,793	2,429,446	1,491,648	1,529,211	2,032,551	10,327,163
Paid-in or Capital Surplus	88,915,375	0	3,139,718	1,556,539	1,656,733	2,065,190	9,248,601	3,578,953	5,826,848	4,539,072	4,524,766	8,551,425	44,227,530
Retained Earnings, Appropriated	724,999	0	27,082	18	112,603	61,874	52,686	106,131	87,535	46,374	28,996	153,830	47,869

Table 9.13 Balance Sheet and Income Statements for U.S. Corporations by Asset Size of Corporation: Services, 1989 (Thousands of Dollars)--Continued

Item	Total	Zero Assets	Zero to Under 100	100 to Under 250	250 to Under 500	500 to Under 1,000	1,000 to Under 5,000	5,000 to Under 10,000	10,000 to Under 25,000	25,000 to Under 50,000	50,000 to Under 100,000	100,000 to Under 250,000	250,000 or More
Retained Earnings, Unappropriated	17,630,584	0	-993,097	3,026,001	2,575,719	1,335,485	-1,298,509	17,291	-1,493,536	-241,202	-440,445	-789,555	15,932,433
Other Retained Earnings (1120S)	1,711,593	0	-4,478,365	-669,785	617,490	1,002,990	1,769,946	856,995	899,218	666,373	355,498	434,634	256,599
Less: Cost of Treasury Stock	9,574,564	0	682,808	639,035	727,264	594,620	1,595,204	405,523	470,803	305,447	241,907	684,155	3,227,797
Total Receipts	7.4E+08	11,620,422	1.1E+08	72,017,079	54,141,274	52,932,644	1.0E+08	37,179,025	36,493,981	29,075,355	25,863,522	43,620,160	1.6E+08
Business Receipts	6.8E+08	10,360,712	1.1E+08	69,828,264	52,552,018	49,599,276	98,882,298	34,776,841	33,177,810	27,010,674	23,262,017	39,466,557	1.3E+08
Total Deductions	7.2E+08	11,806,938	1.1E+08	71,501,317	53,481,421	52,407,750	1.0E+08	36,870,038	36,440,522	28,478,170	25,609,979	43,592,554	1.5E+08
Cost of Sales and Operations	2.7E+08	4,234,910	32,645,562	23,509,464	21,384,071	19,776,105	45,360,124	16,641,693	14,629,675	12,710,692	9,731,682	18,869,563	54,037,758
Net Income (Less Deficit), Total	11,020,194	68,816	1,855,878	513,401	657,672	523,229	639,729	318,744	57,025	574,715	247,055	77,849	5,486,080

Note: Figures that are too large to print are expressed in exponential notation (for example, 5.2E+08 equals 5,200,000,000.

Source: Department of Treasury, Internal Revenue Service, Publication No. 1053, Corporation Income Tax Returns, Sourcebook, 1989.

Table 9.14   Short-Term and Long-Term Loan Rates for Small Commercial and Industrial Loans by All Commercial Banks, February 1986-August 1992[1]

		Short-Term Loans[2]		Prime Rate	Term Loans	
		Fixed Rate	Floating Rate		Fixed Rate	Floating Rate
1992						
	August	8.94	7.48	6.00	9.41	7.71
	May	7.89	7.78	6.50	9.17	7.79
	February	8.18	7.80	6.50	9.07	7.84
1991						
	November	9.35	8.95	7.50	10.05	9.03
	August	11.20	10.16	8.50	11.26	10.37
	May	11.19	10.22	8.50	11.24	10.64
	February	11.29	10.68	9.00	11.73	11.12
1990						
	November	11.90	11.87	10.00	12.30	12.06
	August	12.06	11.84	10.00	12.15	12.08
	May	11.87	11.96	10.00	11.99	12.05
	February	12.12	11.96	10.00	12.29	12.19
1989						
	November	12.38	12.45	10.50	12.28	12.48
	August	12.67	12.49	10.50	12.42	12.66
	May	13.37	13.46	11.50	13.16	13.74
	February	12.26	12.54	10.93	14.08	12.66
1988						
	November	11.94	11.90	10.05	12.65	12.05
	August	11.43	11.48	9.84	11.53	11.59
	May	10.90	10.38	8.84	11.77	10.62
	February	11.17	10.48	8.51	11.90	10.88
1987						
	November	11.29	10.78	8.78	11.93	11.28
	August	10.66	10.15	8.70	12.11	10.15
	May	11.10	9.85	8.25	11.22	10.08
	February	10.51	9.41	7.50	11.04	9.81
1986						
	November	10.55	9.51	7.5	11.35	9.41
	August	10.94	9.90	7.9	11.84	9.99
	May	11.34	10.42	8.5	12.28	10.54
	February	12.52	11.46	9.5	13.02	11.77

[1]Small loans refer to loans under $100,000.

[2]Averages of loan rates for three loan sizes: under $25,000, $25,000 to under $50,000, and $50,000 to under $100,000.

Source: Board of Governors of the Federal Reserve System, Survey of Terms of Bank Lending, Statistical Release E.2, various issues; and Federal Reserve Bulletin, various issues.

Table 9.15 Loan Rates Charged by Banks on Commercial and Industrial Loans Made in August 1991 and May 1992, by Loan Size

| | Loan Size (Thousands of Dollars) | | | |
	1-100	100-499	500-999	1,000+
August 1991				
Large Banks				
Short-Term Loans				
Fixed Rate	9.53	8.56	8.03	7.11*
Floating Rate	9.87	9.48	9.24	7.94*
Term Loans				
Fixed Rate	10.63	9.17	7.80	7.83
Floating Rate	9.92	9.63	9.43	8.92
Small Banks				
Short-Term Loans				
Fixed Rate	11.37	9.55	7.62	6.97*
Floating Rate	10.25	9.73	9.63	8.08
Term Loans				
Fixed Rate	11.29	10.47	9.60	7.55
Floating Rate	10.45	10.06	10.29	9.74
May 1992				
Large Banks				
Short-Term Loans				
Fixed Rate	6.82	5.54	5.12	4.43*
Floating Rate	7.23	6.82	6.62	5.47*
Term Loans				
Fixed Rate	9.64	7.86	7.09	5.06
Floating Rate	7.11	6.85	6.39	6.21
Small Banks				
Short-Term Loans				
Fixed Rate	9.06	6.76	5.23	4.18*
Floating Rate	7.58	7.12	6.86	5.70*
Term Loans				
Fixed Rate	9.40	8.68	8.38	5.70
Floating Rate	7.84	8.33	7.02	6.16

*Averages of loan rates for three loan sizes: $1-5 million, $5-10 million, and $10 million and over.

Source: Board of Governors of the Federal Reserve System, Survey of Terms of Bank Lending, Statistical Release E.2 (September 17, 1991 and June 12, 1992).

Table 9.16 Commercial and Industrial Loans by Large Weekly Reporting and Other Commercial Banks, December 31, 1980-September 1992 (Billions of Dollars)[1]

	All Banks		Large Weekly Reporting Banks		Other Banks		Annual Change in GDP Deflator (Percent)
	Amount	Change (Percent)	Amount	Change (Percent)	Amount	Change (Percent)	
September 30, 1992	593.9	-5.4[2]	278.5	-5.3[2]	315.4	-5.3[2]	2.78[3]
December 31, 1991	619.1	-4.5	290.1	-8.4	329.0	-0.8	3.47
December 31, 1990	648.0	0.8	316.6	-0.7	331.4	2.7	4.72
December 31, 1989	642.6	3.4	318.8	5.6	322.8	6.9	4.26
December 31, 1988	605.0	6.8	302.0	8.1	303.0	4.5	4.24
December 31, 1987	566.4	5.1	279.5	-3.3	289.9	16.0	3.37
December 31, 1986	539.0	7.3	289.1	11.2	249.9	3.2	2.62
December 31, 1985	502.1	5.7	260.0	3.4	242.1	8.1	3.47
December 31, 1984	474.9	14.2	251.4	12.3	223.9	16.7	3.36
December 31, 1983	415.7	4.9	223.9	2.5	191.8	7.9	3.24
December 31, 1982	396.2	10.0	218.5	10.9	177.7	9.0	NA
December 31, 1981	360.1	10.7	197.0	11.9	163.1	9.3	NA
December 31, 1980	325.3		176.1		149.2		

NA = GDP deflator not available for these years.

[1]Not seasonally adjusted. Large weekly reporting banks are banks with domestic assets of $1.4 billion or more as of December 31, 1982.
[2]Annualized rate of change.

[3]Changes from the third quarter of the previous year.

Source: Board of Governors of the Federal Reserve System, Federal Reserve Bulletin, various issues; idem, "Revised Bank Credit Series," March 9, 1988; U.S. Department of Commerce, Bureau of Economic Analysis, Business Conditions Digest, various issues; and idem, Survey of Current Business, various issues.

Table 9.17 Business Loans Outstanding from Finance Companies, December 31, 1980-June 30, 1992

| | Total Receivables Outstanding | | Annual Change In GDP Deflator[1] (Percent) |
	Billions of Dollars	Change (Percent)	
June 30, 1992	293.7	0.7[2]	2.78[2]
December 31, 1991	292.6	-0.3	3.47
December 31, 1990	293.5	14.6	4.72
December 31, 1989	256.0	9.1	4.26
December 31, 1988	234.6	13.9	4.24
December 31, 1987	206.0	19.7	3.37
December 31, 1986	172.1	9.3	2.62
December 31, 1985	157.5	14.3	3.47
December 31, 1984	137.8	21.9	3.36
December 31, 1983	113.4	12.9	3.24
December 31, 1982	100.4	0	NA
December 31, 1981	100.3	11.1	NA
December 31, 1980	90.3		

NA = GDP deflator not available for these years.

[1]Changes from the fourth quarter of the year before.

[2]Annualized rate of change.

Source: Board of Governors of the Federal Reserve System, <u>Federal Reserve Bulletin</u>, Table 1.52, various issues; U.S. Department of Commerce, Bureau of Economic Analysis, <u>Business Conditions Digest</u>, various issues; and idem, <u>Survey of Current Business</u>, February 1992.

Table 9.18 Common Stock Initial Public Offerings by All and Small Issuers, 1984-October 1992 (Millions of Dollars)[1]

	Common Stock	
	Number	Amount
Offerings by All Issuers		
1/1/92-10/31/92	434	21,137.3
1/1/91-10/31/91	273	11,695.5
1/1/91-12/31/91	366	16,407.7
1990	172	4,519.0
1989	204	6,067.5
1988	225	5,738.8
1987	519	17,023.1
1986	701	18,086.2
1985	353	8,347.9
1984	355	3,807.8
Offerings by Issuers with Assets of $10 Million or Less		
1/1/92-10/31/92	170	3,938.0
1/1/91-10/31/91	85	1,015.8
1/1/91-12/31/91	120	1,398.4
1990	81	1,007.3
1989	103	1,171.5
1988	108	1,235.8
1987	258	6,033.3
1986	346	3,662.9
1985	188	3,110.1
1984	355	3,807.8
Offerings by Nonfinancial Issuers with Assets of $10 Million or Less		
1/1/92-10/31/92	161	3,490.3
1/1/91-10/31/91	79	966.5
1/1/91-12/31/91	111	1,328.5
1990	67	952.2
1989	95	1,148.6
1988	83	707.7
1987	224	5,099.2
1986	288	2,464.7
1985	151	969.8
1984	298	3,014.7

[1]Excludes closed-end funds. Registered offerings data from the Securities and Exchange Commission are no longer available. Data provided by Securities Data Company are not as inclusive as those registered with the SEC.

Source: Special tabulations prepared for the U.S. Small Business Administration, Office of Advocacy by Securities Data Company, Inc.

Table 9.19 New Commitments, Disbursements, and Total Capital Pool of the Venture Capital Industry, 1982-1992 (Billions of Dollars)

Year	New Commitments to Venture Capital Firms	Disbursements to Funded Companies	Number of Funded Companies	Total Investment Capital Pool At End of Year[1]
1992[2]	2.5[2]	1.4[2]	633[2]	NA
1991	1.3	1.4	792	NA
1990	1.8	2.3	1,176	36.0
1989	2.4	3.4	1,465	34.4
1988	2.9	3.8	1,530	31.1
1987	4.1	4.0	1,740	29.0
1986	3.3	3.2	1,512	24.1
1985	3.3	2.7	1,388	19.6
1984	4.2	2.7	1,410	16.3
1983	4.5	2.5	1,236	12.1
1982	1.7	1.4	828	6.7

NA = Not available.

[1]The capital pool at year end should equal the total pool at the end of the previous year plus new commitments, minus the amount of net withdrawal (or liquidation) from the funds. For 1983, an additional $600 million was identified which had not been included in the prior estimate.

[2]For the first six months of 1992.

Source: Capital Publishing Corporation, <u>Venture Capital Journal</u> (various issues).

Table 9.20 Sources of Capital Committed to Independent Venture Funds, 1983-1992 (Percent)

	1983	1984	1985	1986	1987	1988	1989	1990	1991	1992
Total (Billions of Dollars)	3.4	3.2	2.3	3.3	4.2	2.8	2.4	0.95	1.3	2.5
Share contributed by:										
Pension Funds	31	34	33	50	39	46	36	49	42	42
Foreign Sources	16	18	23	11	13	14	13	12	12	11
Corporations	12	14	12	11	11	11	20	6	4	3
Endowments	8	6	8	6	10	12	12	17	24	19
Individuals	21	15	13	12	12	8	6	8	12	11
Banks/Insurance COs	12	13	11	10	15	9	13	8	6	15
Total	100	100	100	100	100	100	100	100	100	100

Source: Capital Publishing Corporation, <u>Venture Capital Journal</u>, various issues.

Table 9.21 Disbursements to Small Business by Small Business Investment Companies (SBICs) and 301(d) SBICs, 1980-September 1991 (Millions of Dollars)

Year	Total Number	Total Amount	SBICs Number	SBICs Amount	301(d)[1] Number	301(d)[1] Amount
1992[2]	1,954	534.2	895	425.1	1,059	109.1
1991[3]	2,013	491.6	1,033	324.3	980	167.3
1990	2,367	645.2	1,334	545.9	1,033	99.3
1989	3,322	690.0	1,876	542.4	1,446	147.6
1988	3,724	750.9	2,227	614.4	1,497	136.5
1987	4,128	680.5	2,522	537.9	1,606	142.6
1986	4,333	620.8	2,675	75.9	1,658	144.9
1985	4,205	542.3	2,756	434.6	1,449	107.7
1984	3,990	513.9	2,755	425.5	1,235	88.0
1983	3,247	468.8	2,464	412.9	783	55.9
1982	2,941	369.9	2,177	322.9	764	47.0
1981	3,176	387.1	2,434	332.7	742	54.4
1980	2,637	337.4	2,090	295.2	547	42.2

[1]301(d) companies are minority or economically disadvantaged Small Business Investment Companies.

[2]Figures for 1992 are annualized figures based on disbursements made from January through September.

[3]Figures for 1991 are annualized figures based on disbursements made from January through September.

Source: U.S. Small Business Administration, Investment Division.

Table 9.22 Sources of Credit for Small and Medium-Sized Businesses (Dollars Borrowed as a Percentage of Total Assets)[1]

	All Small and Medium-Sized Firms	Asset Size of Firm		
		Under $1 Million	$1 Million-$10 Million	Over $10 Million
Total Credit	36.1	41.3	35.1	33.5
Total Credit plus Accounts Payable	48.8	48.0	50.2	48.0
Total Credit From Financial Institutions	25.0	25.8	25.5	23.8
Depository Institutions	20.5	21.4	20.6	19.8
Commercial Banks	17.3	15.8	16.4	19.3
Thrifts[2]	3.3	5.6	4.2	0.5
Nondepository Financial Institutions	4.4	4.3	4.9	4.1
Leasing Companies	0.4	0.4	0.5	0.4
Finance Companies	3.0	1.8	3.3	3.6
Other Financial[3]	1.0	2.1	1.0	0.1
Nonfinancial Sources[4]	11.1	15.6	9.6	9.7
Owners	4.2	7.4	3.8	2.4
Accounts Payable	12.7	6.7	15.1	14.5

[1]Average percentages are weighted by asset size. All figures have been weighted to adjust for unequal sampling and response rates.

[2]Thrifts include savings and loan associations, savings banks, and credit unions.

[3]In addition to those listed, nondepository financial institutions include brokerage companies, mortgage companies, and insurance companies.

[4]Other sources include loans from owners, individuals, family and relatives, nonfinancial corporations, and government agencies. This percentage also includes loans for which the source is not known--approximately 3 percent of small and medium-sized business assets.

Source: Preliminary data compiled from the National Survey of Small Business Finances by staff of the Board of Governors of the Federal Reserve System.

Table 9.23 Small and Medium-Sized Firms Obtaining Financial Services from Various Sources, 1990 (Percent)

Source	All Credit	Type of Credit					
		Leasing	Line of Credit	Mortgage	Vehicle	Equipment	Other
All Sources	71.5	7.1	24.0	17.8	25.9	14.7	32.9
All Financial Institutions	57.9	5.3	23.7	14.4	24.8	12.5	8.9
All Depository Institutions	51.5	1.8	23.1	13.7	16.7	9.9	8.0
Commercial Banks	47.5	1.7	21.9	11.3	15.2	9.3	7.0
Thrifts[1]	6.5	0.2	1.7	2.6	1.7	0.6	1.1
All Nondepository Financial Institutions[2]	17.8	3.9	0.9	1.1	9.9	3.2	1.0
Leasing Companies	4.3	2.7	4	4	0.6	1.2	4
Finance Companies	13.3	1.3	0.8	0.6	9.4	2.0	0.5
Other Financial	1.2	0.1	0.2	0.5	4	0.1	0.5
Nonfinancial Sources	28.2	2.2	0.3	3.9	1.3	2.7	21.4
Source Unknown	7.0	0.1	0.1	0.4	0.1	0.1	6.8

[1]Thrifts include savings and loan associations, savings banks, and credit unions.

[2]In addition to those listed, nondepository institutions include: brokerage and money market mutual fund companies, mortgage banks, and insurance companies.

[3]Nonfinancial sources include: venture capital firms, other businesses, family or other individuals, government agencies, and owners.

[4]Indicates percentage less than 0.05.

Source: Computed from the National Survey of Small Business Finances by the staff of Federal Reserve Board. See also Greg Ellihausen and John Wolken, "Banking Markets and the Use of Financial Services by Small and Medium-Sized Business," Staff Study no. 160, (Washington, D.C.: Board of Governors of the Federal Reserve System, 1990).

10 Small Business Economic Indicators

Introduction

The U.S. Small Business Administration's Office of Advocacy compiles the latest small business economic indicators by state. These economic indicators serve as a quick reference guide to current data on small business activity nationwide. The data are collected from various federal and private sources—including the U.S. Department of Labor, U.S. Department of Commerce, and the Dun and Bradstreet Corporation. These economic indicators were selected based on their availability and applicability to small business.

New Business Incorporations

Data on new business incorporations are collected and published by the Dun and Bradstreet Corporation (D&B). These data represent businesses that file for organization as a corporation with the secretary of state in each jurisdiction.

These business incorporation filings may reflect:
- An actual start-up of a new business,
- An intention to start a new business,
- The conversion of an existing sole proprietorship or partnership into the corporate form,
- The creation of a subsidiary of an existing corporation.

Therefore, using these data as a business formation indicator warrants some degree of caution.

New and Successor Firms

New and successor firm data are collected from State Employment Security Agency quarterly reports to the U.S. Department of Labor's Employment and Training Administration. If a firm has employees, it is required to file quarterly income tax withholding for each employee and pay both unemployment insurance (FUTA) and the employer's share of Social Security taxes (FICA). Therefore, the number of new firms with employees is available with little or no lag. A new firm in this case is a firm which has begun to employ people. A successor firm is an existing firm with employees which has changed owners. The new owners are required to file withholding taxes quarterly, and in that manner company records can be updated.

Small Business Income

An approximation of small business income—the income of nonfarm sole proprietorships and partnerships—is collected and published quarterly by the U.S. Department of Commerce's Bureau of Economic Analysis. It represents about 85 percent of small firms but only 20 percent of small firm earnings.

These data represent estimates derived from two sources: (1) quarterly income data interpolated from the U.S. Department of Commerce, Bureau of Economic Analysis, and (2) annual data extrapolated from tax returns (1040C and 1065) and published by the Internal Revenue Service.

These data include inventory valuation and capital consumption adjustments and exclude employer pension contributions and other nonlabor sources of income. While proprietors' income represents about 15 to 20 percent of income in the small business sector, it is not the only source. About half of wage-and-salary income also represents small business income, usually from small corporations. The latter, however, cannot be disaggregated by firm size on a regular basis.

Business Bankruptcies

Business bankruptcy data are provided to the U.S. Small Business Administration by the Statistical Analysis and Reports Division of the Administrative Office of the U.S. Courts. These data are reported under federal bankruptcy regulations when businesses file bankruptcy petitions under Chapters 7, 11, or 12 of the bankruptcy laws.

A business bankruptcy is a legal recognition that a company is insolvent—that is, it cannot satisfy its creditors or discharge its liabilities. Therefore, the company must restructure (Chapter 11) or completely liquidate (Chapter 7). (Farm businesses are liquidated under the provisions of Chapter 12.) Business bankruptcy data are more likely to include self-employed persons and new, very small firms than are business failures.

Business Failures

Business failures are collected and published by the Dun and Bradstreet Corporation (D&B). These data represent businesses that are no longer in D&B's list of active businesses during their latest survey due to failure or the filing of a bankruptcy petition. A business failure is defined as an enterprise that ceases operation with a loss to one or more creditors.

**Business
Terminations**

Data on business terminations are collected from State Employment Security Agencies and submitted quarterly to the U.S. Department of Labor, Employment and Training Administration. If a firm has employees, it is required to withhold quarterly federal income tax for each employee, and pay quarterly unemployment insurance premiums under the FICA and FUTA laws. Therefore, when a firm terminates operations (that is, ceases to employ people), the respective state Employment Security Agency has a record since no more tax payments are received.

Chapter 10 Tables

Table 10.1 New Business Incorporations by SBA Region and by State, 1982-1992

	1982	1983	1984	1985	1986	1987	1988	1989	1990	1991	1992
U.S. Total	566.9	600.4	635.0	662.0	702.1	685.6	685.1	676.6	647.7	628.6	666.8
Region I	26.5	28.7	32.0	37.9	42.0	42.0	40.3	35.3	31.4	28.9	28.7
Connecticut	7.3	7.7	8.1	11.2	12.5	12.1	11.9	10.4	9.1	8.5	7.3
Maine	1.8	2.1	2.2	2.6	3.1	3.2	3.1	2.8	2.4	2.3	2.4
Massachusetts	11.8	12.6	14.2	15.8	17.3	17.2	16.4	14.1	12.5	11.7	12.2
New Hampshire	2.0	2.3	2.8	3.5	3.9	3.7	3.4	2.9	2.7	2.4	2.6
Rhode Island	2.3	2.5	2.8	3.1	3.5	3.7	3.4	3.3	3.0	2.5	2.6
Vermont	1.3	1.5	1.9	1.7	1.8	2.0	2.0	1.8	1.7	1.5	1.6
Region II	82.1	90.4	96.3	102.5	110.0	108.2	110.3	103.8	93.9	91.8	97.5
New Jersey	22.4	26.2	27.6	30.5	33.1	31.9	32.7	30.4	28.3	28.0	30.0
New York	59.7	64.2	68.6	72.1	76.9	76.3	77.7	73.4	65.6	63.8	67.5
Region III	63.0	67.6	72.1	78.3	89.3	91.5	92.8	93.4	88.2	85.0	89.2
Delaware	22.0	23.9	25.9	26.6	31.5	31.4	31.5	30.9	29.9	29.9	33.6
District of Columbia	1.7	2.8	2.1	2.2	2.3	2.3	2.3	2.3	2.4	2.3	2.4
Maryland	10.4	9.6	11.2	14.2	16.0	16.4	16.9	17.3	16.7	16.5	17.2
Pennsylvania	13.4	14.6	15.9	17.7	20.2	21.4	21.8	22.2	19.4	17.3	16.9
Virginia	12.0	13.7	14.6	15.0	16.7	17.2	17.7	18.0	17.4	16.9	16.9
West Virginia	3.4	2.9	2.5	2.5	2.6	2.8	2.7	2.6	2.5	2.2	2.2
Region IV	103.5	114.7	125.7	133.7	141.0	142.3	138.5	144.6	144.3	141.6	152.4
Alabama	4.4	5.5	6.0	6.1	6.8	6.7	6.6	6.6	6.1	6.1	7.1
Florida	56.1	61.3	67.0	71.6	77.6	79.4	75.0	80.0	81.4	81.1	86.0
Georgia	12.5	14.6	17.7	17.3	17.6	18.1	18.7	18.8	18.9	18.1	21.0
Kentucky	6.0	6.4	7.5	7.9	7.7	6.7	7.0	6.9	6.7	6.8	7.2
Mississippi	3.5	3.2	2.9	3.2	3.1	3.8	3.8	3.6	3.4	3.6	3.8
North Carolina	9.6	11.2	11.1	11.8	12.7	12.3	12.8	13.2	12.4	11.9	12.6
South Carolina	4.0	4.7	5.7	7.1	6.2	6.3	6.2	6.9	7.2	5.7	6.2
Tennessee	7.5	7.9	7.7	8.7	9.3	9.1	8.5	8.5	8.3	8.3	8.5
Region V	82.1	86.8	93.8	90.7	95.1	93.7	99.2	100.8	98.3	93.8	102.8
Illinois	28.5	30.0	32.9	26.1	27.0	26.8	28.7	28.9	29.3	29.1	30.9
Indiana	8.3	8.8	9.4	9.9	10.7	11.0	13.0	14.0	11.7	10.2	11.1
Michigan	17.2	18.5	19.5	21.9	22.9	21.8	22.6	22.5	22.2	20.1	24.7
Minnesota	7.4	8.2	9.1	9.2	9.7	9.4	9.5	9.6	9.7	9.6	10.0
Ohio	14.5	15.0	16.3	17.2	18.4	18.4	19.0	18.8	18.1	17.9	18.7
Wisconsin	6.2	6.3	6.6	6.4	6.5	6.2	6.3	7.0	7.3	7.0	7.3
Region VI	76.5	71.6	65.6	69.0	66.4	60.3	55.5	59.3	60.6	58.7	61.0
Arkansas	3.9	4.2	4.9	5.3	5.8	5.7	4.3	6.5	6.1	5.3	6.1
Louisiana	14.3	11.1	9.3	11.4	11.7	10.1	9.1	9.0	9.0	9.0	10.8
New Mexico	2.5	2.5	2.9	2.8	2.5	2.4	2.5	2.6	2.9	2.7	2.8
Oklahoma	13.6	10.1	5.5	8.1	7.6	7.6	7.2	7.2	7.2	7.1	7.2
Texas	42.2	43.9	43.0	41.4	38.8	34.6	32.5	34.0	35.5	34.6	34.0

Table 10.1 New Business Incorporations by SBA Region and by State, 1982-1992--Continued

	1982	1983	1984	1985	1986	1987	1988	1989	1990	1991	1992
Region VII	20.2	22.1	21.8	21.6	22.4	20.9	21.2	21.5	21.3	21.1	22.5
Iowa	4.2	4.4	4.0	4.1	4.2	3.8	3.8	4.6	4.4	4.5	4.9
Kansas	4.4	5.3	5.1	4.8	4.4	4.3	4.4	4.4	4.2	3.9	4.3
Missouri	8.6	9.6	10.0	10.2	11.2	10.3	10.3	10.0	9.8	9.5	10.0
Nebraska	2.9	2.8	2.7	2.6	2.6	2.6	2.7	2.7	2.9	3.1	3.3
Region VIII	20.3	21.4	22.8	22.1	24.1	22.4	24.0	21.3	21.0	23.4	25.3
Colorado	11.8	12.8	14.2	14.2	15.9	14.5	16.2	13.4	12.3	13.6	14.9
Montana	1.6	1.5	1.6	1.4	1.5	1.4	1.3	1.3	1.5	1.6	1.9
North Dakota	1.0	0.9	1.0	0.9	0.9	1.0	0.9	0.8	0.9	0.8	1.0
South Dakota	0.8	1.0	1.0	0.9	1.0	1.0	1.0	1.0	1.1	1.0	1.2
Utah	3.6	4.1	4.0	3.7	3.9	3.8	3.8	3.9	4.1	5.0	4.6
Wyoming	1.4	1.2	1.1	1.0	1.0	0.8	0.8	0.9	1.2	1.4	1.7
Region IX	73.8	77.2	84.6	85.8	92.1	84.7	82.7	75.0	65.1	61.2	62.5
Arizona	9.6	10.7	12.1	12.9	12.5	11.9	12.4	11.6	10.1	9.8	9.1
California	53.7	55.4	61.0	61.1	67.2	59.7	56.4	48.2	39.1	36.6	37.0
Hawaii	2.6	2.5	2.8	3.0	2.8	3.2	3.2	3.8	3.8	3.8	3.8
Nevada	7.9	8.6	8.8	8.7	9.5	9.9	10.7	11.4	12.0	11.0	12.6
Region X	19.1	19.8	20.3	20.3	19.8	19.4	20.5	21.6	23.7	23.1	24.9
Alaska	2.5	2.5	2.5	2.1	1.7	1.5	1.4	1.4	1.3	1.3	1.5
Idaho	1.7	1.8	1.7	1.6	1.8	1.7	1.9	1.7	1.9	1.9	2.1
Oregon	6.1	6.7	6.8	7.2	7.3	6.9	7.2	7.7	8.5	8.4	8.9
Washington	8.7	8.8	9.3	9.4	9.0	9.4	10.1	10.7	11.9	11.5	12.5

Source: Adapted by the U.S. Small Business Administration, Office of Advocacy, from the Dun and Bradstreet Corporation, New Business Incorporations, various issues.

Table 10.2 New and Successor Firms by SBA Region and State, 1982-1992

	1982	1983	1984	1985	1986	1987	1988	1989	1990	1991	1992
U.S. Total	781,009	804,129	854,887	880,839	899,692	911,456	885,087	898,007	915,145	864,220	874,087
Region I	36,552	44,944	45,725	46,592	52,857	56,628	57,725	53,421	45,969	45,542	43,316
Connecticut	9,779	10,860	11,312	11,509	12,947	13,879	14,711	13,856	12,128	10,975	10,599
Maine	3,461	3,673	4,477	3,317	5,612	5,796	5,948	5,671	4,741	4,435	4,708
Massachusetts	14,599	20,776	19,291	18,706	20,649	22,066	22,611	20,658	17,463	15,393	15,912
New Hampshire	3,507	4,362	5,000	5,668	6,593	6,868	6,148	5,624	5,211	4,738	4,756
Rhode Island	3,022	3,072	3,424	3,803	3,817	4,438	4,796	4,325	3,557	7,210	4,622
Vermont	2,184	2,201	2,221	3,589	3,239	3,581	3,511	3,287	2,869	2,791	2,719
Region II	81,262	83,058	90,194	91,629	102,368	104,553	101,871	95,759	91,147	81,269	82,796
New Jersey	24,797	24,731	25,760	28,261	33,453	34,041	32,282	29,480	28,003	24,560	25,036
New York	56,465	58,327	64,434	63,368	68,915	70,512	69,589	66,279	63,144	56,709	57,760
Region III	66,432	69,637	75,858	76,192	79,640	89,162	86,247	92,218	84,784	82,393	82,899
Delaware	1,900	2,299	2,262	2,114	2,423	3,125	2,928	2,849	2,364	3,025	2,919
District of Columbia	2,558	3,209	3,232	3,245	3,284	3,512	3,520	4,014	3,382	3,388	4,688
Maryland	14,064	15,812	17,573	17,655	18,414	21,208	20,630	20,288	19,967	18,953	18,885
Pennsylvania	26,631	26,543	28,735	29,738	30,519	29,867	30,682	36,121	30,661	30,310	29,765
Virginia	16,985	17,217	19,009	18,230	20,314	26,159	23,457	24,014	23,414	21,847	21,719
West Virginia	4,294	4,557	5,047	5,210	4,686	5,291	5,030	4,932	4,996	4,870	4,923
Region IV	133,302	141,118	150,813	164,384	170,373	174,128	171,124	173,686	174,504	165,248	173,240
Alabama	10,158	9,906	10,065	11,529	14,243	12,775	12,570	12,298	12,033	11,702	12,001
Florida	47,299	48,449	53,449	57,170	58,291	60,091	59,875	62,121	58,665	59,604	59,964
Georgia	18,923	20,836	22,568	24,042	24,187	26,837	26,157	25,520	27,039	25,052	26,912
Kentucky	9,876	11,421	11,097	11,108	12,497	12,327	12,340	12,022	11,859	10,947	11,660
Mississippi	6,668	7,190	7,437	7,746	7,451	7,687	6,529	8,008	7,357	6,768	7,293
North Carolina	16,668	18,864	19,545	22,338	25,277	23,088	24,906	25,049	24,857	23,978	27,890
South Carolina	9,259	9,562	10,985	11,296	11,419	13,315	12,391	11,877	12,611	11,451	11,210
Tennessee	14,451	14,890	15,667	19,155	17,008	18,008	16,356	16,791	20,083	15,746	16,310
Region V	119,042	114,443	119,519	116,094	129,847	124,386	119,618	125,837	122,210	117,126	117,975
Illinois	43,224	35,144	34,496	30,767	46,320	38,359	34,043	35,209	32,520	29,353	30,889
Indiana	11,863	11,965	11,846	13,508	12,890	14,890	14,261	15,546	14,645	15,366	15,837
Michigan	20,266	19,624	22,906	21,089	18,348	18,348	21,254	23,649	21,478	20,532	20,786
Minnesota	11,732	11,913	14,649	13,924	14,175	14,102	13,420	13,379	14,948	14,117	13,812
Ohio	20,814	22,584	23,334	24,107	24,883	25,863	25,311	25,215	25,600	24,444	22,859
Wisconsin	11,143	13,213	12,288	12,699	13,231	12,824	13,329	13,239	13,019	13,314	13,792
Region VI	98,200	97,648	100,318	113,309	95,598	102,258	91,050	90,522	93,558	94,866	94,380
Arkansas	7,613	7,928	8,628	8,684	8,404	8,484	7,725	8,059	7,856	7,928	8,891
Louisiana	16,366	13,976	14,500	14,467	12,771	11,398	11,023	11,665	10,735	11,004	12,230
New Mexico	5,608	5,875	5,823	6,242	5,915	5,292	5,878	5,840	5,787	5,406	5,534
Oklahoma	12,106	13,336	12,495	12,138	11,391	9,940	9,641	9,605	9,593	9,534	9,712
Texas	56,507	56,533	58,872	71,778	57,117	67,144	56,783	55,353	59,587	60,994	58,013

Table 10.2 New and Successor Firms by SBA Region and State, 1982-1992--Continued

	1982	1983	1984	1985	1986	1987	1988	1989	1990	1991	1992
Region VII	37,459	37,889	41,137	41,208	41,381	41,503	41,343	41,726	39,655	39,287	39,715
Iowa	7,286	7,764	8,041	7,708	7,124	8,034	7,655	8,041	7,502	8,338	8,231
Kansas	8,630	8,669	9,103	9,356	9,366	8,788	8,960	8,869	8,645	8,218	7,976
Missouri	15,109	15,888	17,970	18,542	19,551	19,378	19,551	19,400	18,145	17,606	18,073
Nebraska	6,434	5,568	6,023	5,602	5,340	5,303	5,177	5,416	5,363	5,125	5,435
Region VIII	36,317	36,075	36,189	34,348	35,117	33,830	29,611	32,540	30,889	31,283	36,056
Colorado	17,842	16,323	15,776	15,190	16,839	15,623	12,089	14,544	13,454	13,218	16,060
Montana	4,119	4,774	4,624	4,252	4,382	3,914	3,798	3,666	3,622	4,379	4,150
North Dakota	2,512	2,731	2,533	2,254	2,259	2,417	2,350	2,205	2,077	1,954	2,081
South Dakota	2,160	2,360	2,517	2,500	2,540	2,583	2,401	2,645	2,632	2,387	2,738
Utah	6,448	6,800	7,805	7,462	6,560	7,271	6,527	6,474	6,630	6,954	8,068
Wyoming	3,236	3,087	2,934	2,690	2,537	2,022	2,446	3,006	2,474	2,391	2,959
Region IX	138,148	139,446	152,288	153,003	149,076	139,565	139,068	144,102	173,004	161,031	149,853
Arizona	12,734	14,074	14,997	14,729	16,979	17,058	15,356	14,301	15,225	13,792	14,788
California	117,094	116,795	128,322	129,004	122,858	112,886	113,601	119,389	147,425	137,117	124,875
Hawaii	3,657	3,654	3,845	3,842	3,745	4,027	4,080	4,065	4,215	3,775	3,787
Nevada	4,663	4,923	5,124	5,428	5,494	5,594	6,031	6,347	6,139	6,347	6,403
Region X	34,295	39,871	42,846	44,080	43,435	45,443	47,430	48,250	59,425	46,605	53,843
Alaska	1,473	3,924	4,497	4,110	4,296	4,886	5,251	3,405	3,015	2,659	2,708
Idaho	3,561	4,049	4,559	4,183	3,948	3,924	4,131	4,148	4,595	4,404	5,215
Oregon	11,321	11,990	12,879	14,903	13,532	13,547	12,759	14,706	16,979	13,996	14,555
Washington	17,940	19,908	20,911	20,884	21,659	23,086	25,289	25,991	34,836	25,546	31,365

Source: Adapted by the Office of Advocacy, U.S. Small Business Administration, from data provided by the U.S. Department of Labor, Employment and Training Administration.

Table 10.3 Wage-and-Salary Income and Nonfarm Proprietors' Income, by SBA Region and State, 1987-1992 (Millions of Dollars)

	1987	1988	1989	1990	1991	1992
U.S. Total						
Wage-and-Salary	2,232,996	2,413,656	2,562,605	2,719,435	2,798,404	2,919,361
Proprietors' Income	279,638	309,401	330,683	352,574	332,206	364,932
Total Earned	2,512,634	2,723,057	2,893,287	3,072,009	3,130,610	3,284,293
Region I						
Wage-and-Salary	144,592	158,970	165,906	169,836	169,278	174,053
Proprietors' Income	17,656	19,943	21,212	21,596	21,017	23,535
Total Earned	162,248	178,913	187,118	191,432	190,294	197,588
Connecticut						
Wage-and-Salary	41,306	45,379	47,419	48,894	49,292	50,229
Proprietors' Income	4,358	4,849	5,127	5,358	5,082	5,724
Total Earned	45,663	50,228	52,546	54,252	54,374	55,953
Maine						
Wage-and-Salary	9,216	10,193	10,943	11,346	11,304	11,573
Proprietors' Income	1,567	1,778	1,924	1,998	1,970	2,225
Total Earned	10,783	11,991	12,868	13,344	13,275	13,798
Massachusetts						
Wage-and-Salary	70,422	77,446	80,297	81,800	81,239	83,568
Proprietors' Income	8,287	9,425	10,006	10,055	9,786	10,887
Total Earned	78,708	86,870	90,303	91,855	91,025	94,455
New Hampshire						
Wage-and-Salary	10,234	11,279	11,709	11,766	11,628	12,127
Proprietors' Income	1,724	1,966	2,094	2,028	2,118	2,391
Total Earned	11,957	13,245	13,802	13,794	13,746	14,518
Rhode Island						
Wage-and-Salary	8,977	9,792	10,300	10,607	10,349	10,831
Proprietors' Income	1,000	1,122	1,197	1,259	1,190	1,328
Total Earned	9,976	10,914	11,496	11,866	11,539	12,159
Vermont						
Wage-and-Salary	4,439	4,882	5,239	5,424	5,486	5,726
Proprietors' Income	722	804	865	898	870	980
Total Earned	5,161	5,685	6,103	6,322	6,336	6,706
Region II						
Wage-and-Salary	291,590	318,005	332,712	349,888	351,399	363,959
Proprietors' Income	34,971	39,240	41,735	44,621	41,430	45,163
Total Earned	326,561	357,245	374,447	394,509	392,829	409,122
New Jersey						
Wage-and-Salary	87,185	95,878	100,735	105,627	106,710	110,798
Proprietors' Income	9,725	10,927	11,614	12,076	11,620	12,861
Total Earned	96,910	106,805	112,349	117,703	118,330	123,658
New York						
Wage-and-Salary	204,405	222,128	231,977	244,261	244,689	253,162
Proprietors' Income	25,246	28,312	30,121	32,546	29,810	32,302
Total Earned	229,651	250,440	262,098	276,806	274,499	285,464
Region III						
Wage-and-Salary	237,772	258,269	283,973	300,219	307,879	319,053
Proprietors' Income	26,540	29,438	32,659	34,469	32,882	36,495
Total Earned	264,312	287,707	316,632	334,687	340,762	355,549
Delaware						
Wage-and-Salary	6,983	7,688	8,380	8,863	9,199	9,437
Proprietors' Income	722	779	837	926	992	1,127
Total Earned	7,705	8,467	9,216	9,789	10,191	10,563

Table 10.3 Wage-and-Salary Income and Nonfarm Proprietors' Income, by SBA Region and State, 1987-1992 (Millions of Dollars)--Continued

	1987	1988	1989	1990	1991	1992
District of Columbia						
Wage-and-Salary	19,646	21,574	22,965	24,390	25,355	26,329
Proprietors' Income	1,189	1,379	1,471	1,369	1,330	1,404
Total Earned	20,836	22,952	24,436	25,759	26,685	27,732
Maryland						
Wage-and-Salary	46,121	50,512	53,868	57,143	58,094	59,498
Proprietors' Income	4,685	5,258	5,664	6,065	5,995	6,717
Total Earned	50,805	55,770	59,532	63,208	64,089	66,215
Pennsylvania						
Wage-and-Salary	102,667	110,835	117,280	124,101	127,311	132,344
Proprietors' Income	13,734	15,117	16,119	17,044	15,969	17,627
Total Earned	116,401	125,952	133,399	141,145	143,280	149,971
Virginia						
Wage-and-Salary	59,511	64,686	69,189	72,581	74,354	77,269
Proprietors' Income	5,876	6,541	7,028	7,394	7,066	7,951
Total Earned	65,387	71,227	76,217	79,975	81,419	85,220
West Virginia						
Wage-and-Salary	11,379	11,901	12,292	13,140	13,567	14,177
Proprietors' Income	1,337	1,458	1,541	1,672	1,531	1,671
Total Earned	12,716	13,359	13,832	14,812	15,098	15,848
Region IV						
Wage-and-Salary	342,670	370,815	393,495	419,411	434,853	459,209
Proprietors' Income	41,874	45,994	48,989	53,418	49,054	54,414
Total Earned	384,544	416,809	442,484	472,829	483,907	513,623
Alabama						
Wage-and-Salary	28,996	31,047	32,767	34,899	36,636	38,676
Proprietors' Income	3,368	3,705	3,943	4,249	3,804	4,168
Total Earned	32,364	34,751	36,710	39,148	40,440	42,844
Florida						
Wage-and-Salary	97,473	106,392	113,517	121,616	125,733	131,266
Proprietors' Income	12,339	13,151	14,057	15,832	12,786	14,233
Total Earned	109,811	119,543	127,574	137,448	138,519	145,499
Georgia						
Wage-and-Salary	57,752	62,281	65,383	69,533	71,746	76,057
Proprietors' Income	6,049	6,693	7,141	7,722	7,104	7,907
Total Earned	63,801	68,974	72,524	77,255	78,851	83,963
Kentucky						
Wage-and-Salary	25,011	26,767	28,293	30,416	31,783	34,004
Proprietors' Income	3,639	4,111	4,383	4,598	4,391	4,920
Total Earned	28,650	30,878	32,676	35,014	36,173	38,924
Mississippi						
Wage-and-Salary	14,558	15,565	16,460	17,362	18,221	19,243
Proprietors' Income	2,218	2,469	2,643	2,814	2,598	2,837
Total Earned	16,777	18,033	19,102	20,176	20,819	22,080
North Carolina						
Wage-and-Salary	54,519	59,152	62,988	66,732	68,857	73,590
Proprietors' Income	6,155	6,847	7,315	7,912	8,133	9,074
Total Earned	60,674	66,008	70,303	74,643	76,990	82,664
South Carolina						
Wage-and-Salary	25,775	28,026	30,133	32,333	33,224	34,610
Proprietors' Income	2,715	2,998	3,063	3,586	3,187	3,512
Total Earned	28,489	31,024	33,197	35,919	36,410	38,122

Table 10.3 Wage-and-Salary Income and Nonfarm Proprietors' Income, by SBA Region and State, 1987-1992 (Millions of Dollars)--Continued

	1987	1988	1989	1990	1991	1992
Tennessee						
Wage-and-Salary	38,587	41,577	43,956	46,521	48,654	51,763
Proprietors' Income	5,391	6,021	6,444	6,706	7,051	7,764
Total Earned	43,978	47,598	50,400	53,227	55,705	59,527
Region V						
Wage-and-Salary	423,808	457,727	482,076	508,529	523,166	549,364
Proprietors' Income	46,470	51,108	54,181	57,522	51,472	56,626
Total Earned	470,278	508,835	536,256	566,051	574,638	605,990
Illinois						
Wage-and-Salary	113,967	123,798	130,251	138,072	142,233	148,545
Proprietors' Income	14,860	16,465	17,475	18,373	16,633	18,176
Total Earned	128,827	140,262	147,726	156,445	158,866	166,720
Indiana						
Wage-and-Salary	46,041	49,734	52,657	55,467	57,650	60,563
Proprietors' Income	5,204	5,710	6,101	6,358	5,918	6,476
Total Earned	51,245	55,444	58,758	61,825	63,568	67,039
Michigan						
Wage-and-Salary	87,023	93,399	98,472	102,368	103,581	108,403
Proprietors' Income	7,697	8,383	8,895	9,629	8,384	9,301
Total Earned	94,720	101,782	107,367	111,997	111,965	117,704
Minnesota						
Wage-and-Salary	40,859	44,295	46,945	49,984	52,286	56,612
Proprietors' Income	4,331	4,800	5,085	5,293	4,994	5,497
Total Earned	45,190	49,095	52,030	55,277	57,280	61,109
Ohio						
Wage-and-Salary	95,811	103,074	107,979	113,625	116,284	121,900
Proprietors' Income	9,728	10,631	11,216	12,229	10,453	11,567
Total Earned	105,539	113,705	119,195	125,854	126,737	133,467
Wisconsin						
Wage-and-Salary	40,107	43,428	45,772	49,012	51,133	54,342
Proprietors' Income	4,651	5,120	5,409	5,642	5,091	5,609
Total Earned	44,758	48,547	51,181	54,654	56,224	59,951
Region VI						
Wage-and-Salary	215,965	228,204	239,699	258,412	273,801	286,790
Proprietors' Income	30,839	33,606	35,762	38,795	36,566	39,707
Total Earned	246,804	261,811	275,460	297,206	310,367	326,496
Arkansas						
Wage-and-Salary	14,554	15,495	16,323	17,538	18,611	19,849
Proprietors' Income	2,310	2,488	2,636	2,825	2,464	2,719
Total Earned	16,863	17,983	18,959	20,363	21,076	22,568
Louisiana						
Wage-and-Salary	29,036	30,630	31,817	34,348	36,393	37,676
Proprietors' Income	4,069	4,470	4,741	5,027	4,537	4,906
Total Earned	33,105	35,101	36,557	39,374	40,931	42,582
New Mexico						
Wage-and-Salary	10,354	10,866	11,422	12,344	13,012	13,700
Proprietors' Income	1,252	1,321	1,401	1,572	1,427	1,600
Total Earned	11,605	12,187	12,823	13,915	14,439	15,300
Oklahoma						
Wage-and-Salary	21,863	22,894	23,928	25,453	26,713	27,669
Proprietors' Income	3,734	4,059	4,294	4,479	3,907	4,244
Total Earned	25,597	26,953	28,222	29,932	30,620	31,913

Table 10.3 Wage-and-Salary Income and Nonfarm Proprietors' Income, by SBA Region and State, 1987-1992 (Millions of Dollars)--Continued

	1987	1988	1989	1990	1991	1992
Texas						
Wage-and-Salary	140,159	148,320	156,208	168,729	179,071	187,896
Proprietors' Income	19,476	21,268	22,691	24,893	24,231	26,238
Total Earned	159,634	169,588	178,899	193,623	203,302	214,133
Region VII						
Wage-and-Salary	96,147	102,596	108,219	114,582	119,248	124,885
Proprietors' Income	14,591	16,079	17,013	17,882	15,909	17,382
Total Earned	110,737	118,675	125,232	132,465	135,157	142,267
Iowa						
Wage-and-Salary	19,624	21,218	22,610	24,103	25,274	26,586
Proprietors' Income	3,494	3,894	4,119	4,334	3,802	4,126
Total Earned	23,118	25,113	26,729	28,437	29,075	30,712
Kansas						
Wage-and-Salary	19,871	21,058	22,067	23,464	24,544	25,871
Proprietors' Income	2,952	3,245	3,428	3,679	3,219	3,531
Total Earned	22,823	24,303	25,495	27,143	27,763	29,402
Missouri						
Wage-and-Salary	44,568	47,395	49,857	52,292	53,822	56,091
Proprietors' Income	6,236	6,847	7,259	7,464	6,779	7,425
Total Earned	50,803	54,243	57,116	59,756	60,601	63,516
Nebraska						
Wage-and-Salary	12,085	12,925	13,686	14,724	15,608	16,337
Proprietors' Income	1,909	2,093	2,208	2,406	2,110	2,300
Total Earned	13,994	15,018	15,893	17,129	17,717	18,638
Region VIII						
Wage-and-Salary	60,267	63,421	66,872	71,673	76,885	81,816
Proprietors' Income	8,872	9,653	10,252	11,004	9,903	10,826
Total Earned	69,139	73,074	77,123	82,677	86,788	92,643
Colorado						
Wage-and-Salary	31,261	32,797	34,548	36,944	39,465	42,051
Proprietors' Income	4,352	4,737	5,048	5,395	4,844	5,308
Total Earned	35,612	37,534	39,596	42,340	44,309	47,359
Montana						
Wage-and-Salary	4,831	5,093	5,334	5,649	6,069	6,491
Proprietors' Income	1,004	1,094	1,154	1,223	1,136	1,256
Total Earned	5,835	6,188	6,488	6,872	7,205	7,747
North Dakota						
Wage-and-Salary	4,315	4,481	4,651	4,922	5,219	5,466
Proprietors' Income	713	770	801	870	735	790
Total Earned	5,028	5,251	5,451	5,791	5,954	6,256
South Dakota						
Wage-and-Salary	4,028	4,298	4,548	4,950	5,364	5,715
Proprietors' Income	873	966	1,020	1,103	969	1,053
Total Earned	4,901	5,263	5,568	6,053	6,333	6,768
Utah						
Wage-and-Salary	12,122	12,930	13,853	15,002	16,338	17,512
Proprietors' Income	1,381	1,515	1,630	1,719	1,692	1,834
Total Earned	13,503	14,445	15,483	16,721	18,030	19,346
Wyoming						
Wage-and-Salary	3,711	3,823	3,937	4,206	4,431	4,581
Proprietors' Income	550	572	600	695	527	587
Total Earned	4,261	4,394	4,537	4,900	4,958	5,167

Table 10.3 Wage-and-Salary Income and Nonfarm Proprietors' Income, by SBA Region and State, 1987-1992 (Millions of Dollars)--Continued

	1987	1988	1989	1990	1991	1992
Region IX						
Wage-and-Salary	345,228	374,506	401,154	430,248	438,974	450,534
Proprietors' Income	46,852	52,123	55,677	59,021	60,584	65,942
Total Earned	392,080	426,629	456,831	489,269	499,558	516,476
Arizona						
Wage-and-Salary	28,987	31,063	32,524	34,178	35,470	37,188
Proprietors' Income	3,054	3,288	3,505	3,646	3,658	4,048
Total Earned	32,041	34,352	36,029	37,825	39,128	41,236
California						
Wage-and-Salary	294,795	319,540	341,999	366,421	372,269	380,416
Proprietors' Income	41,666	46,406	49,498	52,540	53,583	58,284
Total Earned	336,461	365,945	391,497	418,960	425,852	438,700
Hawaii						
Wage-and-Salary	10,691	11,755	12,997	14,394	15,272	15,968
Proprietors' Income	1,177	1,346	1,476	1,499	1,840	1,924
Total Earned	11,868	13,101	14,473	15,893	17,112	17,892
Nevada						
Wage-and-Salary	10,755	12,148	13,633	15,255	15,963	16,963
Proprietors' Income	956	1,083	1,199	1,337	1,504	1,686
Total Earned	11,711	13,232	14,832	16,592	17,467	18,648
Region X						
Wage-and-Salary	74,959	81,143	88,500	96,638	102,923	109,698
Proprietors' Income	10,974	12,218	13,205	14,247	13,389	14,842
Total Earned	85,932	93,361	101,705	110,885	116,312	124,541
Alaska						
Wage-and-Salary	6,449	6,608	7,379	7,799	8,218	8,539
Proprietors' Income	1,152	1,275	1,401	1,591	1,287	1,373
Total Earned	7,601	7,883	8,780	9,390	9,505	9,912
Idaho						
Wage-and-Salary	6,174	6,680	7,208	7,917	8,482	9,218
Proprietors' Income	1,280	1,435	1,545	1,635	1,666	1,877
Total Earned	7,454	8,115	8,752	9,552	10,148	11,095
Oregon						
Wage-and-Salary	21,365	23,386	25,329	27,535	28,904	30,629
Proprietors' Income	3,293	3,694	3,962	4,191	4,116	4,538
Total Earned	24,659	27,080	29,291	31,725	33,020	35,167
Washington						
Wage-and-Salary	40,970	44,469	48,584	53,388	57,319	61,313
Proprietors' Income	5,249	5,814	6,297	6,831	6,320	7,054
Total Earned	46,129	50,284	54,881	60,219	63,640	68,367

Proprietors' Income includes income data from both proprietorship (Form 1040C) and partnership (Form 1065) tax returns.

Note: Personal Income data exclude employer pension contributions and other non-labor income. Also, detail may not add to totals due to rounding.

Source: Adapted by the U.S. Small Business Administration, Office of Advocacy, from the U.S. Department of Commerce, Bureau of Economic Analysis, Regional Economic Measurement Division, unpublished data).

Table 10.4 Number of Business Bankruptcies by SBA Region and State, 1982-1992

	1982	1983	1984	1985	1986	1987	1988	1989	1990	1991	1992
U.S. Total	68,447	61,612	63,377	70,644	79,926	81,463	62,845	62,449	63,912	70,605	69,848
Region I, Total	2,034	1,600	1,355	1,312	1,164	1,170	1,384	2,297	3,597	3,937	3,943
Connecticut	474	437	336	347	204	190	219	218	445	380	379
Maine	294	197	179	184	171	207	215	205	318	353	398
Massachusetts	657	521	497	441	517	512	587	1,158	1,838	2,073	2,420
New Hampshire	214	175	115	140	112	127	186	320	490	598	164
Rhode Island	256	164	129	131	85	80	117	170	327	333	364
Vermont	139	106	99	69	75	54	60	226	179	200	218
Region II, Total	5,035	3,700	3,864	3,589	3,673	3,328	2,865	3,637	3,726	5,333	6,203
New Jersey	1,557	707	1,259	1,013	1,170	1,056	915	2,505	2,606	1,303	1,561
New York	3,478	2,993	2,605	2,576	2,503	2,272	1,950	1,132	1,120	4,030	4,642
Region III, Total	4,865	4,094	3,885	4,302	4,158	4,546	4,004	4,790	6,689	7,859	6,898
Delaware	72	69	52	47	33	65	50	64	114	126	243
District of Columbia	80	90	101	97	85	78	63	73	129	181	134
Maryland	436	477	446	486	457	965	397	480	1,356	1,633	1,642
Pennsylvania	2,121	1,624	1,523	1,354	1,341	1,287	1,125	1,310	1,751	2,173	2,448
Virginia	1,740	1,416	1,327	1,905	1,769	1,680	2,029	2,462	2,958	3,309	1,963
West Virginia	416	418	436	413	473	471	340	401	381	437	468
Region IV, Total	10,001	8,179	8,439	9,089	9,904	11,059	8,641	10,031	11,134	12,419	11,231
Alabama	1,277	891	967	949	1,185	1,627	1,211	1,334	1,356	1,431	1,318
Florida	1,890	1,620	2,107	2,151	2,065	1,837	1,823	2,021	2,842	3,031	2,986
Georgia	1,945	1,672	1,616	1,830	2,229	2,020	1,627	2,339	2,366	2,941	2,475
Kentucky	1,106	749	932	997	985	1,199	998	1,155	1,324	1,016	692
Mississippi	477	357	335	384	580	936	363	337	288	411	481
North Carolina	1,009	920	835	1,005	960	1,270	950	1,005	1,280	1,390	1,179
South Carolina	323	285	233	299	349	330	405	312	404	479	234
Tennessee	1,974	1,685	1,414	1,474	1,551	1,840	1,264	1,528	1,274	1,720	1,866
Region V, Total	13,068	12,082	12,131	13,029	12,250	12,051	9,325	9,075	9,679	9,478	10,159
Illinois	3,644	3,645	3,643	4,009	3,826	3,629	2,780	2,397	2,041	2,354	2,586
Indiana	1,575	1,283	1,285	1,421	1,576	1,550	1,191	1,093	1,090	1,083	1,263
Michigan	1,872	1,632	1,486	1,547	1,684	1,605	1,512	1,579	1,633	1,571	1,793
Minnesota	1,397	1,366	1,379	1,738	1,727	1,729	1,414	1,511	1,771	1,797	1,494
Ohio	2,748	2,442	2,384	2,293	2,080	2,220	1,482	1,447	1,778	1,402	1,862
Wisconsin	1,832	1,714	1,954	2,021	1,357	1,318	946	1,048	1,366	1,271	1,161
Region VI, Total	6,479	7,246	8,294	10,876	14,728	14,426	12,022	10,327	9,187	7,589	7,827
Arkansas	506	419	746	604	589	706	552	454	467	497	577
Louisiana	1,297	1,302	1,317	1,540	2,594	2,555	1,584	1,372	1,338	1,089	865
New Mexico	223	197	278	373	453	410	405	302	348	333	476
Oklahoma	1,001	1,049	1,059	2,000	2,722	2,517	1,932	1,720	1,716	1,258	1,096
Texas	3,452	4,279	4,894	6,359	8,370	8,238	7,549	6,479	5,318	4,412	4,813

Table 10.4 Number of Business Bankruptcies by SBA Region and State, 1982-1992--Continued

	1982	1983	1984	1985	1986	1987	1988	1989	1990	1991	1992
Region VII, Total	4,534	3,500	4,820	5,977	6,688	7,422	3,903	3,072	3,197	2,875	2,644
Iowa	1,378	1,341	1,560	2,272	2,303	2,017	1,148	960	893	748	660
Kansas	711	550	955	1,234	1,517	1,421	764	552	560	527	600
Missouri	1,819	1,075	1,644	1,843	1,893	2,486	1,423	1,169	1,319	1,216	1,034
Nebraska	626	534	661	628	975	1,498	568	391	425	384	350
Region VIII, Total	3,987	3,733	4,343	5,387	7,170	8,589	6,747	5,537	2,939	2,313	2,537
Colorado	1,759	1,492	1,989	2,347	3,659	5,291	4,304	3,805	1,088	611	1,143
Montana	192	269	217	356	438	484	483	354	223	207	240
North Dakota	316	361	317	357	268	302	197	211	209	191	180
South Dakota	441	310	340	611	902	878	369	320	388	356	284
Utah	1,034	935	1,045	1,223	1,388	1,265	1,249	723	895	830	551
Wyoming	245	366	435	493	515	369	145	124	136	118	139
Region IX, Total	14,370	13,849	12,169	12,358	13,990	13,070	9,577	10,030	10,196	15,046	14,968
Arizona	1,308	1,464	1,389	1,441	1,936	1,731	1,586	2,401	2,377	2,194	2,050
California	12,176	11,531	10,045	9,967	11,066	10,763	7,442	7,094	7,391	12,295	12,215
Hawaii	254	276	225	266	257	183	117	129	74	77	163
Nevada	632	578	510	684	731	393	432	406	354	480	540
Region X, Total	4,074	3,629	4,077	4,725	6,201	5,802	4,377	3,653	3,568	3,756	3,438
Alaska	212	152	218	277	343	356	225	208	164	170	196
Idaho	418	602	658	704	609	717	407	359	365	225	
Oregon	1,531	1,339	1,523	2,046	2,604	1,807	1,111	890	1,061	1,177	1,105
Washington	1,913	1,536	1,678	1,698	2,645	2,922	2,634	2,196	1,978	2,184	1,622

Note: Bankruptcy data exclude Guam, Puerto Rico, and the Virgin Islands.

A business bankruptcy is the legal recognition that a company is insolvent (i.e., not able to satisfy creditors or discharge liabilities); must restructure or completely liquidate. A business bankruptcy culminates in the filing of a bankruptcy petition under Chapter 7, 9, 11, 12, or 13 of the federal bankruptcy laws.

Source: Adapted by the U.S. Small Business Administration, Office of Advocacy, from the Administrative Office of the U.S. Courts.

Table 10.5 Number of Business Failures by SBA Region and State, 1985-1992

	1985	1986	1987	1988	1989	1990	1991	1992
U.S. Total	57,252	61,601	61,236	57,099	50,361	60,432	88,140	96,836
Region I	1,228	1,109	1,039	1,051	1,282	3,057	5,654	6,198
Connecticut	307	202	110	151	147	430	911	1,224
Maine	80	59	59	84	132	197	396	463
Massachusetts	683	725	653	556	771	1,898	2,839	3,021
New Hampshire	60	56	135	165	125	275	861	720
Rhode Island	60	38	34	42	56	183	459	511
Vermont	38	29	48	53	51	74	188	259
Region II	2,840	2,426	2,509	3,220	2,570	4,527	8,370	10,684
New Jersey	990	912	776	860	1,964	3,281	2,758	2,821
New York	1,850	1,514	1,733	2,360	606	1,246	5,612	7,863
Region III	3,571	3,066	3,252	3,083	3,252	4,892	8,043	8,757
Delaware	46	46	30	64	31	80	160	189
District of Columbia	60	65	62	53	44	101	198	210
Maryland	450	462	490	424	232	686	1,331	1,710
Pennsylvania	1,657	1,572	1,561	1,399	1,606	2,209	3,658	4,087
Virginia	991	693	875	928	1,177	1,585	2,297	2,159
West Virginia	367	228	234	215	162	231	399	402
Region IV	7,917	7,810	8,513	8,569	8,757	10,692	15,352	14,362
Alabama	608	376	495	635	490	676	1,027	902
Florida	2,793	3,331	3,217	3,135	3,160	3,655	5,229	5,370
Georgia	954	617	1,234	1,379	1,787	1,937	3,390	2,872
Kentucky	983	958	965	701	676	1,048	1,234	1,088
Mississippi	467	501	591	493	536	457	523	497
North Carolina	665	582	584	672	762	1,030	1,351	1,491
South Carolina	230	264	279	385	182	415	603	482
Tennessee	1,217	1,181	1,148	1,169	1,164	1,474	1,995	1,660
Region V	10,501	10,310	10,275	9,603	9,145	8,830	12,368	12,414
Illinois	3,402	3,308	3,308	3,301	3,382	2,124	3,068	3,093
Indiana	1,245	1,094	1,301	923	929	1,164	1,736	1,479
Michigan	1,465	1,620	1,810	1,799	2,080	2,100	2,295	2,427
Minnesota	506	639	690	536	323	522	1,583	1,509
Ohio	2,456	2,082	1,927	1,936	1,713	2,254	2,776	2,682
Wisconsin	1,427	1,567	1,239	1,108	718	666	910	1,224
Region VI	8,300	13,019	12,986	10,886	8,807	10,056	10,854	10,763
Arkansas	622	377	440	363	307	260	480	512
Louisiana	1,384	1,826	1,817	1,438	1,402	1,153	1,103	858
New Mexico	358	271	227	344	393	318	390	456
Oklahoma	1,030	2,869	2,135	868	1,266	1,587	1,845	1,418
Texas	4,906	7,676	8,367	7,873	5,439	6,738	7,036	7,519

Table 10.5 Number of Business Failures by SBA Region and State, 1985-1991--Continued

	1985	1986	1987	1988	1989	1990	1991	1992
Region VII	4,147	4,361	4,165	3,157	2,594	2,886	3,429	4,270
Iowa	830	672	915	661	560	554	295	730
Kansas	1,583	1,689	993	846	668	758	989	1,079
Missouri	1,247	1,632	1,573	1,381	1,150	1,216	1,609	1,829
Nebraska	487	368	684	269	216	358	536	632
Region VIII	3,977	4,558	4,493	3,585	2,353	3,232	3,292	2,943
Colorado	2,693	3,274	2,890	2,233	1,516	2,077	1,959	1,739
Montana	194	184	324	241	191	191	160	211
North Dakota	94	101	111	159	105	145	140	163
South Dakota	145	151	278	148	142	270	315	232
Utah	577	566	611	599	281	372	556	457
Wyoming	274	282	279	205	118	177	162	141
Region IX	11,607	11,555	11,244	11,128	9,465	10,386	17,504	22,755
Arizona	694	668	821	1,442	1,250	1,084	2,230	2,297
California	10,295	10,241	9,969	9,178	7,814	8,902	14,685	19,732
Hawaii	251	283	171	179	170	147	74	289
Nevada	367	363	283	329	231	253	515	437
Region X	3,164	3,387	2,760	2,817	2,136	1,874	3,274	3,690
Alaska	173	288	305	287	143	123	144	103
Idaho	203	314	451	363	233	309	397	360
Oregon	1,151	1,001	712	509	444	588	1,309	1,259
Washington	1,637	1,784	1,292	1,658	1,316	854	1,424	1,968

Note: A business failure is an establishment which ceases operation with creditors.

Source: Adapted by the U.S. Small Business Administration, Office of Advocacy, from Dun and Bradstreet Corporation, various press releases.

Table 10.6 Business Terminations by SBA Region and State, 1982-1992

	1982	1983	1984	1985	1986	1987	1988	1989	1990	1991	1992
U.S. Total	701,582	712,316	579,932	748,438	809,001	723,997	763,299	830,478	837,511	820,445	818,472
Region I	29,910	37,649	31,547	29,479	36,152	35,602	38,944	40,330	40,288	48,274	44,509
Connecticut	13,868	9,263	10,078	9,073	9,946	10,481	11,931	11,741	11,994	12,242	12,017
Maine	689	7,899	4,078	4,064	4,081	4,392	4,366	4,683	4,737	4,593	3,876
Massachusetts	12,231	17,069	13,815	12,601	18,200	16,063	17,385	18,415	17,539	18,914	17,263
New Hampshire	3,122	3,418	3,576	3,741	3,925	4,666	5,262	5,491	6,018	5,599	5,317
Rhode Island	3,108	2,840	3,859	3,040	3,120	3,671	3,511	3,993	3,863	3,963	3,858
Vermont	1,904	1,769	1,794	2,605	2,490	2,764	2,703	2,915	2,687	2,963	2,178
Region II	77,154	74,521	71,731	78,915	90,948	87,707	88,155	90,875	89,165	89,487	91,961
New Jersey	22,203	22,087	21,085	22,814	26,504	26,981	25,432	26,645	25,538	27,472	28,961
New York	54,951	52,434	50,646	56,101	64,444	60,726	62,723	64,230	63,627	62,015	63,000
Region III	62,725	59,733	60,704	62,479	66,014	72,379	76,395	73,637	76,857	79,463	77,204
Delaware	1,643	2,112	1,702	1,912	1,914	2,159	2,206	1,793	1,422	2,490	1,749
District of Columbia	2,658	1,892	3,193	3,320	3,304	3,647	3,620	4,340	3,715	3,998	3,125
Maryland	12,331	11,860	12,955	13,977	14,071	15,539	16,201	16,198	17,945	18,842	18,426
Pennsylvania	27,595	22,791	25,939	24,667	24,978	27,760	29,100	28,019	27,929	29,668	29,731
Virginia	13,515	16,577	12,655	13,261	17,157	18,715	20,527	18,333	21,438	19,820	19,809
West Virginia	4,983	4,501	4,260	5,342	4,590	4,559	4,741	4,954	4,408	4,645	4,364
Region IV	124,425	118,176	115,406	125,793	140,242	145,143	145,917	153,502	159,141	160,386	161,762
Alabama	10,203	9,737	9,368	8,334	10,191	10,877	11,714	11,404	10,927	14,478	11,710
Florida	41,138	37,597	39,043	41,292	49,038	49,044	49,452	51,683	54,009	55,539	55,317
Georgia	17,468	16,502	16,030	17,247	18,630	19,717	21,268	24,136	24,448	24,527	25,481
Kentucky	10,117	9,961	9,598	10,385	11,031	11,368	10,686	11,079	11,276	10,356	10,691
Mississippi	6,482	7,176	6,146	6,761	6,870	7,925	7,131	7,334	7,200	6,768	6,997
North Carolina	15,872	15,424	14,405	16,578	20,323	20,166	21,748	22,153	21,643	22,882	26,103
South Carolina	8,748	8,268	8,496	8,524	9,636	10,750	10,406	10,280	10,736	10,785	10,605
Tennessee	14,397	13,511	13,320	16,672	14,523	15,296	14,052	15,433	18,902	15,051	14,858
Region V	105,468	104,893	100,526	117,144	111,822	103,517	100,669	116,674	117,549	104,090	105,759
Illinois	25,380	30,110	28,979	44,824	37,159	32,423	28,553	34,661	29,173	26,771	31,250
Indiana	11,758	12,049	10,687	11,817	10,869	8,638	12,636	16,338	10,632	15,919	13,462
Michigan	20,798	18,132	11,170	14,837	16,596	16,596	16,372	21,645	28,676	15,055	18,010
Minnesota	11,279	11,046	11,660	12,177	13,092	13,038	11,829	11,097	13,614	12,500	11,041
Ohio	20,906	22,437	29,461	23,588	21,841	21,617	19,520	20,897	23,863	22,490	20,287
Wisconsin	15,347	11,119	8,569	9,901	12,238	11,205	11,759	12,036	11,591	11,355	11,736
Region VI	76,161	88,091	90,163	97,451	98,380	106,767	95,708	89,776	86,306	85,214	81,466
Arkansas	7,281	7,645	7,348	7,429	8,179	7,936	8,211	8,771	7,252	7,348	6,982
Louisiana	13,392	13,280	12,252	14,504	13,153	13,975	12,596	12,178	10,883	10,536	10,719
New Mexico	4,909	4,721	4,464	5,515	5,830	5,563	5,459	5,598	4,943	5,242	4,876
Oklahoma	9,405	13,573	12,754	11,273	12,968	12,130	11,321	8,919	9,397	8,856	8,640
Texas	41,174	48,872	53,345	58,730	58,250	67,163	58,121	54,310	53,831	53,232	50,249

Table 10.6 Business Terminations by SBA Region and State, 1982-1992--Continued

	1982	1983	1984	1985	1986	1987	1988	1989	1990	1991	1992
Region VII	35,449	36,330	39,566	38,917	40,423	40,423	38,592	38,769	38,577	37,772	37,498
Iowa	8,284	7,828	8,395	8,608	8,525	8,503	7,484	7,686	6,971	7,410	7,542
Kansas	7,984	7,730	7,724	8,671	9,054	8,926	8,601	8,958	8,788	8,303	7,364
Missouri	14,230	16,295	18,314	15,717	16,888	17,796	17,294	16,870	16,674	16,764	17,022
Nebraska	4,951	4,477	5,133	5,921	5,956	5,611	5,213	5,255	6,144	5,295	5,570
Region VIII	31,233	32,176	30,699	34,320	33,369	27,729	30,001	33,299	29,626	27,209	29,241
Colorado	13,933	14,112	11,427	15,224	14,092	8,736	12,625	15,722	12,864	11,236	13,011
Montana	3,665	3,955	4,142	4,415	4,642	4,556	3,813	3,613	3,453	3,345	3,536
North Dakota	2,426	2,552	2,652	2,317	2,607	2,561	2,108	2,297	2,265	1,944	2,010
South Dakota	2,174	2,330	2,337	2,308	2,549	2,368	2,280	2,162	2,370	2,194	2,375
Utah	6,312	6,281	7,025	7,018	6,494	7,171	6,781	6,271	5,774	5,754	6,112
Wyoming	2,723	2,946	3,116	3,038	2,985	2,337	2,394	3,234	2,900	2,736	2,197
Region IX	123,189	125,029	104,608	121,319	150,634	65,246	109,033	153,940	158,275	146,170	146,207
Arizona	11,307	10,325	10,707	10,455	14,132	13,528	13,250	13,392	14,235	13,011	12,531
California	104,055	106,268	86,215	102,880	128,356	43,894	87,586	132,141	135,767	124,345	124,137
Hawaii	3,295	3,572	3,438	3,478	3,200	3,230	3,633	3,390	3,385	3,486	3,612
Nevada	4,582	4,864	4,248	4,506	4,946	4,594	4,564	5,017	4,888	5,328	5,927
Region X	35,868	35,718	34,982	42,621	41,017	39,484	39,885	39,676	41,727	42,380	52,865
Alaska	947	3,283	3,200	3,712	5,278	5,733	5,781	3,552	3,382	2,581	11,710
Idaho	3,840	3,648	3,778	3,862	4,090	3,710	3,269	3,835	3,337	3,500	4,028
Oregon	12,635	12,451	11,567	13,650	12,792	12,410	11,390	11,792	11,921	13,347	11,799
Washington	18,446	16,336	16,437	21,397	18,857	17,631	19,445	20,497	23,087	22,952	25,328

Source: Adapted by the Office of Advocacy, U.S. Small Business Administration, from data provided by the Employment and Training Administration, U.S. Department of Labor, February 1993.

11 Miscellaneous Data

The Intellectual Property System

Tables 11.1 through 11.15 present data collected in a study of small and large firms that have used the intellectual property protection system. A random sample was taken of the firms in the Corporate Technology Directory that had patents, copyrights, trademarks, Statutory Invention Registrations, registrations under the Semiconductor Chip Protection Act, or litigation pending in federal courts. Responses were received from 322 small enterprises (under 500 employees) and 54 large enterprises (500 employees or more). Because the small-firm sample was stratified by industry, the small-enterprise results are weighted by the small-firm populations of the individual industries.

Highlights

• Patents are the most important form of intellectual property protection for small enterprises, followed closely by trade secrets. Further down in importance are copyrights, followed closely by trademarks and contractual agreements. A distant last are Statutory Invention Registration and the Semiconductor Chip Protection Act. The pattern is basically similar for large enterprises, with the exception that contractual agreements are a little more important than trademarks, and copyrights are considerably less important (Table 11.3).

• For both small and large enterprises, technology alliances were most likely during development and least likely during basic research as opposed to applied research, testing and evaluation, manufacturing, or marketing. Large enterprises were more likely than small enterprises to have used each kind of technology alliance at each stage of activity (Table 11.5).

• The most likely recipient of a license seems to be an enterprise in the same size category. Sixty percent of small enterprises granting licenses to domestically owned organizations have entered into licensing agreements with other small enterprises. Ninety-four percent of large enterprises granting licenses to domestically owned organizations have granted licenses to other large enterprises (Table 11.8).

• The second favorite recipients of licenses granted by small and large enterprises are each other. Almost half (49 percent) of small enterprises granting licenses to domestically owned organizations have granted licenses to large enterprises. And a little over one-half (53 percent) of large enterprises granting licenses to domestically owned organizations have granted licenses to small enterprises (Table 11.8).

• Small enterprises were most likely to have received licenses from other small enterprises: 53 percent of small enterprises that had received licenses received them from other small domestic enterprises. Large enterprises showed a similar preference for other large enterprises: 81 percent of large enterprises that had received licenses received them from other large domestic enterprises (Table 11.9).

• The median small enterprise was founded in the late 1970s. The median large enterprise was founded in the early 1940s (Table 11.11).

• The median small enterprise had sales in the most recent fiscal year of $1 to $5 million. The median large enterprise had sales of $100 million to $1 billion (Table 11.12).

• The median small enterprise had exports accounting for 6 to 10 percent of sales. The median large enterprise had exports accounting for 11 to 25 percent of sales (Table 11.13).

• The median small enterprise had 25 to 49 employees. The median large enterprise had 2,500 to 4,999 employees (Table 11.14).

• The median large enterprise responding had research and development (R&D) expenses that were 5 percent or less of sales, while the median small enterprise responding had R&D expenses that were 11 percent or more of sales. R&D expenses were 11 to 40 percent of sales for 37 percent of the small enterprises and only 21 percent of the large enterprises. Fourteen percent of the small enterprises had R&D expenses that were more than 40 percent of sales, compared with none of the large enterprises (Table 11.15).

Number of High Technology Firms by Industry

While, according to some, "high technology has become a phrase frequently used and ambiguously applied in both the professional and popular literature," Armington, Harris, and Odle developed a comprehensive and explicit definition of high technology, given in terms of the 88 four-digit Standard Industrial Classification (SIC) codes in Table 11.16.[1] These were the industries with a high per-

1 Catherine Armington, Candee Harris, and Marjorie Odle, "Formation and Growth in High-Technology Firms: A Regional Assessment" in U.S. Office of Technology Assessment, *Technology, Innovation, and Regional Economic Development* (Washington, D.C.: U.S. Government Printing Office, 1984).

centage of scientists, engineers, and technicians at the three-digit level, or a high ratio of research and development (R&D) to sales at the two-digit level, after exclusion of some clearly inappropriate four-digit industries. High technology defined in this way comprised 88,453 firms in 1986, according to the Small Business Data Base.

Procurement Data   Tables 11.17 through 11.24 are from the appendix on procurement in the 1993 edition of *The State of Small Business: A Report of the President.*[2] These tables present data on federal procurement in fiscal year 1991, with breakdowns by state (Table 11.22), by gender and ethnicity of vendor (Tables 11.23 and 11.24), and by type of product or service sold (Table 11.20). Some recent data on the federal government's Small Business Innovation Research program is also included in this section (Table 11.21).

2   Executive Office of the President, *The State of Small Business: A Report of the President* (Washington, D.C.: U.S. Government Printing Office, 1993).

Chapter 11 Tables

Table 11.1 Small and Large Enterprises Indicating Ownership of Intellectual Property Rights
(Percent)

Domestic Intellectual Property Rights	Small Enterprises	Large Enterprises
Patents	58	88
Copyrights	57	60
Trademarks (and Other Marks)	69	88
Semiconductor Chip Protection Act	2	4
Statutory Invention Registrations	1	2

Foreign Intellectual Property Rights	Small Enterprises	Large Enterprises
Patents	26	75
Copyrights	9	27
Trademarks (and Other Marks)	17	75
Mask Works	0	0
Other	0	0

Source: "Survey of Small Business Use of Intellectual Property Protection," prepared under
Contract #SBA-3070-OA-88 for the U.S. Small Business Administration, Mary Seyer Koen,
Principal Investigator, MO-SCI Corporation, 1991, Table 6.

Table 11.2 Small and Large Enterprises by Number of Domestic Intellectual Property Rights Owned (Percent)

| | | Number Owned | | |
		1 - 5	6 - 10	11+
Patents	Small Enterprises	41	9	8
	Large Enterprises	12	2	74
Copyrights	Small Enterprises	29	8	20
	Large Enterprises	14	10	36
Trademarks	Small Enterprises	56	7	6
	Large Enterprises	16	6	66

Source: "Survey of Small Business Use of Intellectual Property Protection," prepared under Contract #SBA-3070-OA-88 for the U.S. Small Business Administration, Mary Seyer Koen, Principal Investigator, MO-SCI Corporation, 1991, Table 8.

Table 11.3 Small and Large Enterprises Ranking Forms of Intellectual Property Protection as First, Second or Third in Importance (Percent)

	Small Enterprises			Large Enterprises		
	Ranking in Importance			Ranking in Importance		
	First	Second	Third	First	Second	Third
Patents	35	16	14	38	23	21
Copyrights	20	16	18	4	8	15
Trademarks	11	24	18	12	23	19
Trade Secrets	28	20	12	40	19	17
SCPA	0	1	0	2	0	0
SIR	0	1	2	0	0	0
Contracts	9	18	18	13	23	17

Source: "Survey of Small Business Use of Intellectual Property Protection," prepared under Contract #SBA-3070-OA-88 for the U.S. Small Business Administration, Mary Seyer Koen, Principal Investigator, MO-SCI Corporation, 1991, Table 9.

Table 11.4 Small and Large Enterprises Indicating Ownership of Intellectual Property Rights Five Years Ago (Percent)

Domestic Intellectual Property Rights	Small Enterprises	Large Enterprises
Patents	49	86
Copyrights	47	43
Trademarks (and Other Marks)	53	84
Statutory Invention Registrations	0	0

Foreign Intellectual Property Rights	Small Enterprises	Large Enterprises
Patents	20	70
Copyrights	7	20
Trademarks (and Other Marks)	14	68
Mask Works	0	0
Other	0	0

Source: "Survey of Small Business Use of Intellectual Property Protection," prepared under Contract #SBA-3070-OA-88 for the U.S. Small Business Administration, Mary Seyer Koen, Principal Investigator, MO-SCI Corporation, 1991, Table 10.

Table 11.5 Small and Large Enterprises Involved in Technology Alliances by Stage of Activity and Type of Alliance (Percent)

Small Enterprises

	Not Used	Licensing	Joint Venture	Contract or Subcontract	Other
Basic Research	77	7	7	14	0
Applied Research	69	9	10	22	0
Development	35	28	23	41	0
Testing and Evaluation	62	9	11	28	0
Manufacturing	44	29	13	24	0
Marketing	44	29	21	19	1

Large Enterprises

	Not Used	Licensing	Joint Venture	Contract or Subcontract	Other
Basic Research	52	24	26	39	0
Applied Research	30	48	30	54	0
Development	9	61	46	67	0
Testing and Evaluation	24	33	24	63	0
Manufacturing	28	50	39	39	0
Marketing	43	33	28	35	0

Source: "Survey of Small Business Use of Intellectual Property Protection," prepared under Contract #SBA-3070-OA-88 for the U.S. Small Business Administration, Mary Seyer Koen, Principal Investigator, MO-SCI Corporation, 1991, Table 14.

Table 11.6 Small and Large Enterprises by Number of Technology Alliances with Various Types of Organizations (Percent)

Small Enterprises

Domestic Owned	Number of Alliances					
	0	1	2-4	5-9	10-24	25+
Small Enterprises	38	16	33	9	4	0
Large Enterprises	51	26	14	7	1	1
Government	74	8	10	5	1	2
Higher Education	88	4	6	1	1	0
Other Nonprofits	97	2	1	0	0	0
Other Organizations	100	0	0	0	0	0

Foreign Owned	Number of Alliances					
	0	1	2-4	5-9	10-24	25+
Small Enterprises	76	7	16	1	0	0
Large Enterprises	79	7	12	1	0	0
Government	97	0	2	0	0	0
Higher Education	99	0	0	0	0	0
Other Nonprofits	100	0	0	0	0	0
Other Organizations	99	0	0	0	1	0

Large Enterprises

Domestic Owned	Number of Alliances					
	0	1	2-4	5-9	10-24	25+
Small Enterprises	46	5	13	10	10	15
Large Enterprises	15	8	33	18	13	13
Government	56	10	18	5	0	10
Higher Education	44	10	18	15	3	10
Other Nonprofits	85	5	10	0	0	0
Other Organizations	100	0	0	0	0	0

Foreign Owned	Number of Alliances					
	0	1	2-4	5-9	10-24	25+
Small Enterprises	56	5	21	8	8	3
Large Enterprises	33	10	21	18	8	10
Government	85	3	8	3	0	3
Higher Education	82	5	5	5	3	0
Other Nonprofits	97	0	0	3	0	0
Other Organizations	100	0	0	0	0	0

Source: "Survey of Small Business Use of Intellectual Property Protection," prepared under Contract #SBA-3070-OA-88 for the U.S. Small Business Administration, Mary Seyer Koen, Principal Investigator, MO-SCI Corporation, 1989, Table 16.

Table 11.7 Small and Large Enterprises Indicating Extent of Difficulties with Protection of Intellectual Property When Discussing Financing with Specific Types of Organizations (Percent)

Small Enterprises

Types of
Organizations

	Extent of Difficulty			
	None	Slight	Moderate	Major
Venture Capitalists	56	14	24	7
Small Enterprises	61	13	17	10
Large Enterprises	33	23	29	15
Government	56	17	10	18
Other	83	11	2	4

Large Enterprises

Types of
Organizations

	Extent of Difficulty			
	None	Slight	Moderate	Major
Venture Capitalists	60	20	20	0
Small Enterprises	20	40	40	0
Large Enterprises	33	33	17	17
Government	43	14	0	43
Other	100	0	0	0

Source: "Survey of Small Business Use of Intellectual Property Protection," prepared under Contract #SBA-3070-OA-88 for the U.S. Small Business Administration, Mary Seyer Koen, Principal Investigator, MO-SCI Corporation, 1991, Table 18.

Table 11.8 Small and Large Enterprises by Number of Licenses Granted to Various Type of Organizations (Percent)

Small Enterprises

	Number of Licenses					
Domestic Owned	0	1	2-4	5-9	10-24	25+
Small Enterprises	40	23	20	6	3	8
Large Enterprises	51	15	24	5	2	4
Government Agencies	88	1	6	2	1	2
Higher Education	94	1	3	1	0	2
Other Nonprofits	97	0	0	0	3	0
Other Organizations	100	0	0	0	0	0
Foreign Owned	0	1	2-4	5-9	10-24	25+
Small Enterprises	76	6	16	0	0	2
Large Enterprises	76	4	14	2	1	3
Government Agencies	98	1	0	1	0	0
Higher Education	99	1	0	0	0	0
Other Nonprofits	100	0	0	0	0	0
Other Organizations	100	0	0	0	0	0

Large Enterprises

	Number of Licenses					
Domestic Owned	0	1	2-4	5-9	10-24	25+
Small Enterprises	47	0	28	9	6	9
Large Enterprises	6	9	38	13	16	19
Government Agencies	75	0	3	13	3	6
Higher Education	84	3	6	0	3	3
Other Nonprofits	91	0	3	3	0	3
Other Organizations	97	0	0	3	0	0
Foreign Owned	0	1	2-4	5-9	10-24	25+
Small Enterprises	59	13	16	6	3	3
Large Enterprises	25	16	19	16	25	0
Government Agencies	91	0	0	6	3	0
Higher Education	88	3	3	3	3	0
Other Nonprofits	97	0	3	0	0	0
Other Organizations	100	0	0	0	0	0

Source: "Survey of Small Business Use of Intellectual Property Protection," prepared under Contract #SBA-3070-OA-88 for the U.S. Small Business Administration, Mary Seyer Koen, Principal Investigator, MO-SCI Corporation, 1991, Table 28.

Table 11.9 Small and Large Enterprises by Number of Licenses Received from Various Types of Organizations (Percent)

Small Enterprises

Domestic Owned	Number of Licenses					
	0	1	2-4	5-9	10-24	25+
Small Enterprises	47	31	22	0	0	0
Large Enterprises	63	18	14	2	3	0
Government Agencies	94	4	1	1	0	0
Higher Education	93	1	5	1	0	0
Other Nonprofits	98	1	1	0	0	0
Other Organizations	99	0	1	0	0	0
Foreign Owned	0	1	2-4	5-9	10-24	25+
Small Enterprises	92	7	1	0	0	0
Large Enterprises	86	11	2	0	0	0
Government Agencies	100	0	0	0	0	0
Higher Education	99	0	0	0	0	0
Other Nonprofits	100	0	0	0	0	0
Other Organizations	100	0	0	0	0	0

Large Enterprises

Domestic Owned	Number of Licenses					
	0	1	2-4	5-9	10-24	25+
Small Enterprises	35	6	26	10	13	10
Large Enterprises	19	3	32	19	10	16
Government Agencies	74	0	10	10	6	0
Higher Education	65	6	1	10	3	0
Other Nonprofits	94	0	6	0	0	0
Other Organizations	100	0	0	0	0	0
Foreign Owned	0	1	2-4	5-9	10-24	25+
Small Enterprises	71	6	6	6	6	3
Large Enterprises	35	23	26	6	10	0
Government Agencies	84	3	6	3	3	0
Higher Education	84	0	10	6	0	0
Other Nonprofits	97	0	0	3	0	0
Other Organizations	100	0	0	0	0	0

Source: "Survey of Small Business Use of Intellectual Property Protection," prepared under Contract #SBA-3070-OA-88 for the U.S. Small Business Administration, Mary Seyer Koen, Principal Investigator, MO-SCI Corporation, 1991, Table 44

Table 11.10 Small and Large Enterprises in Each Field of Technology (Percent)

Field	Small Enterprises	Large Enterprises
Automation	7.5	11.1
Biotechnology	3.5	3.7
Chemicals	1.8	11.1
Computers	8.6	12.9
Defense	4.8	9.3
Energy	1.8	9.3
Advanced Materials	3.3	9.3
Medical	5.6	0.0
Pharmaceutical	2.6	3.7
Photonics and Optics	4.4	3.7
Software	27.7	11.1
Subassembly	13.1	3.7
Testing and Measurement	4.8	1.8
Telecommunications	10.5	7.4
Transportation	0.1	1.9

Source: "Survey of Small Business Use of Intellectual Property Protection," prepared under Contract #SBA-3070-OA-88 for the U.S. Small Business Administration, Mary Seyer Koen, Principal Investigator, MO-SCI Corporation, 1991, Table 100.

Table 11.11   Small and Large Enterprises Founded in Successive Five Year Periods (Percent)

	Small Enterprises	Large Enterprises
1985-1990	10.1	2.1
1980-1984	32.3	8.5
1975-1979	22.5	0.0
1970-1974	11.4	4.3
1965-1969	7.5	14.8
1960-1964	4.9	4.3
1955-1959	2.9	4.3
1950-1954	1.2	4.3
1945-1949	1.5	6.4
1940-1944	0.2	4.3
1935-1939	1.5	4.3
1930-1934	1.1	2.1
1925-1929	0.0	6.4
1920-1924	0.6	4.3
1915-1919	0.6	2.1
1910-1914	0.2	2.1
1905-1909	0.1	2.1
1900-1904	1.1	6.4
before 1900	0.2	17.0

Source: "Survey of Small Business Use of Intellectual Property Protection," prepared under Contract #SBA-3070-OA-88 for the U.S. Small Business Administration, Mary Seyer Koen, Principal Investigator, MO-SCI Corporation, 1991, Table 101.

Table 11.12 Small and Large Enterprises in Various Sales Ranges (Percent)

Sales Volume	Small Enterprises	Large Enterprises
$0-$25,000	2.6	0.0
$25,000-$100,000	3.6	0.0
$100,000-$500,000	12.7	0.0
$500,000-$1 million	12.9	0.0
$1 million-$5 million	36.9	0.0
$5 Million-$10 Million	12.3	2.0
$10 Million-$25 Million	15.2	0.0
$25 Million-$50 Million	3.1	4.1
$50 Million-$100 Million	0.6	10.2
$100 Million-$1 Billion	0.1	46.9
over $1 Billion	0.0	36.7

Source: "Survey of Small Business Use of Intellectual Property Protection," prepared under Contract #SBA-3070-OA-88 for the U.S. Small Business Administration, Mary Seyer Koen, Principal Investigator, MO-SCI Corporation, 1991, Table 103.

Table 11.13 Small and Large Enterprises by Export Sales (As a Percent of Total Sales) in the Following Ranges (Percent)

Export Sales	Small Enterprises	Large Enterprises
0	24.7	10.4
1-5	20.4	18.8
6-10	14.5	14.6
11-25	19.9	25.0
26-40	14.2	12.5
41-60	4.7	14.6
61-80	1.5	4.2
81-100	0.0	0.0

Source: Survey of Small Business Use of Intellectual Property Protection, prepared under Contract #SBA-3070-OA-88 for the U.S. Small Business Administration, Mary Seyer Koen, Principal Investigator, MO-SCI Corporation, 1991, Table 104.

Table 11.14 Small and Large Enterprises by Number of Employees (Percent)

Small Enterprises

Number of Employees	Percent
0-9	20.9
10-24	27.1
25-49	16.2
50-99	13.9
100-249	16.9
250-499	5.0

Large Enterprises

Number of Employees	Percent
500-999	27.1
1000-2499	20.8
2500-4999	12.5
5000+	39.6

Source: "Survey of Small Business Use of Intellectual Property Protection," prepared under Contract #SBA-3070-OA-88 for the U.S. Small Business Administration, Mary Seyer Koen, Principal Investigator, MO-SCI Corporation, 1991, Table 106.

Table 11.15 Small and Large Enterprises with R and D Expenses (As a Percent of Sales) in the Following Ranges (Percent)

R and D Expenses (As a Percent of Sales)	Small Enterprises	Large Enterprises
0	6.0	6.4
1-5	21.3	51.1
6-10	21.5	21.3
11-25	28.2	19.1
26-40	8.7	2.1
41-60	4.8	0.0
61-80	3.6	0.0
81-100	6.0	0.0

Source: "Survey of Small Business Use of Intellectual Property Protection," prepared under Contract #SBA-3070-OA-88 for the U.S. Small Business Administration, Mary Seyer Koen, Principal Investigator, MO-SCI Corporation, 1991, Table 108.

Table 11.16 Number of Firms by Employment Size and by High Technology Standard Industrial Classification Industry, 1986

SIC	1-4	5-9	10-19	20-49	50-99	100-249	250-499	500-999	1000-4999	5000-9999	10000-and up	Total
1311	7,353	2,523	1,122	565	184	90	34	13	15	5	13	11,917
1321	29	19	10	5	3	0	0	0	0	1	0	67
2812	5	9	4	3	1	3	0	2	0	0	2	29
2813	22	22	23	11	4	3	4	1	1	0	2	93
2816	14	16	17	25	9	2	2	2	0	0	0	87
2821	84	94	115	109	63	38	15	1	14	2	4	539
2822	26	27	18	27	15	8	4	3	2	1	0	131
2823	3	5	2	3	1	1	0	1	5	0	2	23
2824	13	9	13	10	9	8	1	2	3	1	0	69
2831	55	58	52	53	17	13	3	1	2	0	0	254
2833	78	74	62	55	23	6	4	4	2	0	2	310
2834	195	186	125	141	76	43	24	13	12	4	16	835
2861	20	20	9	8	5	1	1	0	0	0	1	65
2865	22	28	28	20	10	9	7	3	1	0	1	129
2891	136	139	137	112	36	13	6	2	3	0	0	584
2892	8	12	8	13	8	3	1	0	2	0	0	55
2893	46	57	61	40	17	9	2	2	2	1	0	237
2895	0	0	1	0	1	0	1	0	0	1	0	4
2899	475	327	257	166	74	28	9	9	7	2	0	1,354
2911	83	76	40	55	22	20	7	7	11	4	6	331
3482	77	24	15	3	1	2	1	0	2	0	0	125
3483	13	5	6	8	5	2	3	1	1	1	0	45
3484	92	51	30	23	6	5	4	2	1	0	0	214
3489	20	12	8	8	3	6	2	0	2	0	0	61
3511	39	27	16	13	6	2	3	0	0	0	1	107
3519	74	58	35	19	10	8	4	2	0	2	2	214
3531	217	169	147	154	75	41	15	10	10	1	1	840
3532	100	78	56	59	21	20	4	2	3	0	3	346
3533	229	216	150	133	30	29	9	5	8	3	3	815
3534	30	23	33	27	20	14	6	1	3	0	1	158
3535	120	147	155	150	74	44	10	4	3	0	0	707
3536	64	50	54	55	31	18	10	1	1	0	1	285
3537	138	103	91	106	35	35	4	1	3	1	0	517
3561	165	115	74	93	38	39	11	6	6	0	2	549
3562	21	22	21	25	16	7	2	10	6	1	1	132
3563	63	68	48	48	26	15	4	3	3	0	0	278
3564	118	110	125	115	39	32	16	6	3	1	0	565
3565	332	243	159	95	19	6	1	0	0	0	0	845
3566	17	31	36	51	22	10	5	3	2	0	0	177
3567	105	88	94	89	39	35	13	4	3	0	1	471
3568	26	31	31	33	14	13	4	3	3	0	1	159
3569	520	455	404	362	142	83	22	6	8	0	1	2,003
3572	5	5	2	1	4	1	1	0	0	0	0	19
3573	467	471	415	448	215	166	68	39	50	6	12	2,357
3574	13	7	5	10	3	3	2	2	1	0	0	46
3576	21	25	26	21	11	5	1	2	1	0	0	113
3579	55	44	37	34	21	6	5	3	5	0	2	212
3622	290	231	207	178	67	29	13	5	6	0	1	1,027
3623	37	29	28	41	13	8	3	5	5	0	0	169
3624	8	11	7	10	8	6	3	2	2	0	0	57
3629	59	56	46	47	22	17	4	4	2	0	0	257
3651	224	144	131	87	36	31	10	4	4	1	2	674
3652	594	269	119	86	30	12	6	5	0	0	0	1,121
3661	134	97	97	94	45	52	16	8	11	0	1	555
3662	698	606	554	574	222	174	50	24	26	6	11	2,945
3671	5	5	1	3	0	0	0	0	0	0	0	14
3672	16	8	10	2	0	1	2	1	0	0	0	40
3673	10	9	7	11	2	6	1	1	0	0	0	47
3674	379	325	290	264	108	85	27	17	13	0	6	1,514
3675	8	10	12	17	9	16	3	3	2	1	1	82
3676	6	7	8	7	7	8	3	2	1	0	0	49
3677	44	52	50	68	49	26	10	3	1	0	0	303
3678	15	9	12	15	16	13	6	2	2	0	1	91
3679	791	700	760	883	370	288	89	40	26	2	1	3,950
3721	56	39	30	20	6	6	3	2	0	0	7	169
3724	55	34	43	62	32	30	12	5	4	0	3	280

Table 11.16 Number of Firms by Employment Size and by High Technology Standard Industrial Classification Industry, 1986 (Continued)

SIC	1-4	5-9	10-19	20-49	50-99	100-249	250-499	500-999	1000-4999	5000-9999	10000-and up	Total
3728	245	224	177	209	104	70	23	5	11	2	1	1,071
3761	5	0	1	1	0	1	0	1	0	0	3	12
3764	2	0	2	0	1	0	1	0	1	0	1	8
3769	4	5	4	6	2	2	1	1	1	0	0	26
3811	313	245	166	181	79	44	18	8	10	1	2	1,067
3822	133	84	75	81	30	26	4	0	1	3	1	438
3823	468	371	322	294	93	62	26	5	7	1	0	1,649
3824	44	46	29	29	11	15	3	2	3	0	0	182
3829	256	188	148	124	71	39	6	7	4	0	0	843
3832	186	124	126	105	43	27	10	7	1	0	0	629
3841	311	278	231	184	85	67	15	13	11	1	1	1,197
3842	610	453	281	216	80	50	19	7	11	1	0	1,728
3843	384	190	111	60	21	18	6	2	2	0	0	794
3851	297	234	178	137	53	37	9	5	4	2	0	956
3861	274	202	166	135	61	31	14	4	4	1	5	897
3873	152	63	40	39	18	14	5	2	1	1	0	335
7372	5,838	3,471	2,059	1,127	317	185	65	29	22	1	1	13,115
7374	1,677	1,292	755	565	220	138	42	9	15	1	1	4,715
7379	4,636	1,770	894	472	133	64	16	5	2	0	0	7,992
7391	1,938	1,164	612	376	112	74	28	9	11	4	3	4,331
7397	653	543	384	275	82	44	7	3	2	0	0	1,993
8922	467	417	283	247	115	74	20	20	11	3	1	1,658
Total	34,120	20,384	13,833	10,936	4,277	2,835	954	459	450	70	135	88,453

Source: U.S. Small Business Administration, Office of Advocacy, Small Business Data Base, USEEM File, version 8, December 1987.

Table 11.17 Total Federal Contract Actions, 1991

	Thousands of Dollars		Small Business Share (Percent)
	Total	Small Business	
Total	210,689,057	39,660,931	18.8
Actions under $25,000 (Reported in Summary Form)	21,086,837	10,813,573	51.3
Actions over $25,000 (Reported Individually)	189,602,220	28,847,358	15.2

Source: Federal Procurement Data System, <u>Federal Procurement Report</u> (Washington, D.C.: U.S. Government Printing Office, February 13, 1992).

Table 11.18 Federal Contract Actions Over $25,000, FY 1979-FY 1991

Fiscal Year	Thousands of Dollars		Small Business Share (Percent)
	Total	Small Business	
1991	189,602,220	28,847,358	15.2
1990	171,300,890	25,401,626	14.8
1989	168,694,981	23,716,171	14.1
1988	174,097,585	25,671,318	14.7
1987	181,538,592	27,927,719	15.4
1986	183,650,227	28,780,092	15.7
1985	187,985,466	26,702,695	14.2
1984	167,933,486	25,506,023	15.2
1983	155,588,106	22,080,024	14.2
1982	152,397,884	23,558,563	15.5
1981	128,864,744	20,068,789	15.6
1980	100,893,385	15,326,121	15.2
1979	88,293,438	14,012,838	15.9

Note: Starting FY 1983, the dollar threshold for reporting detailed information on DOD procurement actions increased from $10,000 to $25,000. For civilian agencies, a similar change was made starting in FY 1986.

Source: Federal Procurement Data System, Federal Procurement Report (Washington, D.C.: U.S. Government Printing Office, February 13,1992); and idem, "Special Report S89522C" (prepared for the U.S. Small Business Administration, Office of Advocacy, June 12, 1989).

Table 11.19 Small Business Share of Contract Actions Over $25,000 by Major Product of Service Category, FY 1980, FY 1990, and FY 1991

Product/Service Category	FY 1980		FY 1990		FY 1991	
	Thousands of Dollars	Small Business Share (Percent)	Thousands of Dollars	Small Business Share (Percent)	Thousands of Dollars	Small Business Share (Percent)
Research and Development						
Total	14,195,369		28,423,371		29,069,489	
Small Business	958,063	6.7	2,184,656	7.7	2,159,151	7.4
Construction						
Total	8,592,397		9,577,817		14,051,582	
Small Business	3,627,308	42.2	4,691,269	49.0	5,892,026	41.9
Services						
Total	26,383,173		55,109,161		65,771,692	
Small Business	3,492,741	13.2	8,758,243	15.9	10,244,892	15.6
Supplies and Equipment						
Total	51,668,061		80,873,206		91,301,286	
Small Business	7,210,216	14.0	10,405,320	12.9	14,487,660	12.6

Source: Federal Procurement Data System, "Special Report S89522A" (prepared for the Small Business Administration, Office of Advocacy, June 7, 1989); and "Special Report S92132E" (prepared for the U.S. Small Business Administration, Office of Procurement Assistance by Federal Procurement Data System, Washington, D.C., May 30, 1991).

Table 11.20 Annual Change in Dollar Volume of Contract Actions Reported Individually, by Major Product or Service Category, FY 1979-FY 1991 (Percent)

Product/Service Category	1979-1980	1980-1981	1981-1982	1982-1983	1983-1984	1984-1985	1985-1986	1986-1987	1987-1988	1988-1989	1989-1990	1990-1991
Research and Development												
Total	11.0	17.9	19.9	10.4	10.3	5.3	-0.2	5.0	1.4	4.6	-0.7	2.2
Small Business	13.2	3.0	-3.2	10.4	13.4	27.5	8.8	13.5	-1.9	2.0	15.8	-1.2
Construction												
Total	13.7	11.6	10.4	-0.4	6.0	11.5	-1.6	14.2	-16.9	-10.6	-8.0	46.7
Small Business	0.5	15.0	9.7	20.0	15.7	13.8	-10.6	11.1	-14.4	-10.2	-15.0	25.6
Other Services												
Total	13.3	25.3	16.8	1.2	6.1	9.3	1.5	9.2	-1.6	-6.4	18.7	19.3
Small Business	14.4	36.1	12.6	-1.1	8.9	10.5	3.5	12.4	6.2	-14.2	28.5	17.0
Supplies and Equipment												
Total	15.8	34.3	19.6	0.8	8.4	15.0	-4.6	-9.5	-5.2	-7.4	2.1	12.9
Small Business	11.4	40.2	24.9	19.3	19.1	-5.1	21.6	-18.7	-15.5	-5.0	12.5	10.4

(Annual Change, Fiscal Year)

Source: Federal Procurement Data System, "Special Report S89522A" (prepared for the Small Business Administration, Office of Advocacy, June 7, 1989); and idem, "Special Report T4SBRPT5" (prepared September 12, 1990); "Special Report F" (prepared for the U.S. Small Business Administration, Office of Procurement Assistance by Riley and Johnson, Washington, D.C., May 30, 1991); and "Special Report S92132E" (prepared for the U.S. Small Business Administration, Office of Procurement Assistance, Washington, D.C., June 18, 1992).

Table 11.21 Small Business Innovation Research Program, FY 1983-FY 1991

Fiscal Year	Phase I			Phase I		
	Number of Proposals	Number of Awards	Amount of Awards (Thousands of Dollars)	Number of Proposals	Number of Awards	Amount of Awards (Thousands of Dollars)
Total	129,176	16,265	815,492	12,381	5,236	1,924,745
1991	20,920	2,553	127,858	1,734	788	335,856
1990	20,957	2,346	118,098	2,019	837	341,836
1989	17,233	2,137	107,728	1,776	749	321,674
1988	17,039	2,013	101,935	1,899	711	284,867
1987	14,723	2,189	109,585	2,390	768	240,883
1986	12,449	1,945	98,494	1,112	564	199,394
1985	9,086	1,397	69,126	765	407	130,003
1984	7,955	999	48,020	559	338	60,422
1983	8,814	686	34,648	127	74	9,810

Note: Phase I evaluates the scientific and technical merit and feasibility of an idea. Phase II expands on the results and further pursues the development of Phase I. Phase III commercializes the results of Phase II and requires the use of private or non-SBIR federal funding. The Phase II awards in FY 1983 were pursuant to predecessor programs that qualified as SBIR funding.

Source: U.S. Small Business Administration, Office of Innovation, Research and Technology, annual reports for FY 1983-FY 1991.

Table 11.22 Small Business Share of Prime Contract Dollars by State, FY 1991

	FY 1991 (Thousands of Dollars		Small Business Share	Dollar Rank by State	Rank Per Capita by State
	Total	Small Business			
Total Federal	189,602,220	28,847,358	15.2		
Alabama	3,374,915	689,171	20.4	19	16
Alaska	785,424	316,193	40.3	37	6
Arizona	3,008,251	315,005	10.5	21	17
Arkansas	434,039	175,560	40.4	43	18
California	31,263,649	3,316,109	10.6	1	10
Colorado	4,505,663	470,549	10.4	12	8
Connecticut	5,222,234	289,252	5.5	10	4
Delaware	154,556	50,008	32.4	49	46
District of Columbia	3,587,782	1,153,012	32.1	15	1
Florida	7,101,062	1,161,059	16.4	8	26
Georgia	2,329,108	543,793	23.3	22	36
Hawaii	736,365	276,343	37.5	38	23
Idaho	1,000,000	109,550	10.9	35	11
Illinois	3,569,164	783,330	21.9	18	39
Indiana	2,313,103	197,606	8.5	23	34
Iowa	635,010	109,428	17.2	39	47
Kansas	1,066,963	194,725	18.3	34	31
Kentucky	1,962,161	703,770	35.9	29	27
Louisiana	2,060,394	482,736	23.4	25	29
Maine	1,121,637	82,755	7.4	32	14
Maryland	7,230,361	1,689,281	23.4	6	5
Massachusetts	7,920,127	834,741	10.5	5	9
Michigan	2,063,268	369,999	17.9	24	49
Minnesota	1,975,887	146,488	7.4	28	30
Mississippi	2,010,078	312,714	15.5	26	20
Missouri	7,113,729	461,001	6.5	7	7
Montana	172,701	134,334	77.8	48	48
Nebraska	426,777	141,690	33.2	45	45
Nevada	1,103,379	102,956	9.3	33	13
New Hampshire	464,846	62,163	13.4	42	33
New Jersey	4,299,684	944,640	22.0	14	25
New Mexico	3,429,306	341,337	10.0	18	2
New York	9,241,450	1,187,290	12.8	4	28
North Carolina	2,006,797	541,025	27.0	27	40
North Dakota	223,368	133,179	59.6	46	37

Table 11.22 Small Business Share of Prime Contract Dollars by State, FY 1991 (Continued)

	FY 1991 (Thousands of Dollars		Small Business Share	Dollar Rank by State	Rank Per Capita by State
	Total	Small Business			
Ohio	6,392,075	988,251	15.5	9	24
Oklahoma	953,152	355,400	37.3	36	41
Oregon	568,944	310,527	54.6	41	50
Pennsylvania	4,446,697	931,084	20.9	13	35
Rhode Island	429,295	100,886	23.5	44	32
South Carolina	3,178,393	385,413	12.1	20	15
South Dakota	192,493	96,493	50.3	47	43
Tennessee	4,742,274	505,178	10.7	11	12
Texas	12,716,233	1,629,349	12.8	2	21
Utah	1,399,034	222,835	15.9	30	19
Vermont	99,063	27,908	28.2	51	51
Virginia	9,793,574	2,922,629	29.8	3	3
Washington	3,445,798	569,590	16.5	17	22
West Virginia	583,579	105,010	18.0	40	38
Wisconsin	1,379,556	235,140	17.0	31	42
Wyoming	124,508	76,330	61.3	50	44
All Others	13,243,424	562,243	4.2	-	-

Source: Adapted from Federal Procurement Data System, <u>Federal Procurement Report</u> (Washington, D.C.: U.S. Government Printing Office, February 13, 1992).

Table 11.23 Total Federal Contract Actions to Small, Women-Owned, and Minority-Owned Businesses, FY 1991 (Thousands of Dollars)

	Total	Actions Over $25,000	$25,000 Or Less
Total	210,689,057	189,602,220	21,086,837
Small Business	40,388,923	28,847,358	10,813,523
Percent of Total	19.2	15.2	51.3
Women-Owned Business	2,408,795	1,765,166	643,629
Percent of Total	1.1	0.9	3.1
Minority-Owned Business	6,951,075	6,486,289	464,786
Percent of Total	3.2	3.4	2.2

Source: Adapted from Federal Procurement Data System, <u>Federal Procurement Report</u> (Washington, D.C.: U.S. Government Printing Office, February 13, 1992).

Table 11.24 Annual Change in the Dollar Volume of Contract Actions Over $25,000 Awarded to Small, Women-Owned, and Minority-Owned Businesses FY 1980-FY 1991 (Thousands of Dollars)

	Total, All Business			Small Business			Women-Owned Business			Minority-Owned Business		
	Total Actions	Change From Prior Year Dollars	Percent	Total Actions	Change From Prior Year Dollars	Percent	Total Actions	Change From Prior Year Dollars	Percent	Total Actions	Change From Prior Year Dollars	Percent
1991	189,602,220	18,301,330	10.7	28,847,358	3,445,732	11.9	1,765,166	287,272	19.4	6,486,289	796,229	14.0
1990	171,300,890	2,605,909	1.5	25,401,626	1,685,455	7.1	1,447,894	74,955	5.3	5,690,060	356,172	6.7
1989	168,694,981	-5,402,604	-3.1	23,716,171	-1,955,147	-7.6	1,402,939	75,215	5.7	5,333,888	141,382	2.7
1988	174,097,585	-7,441,007	-4.1	25,671,318	-2,256,401	-8.1	1,327,724	74,839	6.0	5,192,506	343,381	7.1
1987	181,538,592	-2,111,635	-1.1	27,927,719	-852,373	-3.0	1,252,885	56,034	4.7	4,849,125	563,200	13.1
1986	183,650,227	-4,335,239	-2.3	28,780,092	2,077,397	7.8	1,196,851	102,643	9.4	4,285,925	401,286	10.3
1985	187,985,466	20,051,980	11.9	26,702,695	1,196,672	4.7	1,094,208	238,077	27.8	3,884,639	-119,500	-3.0
1984	167,933,846	12,345,380	7.9	25,506,023	3,425,999	15.5	856,131	244,755	40.0	4,004,139	817,048	25.6
1983	115,588,106	3,190,222	2.1	22,080,024	-1,478,539	-6.3	611,376	60,775	11.0	3,187,091	328,180	11.5
1982	152,397,884	23,553,140	18.3	23,558,563	3,489,774	17.4	550,601	-534,772	-49.3	2,858,911	223,903	8.5
1981	128,864,744	27,971,359	27.7	20,068,789	4,742,668	30.9	1,085,373	297,844	37.8	2,635,008	813,087	44.6
1980	100,893,385	-	-	15,326,121	-	-	787,529	-	-	1,821,921	-	-

Source: Federal Procurement Data System, "Special Report S89522C" (prepared for the U.S. Small Business Administration, Office of Advocacy, June 12, 1989); and idem, *Federal Procurement Report* (Washington, D.C.: U.S. Government Printing Office, July 10, 1990 and March 13, 1991).

Appendix: List of States by SBA Region

SBA Region I
Connecticut
Maine
Massachusetts
New Hampshire
Rhode Island
Vermont

SBA Region II
New Jersey
New York

SBA Region III
Delaware
District of
  Columbia
Maryland
Pennsylvania
Virginia
West Virginia

SBA Region IV
Alabama
Florida
Georgia
Kentucky
Mississippi
North Carolina
South Carolina
Tennessee

SBA Region V
Illinois
Indiana
Michigan
Minnesota
Ohio
Wisconsin

SBA Region VI
Arkansas
Louisiana
New Mexico
Oklahoma
Texas

SBA Region VII
Missouri
Iowa
Kansas
Nebraska

SBA Region VIII
Colorado
Montana
North Dakota
South Dakota
Utah
Wyoming

SBA Region IX
Arizona
California
Hawaii
Nevada

SBA Region X
Alaska
Idaho
Oregon
Washington

Glossary

Asians as used by the Bureau of the Census in the Survey of Minority-Owned Business Enterprises, this minority category represents a diverse group that includes Aleuts, Eskimos, American Indians, Asian Indians, Chinese, Japanese, Koreans, Vietnamese, Filipinos, Hawaiians, and other Pacific Islanders.

balance sheet data on assets, liabilities, and equity derived from income tax returns filed by businesses.

bankruptcy condition in which a business cannot meet its debt obligations and petitions a federal district court for either reorganization of its debts or liquidation of its assets.

branch an affiliate establishment of a multiestablishment enterprise that is not a parent of any other establishment.

Characteristics of Business Owners a follow-on survey to the Census Bureau's 1982 economic census. Using samples derived from tax returns, it provides information on sole proprietorships, partnerships, and subchapter S corporations.

corporation a firm granted a state charter to incorporate, thereby limiting the liability of its owners.

County Business Patterns an establishment-based data base on employment and payroll that is assembled and published annually by the Bureau of the Census. It is based on employers' Social Security witholding reports to the federal government.

Current Population Survey a monthly survey of households that is conducted by the Census Bureau.

economic census a census of business that has been conducted by the Census Bureau every five years since 1967, collecting data for years ending in a 2 or 7.

employer identification number a unique number assigned by the Internal Revenue Service to any business or individual required to withold income and Social Security taxes from the wages of an employee.

enterprise aggregation of all establishments owned by a parent company. An enterprise may consist of a single, independent establishment, or it can include subsidiaries or other branch establishments under the same ownership and control.

Enterprise Statistics an enterprise-based data base on employment, payroll, and sales that is derived from the Census Bureau's quinquennial economic census.

establishment smallest unit in which business activity is conducted and on which statistical information is collected. Establishments may be independent—called a single-establishment enterprise—or they may be branches of larger firms. Most federal data are available only for establishments.

failure the closure of a business causing a loss to at least one creditor.

Federal Insurance Contributions Act (FICA) federal law passed in 1935 that mandated the payroll witholding mechanism used to fund the Social Security system.

Federal Unemployment Tax Act (FUTA) federal law passed in 1939 that created the state-administered unemployment insurance system and its funding source of payroll taxes.

goods-producing sector all businesses producing tangible goods; includes agriculture, mining, construction, and manufacturing.

Hispanic According to the Census Bureau, those of Cuban, Mexican, Puerto Rican, Latin American (Central or South American), European Spanish, or other Spanish-speaking origin or ancestry. As many as 2.7 percent of Hispanic-owned businesses might also be categorized as Black-owned businesses.

household data data that is derived by surveying workers and other members of households.

income statement data on revenues and cost of operations derived from income tax returns filed by businesses.

incorporation filing of a certificate of incorporation with a state's secretary of state, thereby limiting the owner's liability. It is one of the major indicators of business formation.

Metropolitan Statistical Area a geographic area defined by the Office of Management and Budget as a large population nucleus with at least 50,000 persons, together with adjacent communities that have a high degree of economic and social integration with that nucleus, usually through employment and commuting patterns.

minority-owned business businesses owned by Blacks, persons of Spanish or Latin American ancestry, and persons of American Indian or Asian origin or descent. *See also* Hispanic.

National Survey of Small Business Finances a survey of 3,400 small businesses conducted in 1988–1989 under the sponsorship of the Federal Reserve Board and the U.S. Small Business Administration. Its purpose was to ascertain the uses of different financing sources by small businesses, examine their use of financial and banking services, and obtain balance sheet and income statement information.

new firm either a new registration of incorporation with a state or, for data collected by the U.S. Department of Labor's Employment and Training Administration, the application for a new account number with a state's department of employment security.

partnership two or more parties who enter into a legal relationship to conduct business for profit. Defined by the Internal Revenue Code as joint ventures, syndicates, groups, pools, and other associations of two or more persons that are not specifically classed in the tax code as corporations or proprietorships.

proprietorship *see* sole proprietorship.

reporting unit term used by the U.S. Department of Labor to describe entities that are included in the quarterly ES-202 reports made by each state's department of employment to the federal government. These reports provide payroll and employment information by establishment.

service-producing sector broadly defined, all U.S. industries that produce intangibles, including the five major industry divisions of transportation, communications, and utilities; wholesale trade; retail trade; finance, insurance, and real estate; and services.

Small Business Data Base a dynamic, micro-level data base created by the U.S. Small Business Administration, based on data edited from the Dun and Bradstreet Corporation's Dun's Market Identifier (DMI) file. It contains data for 1976 through 1990, and was phased out in 1992.

Small Business Innovation Research (SBIR) program program mandated by the Small Business Innovation Development Act of 1982, requiring federal agencies with $100 million or more of extramural R&D obligations to set aside 1.25 percent of these funds for small business.

sole proprietorship unincorporated, one-owner business, farm, or professional practice. It is the most common legal form of business ownership: about 85 percent of all small businesses are proprietorships. The liability of the owner is unlimited in this form of ownership.

Standard Industrial Classification (SIC) codes a system of industrial classification established by the federal government and used to categorize businesses by type of economic activity. The codes are published in the *Standard Industrial Classification Manual* published by the Office of Management and Budget. Data reported by industry in this edition of the *Handbook of Small Business Data* conform to the 1987 edition of the manual.

subchapter S corporation a form of corporation with a limited number of shareholders that is treated as a partnership for tax purposes by the Internal Revenue Code.

successor firm the take-over of an existing firm by a new or existing firm.

Survey of Minority-Owned Business Enterprises a survey conducted by the Census Bureau every five years as part of its economic census. It provides information on sole proprietorships, partnerships, and subchapter S corporations owned by American Indians, Alaska Natives, Asian Americans, Blacks, and Hispanics.

Survey of Women-Owned Business Enterprises a survey conducted by the Census Bureau every five years as part of its economic census. It provides information on proprietorships, partnerships, and subchapter S corporations owned by women.

termination for data collected by the U.S. Department of Labor's Employment and Training Administration, a firm that either reported being out of business or reported no employment for two years.

unemployment insurance a federally mandated, state-administered system of payments to unemployed workers. *See* Federal Unemployment Tax Act.

wage-and-salary worker a worker who receives wages, salary, commissions, tips, or pay in kind from a private employer or governmental unit.

Index of Tables

Note: index entries refer to table numbers.

Note: index entries refer to table numbers.

Note: index entries refer to table numbers.

Note: index entries refer to table numbers.

Note: index entries refer to table numbers.

Note: index entries refer to table numbers.